Dr. Doina Frumuselu, a distinguished expert and consultant with a PhD in Visual Arts and a PhD in Climatology, has made notable scholarly contributions through 90 articles and 33 books. She specializes in the life and works of Constantin Brancusi, in addition to her research on corrosion control and environmental effects.

In memory of my friend, Sidney Geist.

Doina Frumuselu

BRANCUSI BIOGRAPHY

AUSTIN MACAULEY PUBLISHERS
LONDON * CAMBRIDGE * NEW YORK * SHARJAH

Copyright © Doina Frumuselu 2025

All rights reserved. No part of this publication may be reproduced, distributed, or transmitted in any form or by any means, including photocopying, recording, or other electronic or mechanical methods, without the prior written permission of the publisher, except in the case of brief quotations embodied in critical reviews and certain other non-commercial uses permitted by copyright law. For permission requests, write to the publisher.

Any person who commits any unauthorized act in relation to this publication may be liable to criminal prosecution and civil claims for damages.

All of the events in this memoir are true to the best of author's memory. The views expressed in this memoir are solely those of the author.

Ordering Information
Quantity sales: Special discounts are available on quantity purchases by corporations, associations, and others. For details, contact the publisher at the address below.

Publisher's Cataloging-in-Publication data
Frumuselu, Doina
Brancusi Biography

ISBN 9798891551305 (Paperback)
ISBN 9798891551312 (Hardback)
ISBN 9798891551329 (ePub e-book)

Library of Congress Control Number: 2024913502

www.austinmacauley.com/us

First Published 2025
Austin Macauley Publishers LLC
40 Wall Street, 33rd Floor, Suite 3302
New York, NY 10005
USA

mail-usa@austinmacauley.com
+1 (646) 5125767

Table of Contents

Introduction	9
Childhood in Hobita	13
Years of Searching for His Path in Life	18
School of Crafts in Craiova	22
School of Beaux Arts in Bucharest	35
First Years of Life in Paris	63
The American Dream	115
To the Peaks of Glory	127
The Romanian Dream	253
Senior Years	292
Preparing for the Final Voyage	328
Departure	350
They Have Met Brancusi…	359
Abbreviations	400
Bibliography	401
List/Source of Illustrations	457
Endnotes	477

Introduction

Brancusi was born in 1876, in the poorest village of Gorj County, at the feet of Carpathian Mountains, the poorest county from the Old Kingdom, as Romania was called then. The poverty was owed to the infertile land, which was divided among many family members as people had many children back then, and that was his case as well. He was born during a time of great changes in Romanian history, which meant great sacrifices in human and material terms.

The poverty of the place was compensated by the beauty of landscapes, by traditions and customs and by the villagers' crafts, among which wood processing reached handcraftsmanship and the child Brancusi kept marveling at everything he saw and witnessed and wanted to master such crafts himself as well.

He spent his childhood years between the coppice of Bistrita River, the surrounding hills, Tismana Monastery and Valcan Mountains, where he would climb the sheep together with shepherds in spring and come down back to the village in autumn. The beauty of places around Tismana Monastery charmed him, as his mother took the children there to pray for the family, left early without the support of the father who had died. Later on, Brancusi would say about his studio he wanted it to be a *subsidiary* of Tismana in Paris.

Since his childhood, under the influence of his older brothers he endeavored to reach a better condition and live well, even to strike rich. After several travels, he stopped in Craiova, where he received the support of some protectors and attended the School of Crafts of Dolj County, wood sculpture section. Brancusi was drawn by wood architecture, by the inner structure of the material, which he could render only by chisel and hatchet, having learned no less than 33 joining modes.

Wood processing led him to sculpture: "Wood took me to sculpture and then stone after wood, which is also confirmed by sculpture stages, as Xoanon received the stone pattern." He considered the years he spent in Craiova as the most important of his life: "I was born a second time in Craiova." About the place the School of Crafts held in his life, Brancusi would tell V.G. Paleolog: "I have learned whole-heartedly and managed to acquire solid knowledge, thus departing from hearsay lessons and using the available books, tools and competent people who taught me; I needed a long time to leave off the pulling mode of the saw which I had not learned to agree with the breathing pace, as well as the handling of the hatchet and chisel by keeping my head high and swelling up my chest."

The 20th century found him a student in the School of Beaux Arts of Bucharest, where he attended very seriously the courses and practical sessions, even with dedication, which drew the attention of the school's heads, professors and colleagues. He got involved in the cultural life of the Capital City; he read a lot and worked enormously, to the great amazement of his colleagues and friends.

In 1904, Brancusi attempted getting a stipend for Italy, but he did not manage it and then followed his destiny, leaving abroad on his own and such route ended in Paris. By contest, he was admitted in the National School of Beaux Arts, where he would be student subsidized by the Romanian state and got very good results, until 1907. In Paris he worked in the studio of Professor Antonin Mercié and in that of Auguste Rodin, and then he continued alone.

About such beginner years spent in destitution Brancusi would tell: "I had a hard time at the beginning. Sometimes I had to lean on the walls lest I should fall from hunger or illness. I had hung over my bed card boards where I wrote the pieces of advice I was repeating to myself, in my moments of doubt;" then, detached and wise he explained how useful suffering is to forge strong characters in life: "suffering hardens the human being and is more necessary than pleasure in forging the character."

Brancusi could not be defeated because he always, from childhood to his dying day was guided by birds, be they magic, golden or of fire, and he believed strongly in their help. "As a child I have always dreamt of flying to the trees and into the sky." When Constantin Brancusi was asked about his favorite piece, he answered decidedly: "*Maiastra!* I have been working to it since 1908 and have not finished yet." The fascination of flight drew him near the genial inventors Traian Vuia, Aurel Vlaicu and Henri Coanda.

The first participation of Brancusi with pieces to an exhibition was in 1898 in Craiova, when the chroniclers of the time appreciated him. And abroad, the first participation to an exhibition was in 1906 in Paris at the Salon organized by the National Society of Beaux Arts. However, he met success only at the first modern art exhibition in the world, the Armory Show 1913, organized in New York where he dispatched five sculptures, which have drawn his fellow sculptors, collectors and the public. After this reference date, America would adore him and included him in the international artistic life. It is not by mere chance that Sidney Geist called him, half-jokingly, half in earnest, "Brancusi, American sculptor!" Although the artist went to America only three times (twice in 1926 and once in 1939), he has known, understood and loved the Americans for their sincere childish manner of behavior, for their open mind to artistic novelty, for the sincere appreciation of his sculpture and for their unconditional friendship. From more than 190 exhibitions mentioned in this volume half were organized in the United States, and the path to glory was traced in New York with the Armory Show, while the last exhibitions during his life were arranged at New York, Palm Beach, and Philadelphia in February 1957.

Attempting to decipher the Brancusi code we have the feeling each door open to his knowing leads to yet other rooms, with other doors, in an unending line. Everything was without end with him. This is why Brancusi never mentioned what piece ended a sculptural cycle because he considered he still had to add something new to each sculpture.

In 1934, when sculptor Constantin Brancusi began discussing with Arethia and Gheorghe Tatarescu about the possible construction of a monument to the memory of Gorj heroes who had died for the country, he was 58. He was mature, his fame was worldwide, his artistic and technical skill was unmatched, and therefore he was ready for some fundamental work. The topic was inciting for philosopher Brancusi as well, not only for the artist, as in Gorj there is an impressive cult of the departed for all those that studied it. In 1922, Brancusi intended building a monument for the heroes of Pestisani villages but things did not go his way; his fellow countrymen forgot the project but he did not.

The sculptural ensemble *Heroes' Road* from Targu-Jiu is the current name of the monumental trilogy that the artist called the *Road of Heroes' Souls*. To construct it, in 1937 and 1938 the sculptor proposed the *Column* at the beginning and then the *Gate*. Brancusian creation being spontaneous, it was subject to major changes: including a table with chairs around it in the ensemble, then the first *Table* was replaced as well as the position of *Chairs* around it. In this monument Brancusi put to value the engineering side of his personality. As a matter of fact, all masters and workers from the Targu-Jiu site were respectfully calling him "Mr. Engineer."

Having returned to Paris, one project finished in Targu-Jiu and another one failed, the *temple of deliverance* in Indore, while the black tempest of the war hung over Europe, Brancusi concerned himself only with the fate of his studio that he deemed being a living museum, open to all the visitors and himself, included in the "scenery."

On Brancusi there have been many writings and more still are issued—valuable or fiction volumes, more essays than documentaries. Brancusi phenomenon is more difficult to understand given his complex personality with thorough education and instruction in an Orthodox Conservatory country, impoverished by the wars of the ending 19th century, an environment he would be attached to until the end of his life; then he was transplanted in a progressive environment open to all artistic currents, as was Paris in the first decades of the 20th century. The artist got perfectly integrated in this environment, which he influenced by his native intelligence and talent.

Brancusi liked telling stories about himself in personal a-temporal and a-spatial manner; therefore, many times it was difficult to separate truth from fiction. This is the specific language of Gorj inhabitants with many meanings, spoken with detachment given by the conviction that everything is relative—facts, places, and dates.

The book has been devised and written as a journal of the artist's life, reconstituted using the writings of those he knew and of those who studied his life and work in Romania and abroad, the publications and archives from France and other European countries, the worthy archives of American institutions, etc. The volume ends with a series of testimonies less known in Romania and new abroad.

Brancusi passed away in 1957 but he remains with us forever!

Childhood in Hobita

1876-1887

Hobita, Pestisani, Bradiceni (Gorj County)

On 19 February 1876, according to the Julian calendar, Constantin Brancusi was born in Hobita village of Pestisani, locality found north-west in Gorj County along the road connecting Targu-Jiu town to Tismana (Fig.1).

Fig. 1. Tismana Monastery, 1860

At the end of the 19th century Hobita, was one of the poorest villages in Gorj County, which in turn was one of the poorest in Romania (Fig. 2). To a great extent the poverty was owed to the fact that the same parcel of land was continuously divided between a growing number of family members.

Fig. 2. Village surrounding Targu-Jiu, 1860

The birth certificate of Constantin Brancusi, found in the State Archives of Craiova, the Civil Status Register for births in Pestisani village, in 1876 under no. 17 mentions: "Birth certificate—Constantin, son of Nicolae Brancusi of year one thousand eight hundred seventy-six, month February, day twenty-one, nine o'clock in the morning. Birth certificate of Constantin—male gender, born the day before yesterday in his parents' home of Pestisani, son of Mr. Nicolae Brancusi, forty-five, farmer of trade, domiciled in Pestisani village and of Mrs. Maria Brancusi, twenty-four, of the agricultural domain, domiciled in Pestisani village, according to the father's statement who came also showing us the infant..."[1] It was just habitual practice those days, when roads became impracticable with bad weather and consequently the important events of peasants' lives were registered before witnesses, but quite late. In 1919, the Kingdom of Romania introduced the Gregorian calendar and 1 April became 14 April, thus we deem it more accurate to observe the artist's birth date as being 19 February/2 March.

The name of the artist's father was Nicolae Brancusi (1832-1884), but being the sickling, the parents changed it into Radu according to an ancient custom that attempted cheating evil spirits and death[2]. He was 40 on January 27, 1872 when he married his second wife, Maria Deaconescu (1851-1919), 21 years old spinster of Pestisani. He had three sons from his first marriage, Ion, Gheorghe and Vasile, and he would have four more children from his second wife, Maria-Grigore (1873-1933), Constantin (1876-1957), Dumitru (1878-1930) and Eufrosina (1884-1948).

In terms of fortune, Nicolae-Radu Brancusi had around 7 hectares of land along the Bistrita River and on the hills surrounding Hobita, which he worked with his family and paid his dues to the state for. Lawyer and erudite publicist

Petre Pandrea writes about the sculptor's family in his memoires: "it was the poorest branch of the somewhat richer freeholder Brancusi's of the plains," whom he considered even well-off compared to the other villagers, since Nicolae-Radu had "two to three helping hands" that he used "in agriculture and carpentry"[3]. Artist Constantin Brancusi would proudly narrate about his father's habit of traveling, and upon his return he would introduce foreign innovations from the town. This is what happened to the house windows—he enlarged and made them open, which was afterwards mimicked by other villagers[4] (Fig. 3).

Fig. 3. *Constantin Brancusi* house museum of Hobita, reconstituted in 1971

There are his village friends' memories about the childhood of Costache, name of endearment among his family and friends, which they related much later to his biographers. Costache knew poverty from early childhood. He helped his mother as best he could with household chores, in the orchard, in the fields and also watched his younger brothers. When he grew a little, he was sent to the pasture with the geese, sheep and pigs. All the hardships of a destitute life no longer mattered for Costache when he was facing the wonders of nature, discovering the fairy tales and stories of old people, the village habits and community feasting days.

When grazing the geese and sheep on the banks of Bistrita River (Fig. 4) Constantin used to select stones of various shapes and colors from the gravel, filling up his pockets. He also liked carving wood toys selected by rules known only to him; he liked modeling clay figures and making snowmen in winter[5]. Later on, the artist would confess to the sculptress Irina Codreanu and to the composer Marcel Mihalovici that he always remembered the "image of these sculptures in the hard snow, when I was a child"[6].

Fig. 4. Coppice of Bistrita River

In 1958, Vasile Blendea called Trifu, a childhood friend, who would tell art critic Vasile Dragut that Costache was very droll: "he kept playing pranks and did not like staying with pigs for pasture," but in exchange he liked carving sticks with his pocket knife[7].

At the age of seven, Constantin began a shepherd's life at the pen in the mountains, where he went up at Easter (April) and returned at Saint Demeter (October). Losing his father in 1884 and growing family poverty compelled him to work harder and harder[8].

Brancusi began primary classes in 1883, in Pestisani, where children learned in a school building made of wattle. In 1884, when he was in the second grade, the school teacher punished him for carving the bench with his pocket knife. It was then he ran away, but his mother found him quickly and brought him back home. He continued his primary studies in Bradiceni, where he attended two primary classes.

Constantin attended the 3rd year of the primary school (1885-1886) in Bradiceni where his uncle Grigore Brancusi was teaching. It was still there he began also the 4th grade with the same teacher (1886-1887) but he could not finish it because of the harsh winter, which prevented him going to school so he did not graduate. "He had a good head, he understood quickly and liked knowing everything," Vasile Blendea-Trifu told[9].

Targu-Jiu, Hobita

In March 1887, before finishing his primary classes he ran away again to Targu-Jiu (Fig. 5) and got hired as apprentice in Ion Mosculescu's dye shop, thus entering the world of pigments, colors and painting recipes, but his mother took him back to Hobita. At 12, poverty chased him again from home!

Six months after coming home, Constantin worked as shop assistant with his step brother Ion (Chijnea), whom he also helped in the household. His mother wanted very much to see him turning a priest, but she usually said she felt "he would not stay around much."

Fig. 5. Targu-Jiu at the end of the 19th century

Years of Searching for His Path in Life

1888-1890

Slatina

In 1888, he left home again, this time to Slatina with his mother's will (Fig. 6), where he maintained himself as shop assistant for several months[10].

Fig. 6. Central area of Slatina town

Craiova

In 1889, he left Slatina and went to Craiova, where he got hired by the *Spirtaru Bros.* restaurant that faced the railroad station (Fig. 7), which was actually an eating house located in the place of a great resort. He would work hard for two years there, sometimes even "18 hours a day," still for "gain"[11].

Fig. 7. Train station of Craiova

1891-1894

Craiova

Pushed by this obsession to "gain" and with Spirtaru's aid, from June 1891 to September 1892, he was hired as shop assistant in the "goods and colonial produce store" of the famous merchant Ion Zamfirescu[12], located on the 19 Madonna Dudu Street, the main one in Craiova until the beginning of the 20th century. Zamfirescu also had a tavern with "fine wines and spirits" in central Craiova. Constantin would inhabit the attic of Zamfirescu's house across the street. He stayed until September 1892, when the merchant began building a house and gave up his services.

Slatina

He got hired in the colonial shop of Mrs. Stanculescu, who had a beautiful daughter, Stela. Constantin fell in love with the girl[13] and stayed there from September 1892 until March 1893, when he left for unknown reasons and never returned.

Bucharest, Pitesti

After his departure from Slatina, Constantin went to Bucharest where he stayed only a few days, then he went further to Pitesti where he worked for three months in the pub of Serbanescu, in the area of the town train station[14] (Fig. 8).

Fig. 8. Pitesti train station area

Craiova

In the summer of 1893, Constantin returned to Craiova to his old employer, Ion Zamfirescu. In 1890, there he had met Ion Ciobanu, also called Ion Georgescu-Gorjan, 7 years' older than him, born in Godinesti (Gorj County), who was shop seller and trusted person of Ghita Ionescu, owner of the merchandise and colonial goods shop "Colored Star" of 23 Madonna Dudu Street. Ion Georgescu-Gorjan took him in his house rented from Ghita Ionescu in 14 C.A. Rosetti Street, where he kept two rooms and lived with his brother Gheorghe. Constantin would share a room upstairs with Gheorghe until 1894[15].

In his spare time, he wandered about town in order to get acquainted with it, went to churches and especially to Madonna Dudu, St. Elijah, Saint Trinity (Figs. 9a-c) and Obedeanu, he carved and modeled. He liked to offer his employer and protectors household objects ingeniously devised and artfully made such as little chairs, wall hangers, shelves, games, frames, etc.

In the winter of 1893-1894, Brancusi manufactured a violin from the laths of an orange crate, which he treated as best he could to get good resonance. The sounds of this violin amazed Mihalache the Fiddler and all the clients of Ion Zamfirescu, among whom were many persons of influence in the town—Costica I. Grecescu called Perieru, Enache Manea, Ghita Ionescu, Ion Mitescu, a.o. They decided to help the talented young man to attend the School of Crafts[16].

Figs. 9a-c. Churches of Craiova, 1908:
a—Madonna Dudu; b—St. Elijah; c—Saint Trinity

Professor Petre Ceaureanu of Hobita whose father had also been shop assistant in Craiova would narrate about this period of Constantin's life: "Father told me that in Craiova as well, where Brancusi was shop assistant, he went on sculpting as soon as he got there. Brancusi had clay in the attic where he slept. When he delivered his basket to the customers—he was working in a pub, which was also colonial goods shop—he would climb in the attic and made clay figures—people heads, animals. As soon as his shop hours ended, he started working. Finding this out a good man and client in the shop told it to the headmaster of the School of Crafts in Craiova. This one came by carriage and took him to school, looking after him always."[17]

School of Crafts in Craiova

1895

Craiova

By the intervention of Costica I. Grecescu-Perieru, county counselor, the necessary steps were taken to enlist Brancusi in the School of Crafts, despite the absence of his graduation certificate for the four compulsory primary classes. In the autumn of 1894, on 1 September, Brancusi became a freshman in the School of Crafts, Wood Sculpture division.

The School of Crafts was state-owned, established in 1871 by the Craiova born Minister Gheorghe Chitu and financed from the budget of the Prefect's Office from Dolj County, which also tended to its smooth operation. It was the second school of its kind in the country, after Bucharest. In school students got theoretical and practical instruction with the purpose of training Romanian professors and masters, who in time were meant to replace the foreigners, mainly from Vienna. They were taught calligraphy, notions of physics and applied mechanics, arithmetic and practical geometry, notions of technology, agricultural machines, shop accounting, drawing and sketching.

Drawing Professor, Petre B. Popescu, with a background in polytechnic studies in Switzerland, was school principal. The wood sculpture foreman was the Austrian Joseph Sicherl. Another Austrian foreman, Karl Seffeld, was head of the turnery shop. Mihail Burlan, graduate of the school of decorative arts in Paris, was the head of the carpentry section[18] (Fig. 10). Students could choose the following specialties: blacksmith, locksmith and tinsmith, fitting, turnery, carpentry, wheelwright's and carts, wood sculpture. [19][20][21]

Fig. 10. Workshops of the School of Crafts, Craiova

Craiova at the end of the 19th century is shown in the documents to have been a town without public monuments, just some triptych crosses at fountains of the town limits, and without museums. The only place where Brancusi could get an idea about sculpture was in the graveyards, where some bust or statue could be seen among the wooden and stone crosses. When V.G. Paleolog asked him how he got to sculpture, Brancusi answered that he began with wood "and stone followed wood, which is also confirmed by the development stages in sculpture history"[22].

At the beginning of 1895, after four months of courses Brancusi asked the school management to enlist him in the 2nd year of study and his demand was approved given his older age than his colleagues', "after proper examination upon his request" as the school headmaster, Professor Petre B. Popescu wrote in his curriculum[23].

Scarcity compelled Brancusi to find some work after school hours and also to take the necessary steps in order to get some stipend. On 20 August, he submitted an application for the scholarship contest and the file with the following documents required by the school management: the consent of his mother Maria Brancusi, dated 8 August 1895, authenticated by Pestisani Town Hall, and certificate 56 of 15 August 1895 issued by the management of the School of Crafts in Craiova showing he got 8.75/10 after the two years.

On 31 August, after examination passed before a commission chaired by the prefect of Dolj County and including three members, of whom one was Petru P. Popescu, school headmaster Brancusi was admitted as scholarship recipient in the sculpture section, as also written in the minutes (Fig. 11)[24]. He got 7/10 in arithmetic and 8/10 in geometry at the exam[25]. The benefits of internship consisted of free accommodation, meals and school uniform, as well as exemption from certain taxes.

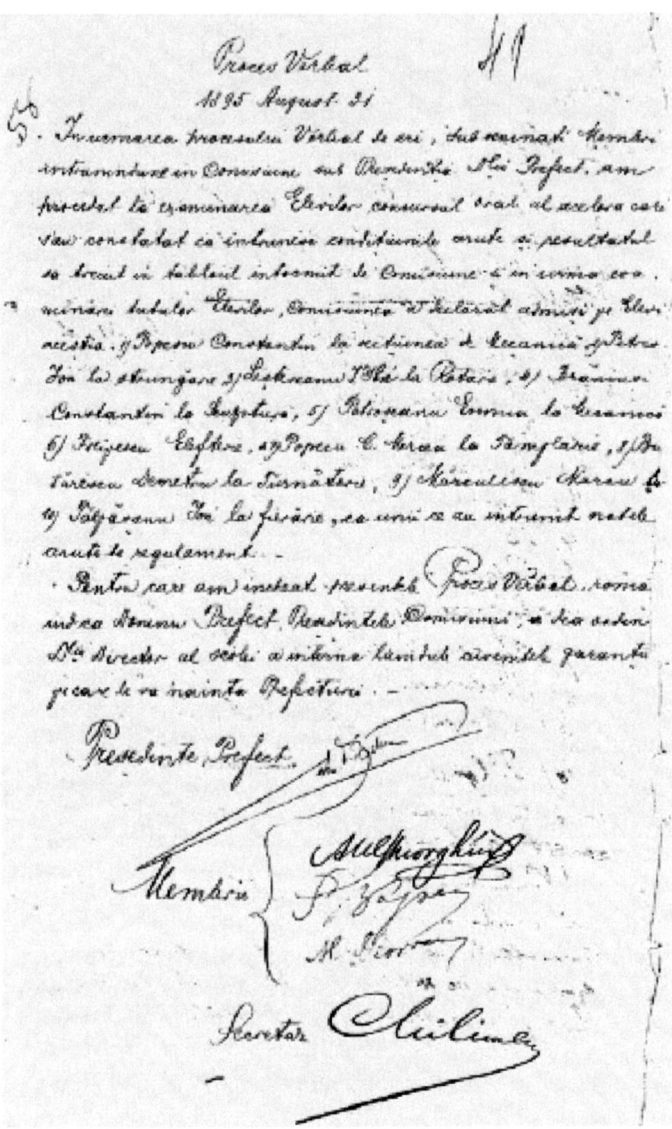

Fig. 11. Minutes of the Commission attributing stipends in the School of Crafts in Craiova, 31 August 1895

On 20 August he sent a letter to the mayor of Pestisani in which he offered to sculpt a marble bust in front of the Town Hall and made the gift of a marble beetle to him, present for which the mayor of Pestisani thanked him (Figs. 12 and 13)[26].

From the first scholarship he took his mother to Craiova in order to show her the places where he worked and studied. He enlisted in the 3rd year of study in autumn.

From 1895 to 1898, in addition to the school stipend, Brancusi also benefited from a "study aid" amounting to 200 Lei annually from the Trusteeship of Madonna Dudu Church, a sum he would receive until the completion of his studies in the country[27].

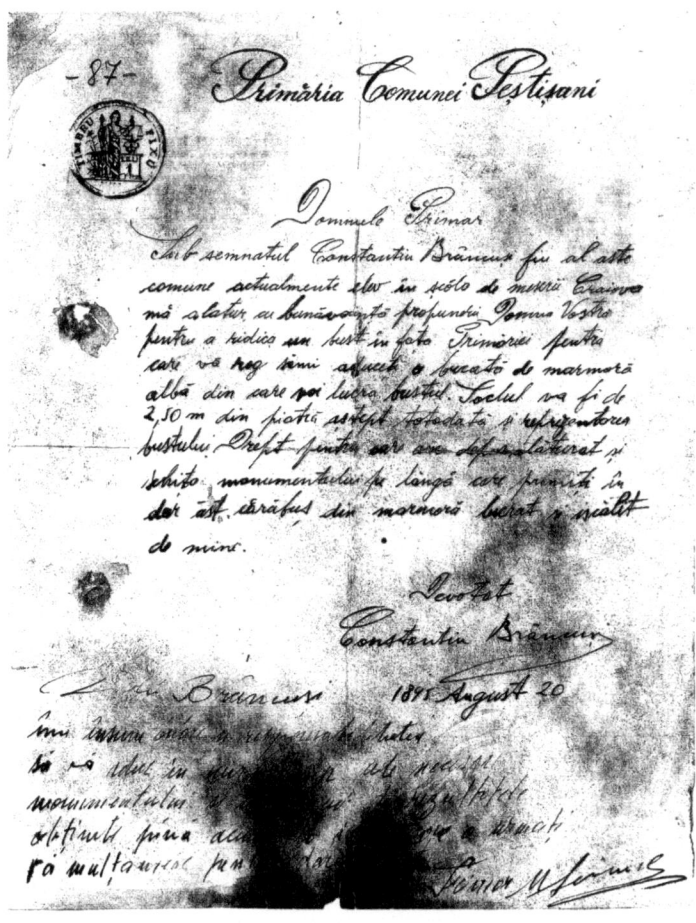

Fig. 12. Letter of Brancusi to the mayor of Pestisani, 20 August 1895

Fig. 13. *Beetle*

1896

Craiova

On 1 January, Brancusi's mother signed a guarantee document (Fig. 14) stating she agreed to cover all expenses incurred by the School of Crafts, in case her son abandoned school or was expelled[28].

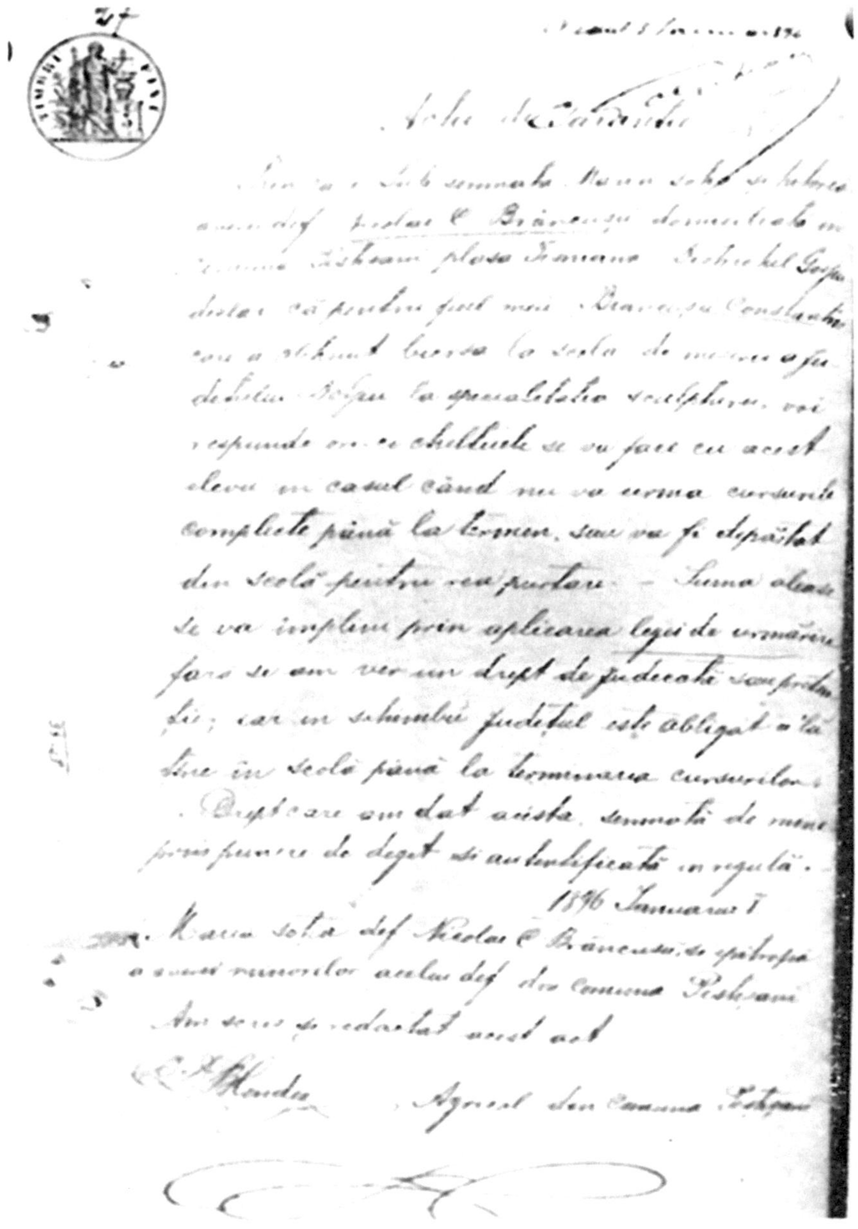

elevu în casul când nu va urma cursurile complecte până la termen, sau va fi depărtat din școlă pentru rea purtare – Suma aleasă se va împlini prin aplicarea legei de urmărire fără să am vr'un drept de judecată sau protestie; iar în schimbul judeţul este obligat a'l ține în școlă până la terminarea cursurilor.

Drept care am dat acesta semnată de mine prin punere de deget și autentificată în regulă.

1896 Ianuarie 1

Fig. 14. Guarantee deed signed by Brancusi's mother, Pestisani, 1 January 1896

He graduated the 3rd year of study with 9.32/10, being the first of 16 students[29] (Fig. 15).

Fig. 15. Brancusi wearing the uniform of the School of Crafts in Craiova

A photo document published by Professor Ion Schintee in Ramuri magazine, issue of August 1964, pointed out a loom sculpted by Brancusi of sycamore maple wood dated 1896 on the upper side. The object is a gift for Maria, wife of tradesman Ghita Ionescu[30] (Fig. 16a). Lotto pieces made of cherry wood (Fig.16b), given to Marilena, the daughter of tradesman, date back this same year[31].

Figs. 16a, b. Wood pieces executed outside the curriculum, Craiova, 1896:
a—loom; b—lotto pieces

On 12 July, he donated a marble box to keep the holy oil, making a donation deed to priest G. Haiduc from St. Elijah Church, the father of doctor Dimitrie Gerota (Figs. 17 and 18)[32].

Fig. 17. Aspects of the sculpted walls of a marble box to keep holy oil, Craiova, 1896

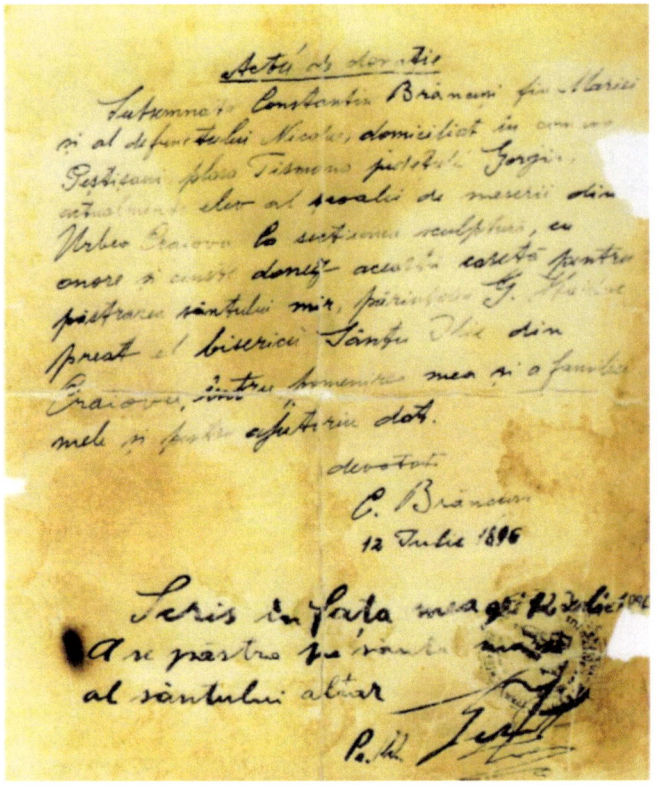

Fig. 18. Donation deed to priest G. Haiduc from St. Elijah Church in Craiova, 12 July 1896

Brancusi's poverty and of other colleagues was well known to the school management that for their assistance requested the prefect's office, guardianship authority, to allow accommodating and feeding seven students, among whom Brancusi, during the Christmas holiday[33].

Letter 14258 of 23.12.1896 from the Prefect Office of Dolj County agreed with the proposal of the school management: "I approve the proposal you submitted in report no. 373 and permit feeding these seven intern students in the school during the Christmas holiday."[34]

Brancusi sculpted much during his four years of study, both under the school curriculum but also to support himself and improve his technique—furniture items, painting frames, household and interior decoration objects and other pieces that he generously offered to his friends, protectors, and noteworthy people; he also contributed to the altar screen and furniture of the Madonna Dudu Church[35].

1897

Vienna

Student Brancusi's cleverness, artistic talent and hard work were highly praised, therefore in the 1897 summer holiday, endowed with a recommendation letter from his Austrian foremen Sicherl and Seffeld, Brancusi (Fig. 19) went to Vienna, getting on board a ship in Turnu Severin. Once he got to his destination, he took a two months' job with the owner of a shop where wood was processed in an artistic mode, supplier of the famous Thonet House[36]. Such an experience was useful to Brancusi because in school, he dealt with fine furniture carpentry, as demanded by the little bourgeoisie of Craiova that got in touch with foreign countries and acquired luxurious tastes, quite doubtful at first.

Fig. 19. Brancusi in the School of Crafts, Craiova, 1897

In Vienna (Fig. 20), Brancusi encountered a different and new world, which would influence his future undertakings to a great extent. After a few hours in the Antique Art Museum, he narrated: "I got out weary, soft headed, dizzy, and my mind scattered and callous," nevertheless he would have liked to stay more, being immersed in the exhibits, but closing time rang and the guards took him out. About the Mineralogical Museum, Brancusi said it "lightened his brain with mineral beauties," and that he felt like he was at home in the Ethnographic Museum.

Being an organized person, Brancusi asked his employer to issue him a qualification certificate, and then he returned to the country by train[37].

Craiova

In view of the regional autumn 1898 exhibition of Craiova, the managerial team of the School of Crafts asked him to sculpt two frames, with drawings and molds contributed by the wood sculpture foreman, Joseph Sicherl and by the carpentry section head, Mihail Burlan. The two frames were sculpted in lime tree wood, ornamented with rococo garlands, leaves and bouquets (Fig. 21a)[38].

Fig. 20. Vienna, 1897

Figs. 21a, b. Wood pieces executed in the School of Crafts shop, Craiova: a—frame; b—corner chair

Two more wood pieces remained from his school years—a case box (cherry wood, 1897) and a corner chair (oak wood, 1894-1898, Fig. 21b)[39], as well as a marble sculpture made outside the school curriculum upon an order for funerary monument, *Prayer* (marble, 1897, Fig. 22)[40].

Romanesti (Gorj County)

In 1897-1901 then in 1914 and 1922 Brancusi visited priest Craciun Smantanescu, one of his friends from Romanesti village, 4 km away from Targu-Jiu. Professor Dan Smantanescu's testimonies recorded in time showed that about in 1897-1898 Brancusi asked the permission of Father Craciun to engrave the "house pillars of oak wood, as hard as ebony" (Fig. 23)[41][42]. Wood architecture had drawn Brancusi from an early age, by its inner structure which he could only render with the chisel and hatchet. He was also concerned with the joining manner of wood, as he had seen in the houses built by Gorj handicraftsmen, and he praised knowing no less than 33 joints[43].

Fig. 22. *Prayer*

Fig. 23. Priest C. Smantanescu's house with pillars carved by Brancusi, Curtisoara Museum (Gorj County)

School of Beaux Arts in Bucharest

1898

Craiova

Professor Petre B. Popescu wanted to pay homage to Gheorghe Chitu, great personality of Craiova, former mayor of the town and minister of Public Instruction, minister of Internal Affairs, minister of Justice and minister of Finance, deputy and senator, member of the Romanian Academy and founder of the School of Crafts who died in 1897, so he asked Brancusi, recent graduate of this school (Fig. 24) to execute a bust of the illustrious departed by his photograph and display it in the regional exhibition. During work, he would meet Lucilla Chitu, niece of Gheorghe Chitu (Fig. 25), who graduated magna cum laude the Literature Faculty of Bucharest and whom he fell in love with[44]. Some colleague narrated the sculptor worked all summer and managed to finish the sculpture in autumn, before the exhibition opened[45].

Fig. 24. Brancusi near his colleagues upon graduation of the School of Crafts, Craiova, June 1898

Fig. 25. Lucilla Chitu, Craiova

On 28 September, Brancusi received from Petre B. Popescu, principal of the School of Crafts from Dolj County, certificate no. 145, indicating that "he graduated with great success the full theoretical and practical courses," and during his years of study he showed "great application both in practice and in theory, as well as exemplary conduct"[46]. Principal Petre B. Popescu offered Brancusi the position of professor in the school from which he had just graduated, but the young man turned down his proposal because his was a different destiny.

The courses in the School of Crafts last five years, but Brancusi graduated in just four (1894-1898). The sculptor would confess to V.G. Paleolog about the place this school had in his life, that he learned "full heartedly", acquiring "sound knowledge," thus managing to get rid of "hear-say learning" because he had "books, tools and competent people" at hand. It was in this school that he acquired the correct technique of the saw, hatchet, and chisel[47].

Petru Comarnescu would say later about Brancusi's life in Craiova that his hard work, most times over 18 hours a day, did nothing else than to fine shape Brancusi (*Frotter le diamant*). In his adult years, the artist remembered this time period without resentment. On the contrary, he recognized the hard life as the foundation of his success in life[48].

Bucharest

On 30 September, he enlisted with the *National Beaux Arts School* in Bucharest, known as *Belle Arte School* or *School of Beaux Arts*, sculpture section, headed by the sculpture and perspective Professor Ion Georgescu (Fig. 26). Other professors Brancusi had in this school included doctor Dimitrie Gerota (anatomy), A.D. Atanasiu (perspective and geometry), Alexandru Tzigara-Samurcas (art history, aesthetics and ethnography), Grigore Tocilescu (history), and Ipolit Strambulescu (drawing)[49].

The school had run from 1869 in the building of Bucharest University (Figs. 27a, b), providing sections of painting, sculpture, engraving, architecture, drawing, aesthetics, history and perspective[50]. During the time of Brancusi's studies, the painter George Demetrescu Mirea was principal, and painting and sculpture courses took place in the school building. The world of sculptors of Bucharest was small at that time. Dimitrie Demetrescu Mirea, Filip Marin, Constantin Balacescu, Ioan Iordanescu, the Spaethes (father and son), and the Storcks (father and two sons) stood out.

Brancusi found a landlord near the school studios: "on Buzesti Street, at the end of Mogosoaia *bridge*, in a blind lane of the street that, had it been extended beyond the garden would have come across Victoriei Avenue, more uptown than Sevastopol Street and Clopotari, nowadays Grigore Alexandrescu. It was some sordid but picturesque cul-de-sac: a stream of roomlets so-called chambers, one stuck to the other with doors opening straight into the narrow alley where an ox-pulled cart or the horse wagon could not pass, in case the doors, opening to the outside, were open"[51] (Fig. 28).

Fig. 26. Professor sculptor I. Georgescu during a perspective class,
School of Beaux Arts in Bucharest, 1896-1897

Figs. 27a, b. Bucharest: a—University Palace during construction;
b—letterhead of the School of Beaux Arts

Fig. 28. Buzesti Street, Bucharest, 1900

During Brancusi's years of study there, Bucharest was in a period of cultural development against the background of a strong return current to Romanian traditional values. Mention is made here of several great personalities of Romanian culture that were active then and there—scholar Nicolae Iorga, professors B.P. Hasdeu, A.D. Xenopol and Spiru Haret, scientists Victor Babes, Petru Poni, Ion Cantacuzino and Emil Racovita, painters Nicolae Grigorescu, Stefan Luchian, Camil Ressu, Jean A. Steriadi, Iosif Iser, Theodor Pallady and Francisc Sirato, sculptor Dimitrie Paciurea, writers I.L. Caragiale, Constantin Dobrogeanu-Gherea and Garabet Ibraileanu, poets Alexandru Macedonski and George Cosbuc, architects Ion Mincu, Grigore Cerchez, Ion N. Socolescu, I.D. Trajanescu and Stefan Ciocarlan, art critics Leo Bachelin, Alexandru Tzigara-Samurcas and Alexandru Bogdan-Pitesti.

At the time, the musician George Enescu acquired success, and a group of young people that studied in Paris established the *Artistic Youth* Society (1901), the most important artistic group until World War I. The *Romanian Philharmonic* Society set up in 1868 organized concerts at the Athenaeum Palace. Brancusi, inquisitive and curious by nature like any other native of Oltenia, was actually updated on everything that happened in Bucharest, and he even got involved in the *Carmen* Choral Society, established in 1901 by D.G. Kiriac, where he would be quite active because he had good tenor voice[52].

As he told Eileen Lane in 1922, the artist was not afraid of poverty because in case he could no longer sculpt, he was ready to wander the whole world singing and would not die of hunger[53].

Craiova

The first articles on Brancusi in the printed press of the time related to the *Regional Agricultural Exhibition*, organized in Craiova in the Bibescu Park, 14-20 October, inaugurated in front of Ministers D. Sturdza, A. Stolojan, C. Stoicescu, and Ionel Bratianu, and of local authorities headed by the town's mayor M. Maldarescu. The *Bust of Gheorghe Chitu* was exhibited in the entrance of the school's pavilion, being noticed by Craiova visitors and chroniclers who in Bucharest and Craiova newspapers wrote how interesting the bust was, being made by "a beginner, Mr. C. Brancusi" (Figs. 29 and 30)[54] [55] [56].

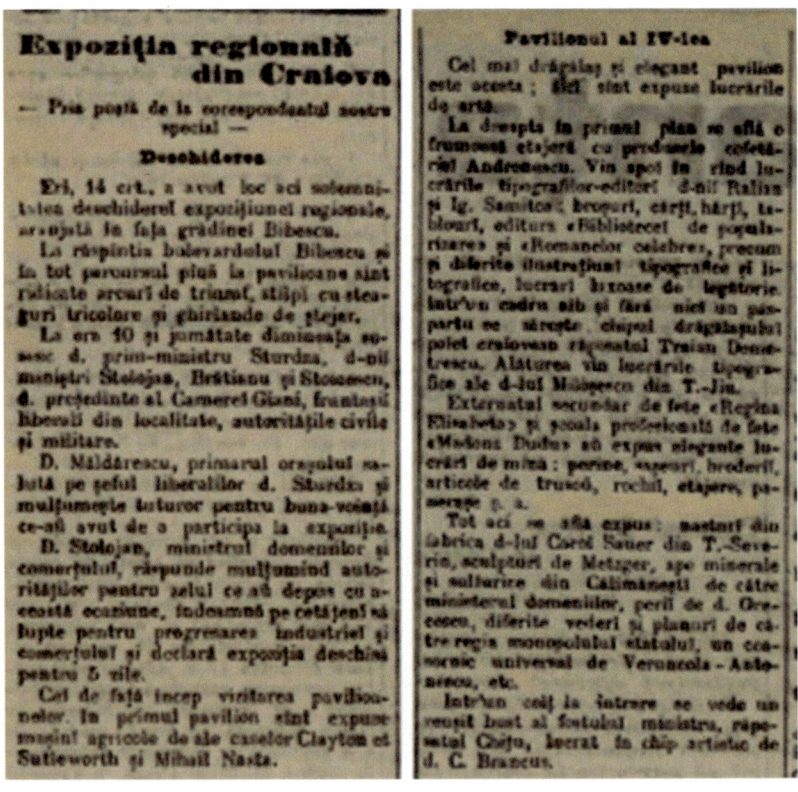

Fig. 29. Adeverul, Bucharest, 16 October 1898

Fig. 30. Albina, Bucharest, 8 November 1898

Bucharest

At the beginning of his studies, Brancusi received a 200 Lei per year stipend from the Trusteeship of the Madonna Dudu Church in Craiova. However, it was insufficient for his expenses and studies, so he was compelled to work as a dishwasher in the beer house of Osvald on Campineanu Street[57](Fig. 31).

Fig. 31. Ion Campineanu Street where Osvald's beer and spirits pub was found, Bucharest

On 30 November 1898, sculptor Ion Georgescu died suddenly and Brancusi, impacted by this event, drew him a *homage drawing*. Petru Comarnescu held that Brancusi had acquired a lot from his professor, given this one's "human qualities" and "ideas," as well as his "portraitist skill"[58]. Vladimir C. Hegel, Polish, followed at the chair; he had studied in Paris and even lived there for a while, and had previously been pedagogue and professor in the School of Arts and Crafts of Bucharest. In his capacity as the sculpture and drawing professor, prone to monumental art, in 1898-1902 V. Hegel would greatly contribute to Brancusi's training as a sculptor.

On 23 December, Brancusi received Mention II[59]—his first success—at the *Sculpture / Antique Bust* contest (*Bust of Vitellius*, gypsum, 1898). It was made during his first few weeks at the Beaux Arts School for a study subject from some mold from the school stocks. He received another honorary mention on 23 December 1899[60] and a bronze medal on 30 June 1900[61].

Hobita, Targu-Jiu

To earn money in order to keep studying, in October 1898 Brancusi sold his share of the inheritance given to him by his parents[62], which was very shameful at that time and the community condemned it harshly, as even a "slice" of land was more expensive than gold. In fact, Brancusi had thus cut his connection with his native land, getting free of this last link in order to follow his destiny!

In 1898, Brancusi spent Christmas with his family in Hobita. Passing by Targu-Jiu he admired the monument erected in honor of Tudor Vladimirescu by the sculptor Constantin Balacescu (Fig. 32), a former student of the School of Crafts from Craiova. The statue was cast in bronze in Milan (Italy). The monument provided him with grand impressions, of which proofs remained in the drawings he sketched in the booklet he would eventually give to his friend Ion Croitoru, when he left the country in 1904[63] (Fig. 33).

Fig. 32. Monument of Tudor Vladimirescu by C. Balacescu, Targu-Jiu

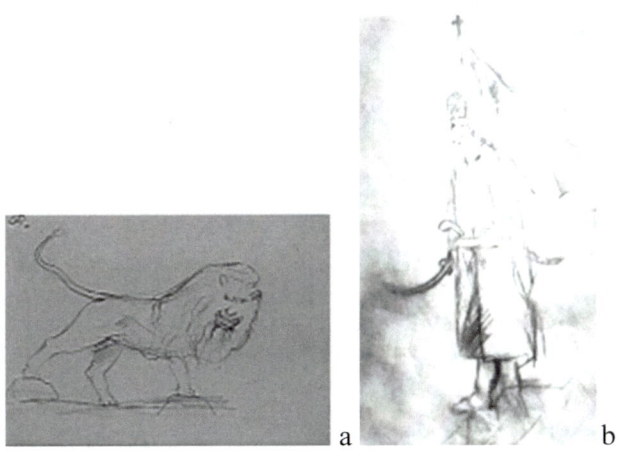

a   b

Figs. 33a, b. Drawings by Brancusi after the monument of Tudor Vladimirecu

1899

Bucharest, Craiova

In the School of Beaux Arts aids were quite small and few in number, and the situation of students attending the art course was not the happiest, many of them being on the brink of poverty. As the art historian, I.D. Stefanescu wrote: "poorer students, some of them too poor, ate when and where they could. They slept hidden in the attic of the School from Grivita Road (where the studios of practical studies were found—A/N), often times without eating anything. I have heard none of them complain. They made parade of the most touching self-pride."[64] (Fig. 34)

Fig. 34. Brancusi in the studio of the School of Beaux Arts, Bucharest, 1899-1901(?)

Now in his second year of studies, on 5 December, student Brancusi requested the Trusteeship of Madonna Dudu Church to increase his stipend, as he deemed the granted aid "wholly insufficient even for study books." The trustees approved doubling his aid to 400 Lei/year, and to get this sum Brancusi provided Costica I. Grecescu-Perieru with proxy on 2 April 1899 and then on 21 March 1900[65].

In view of the country's participation to the Paris Universal Exhibition of 1900 the Government appointed the General Commissariat meant to organize Romania's Pavilion, chaired by commissioner general Dimitrie Olanescu. Brancusi submitted several sculptures but the jury did not accept them for the exhibition.

1900-1901

Craiova

The Council of the Prefect's Office in Dolj County granted him 150 Lei scholarship in the university year 1900-1901. As gratitude for the support offered by the Madonna Dudu Church Brancusi sculpted an icon in bas-relief which he donated to the ecclesiastical establishment (marble, 1900, Fig. 35)[66].

Fig. 35. *Madonna*

Bucharest

For some time, Brancusi lived in the attic of the parish house on 18 Izvor Street, in the same room with Ion Gheorghian-Popescu, a medical student, and with Ion Croitoru, a conservatory student, and was a neighbor to Peter Neagoe, a painting student in the Beaux Arts School, to Ion Comanescu and Daniel Poiana. They were all united by friendship and poverty. Before this accommodation, Brancusi lodged while in school in some unheated dwelling on Dr. Marcovici Street, close to Cismigiu public garden, where he found it impossible to stay during winter. He then took refuge at a friend's in Bonaparte Avenue, close to Clopotarilor suburb where he recruited as model Dimache, bell manufacturer, for the students of the School of Beaux Arts, who also modeled for his anatomic studies after nature. Brancusi also dwelled in the parish house of Mavrogheni Church, where he sang in the choir and pulled the bells[67].

Talking to the musicologist Petru Comarnescu, Ion Croitoru described Brancusi as he had known him: "sober, moderate, *good*, but also a joker." He was "eager to learn, amateur to know everything," he studied with great interest "physics and chemistry books, some even authored by scholar Petru

Poni" as well as "mathematics and descriptive geometry." He loved music, he liked playing the violin, "went to concerts" and sang in the *Carmen* choir[68].

The school program was strictly respected. Brancusi modeled *Head of Laocoön* (clay, 1900) for a study subject from a mold from the stocks of the School of Beaux Arts. At the 30 June 1900 competitions, he was rewarded with an honorary mention for the subjects "Expression Head," "Anatomy," and "Nature Sculpture." He received an honorary mention for this last subject on 19 June 1901, and the silver medal on 23 December 1901[69].

On 21 December 1900, he received a bronze medal for *Expression Head*, and on 19 June 1901 another bronze medal for *Anatomic Study* modeled "by nature" under Professor doctor Dimitrie Gerota's guidance; he also received honorary mentions for "Expression Head" and "Composition" subjects. On 23 December 1901, he received a further honorary mention for both "Aesthetics and Art History" and "Perspective" contests[70].

Being aware that an artist cannot succeed without a sound education, Brancusi read many books of physics, chemistry, mathematics, literature, history, etc. and he was actively participating in all the practical work in the school studio (Figs. 36a, b). Brancusi enjoyed the school's support, headed by Principal G.D. Mirea, professor of anatomy, and undoubtedly the sculpture professor as well; everybody admired and respected him. Painter Theodor Pallady made him a portrait dedicated "Let him die of exhaustion! Brancus 1900," a hint to the sculptor's diligence and hard labor (Fig. 37)[71].

Figs. 36a, b. Brancusi next to his colleagues in the studio of the School of Beaux Arts, Bucharest, 1901

Fig. 37. Brancusi by Th. Pallady, Bucharest, 1900

In 1901 and 1902, Brancusi, guided by doctor Dimitrie Gerota, studied dead bodies for a long time in the Medical Faculty and at the mortuary; he participated in the dissections of muscles and bones, and made measurements and comparisons between living and dead people[72] (Fig. 38).

Fig. 38. Brancoveanu Hospital of Bucharest where the School of Beaux Arts students attended artistic anatomy classes

Principal G.D. Mirea enabled his access to the school during the summer holiday in order to complete the *Écorché* (Fig. 39), under the direction of doctor Dimitrie Gerota and he granted him the 28 August 1901 certificate[73]. *Mars Borghese* and *Allegory* (clay, 1900-1901)[74] are among Brancusi's sculptures modeled in the school studio.

Fig. 39. Studio of the School of Beaux Arts, Bucharest, 1901

Craiova

He sold one marble sculpture and executed sale-purchase deed before the notary (Fig. 40). This deed represents the first document certifying that Brancusi sculpted marble in Romania[75].

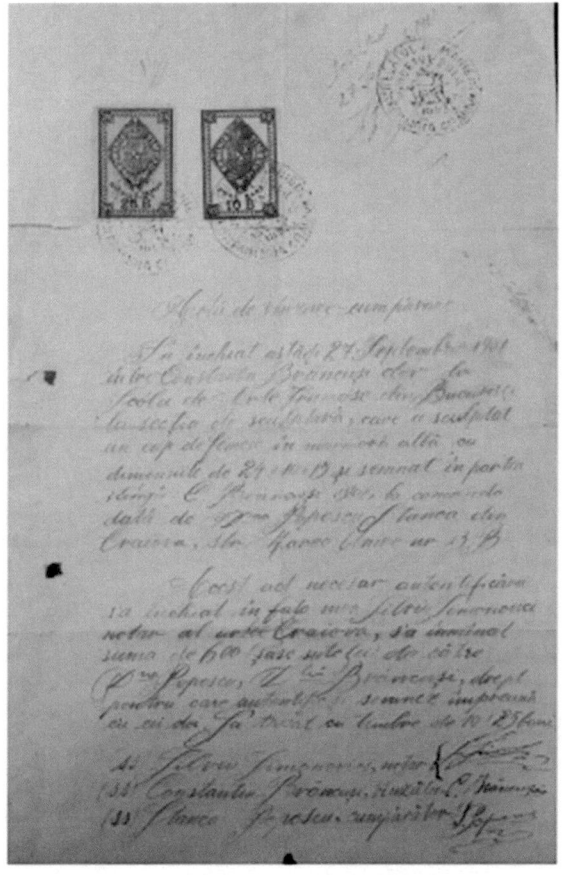

Fig. 40. Sale-purchase deed of a marble woman's head, Craiova, 27 September 1901

1902

Bucharest

Again, to earn money during his school years, Brancusi (Figs. 41a, b) worked in stonecutters' shops, he sculpted, washed dishes in restaurants, made drawings and painted. Proof of that is also the 1902 Typographic Almanac which on page 204 included *C. Brancusi, 18 Elisabeta Boulevard* in the section with painters' addresses from the printing domain (Figs. 42 and 43). His name and address would be still mentioned in the following editions. In the printing domain, Brancusi was introduced by Professor V. Rola Piekarski[76]. Brancusi needed the money to support himself—in the photographs we can notice he was an agreeable young man, self-assured and very well-dressed —as well as his family of Hobita left behind in poverty.

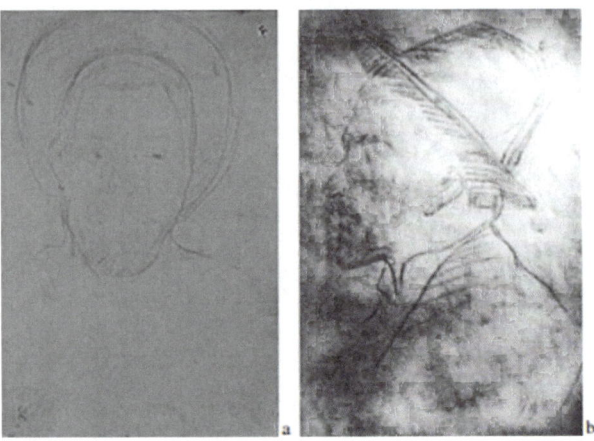

Figs. 41a, b. Brancusi self-portraits, Bucharest, 1901-1902

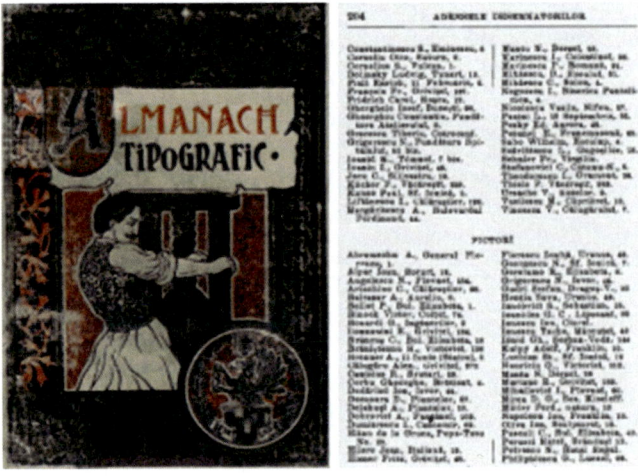

Fig. 42. 1902 Typographic Almanac, Bucharest

Fig. 43. Elisabeta Blvd, Bucharest

During his studies in the School of Beaux Arts of Bucharest Brancusi fell in love with Ana (Fig. 44), sister of his colleague. He did not benefit of long vicinity with his inspiring muse because Ana went to Paris in 1903. A photograph is left of her[77].

Fig. 44. Ana Stefanescu, Bucharest, 1903

Craiova

At the beginning of 1902 Brancusi was conscripted for short term military duty in Craiova (15 January 1902-15 January 1903, Figs. 45a, b), when "thanks to Jean Steriadi he managed doing it by being more on leave"[78]. His relatives in the family of his brother Dumitru from Hobita kept the conscription document entitled "Certificate of presence under the flag" issued by Rovine Regiment no. 26. From it, we can find what he looked like at 26: "Young Constantin Brancusi, son of Nicolae and Maria, born on 18 February 1876 in Gorj district, area Vulcan, village Pestisani, being 1.63 m high, black hair, dusky visage, front—adequate, eyebrows—black, eyes—brown, nose, mouth and chin—adequate, particular signs—none, was registered on 15 January 1902 as plain soldier […]"[79]

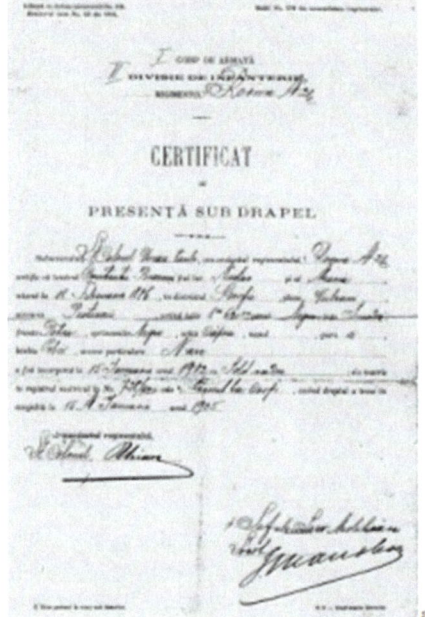

Figs. 45a, b. Rovine Regiment no. 26, Craiova, 1902: a—Brancusi's conscription order; b—barracks of the regiment

Bucharest

Brancusi participated in the rehearsals of the *Carmen* Choral Society, founded by composer Dumitru Georgescu-Kiriac in 1901[80]. As a token of friendship and respect for Georgescu-Kiriac's activity, Brancusi sculpted a statue symbolizing Romanian choir music, which he gave to the society. The sculpture composition entitled *Offering for Chorus "Carmen"* (gypsum, 1902) represents a woman—music—with a group of violin-playing peasants at her feet.

On 5 April, G.D. Mirea issued Brancusi a certificate specifying that he had continued practical courses after graduation of the sculpture section in the School of Beaux Arts[81]. After graduating from the courses of the School of Beaux Arts, and following Principal Mirea's memoir no. 136 of 9 September 1902, Brancusi got the Graduation Diploma no. 2 on 24 September 1902 (Fig. 46)[82].

Craiova

On 30 January he sent a letter to the Trusteeship of Madonna Dudu Church requesting monetary aid for his studies[83], which he was granted (Fig. 47a). As shown by documents, besides Brancusi even Nicolae Titulescu, future politician and chairman of the League of Nations, received stipend from the same church establishment (400 Lei aid, Belle Arte, Bucharest, namely 1,000 Lei, Law Faculty, Paris, Fig. 47b).

During his military stage, in Craiova he was accommodated by Ion Georgescu-Gorjan who lodged in the house of the tradesman Ghita Ionescu (Fig. 48)[84]. In October he modeled the *Bust of Ion Georgescu-Gorjan*[85] (gypsum, Figs. 49a, b).

On 30 November 1902, he sent a letter to the Trusteeship of the Madonna Dudu Church thanking them for their support during his years at the School of Beaux Arts, and once more requested monetary aid to continue his studies in Italy (Fig. 50). Brancusi attached to this aid request twelve photos of sculptures made by him[86]. His application was not approved and the documents were returned to him; some of the photographs were kept and published by the "commentators of Brancusi's creation"[87]. Brancusi was concerned with the photographic art during school. His Professor, A. Tzigara-Samurcas, wrote in his memoirs that he introduced projection in his lectures and used photography as a working method in art history.

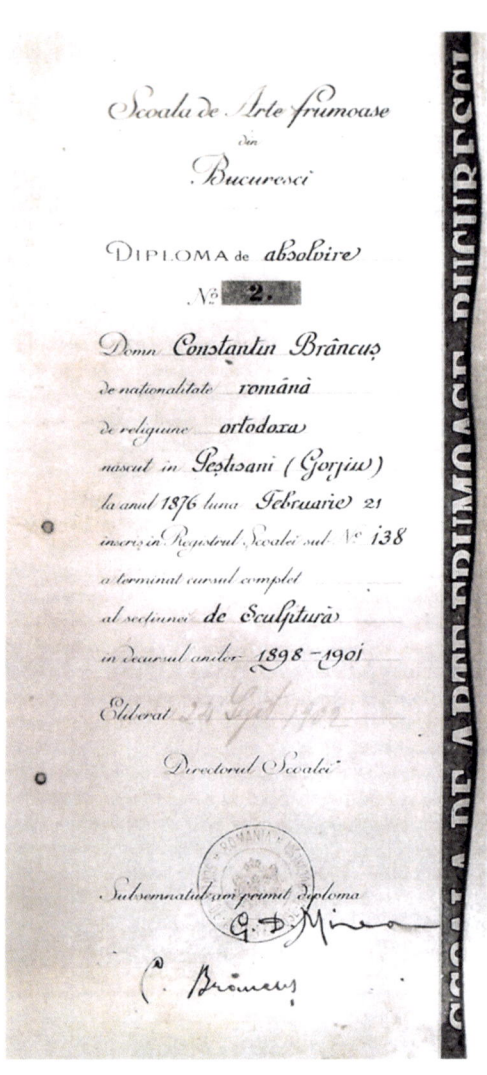

Fig. 46. Graduation Diploma of the School of Beaux Arts, Bucharest, 24 September 1902

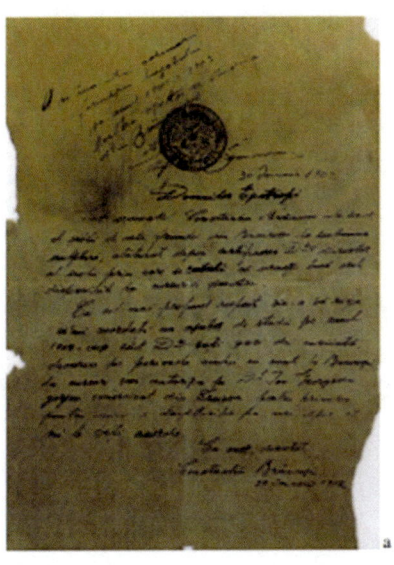

Figs. 47a, b. Trusteeship of Madonna Dudu Church, Craiova: a—Brancusi's letter, 30 January 1902; b—Brancusi and N. Titulescu as scholars, 1902-1903

Fig. 48. House of G. Ionescu, Craiova, 1902

Figs. 49a, b. Ion Georgescu-Gorjan (a) and his bust (b), Craiova, 1902

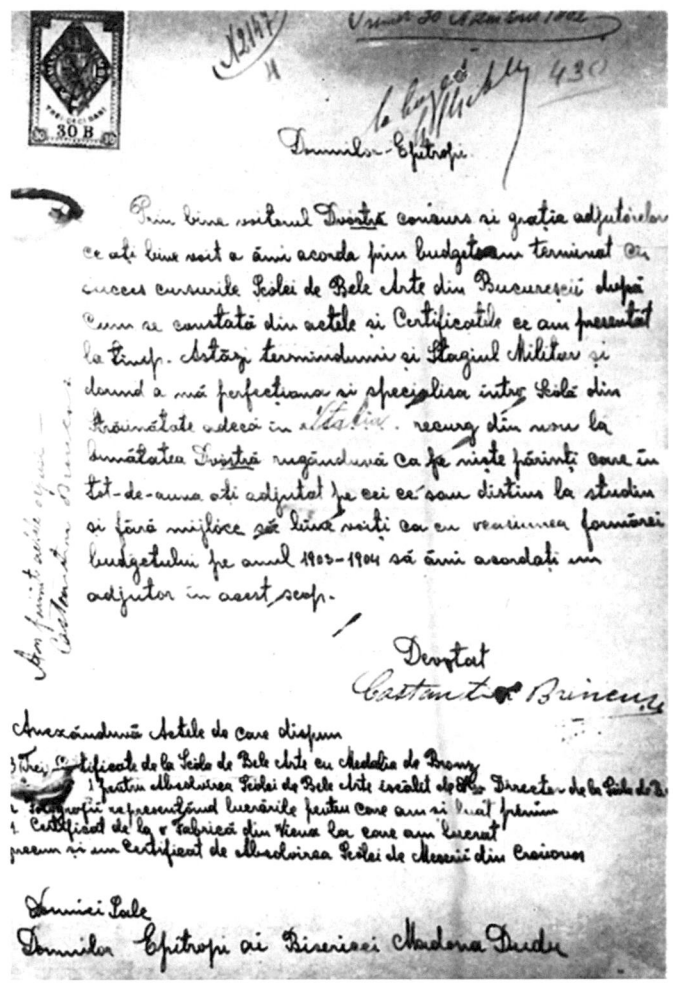

Fig. 50. Letter of Brancusi to the Trusteeship of Madonna Dudu Church, Craiova, 1902

1903

Bucharest

Brancusi exhibited the *Écorché* (gypsum, 1901-1902) between May and June in the Athenaeum Palace (Fig. 51a). In order to make it, the sculptor "has made countless studies on corpses and theoretical ones as well under Dr. Gerota's direction"[88] (Fig. 51b). We can read in the press of that time about this sculpture's success, specifying it could serve as a model for the study of myology in secondary and academic schools and, being the first work of this kind in the country, it was "worth everybody's attention"[89] (Fig. 51c).

All these praiseworthy articles echoed among the ranks of young people and, on 20 May, a letter was registered from the School of Beaux Arts students, written on 14 May and addressed to Spiru Haret, minister of Cults and Public Instruction, whereby they asked his support in procuring a copy of the *Écorché* that was necessary for the study of human anatomy[90] (Fig. 52). The resolution "to be filed" was marked on the letter, which was not good for the request, but by doctor Dimitrie Gerota's intervention two gypsum copies were procured by the Ministry of Cults and Public Instruction, which were meant to be distributed to the school for didactic purposes.

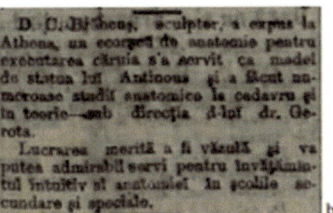

Figs. 51a-c. Bucharest, 1903: a—Athenaeum Palace; b—Adeverul, 7 May, c—Gazeta Artelor, 11 May

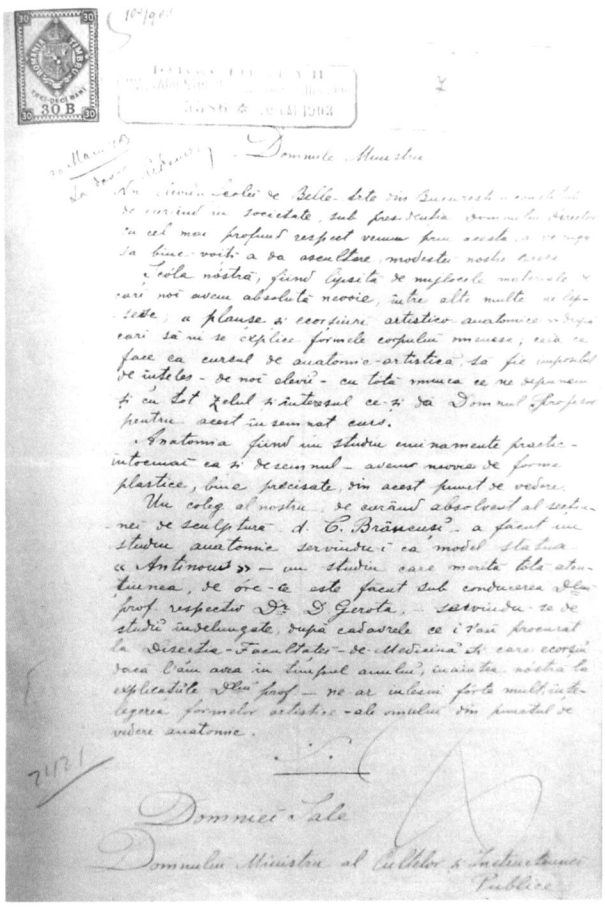

Fig. 52. Letter of the School of Beaux Arts students, Bucharest, 14 May 1903

Francisc Sirato, former school colleague of Brancusi, told Oscar Han that the artist had worked almost two years to the *Écorché*[91]. Camil Ressu, another former colleague of the sculptor, would remember this period later on[92]. There are several opinions[93][94][95] about the number of original pieces and executed copies, as well as about the place where they can be found.

Another Brancusi sculpture—*Bust of General Doctor Carol Davila*—was expected to be completed and journalists were briefed about the development, as seen the publications of that time (Fig. 53a)[96]. During his military service, with the help of doctor Dimitrie Gerota and of his former school colleague Jean A. Steriadi, Brancusi was transferred to Bucharest to execute the *Bust of General Doctor Carol Davila*, which the doctors and the military sanitary corps wanted to place in front of the Military Hospital. Failing to collect an amount fit for a famous artist, the military decided to place the order with Brancusi, who settled for much less but wanted to be exempted of all military duty.

The sculptor worked the bust on the basis of doctor Carol Davila's funeral mask and a photograph (Fig. 53b), perhaps in the studio of the School of Beaux Arts, and gypsum was cast there in March[97] (Fig. 53c). He also modeled a bas-relief of doctor Davila's profile wearing his military uniform (Fig. 53d), a study made after a photograph[98].

The bust of doctor Davila by Brancusi was not to the liking of the institution that placed the order, so the two parties could not strike terms before Brancusi's departure from the country (1904). The order was mediated, moreover, by Doctor Gerota, who wanted to help Brancusi get the necessary funds to go abroad. He received the first installment before making the sculpture and remained only with it, because the bust was not admitted by the military doctors' council that expressed some requests considered ridiculous by the sculptor—to diminish the nose, to change the epaulets, etc. Then Brancusi, to everybody's general amazement, left the room.

Later on, Brancusi explained that it would not have been difficult to comply with the council's requests, but he considered it "easy but prostitute work" to get some train money to Paris. The Oltenian quick spirit and confidence in his own capabilities made him react harshly, to the astonishment of the audience, but also "to the great panic and fright of Doctor Gerota"[99]. Ion Croitoru remembered that "Brancusi left the country in indignation" because "the military" had not paid him for Davila's bust[100].

Figs. 53a-d. General Doctor Carol Davila, Bucharest: a—Adeverul, 28 October 1903; b—Davila's photograph; c—bust; d—bas-relief

First Years of Life in Paris

1904

Bucharest

Brancusi sent a letter to the Medical Students' Society, registered 102 of 18 May 1904 asking for support in order to sell a *Écorché*, being in need of money for studies abroad. The demand was favorably endorsed by the society's committee on the 23 May meeting[101].

Craiova, Hobita, Bahna (Mehedinti County)

In the spring he prepared for departure to Paris, having got 1,000 Lei travel money from Ion Croitoru who Brancusi gave the sketch book to (1900-1902) in token of gratitude, some monetary aid from the Trusteeship of Madonna Dudu Church and from doctor Dimitrie Gerota; also some borrowed money and personal sums from the sale of a few sculptures. He first got to Craiova and Hobita to say good-bye to his friends, relatives and especially his beloved mother whom he left with a broken heart.

In the second half of May, he left Hobita via Tismana, passed by the monastery to ask the priest's blessing, crossed the Motru Rivulet and reached to Baia de Arama; he crossed the lilac forest of Ponoare and arrived to Bahna near Varciorova, close to the Danube River. Brancusi had walked the Hobita-Bahna route in two days, backpack containing some food and a spare pair of shoes. Bahna locality of Mehedinti County is frontier point, and his passport mentioned "country exit will be in the Bahna—Varciorova border point. […] The Romanian canton of the frontier was only a few yards away and, once his passport syllabified and stamped with eight-cornered stamp clearly marked *Exited*, the barrier was lifted—painted differently than the identical one across the road—which, when reached, a haughty soldier came before him wearing hat-like uniform cap adorned with the entire cocktail."[102] The pennate soldier was the Hungarian representative of the Austro-Hungarian Empire's authority.

Vienna

In the country he had decided the following route—Budapest, Vienna, Munich and, perhaps, Paris. He chose the Munich variant taking his protector's advice, doctor Dimitrie Gerota who had been studying there and of Professor Alexandru Tzigara-Samurcas'. Peter Neagoe as well, his former school colleague and house neighbor in Bucharest had studied in Munich so his word also was of significance for Brancusi. He traveled to Vienna by train via Budapest, the same way as in the summer of 1897, when returning from that city. Brancusi stayed in Vienna (Fig. 54) only a few days visiting museums, art galleries, public monuments, etc.

Brancusi did not leave the country as a poor man, as the story goes. This 1904 photograph shows him a tourist wearing fashionable clothes—long comfortable jacket, baggy trousers, ankle boots and leather leggings; brimless hat on his head, backpack and Alpenstock in hand (Fig. 55). It is no wonder he traveled some part of the road by foot since he got used with long distances from his childhood, and the beauty of landscapes just fascinated him. People's hospitality charmed him as well as the local customs and the architecture of new places he visited. All these did not let him feel tired.

Fig. 54. Vienna, 1904

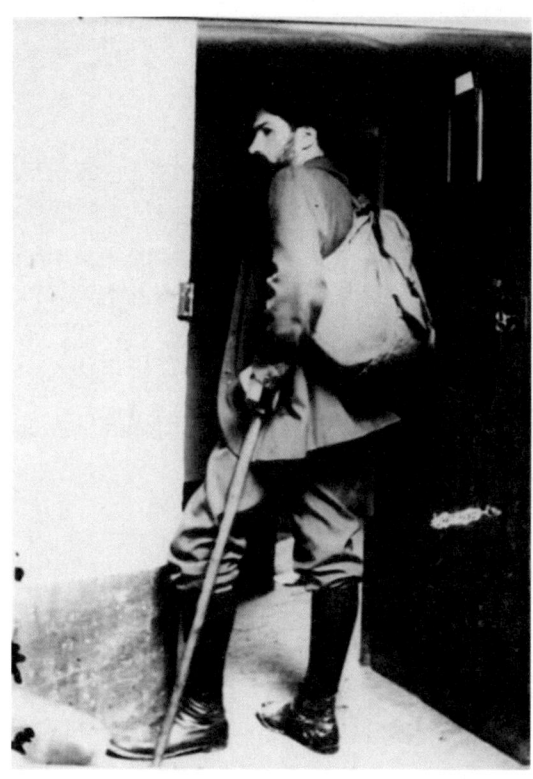

Fig. 55. Brancusi on the way to Paris, 1904

Munich

When recounting with friends, Brancusi told them in Munich: "I arrived with only twenty Lei in my pocket"[103], via Gmunden, Ischl, and Salzburg, and was thus compelled to find some work[104]. He stayed for two weeks in Munich (Fig. 56), went to the studios of the Royal Beaux Arts Academy, and visited museums, exhibitions, the city's Picture Gallery and Gliptotech, along with monuments and so on. It was at this time he became acquainted with the Secession movement, which occurred in Germany in 1892 and initiated the dissidence against the academic art promoted by the Munich Artists' Association (*Münchener Künstlergenossenschaft*). There he decided to go to Paris because: "having got to Munich to work, I realized it is only in Paris one can reach full achievement"[105].

Fig. 56. Munich, 1904

Basel

He passed by Rorschach and Zurich and crossed the Saint-Bernard Gorge. A torrential rain caught him near Basel (Fig. 57), where he fell seriously ill and was cared for by a Church-managed hospital. Escaping from this ordeal—double pneumonia—he would then go on to sculpt a wood crucifix in token of his gratitude[106]. Brancusi bore the marks of this illness his entire life, only his iron will and nerves would help him later cut marble blocks and wood girders by saw and then sculpt them by chisel and hatchet.

Fig. 57. Provisional bridge, Basel, 1904

Langres

He crossed Alsace on foot, reaching to Langres (Haute-Marne). Weakened by the illness Brancusi sent a telegram to Daniel Poiana, his friend who got to Paris in 1903, and asked him for travel money by post[107], thus he could buy a train ticket from Langres to Paris (Fig. 58).

Paris

Brancusi got in the East Station (Fig. 59a) on 14 July and stayed at Daniel Poiana's until an 8th floor dwelling place was found for him at 9 Cité Condorcet (Fig. 59b), for September to November, near Chartier Pub where Daniel again found him a dish washer job (Figs. 60a, b). After some time, he would work in the Mollard Pub still as dishwasher[108].

To come to his help, Archimandrite Chesarie Stefano admitted him as a sexton and caretaker of the Romanian Orthodox Church in Cartier Latin, 9bis Jean de Beauvais Street. A photo of Brancusi wearing the surplice was kept of that time and included an inscription entitled "Memories of Hard Times" (Figs. 61a, b).

This period of Brancusi's life was marked by "destitution, disproportionate absurd destitution which was close to Gorki's teens"[109].

Fig. 58. Rack bar railroad, Langres, 1904

Figs. 59a, b. Paris, 1904: a—East Station; b—Cité Condorcet

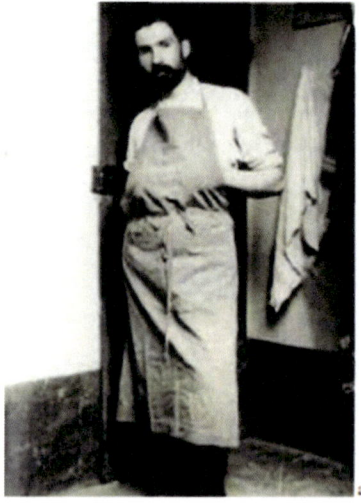 

Figs. 60a, b. Paris, 1904: a—Brancusi working as dishwasher; b—Chartier Beer House

Figs. 61a, b. Paris, 1904: a—Romanian Orthodox Church; b—Brancusi parish clerk

1905

Paris

From April to June, he lived in the attic of a building at 10 Place de la Bourse (Fig. 62) as mentioned in several letters and official documents. There is also one archive photograph with the artist's sculptures made in this home-studio (Fig. 63).

Fig. 62. Place de la Bourse, Paris, 1905

Fig. 63. View from the home-studio of Brancusi, Paris, 1905

In need of money to support his school studies, on 2 April 1905, Brancusi addressed the goodwill of the Ministry of Cults and Public Instruction in Bucharest and asked for a stipend[110]. With the help of Doctor Gerota, he managed to obtain a 600 Lei scholarship from the Raducanu-Simonide study fund, while also receiving 100 Lei each semester from Madonna Dudu.

In May 1905 Brancusi moved to the attic from 16 Place Dauphine (Fig. 64), becoming a neighbor to Louis Herbette, state counselor, Theodor Pallady, Romanian painter, and Otilia Cosmuta, a lesser-known writer in Romania that settled in Paris in 1905, where she was quite active in literary and artistic circles. She became Anatole France's secretary and was a great admirer of Bourdelle, which she skillfully commented the creation of [111] [112]. Despite the true friendship between Brancusi and Otilia Cosmuta, in 1909 Brancusi refused to sculpt A. France's portrait. Brancusi was noted as having said: "I can make nobody's bust since I cannot render something that gives resemblance to the subject—life."[113]

Fig. 64. Place Dauphine, Paris, 1905

On 12 June 1905, state counselor Louis Herbette approached Ernest Henri Dubois, Director of the National School of Beaux Arts[114] for Brancusi's admission to Antonin Mercié's studio. The two French sculptors, Dubois, and Mercié, were well-known in Romania due to having crafted several artistic monuments for public forums. When Brancusi was still in Romania, Ernest Henri Dubois, a great neo-classical sculptor highly appreciated by Romanian politicians, had sculpted the *Monument of Ion C. Bratianu* from University Square of Bucharest, the *Monument of G.C. Cantacuzino* at the entry of Gradina Icoanei Park, and the *Monument of George D. Pallade* in Barlad.

Romania's Legation administered by Minister Grigore G. Ghika addressed the Director of the National School of Beaux Arts to have Brancusi admitted at the approaching entrance exam[115]. Having been admitted, Brancusi obtained the new Director Léon Bonnat's agreement and began working in the studio of Professor Antonin Mercié, from the dates 23 June 1905 until 19 January 1906 (Figs. 65a, b).

Figs. 65a, b. Paris, 1905-1906: a—National School of Beaux Arts; b—Brancusi next to his colleagues

Professor Marius Jean Antonin Mercié was an academic sculptor who innovated nothing in art, being more inspired by Rodin's works where his sculptures paid great attention to details. In Romania when Brancusi was a Beaux Arts student, Mercié completed the *Monument of Alexandru N. Lahovary*. Although the Professor was very fond of Brancusi, he was "misfortunate" due to only crafting "a sculpture a day in Rodin style" with "great technical skill." Mercié thought this was no good for Brancusi as an artist. He stoically endured the time spent in Mercié's studio, as he would later tell P. Pandrea: "These were the hardest years as I was looking for my style, my own path."[116] And he left in order to find his own way in art.

On 1 July 1905, the National School of Beaux Arts issued to student Brancusi, "subsidized by the Romanian government," a certificate signed by Professor Mercié, head of the sculpture studio, which specified his learning as highly satisfactory[117] (Fig. 66).

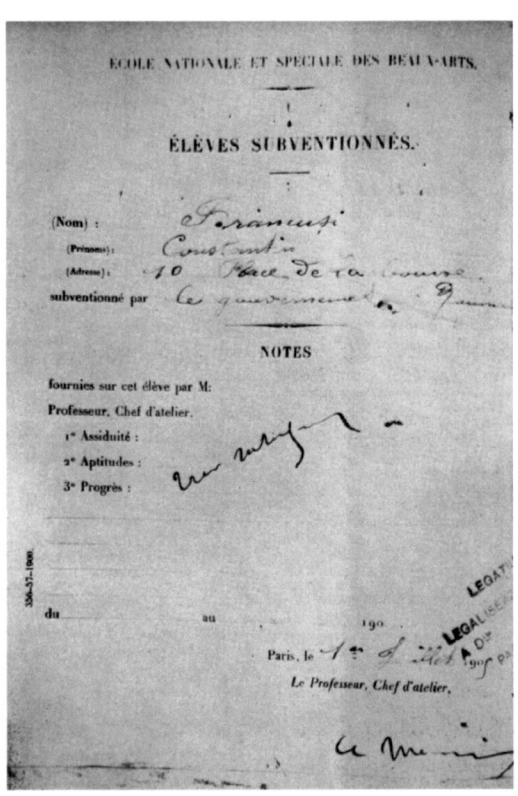

Fig. 66. School grade given to Brancusi by Professor A. Mercié, Paris, 1 July 1905

On 10 November 1905, Director Léon Bonnat issued him a certificate to be sent to Romania's Ministry of Cults and Public Instruction and on 5 December the dean mentioned Professor Mercié's high appreciation [118] concerning the student Brancusi.

He became a member of the Circle of Romanian Students in Paris (*Cercle des étudiants roumains de Paris*) attended by the following attendees: Traian Vuia, Theodor Pallady, Constantin Levaditi, George Enescu, Aurel Vlaicu, Henri Coanda, Ion Theodorescu-Sion, Eustatiu Stoenescu, Theodor Cornel, Emil Damian, Nicolae Darascu, Stefan Popescu, Constantin Nedelcu, Duiliu Marcu, Camil Ressu, Ion and Niculae Pillat, Gheorghita C. Lupescu, Solomon Basile Marbé, a.o. Professor C. Nedelcu remembered Brancusi as having been "sincere, very honest, careful and orderly," showing "original profound independent personality"[119].

During this time, to support himself and progress in sculpture, Brancusi worked with models and photos of male and female busts modeled or cast in gypsum, of which only a few photographs remain. Works made during this time include *Pride*, first bronze cast sculpture. As token of his appreciation for Traian Vuia, Brancusi gave him the *Leaf of the Life* (Fig. 67) made of wood, representing a leaf of the sacred oak tree, symbol of strength for the Romanian people[120].

Fig. 67. *Leaf of the Life*

Brancusi was aware of all artistic movements in Paris. From 1905 to 1914 he participated to the Tuesday soirées that Paul Fort gave at the Closerie des Lilas[121] (Fig. 68), where he would usually meet Guillaume Apollinaire, Filippo T. Marinetti, Amedeo Modigliani, Fernand Léger, Pablo Picasso, as well as other notable figures.

Fig. 68. Closerie des Lilas, Paris

1906

Paris

On 1 February 1906, "feeling the absolute need to study more in order to be able to *produce something*."

Brancusi asked for his scholarship to be extended to 1907. His application was supported by certificates of Parisian professors and by a laudatory report by Professor C.I. Stancescu, then interim dean of the School of Beaux Arts from Bucharest. Professor Stancescu mentioned Brancusi's merits[122].

Brancusi attended the historical flight of Montesson, near Paris on 18 March, when Traian Vuia managed to detach himself 1 meter above ground with his *Vuia I* machine, air-born along 12 m[123] [124] (Fig. 69). There is one Brancusi sculpture from this period dedicated to Vuia as incised in marble, actually an allegorical portrait of the Romanian inventor seen by the sculptor as the bird-man and at the same time a hint to his inquisitive prying spirit, in

Oltenia branded language "he poked his nose everywhere" (1906-1907?, Figs. 70a, b)[125].

Fig. 69. L'Aérophile, Paris, 1906, *9*

Figs. 70a, b. Traian Vuia (a) and his portrait by Brancusi (b)

1906 Salon of the National Society of Beaux Arts (*Société nationale des beaux-arts. Salon 1906*) was organized from 15 April to 16 June where he participated with a gypsum sculpture. Ever since he arrived in France that was the first salon where the sculptor was admitted to participate.

Bucharest

Two articles on this event were published in L'Indépendance Roumaine, one signed by scientist Nicolae Vaschide, a worldwide famous psychiatrist, where he also described the sculptor's studio[126] and the second one authored by Maria Bengescu[127]. Vaschide wrote in his article about the sculptor that "despite the vicissitudes of a needy life full of struggle, [Brancusi] has unflinching faith in his talent."

The *General Romanian Exhibition* (6 June-23 November) was organized on Filaret Hill on the occasion of the 40 years' royal jubilee, where the *Écorché* was exhibited in doctor Dimitrie Gerota's pavilion (Figs. 71a, b).

Figs. 71a, b. *General Romanian Exhibition*—1906, Bucharest: a—general view; b—pavilion of doctor D. Gerota

Paris

On 28 September 1906, Brancusi sent a postcard to his friend Ion Gheorghian-Popescu (Fig. 72) and informed him with justified pride about his participation to the Autumn Salon (*Salon d'Automne*)[128].

Fig. 72. Card sent to I. Gheorghian-Popescu, Paris, 28 September 1906

The 4th exhibition of the Autumn Salon Society (*Société du Salon d'automne/4ᵉ Exposition*) opened from 6 October to 15 November in the Grand Palais of Champs-Élysées. The jury of the sculpture section including Bourdelle, Maillol and Metardo Rosso accepted three of his works.

In 1906, he modeled in clay a few children heads and busts, of which some are cast in gypsum and bronze. To help Brancusi, lottery was organized in the country in November upon the initiative of painter Stefan Popescu. The winner coupon was for the *Child*. Two lists were drawn up, one to be covered by the Circle of Romanian Students in Paris and the second was sent to V.G. Mortun who printed it in L'Indépendance Roumaine of Bucharest on 10 November.

They managed to collect 1,000 FF of which 200 was the cost of bronze casting two copies with Valsuani. The winner of the lottery was Victor N. Popp of Craiova, law student in Paris, who in 1907, would take the work to the country and initiate there a valuable collection of Brancusi sculptures.

Otilia Cosmuta (Fig. 73) wrote in a chronicle about Brancusi and his participation to the Autumn Salon in Paris, published in L'Indépendance Roumaine; she pointed out that Rodin "speaks highly of Brancusi's talent"[129].

Fig. 73. Sofia, wife of painter Stefan Popescu, and Otilia Cosmuta in Brancusi's studio of 16 Place Dauphine, Paris

He was granted 600 Lei from the 1906-1907 budget and in 1907-1908 they dispatched him 1,200 Lei to Paris through the National Bank (21 January 1908), thus ensuing the Romanian government aided Brancusi until he was 32[130].

Brancusi said about his first years in Paris: "At first I had a very difficult time. Sometimes I leaned on walls lest I should fall—of hunger or illness. I have hanged cardboards over my bed marked with all the works of advice I was telling to myself in moments of doubt.;" detached and wise, he assessed the role and use of the hardships endured since he was a child: "suffering strengthens people and is more necessary than pleasure in forging a character.

And then I find everyone is to blame for what happens to one…As a matter of fact, what has sustained me all along the route I took since I left my Gorj village…was this sentiment of personal responsibility for everything. There was no envy or hatred in my heart but only the happiness one can gather everywhere, anytime. I believe the sentiment of our permanent childhood makes us truly alive…"[131]

The 1904 Bucharest Yearbook, page 204 and 1906, page 304 indicated Brancusi's name in the painters' trade, his Bucharest address being 18 Elisabeta Blvd (Fig. 74). Therefore, the sculptor had kept his Bucharest address after settling in Paris, showing he had not broken his connections to the country and was not fully convinced he would stay abroad for good.

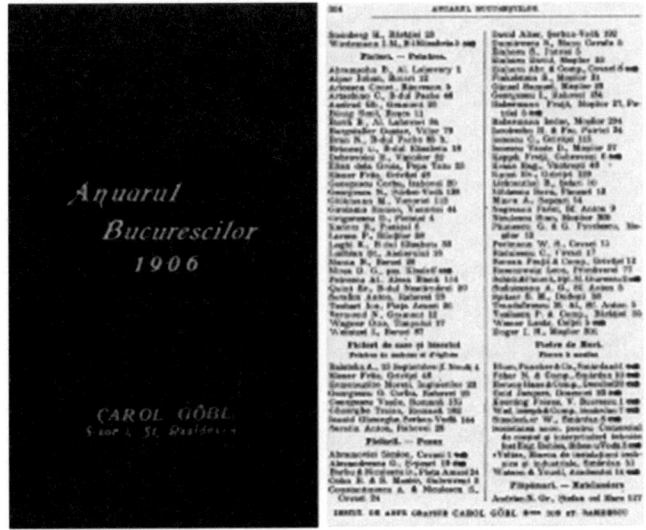

Fig. 74. 1906 Bucharest Yearbook

1907

Paris

At the age of 30, Brancusi was forced by the organization and functioning regulation to leave the National School of Fine Arts. From 24 March to 27 April 1907, Brancusi was hired by Rodin to work as a practitioner in his studio upon the intervention of Queen Elisabeta of Romania visiting Paris, and upon the young sculptor's laudatory introduction by Maria Bengescu and Otilia

Cosmuta. Brancusi's meeting with Rodin has not been fully clarified. Vasile G. Paleolog mentioned in his writing that Maria Bengescu, "arduous apprentice appreciative of arts" and friend of Elena Vacarescu, "understood Brancusi's genius" and mediated the meeting between the two artists in Meudon[132].

Brancusi's relation to Maria Bengescu was short due to having refused to stay in Rodin's studio. In exchange, Otilia Cosmuta wrote that she was thinking of introducing Brancusi to Rodin[133]. Later, studies in Rodin Museum's archive proved she did so.

In 1907, when Brancusi entered as practitioner at Rodin's, the master had developed an *industry* of sculpture, being overwhelmed with orders from Europe and the United States. His studio thronged with students who modeled, cut marble, thinned, finished, and followed bronze casting and metal patina, while Rodin took charge of the concept and coordination. In Rodin's studio, Brancusi became acquainted with American photographer Edward Steichen and with Henri Coanda, a future scientist that would leave important testimonies with respect to the time they spent together, admitting he owed it to Brancusi to have given up sculpture and followed his vocation of scientist and inventor[134].

We think this brief period spent in Rodin's shadow helped Brancusi understand the secrets of artistic bronze casting and finishing techniques, where he could meet a select world just by crossing the master's threshold and being noticed by the personalities of the time. When Brancusi understood Rodin had nothing more to say in sculpture and that everybody else was compelled to line up after him unless they made new revolutions in art, Brancusi left the master's studio. Rodin understood his intentions and bore no grudge. Brancusi did the same that Rodin had done many years before. He chose to return to originally primitive shapes, when man was sincere and clean within creation, untouched by corrupting civilization. Whatever he had seen and practiced in his native places helped him in this return, as his childhood realm had been isolated from the rest of the world and people there expressed their feelings in creation un-impacted by dogmas and progress.

In April, he received an important order of funerary monument from Eliza Stanescu of Buzau. The sculptor was recommended by doctor Dimitrie Gerota and his brother Sava, apothecary in Buzau, as well as by painter Stefan Popescu with his wife Sofia and by Nicolae Vaschide, all three of Buzau. Brancusi signed the contract on 18 April for this monument and received significant amount of money, dispatched in several installments (Fig. 75)[135].

To be able to execute this order the sculptor moved in a bigger studio of Montparnasse district (Figs. 76 and 77). His work to the two ensemble pieces—*Prayer* and *Bust of Petre Stanescu*—lasted more than he estimated and the funerary ensemble would be finished only in 1914.

Sibiu, Craiova

Luceafarul magazine printed in its March issue the first photographs of Brancusi sculptures—*Study* (*Bust of M. G. Lupescu*—A/N), *Study* (*Pride*—A/N) and *Child* (Fig. 78)[136]. These photos were also published in the 1908 Ramuri magazine calendar in Craiova (Fig. 79).

Bucharest

The *6th Painting and Sculpture Exhibition of the "Artistic Youth" Society Under the High Patronage of HRH Princess of Romania* was organized at the Athenaeum Palace (15 March-1 May).

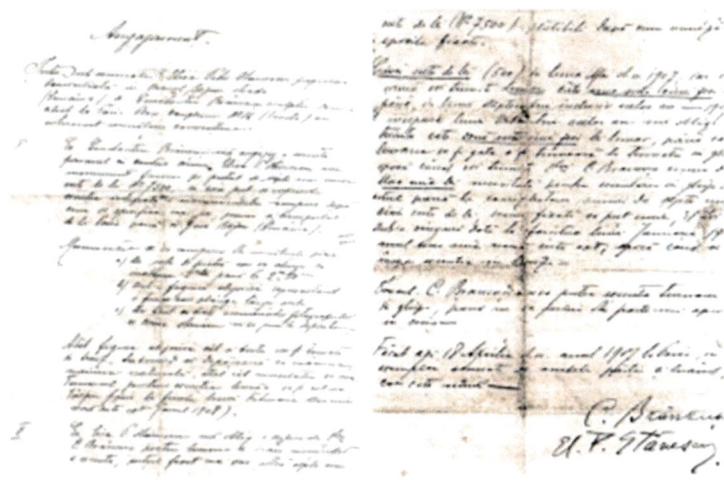

Fig. 75. Commitment to make the funerary ensemble of Buzau, Paris, 18 April 1907

Fig. 76. Montparnasse Street, Paris

Fig. 77. Daniel Poiana and his daughter Alicia in Brancusi's studio of 54 Montparnasse Street, Paris, 1907

Fig. 78. Luceafarul, Sibiu, 1 March 1907

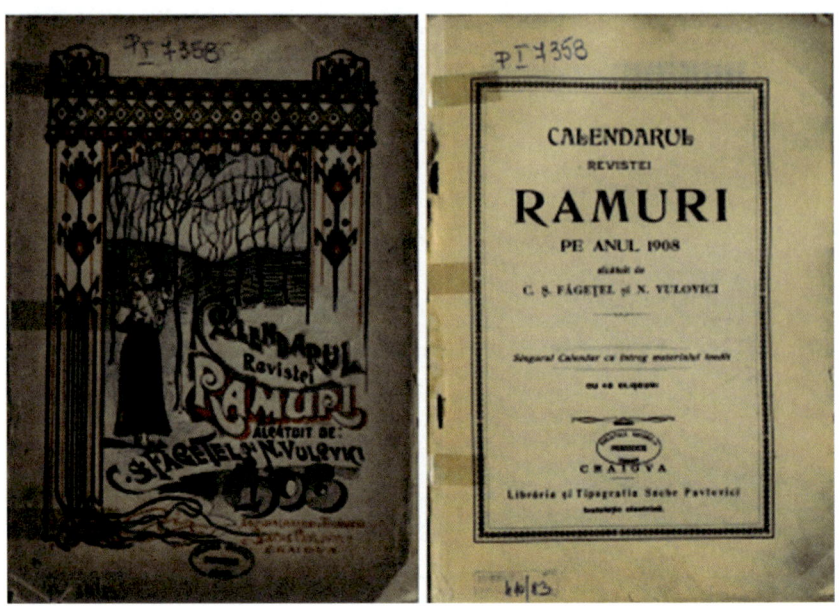

Fig. 79. 1908 Ramuri magazine calendar, Craiova

Paris, Creteil

The 17th exhibition of the National Society of Beaux Arts (*Société nationale des beaux-arts/XVIIe Exposition*) was organized from 14 April to 30 June at the Grand Palais of Champs-Élysées. Brancusi was accepted with four works appreciated by Rodin, Salon chairman. Brancusi told his friends that while Rodin contemplated pensively his sculptures, he had respectfully asked for his opinion: *Maître, dites un mot* [Master, just one word], to which the great artist answered: *Ne travaillez pas trop vite et n'exposez pas de trop* [Don't work too fast and don't exhibit too much][137]. Art critic Theodor Cornel wrote from Paris about Brancusi and the event for newspaper Adeverul, considering him a "talented artist" who was "undoubtedly constructing his artistic future"[138].

Together with Albert Gleizes he participated to the celebration and exhibition organized on 21 July in the phalanstery of Créteil Abbey (L'Abbaye de Créteil), established by Charles Vildrac. There, he befriended writer Alexandre Mercereau.

In autumn, he installed his own forge and anvil in the studio, which would enable his making the working tools needed for stone and marble sculpture.

Though his want of money prevented him from having procured until then, we can thus explain his "road finding" and passage to the direct cut.

The 5th exhibition of the Autumn Salon Society (*Société du Salon d'automne/5ᵉ Exposition*) was organized on 1-22 October at the Grand Palais of Champs-Élysées, where Brancusi exhibited a *Study*.

On 13 October, Brancusi received a harsh blow by losing his friend and mentor Dr. Nicolae Vaschide (Fig. 80) after a heart attack.

On 11 December, Brancusi notified to the Ministry of Cults and Public Instruction of Romania the address where they should send the subsidy: 54 Montparnasse Street, and on 19 December the Bucharest Ministry decided sending him 1,200 Lei.

He met Duchamp brothers, writer Max Jacob, artists Matisse, Juan Gris, Henry de Waroquier, a.o. He became good friend of the painter Henri Rousseau le Douanier.

The same year, Brancusi sculpted a few referential works of his creation, which included: *Prayer* (gypsum, Fig. 81a), *Torment* (gypsum), *Kiss* (stone, Fig. 81b)—opening the series of sculptures on this theme —and *Wisdom of the Earth* (stone).

Fig. 80. Victoria and Nicolae Vaschide and many other friends in Brancusi's studio, Paris, 1907

Figs. 81a, b. Paris, 1907: a—*Prayer*; b—*Kiss*

1908

Sibiu

The Luceafarul magazine in its 1 February issue published Otilia Cosmuta's chronicle about the Autumn Salon of Paris organized in October 1907, where Brancusi also participated who the writer considered "the only valuable artist" of the exhibition. She pointed out the "burning passion" of the sculptor in search of the "models' characteristic," which he then "renders with unutterable love" on the faces of his portraits and busts. The magazine published three photos of Brancusi works (Fig. 82)[139].

Fig. 82. Luceafarul, Sibiu, 1 February 1908

Paris, Craiova

Victor N. Popp, being in Paris in 1907, ordered Brancusi a bust to be made for Traian Demetrescu, poet forerunner of symbolism in Romania, who had died at the age of 30 of tuberculosis, who the young Maecenas wanted to pay homage to. When Brancusi was in Craiova, T. Demetrescu had nurtured his heart and mind with the creation of the national poet Mihai Eminescu, so the sculptor accepted the order unconditionally. The press of Craiova recorded their agreement[140]. Brancusi fell ill with typhoid fever and could not keep up with the order for one year, the bust no longer achieved. Painter Leon Biju, former school colleague in Bucharest, executed a drawing of the artist on his suffering bed, dated 18 February (Fig. 83)[141].

Fig. 83. Brancusi ill with typhoid fever—drawing by L. Biju, Paris, 18 February 1908

Bucharest, Sibiu

The *7th Painting and Sculpture Exhibition of the "Artistic Youth" Society Under the High Patronage of HRH Princess of Romania* was organized at the Athenaeum Palace (20 March-1 May). The exhibition was attended by 39 visual artists with 185 works. Brancusi exhibited two sculptures.

The Luceafarul magazine in its 1 May issue published an exhibition chronicle written by George Murnu that considered Brancusi's works represented "the greatest defiance of pedantry and academism" in Romania, as the artist borrowed from Rodin the "picturesque pathetic treatment of faces, life spontaneity and intensity" (Fig. 84)[142].

Paris, Sibiu

The 18th exhibition of the National Society of Beaux Arts (*Société nationale des beaux-arts/XVIIIe Exposition*) was organized from 15 April to 30 June at the Grand Palais.

Writer Otilia Cosmuta informed her readers about the sculptor, "already widely known" that participated to the National Society of Beaux Arts Salon of Paris, providing also three photographs in her article (Fig. 85). She explained why Brancusi could dispatch only one sculpture, because he was in a hurry to complete a "great funerary monument," however the writer was convinced the artist would soon exhibit new valuable works due to his "serious art"[143].

He frequented the group of modern artists having their studios on the *Bateau Lavoir* (Fig. 86).

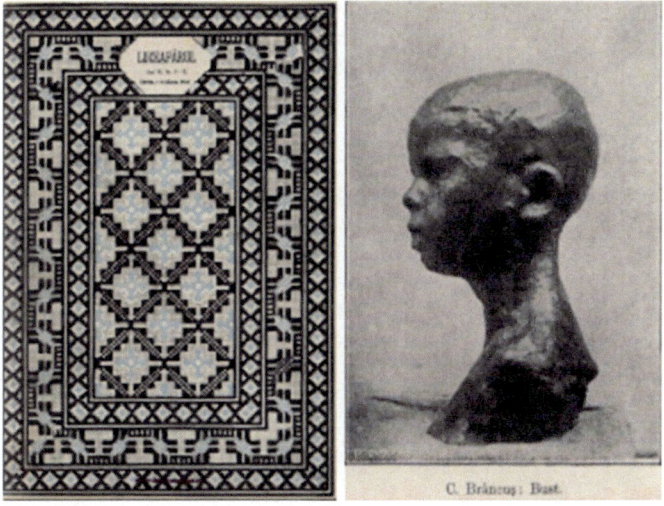

Fig. 84. Luceafarul, Sibiu, 1 May 1908

Fig. 85. Luceafarul, Sibiu, 1 October 1908

Fig. 86. Bateau Lavoir, Paris, 1910

About 1908-1910 Brancusi met Léonie Ricou (Fig. 87a), who from 1908 until the beginning of World War I, kept a salon in central Montparnasse at 270 Raspail Blvd (Fig. 88), frequented by Apollinaire, Ungaretti, Picasso, Severini, González, Modigliani and many other writers and artists of the time. Professor George Oprescu described her as "rich, beautiful, knowing much on art and literature, of delicate constitution, craving any new thing"[144].

Her fine facial traits, expressive eyes and well-delineated mouth, and moreover her spirit and vividness inspired Picasso, Modigliani and Brancusi that made all her portrait, each one by his own vision. In 1914(?)-1917 Brancusi sculpted a stylized portrait, a totem apparently, of Mrs. Ricou using oak wood from the girders of demolished houses, which he liked for the patina. They say this portrait was achieved without the model whose name—*Madame L.R.* (Fig. 87b)—it bears, since she had left Paris because of the war.

The correspondence between Léonie Ricou and Brancusi dates from 1914 to 1921 and can be found in Pompidou Center. The letters show their relationship relied on Léonie Ricou's huge admiration for the sculptor[145].

Baroness Renée Irana Frachon came to the studio and Brancusi executed a few portraits, which, following a laborious process of stylization and refinement, will lead him in 1909-1910 to the *Sleeping Muse* (polished bronze, Figs. 89a, b). The correspondence of Brancusi with baroness Frachon does not hint friendship was trespassed; the publications about the master and his model also indicate Renée Frachon as good friend until the end of the artist's life[146].

Figs. 87a, b. Paris: a—Léonie Ricou; b—*Madame L.R.*

Fig. 88. Raspail Blvd, Paris

Figs. 89a, b. Paris: a—Baroness Renée Irana Frachon; b—*Sleeping Muse*

Bucharest

Danaide was sculpted in Vratsa stone used by Romanian artists. The sculpture authenticity issue was raised because they could not know whether Brancusi had been to Romania at that time. Research studies have shown the work was sculpted in the studio of art collector Alexandru Bogdan-Pitesti, arranged in his house of Brezoianu Street, which he equipped with all the required items and placed at the disposal of a group of painters and sculptors he liked, most of them poor and talented, among whom Brancusi. This assumption is supported by the testimony of poet Tudor Arghezi[147].

Another proof of the fact this work was made by Brancusi in Bucharest during his recovery after the serious illness he endured, typhoid fever, is a photograph inscribed "Tête de jeune fille 1908, pierre sculptée à Bucarest, colectia Bogda [sic], 1908" [Head of young girl 1908, stone sculpted in Bucharest, Bogda collection, 1908][148] [149].

1909

Sibiu

Charles Morice, famous art critic of Mercure de France in Paris, published an article in the Luceafarul magazine on 1 March praising sculptor Brancusi and considering him "one of the best skilled in his generation." The issue also provided three photos of some works exhibited at the Autumn Salon in Paris: *Study* (*Bust of Victoria Vaschide*—A/N), *Study Head* and *Sleep* (Fig. 90)[150].

Fig. 90. Luceafarul, Sibiu, 1 March 1909

Bucharest

The *8th Painting and Sculpture Exhibition of the "Artistic Youth" Society Under the High Patronage of HRH Princess of Romania* was organized at the Athenaeum Palace (15 March-15 April). The exhibition catalogue shows 47 painters and sculptors participated with 201 works of the most different styles. Brancusi sent three sculptures.

The *Official Exhibition of Painting, Sculpture and Architecture* was organized from April to May and Brancusi participated with two works. The exhibition jury, including G.D. Mirea, W. Hegel, A. Tzigara-Samurcas, D. Serafim—former professors of Brancusi in the School of Beaux Arts —I. Mincu and E. Panaitescu-Bardasare, chaired by Spiru Haret granted the 2nd sculpture prize *ex aequo* (amounting to 1,000 Lei) to sculptors Brancusi and Paciurea. There was no first prize.

The Ministry of Cults and Public Instruction purchased the patina gypsum *Bust of Painter Nicolae Darascu* with 2,000 Lei, but this sum was paid in several installments, the last one on 18 March 1910 and only when, upon official request, the sculptor discounted 250 Lei of the initially set price[151].

King Carol I conferred the *Bene Merenti Medal*, 1st class to "Mr. Brancusi C., architect, for his artistic merits" under royal decree upon the proposal of Spiru Haret, minister of Cults and Public Instruction; this was recorded in the Official Gazette no. 48 of 31 May/13 June 1909, page 1921.

Paris

The 7th exhibition of the Autumn Salon Society (*Société du Salon d'automne/7ᵉ Exposition*) from 1 October to 8 November was organized at the Grand Palais of Champs-Élysées. Brancusi participated with a *head of a child* in bronze.

Wilhelm Lehmbruck called on him in his studio. That year he was also visited by his countryman sculptor Anghel Chiciu, former student of the School of Crafts in Craiova, then student of the National School of Beaux Arts in Paris.

In the autumn of 1909, Brancusi received the call of Cecilia Cutescu-Storck and they visited together exhibitions, museums (Louvre, Guimet), cathedrals (Notre-Dame, Chartres), and other destinations[152].

At the Closerie des Lilas Pub, he met with Apollinaire, Picasso, Max Jacob, Maurice de Vlaminck, André Derain, Braque, Henri Rousseau le Douanier, Fernand Léger and Gino Severini. He would meet Modigliani, whom he nurtured sincere long-lasting friendship for through a mutual friend, doctor Paul Alexandre[153] at one of the latter's famous parties he used to throw in the building of 7 Delta Street (Fig. 91). To be closer to Brancusi Modigliani moved at 14 Cité Falguière, a colony of poor artists that rented studio-rooms at affordable prices.

Fig. 91. Façade of the building from 7 Delta Street, Paris

From 1909 to 1911, Modigliani worked passionately in Brancusi's studio, being interested by sculpture in general and by the *direct cut* in particular. He kept going to Brancusi's studio until the beginning of World War I, after which the two friends saw each other less and less. Modigliani focused on sculpture without however neglecting drawing and painting, which he would dedicate to after 1916 until the end of his life. Modigliani made several portraits of Brancusi (Figs. 92a-f), and Brancusi answered him by an artistic gesture, an allegorical portrait referring directly to his bohemian life *De Modi Oiseau de nuit* [To Modi Night Bird] (stone, 1909-1914, Fig. 93)[154].

Figs. 92a-f. *Brancusi* by Modigliani—drawings and paintings: a—*Portrait of Brancusi Seated in an Armchair*, 1908-1909; b—*Portrait of Brancusi*, 1909; c—*Portrait of Constantin Brancusi*, 1909; d—*The Cellist*, 1909; e—*Portrait of Brancusi*, 1909-1910; f—*Bearded Man Seated*, 1909-1910

Fig. 93. *De Modi Oiseau de nuit*

During this time, too, he sculpted his first *Torso* (marble), the model being his friend Lilly Waldenberg[155], and this work opened the same series. Among his other achievements during the year 1909, Brancusi sculpted the following: *Woman Looking in the Mirror* (marble), *Kiss* (stone, funerary stela) and *Sleeping Muse* (marble).

In 1909-1912, the artist got in touch with the futurist movement initiated by Filippo T. Marinetti that in 1909 published the *Futurist Manifesto*.

1910

Paris

The 26th exhibition of the Independent Artists' Society (*Société des artistes indépendants/26e Exposition*) was organized from 18 March to 1 May at the Pont des Invalides. He participated with *Prayer* (gypsum) and a *Sculpted Stone*.

The Friendship Association of Romanians in Paris (*Association amicale des roumains de Paris*) was established in the spring of 1910 in view of helping those that had subsistence problems. Brancusi was an association founder together with composer George Enescu, actor Edouard de Max, painters Theodor Pallady, Stefan Popescu, Gheorghe Marculescu, doctors Solomon Basile Marbé, Constantin Levaditi, lawyer Virgil V. Stanescu, and Professor Constantin Nedelcu elected chairman, among others[156].

Bucharest

The *9th Painting and Sculpture Exhibition of the "Artistic Youth" Society Under the High Patronage of HRH Princess Maria of Romania* (11 April-May) was organized in the society's own building near the Capital City Municipality (Fig. 94). Brancusi exhibited *Wisdom of the Earth* (stone, Fig. 95) that aroused vivid pro and con debates of the artists and art critics. The sculpture of Brancusi started a scandal, especially in the ranks of academic portrait painters appreciated by officials (G.D. Mirea, O. Spaethe, E. Stoenescu and A. Verona).

The *primitivism* of Brancusi was understood only by a limited set of people perceptive of the new trends in art. Nicolae D. Cocea, Camil Ressu, Theodor Cornel, Cecilia Cutescu-Storck and Frederic Storck rallied with Brancusi while

A. Tzigara-Samurcas, Léo Bachelin and Olimp Grigore Ioan were on the other side.

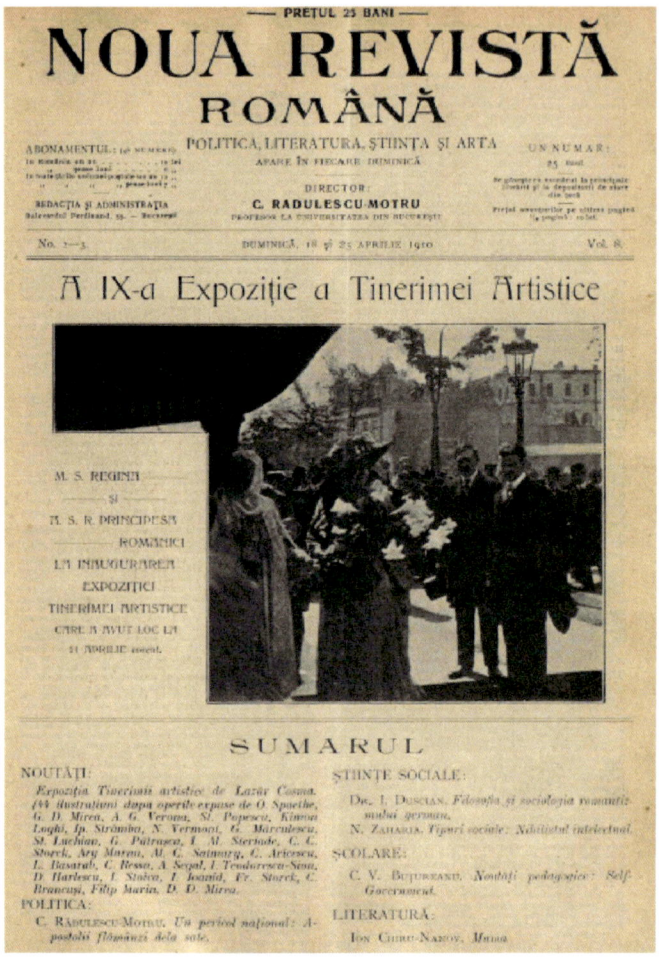

Fig. 94. Queen Elisabeta of Romania and Princess Maria at the exhibition entrance, Bucharest, 1910

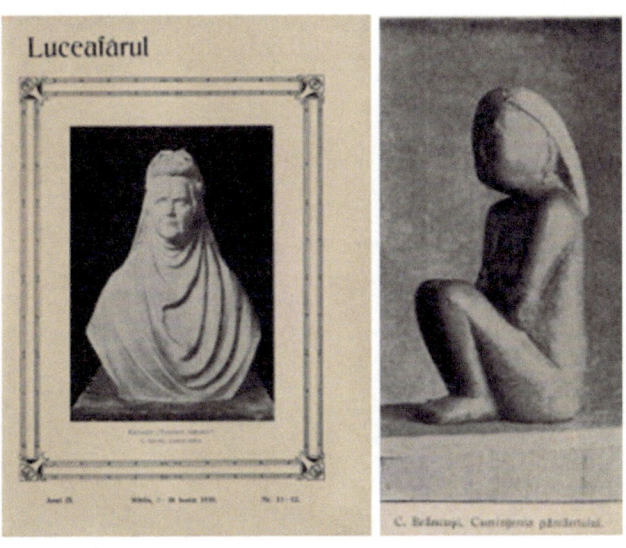

Fig. 95. Luceafărul, Sibiu, 1-16 June 1910

Paris, Bucharest

On 1 July Hungarian painter Margit Pogany (Fig. 96a), whom Otilia Cosmuta introduced to him in 1909, paid a visit to Brancusi and thought she could see her portrait in a sculpture from the studio. Fascinated with her eyes, the artist asked her to pose for a bust. Margit accepted and would pose to him from December 1910 until January 1911[157], and after her departing, he continued to sculpt his portrait without a model (gypsum, 1912-1913, Fig. 96b).

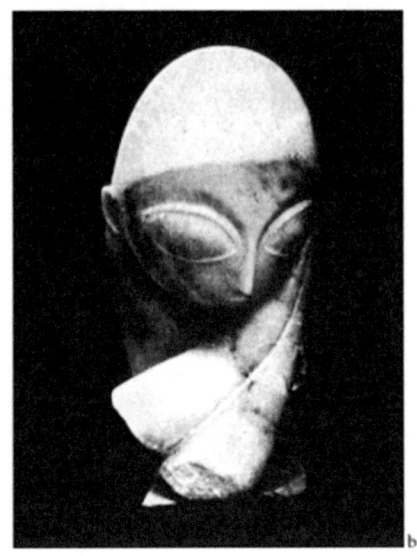

Figs. 96a, b. Margit Pogany, 1910—a; *Miss Pogany*—b

On 2 September his good friend Henri Rousseau le Douanier passed away and the artist was deeply grieved by the painter's death.

On 22 October the Romanian collector Anastase Simu purchased the *Bust of Painter Nicolae Darascu* (bronze, 1906), the "single copy" existing in Brancusi's studio, upon recommendation of art critic Nicolae Pora[158], and paid 1,000 FF. Simu had bought before a marble work, which he saw in the studio—the *Sleep* (1908), a work of Rodin inspiration. The sculptures are exhibited in the Simu Museum of Bucharest, founded in 1910 (Fig. 97).

Fig. 97. *Bust of Painter Nicolae Darascu* and *Sleep* in the Simu Museum

Bucharest

Brancusi befriended his neighbors, the American painters Edward Steichen and Walter Pach. He frequented the studios of vanguard artists from *La Ruche* (Fig. 98), where he met Chagall, Léger, Zadkine, Soutine, a.o.[159]

The first exegete of Brancusi and faithful friend of the artist, V.G. Paleolog remembered how he met Brancusi in 1910 through Modigliani, in the Falguière villa where they both lived and the sculptor was visiting[160].

Fig. 98. Colony of artists *La Ruche*, Paris

On 17 June, engineer Aurel Vlaicu, Brancusi's friend, ran a few meters as pilot on his airplane *A. Vlaicu No. I*, took off and flew, about 50 meters, 3-4 m high, then he landed[161] (Fig. 99a). This moment was registered in the history of Romanian and worldwide aeronautics producing strong impression on the artist who was concerned with flying. It was during this period, he sculpted the *Maiastra* (marble, 1910-1912, Fig. 99b).

Figs. 99a, b. Aurel Vlaicu pilot of *Vlaicu No. I* airplane, Bucharest, June 1910—a; *Maiastra* in the garden of Katherine S. Dreier's West Redding home (CT)—b

Bucharest

The *Autumn Painting and Sculpture Exhibition of the "Artistic Youth" Society Under the High Patronage of HRH Princess Maria of Romania 14 November-December* was organized in the society's own offices. Brancusi exhibited the *Kiss* (stone, 1907), this being considered the first modern sculpture in the world, which was exhibited to the public for the first time. Victor N. Popp purchased the sculpture after the exhibition. Brancusi used to say about the *Kiss* he meant to remind people of the pure eternal love on earth[162].

Again, the exhibition parted the ranks of critics. The only ones that approved the new style of Brancusian sculpture were the artists A. Baltazar, G. Petrascu, A. Steriadi, N. Darascu, I. Theodorescu-Sion, S. Popescu, D. Paciurea and the Storcks.

Paris

The second Paris Air Show (*Salon de locomotion aérienne*) opened at the Grand Palais in autumn and Henri Coanda introduced there the first reaction airplane in the world called *Coanda-10*[163], which was tested when the Salon closed (Fig. 100[164]). The friendship and cooperation relationships of the two universal Romanians—Henri Coanda and Constantin Brancusi—would be kept under big secret, which can be explained in their lifetime but not after their death. From the accounts of scientist Coanda we learn more about their apprenticeship at Rodin's and about the master's high appreciation of his student[165].

On 5 December 1910, young Tatiana Rashevskaia, a Russian woman from Kiev, killed herself due to the unrequited love she had for Doctor Solomon Basile Marbe, Brancusi's friend. Upon the doctor's request, the sculptor executed her mortuary mask and gave the *Kiss* (stone, Fig. 101a) shaped as stela to be placed on the tombstone in Montparnasse. This work is the size of a funerary monument. Upon Rashevskaia's burial on 12 December, Brancusi engraved the epitaph in Cyrillic letters on the pedestal of the funerary stela[166] (Fig. 101b).

Fig. 100. Brancusi, H. Coanda and his wife near the *Coanda-10* airplane, Paris Air Show, 1910

Figs. 101a, b. Montparnasse Cemetery, Paris: a—The *Kiss* on the tomb of Tatiana Rashevskaia; b—the epitaph engraved by Brancusi on the pedestal

1911

Bucharest

Theodor Cornel published the Romanian-French illustrated biographical dictionary where he dedicated two pages to Brancusi and photos of the *Bust of Painter Nicolae Darascu* (gypsum), *Child Head* (marble) and *Wisdom of the Earth* (stone)[167].

Paris

He sculpted *Prometheus* (gypsum), his model being Corneliu, son of Otilia Cosmuta (Figs. 102a, b). Corneliu accounted how Brancusi would make him stand when he posed and how the artist told him stories and sang while modeling the clay[168].

Figs. 102a, b. Corneliu Cosmuta—a; *Prometheus*—b

Impressed by the photographs shown at Jean-Baptiste Charcot's conference on his second expedition to the Antarctic (1908-1910, Fig. 103a), Brancusi began working to the marble sculptures *Three Penguins* (1911-1912, Fig. 103b) and *Two Penguins* (1911-1914). It is possible to have been also influenced by Anatole France's novel *L'Île des pingouins* [Penguin Island] printed in 1908—a great public success.

In 1911, Montparnasse quarter purchased a new Ale House, La Rotonde, which would make history in the Parisian bohemian world at the beginning of the 20th century (Fig. 104). Brancusi would meet here with Modigliani, de Waroquier, González, Cendrars, Picasso, Derain, Delaunay, Soutine, Manuel Ortiz de Zarate Pinto and many other artists, writers and poets[169].

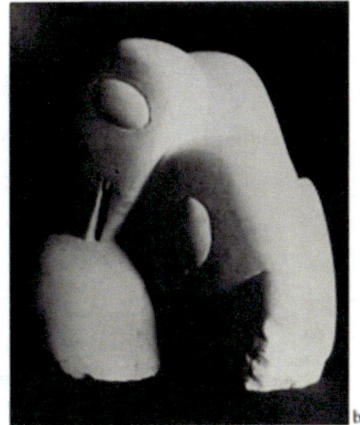

Figs. 103a, b. Jean-Baptiste Charcot surrounded by penguins at the South Pole, 1908—a; *Three Penguins*—b

Fig. 104. La Rotonde, Paris

1912

Paris

From 5 to 24 February, the Italian futurist painters (*Les peintres futuristes italiens*) exhibition was organized at Bernheim-Jeune Gallery, which Brancusi visited and met Gino Severini and Umberto Boccioni that would come to his studio.

From 20 March to 16 May, the 28th exhibition of the Independent Artists' Society (*Société des artistes indépendants/28ᵉ Exposition*) was organized at Quai d'Orsay, Pont de l'Alma. The exhibition was considered the first public demonstration of cubism and participating artists were—Archipenko, Brancusi, Chagall, Delaunay, Duchamp, Gleizes, Gris, de La Fresnaye, Marie Laurencin, Le Fauconnier, Léger, Lhote, Metzinger, Mondrian, Rivera, Lehmbruck, a.o. Brancusi exhibited three sculptures. Guillaume Apollinaire noticed the Romanian artist's works: "Brancusi, delicate and highly personal sculptor with very refined works"[170].

Fig. 105. Brancusi working at the forge in the studio courtyard, Paris, 1912

Fig. 106. Châtillon Avenue, Paris

On 15 May, he rented at 47 Montparnasse Street, a studio with garden where he installed his forge (Fig. 105), and on 19 July, he rented a studio at 36 Châtillon Avenue (Fig. 106).

Bucharest

In 1912, Brancusi announced his participation in Bucharest simultaneously to the *11th Exhibition of the "Artistic Youth" Society* and to the *Official Salon*. On 28 April the Custom Offices in Bucharest refused to release "some sculptures" sent by Brancusi from Paris for the Official Salon, pretexting they did not comply with custom guidelines. The Ministry of Cults and Public Instruction interfered and the works were released on the eve of the exhibition opening[171].

On 1 May, some jury members of the exhibition organized by the *Artistic Youth* invoked an article in the Society's Regulation and voted against hosting Brancusi's sculptures in their exhibition under the pretext he had announced his participation to the Official Salon as well. A few chroniclers, among whom Tudor Arghezi condemned the injustice inflicted to our "most personal" artist when the *Artistic Youth* Society decided "not to exhibit any more, on infidelity grounds"[172].

The *Official Salon* opened May-June and Brancusi exhibited three sculptures. On 5 June the Salon jury decided exceptionally and unanimously to grant the 2,000 Lei 1st prize to Sculpture; it was thus attributed to the "merit-full sculptor" Brancusi for his *Study* (*Torso*—A/N)[173].

Paris

Agnes E. Meyer met Brancusi through a mutual friend—Ed. Steichen[174] (Fig. 107a). She was one of the first woman reporters hired by The New York Sun after her 1907 graduation. A year later, she resumed her literary studies in Sorbonne, where she befriended Gertrude Stein and Edward Steichen. She returned to New York in 1909 and married multi-millionaire Eugene Meyer, who would hold influential financial positions in the federal government. and in 1916-1933 (the precise year is unknown) Brancusi made the *Study for the Portrait of Mrs. Eugene Meyer Jr.* (walnut wood, Fig. 107b). Brancusi provided the following sub-title *A non-despising queen*, as he wanted to suggest Agnes E. Meyer's authoritative but also magnanimous spirit[175].

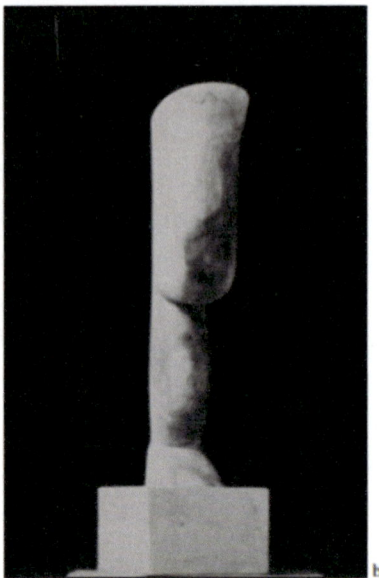

Figs. 107a, b. Agnes E. Meyer, 1910—a; *Study for the Portrait of Mrs. Eugene Meyer Jr.*—b

In 1912, passioned with flight and the shapes of ground-detaching machines, Brancusi with Fernand Léger and Marcel Duchamp went to the 4th Paris Air Show (*4ᵉ Exposition de la locomotion aérienne*) opened in the Grand Palace, 26 October-10 November. Standing before a big plane propeller Brancusi would have exclaimed: "Behold there a sculpture! From now on sculpture should not be inferior to it!"[176], and Duchamp asked his friends whether an artist was capable of making a piece as beautiful as that[177].

Fashion designer Paul Poiret and his wife Denise visited Brancusi's studio and the sculptor invited them to a dinner cooked by him. The guests had a great time and upon leaving they bought a *Maiastra* sculpture against 10,000 FF (polished bronze, 1912)[178][179]. In 1921, Man Ray would make a reference photo of Denise Poiret by the *Maiastra* (Fig. 108) of whom the photographic artist would say: "I had her stand near the Brancusi sculpture, which threw off beams of golden light, blending with the colors of the dress. This was to be the picture, I decided: I'd combine art and fashion."[180]

Fig. 108. Denise Poiret with *Maiastra*, Paris, 1921

In November 1912, his good friend Alexandre Mercereau came to his studio with the American painters Arthur B. Davies, Walt Kuhn, and Walter Pach. Here, they selected works for a great modern art exhibition in New York, scheduled for the year 1913. They loved Brancusi's sculptures and Davies bought a marble *Torso of Girl* and selected four other works for the exhibition.

At the end of 1912, Parisian police covered Jacob Epstein's sculpture from Oscar Wilde's tomb in Pere Lachaise cemetery (Fig. 109), claiming it as an attempt to instill public decency. Brancusi was part of the group that accompanied Epstein daily to the graveyard to take the cloth off the funerary monument[181].

Fig. 109. Oscar Wilde's tomb, Père Lachaise Cemetery, Paris: funerary monument covered with a cloth by the police.

The American Dream

1913

New York

Five Brancusi sculptures were displayed in the *International Exhibition of Modern Art—The Armory Show* (17 February-15 March) organized by the Association of American Painters and Sculptors, chairman Arthur B. Davies.

Davies and secretary Walt Kuhn, in the offices of the infantry regiment The Sixty-ninth Regiment Armory in the New York City (69 Inf'ty Regt Armory), where about 300,000 people attended. It was the first international demonstration of modern art where, according to the exhibition catalogue, 1,112 works were displayed made by more than 300 artists among whom Ingres, Braque, Delacroix, Courbet, Cézanne, Gauguin, Manet, Degas, Toulouse-Lautrec, Matisse, Dufy, Kandinsky, Rodin, Bourdelle, Maillol, Brancusi, Léger, Lehmbruck, Duchamp, Archipenko, Villon, Picasso, Picabia, and others were shown[182].

The *Kiss*, and *Miss Pogany* by Brancusi and Marcel Duchamp's painting *Nude Climbing Downstairs* provoked controversial reactions in the press of the time (Figs. 110a-d)[183][184][185][186]. The aroused scandal brought worldwide fame to Brancusi. There and then he sold *Miss Pogany* to Robert W. Chanler, eccentric American artist, against $540, a good price for that time, then the *Sleeping Muse* was purchased by Mary Harriman Rumsey, *A Muse* by Walt Kuhl and the *Kiss* was Brancusi's wedding present for Walter Pach[187][188]. The sale of his sculptures made Brancusi confess later it was the Americans that helped him overcome the hard times of his life.

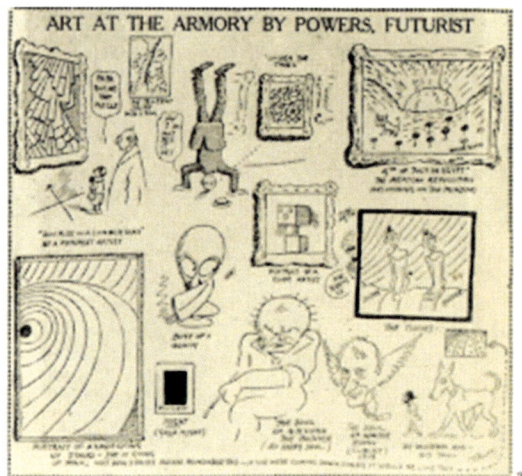 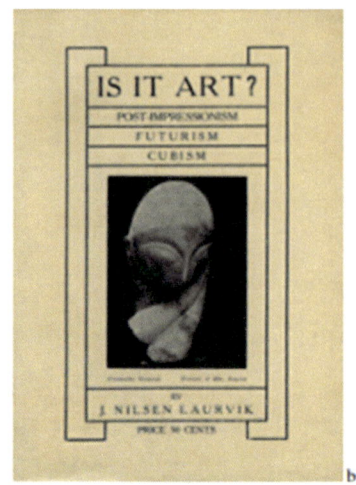

 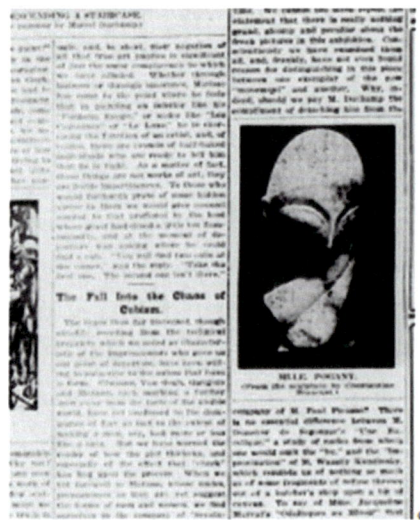

Figs. 110a-d. Echoes in the media, New York, February 1913: a—New York American; b—The International Press; c—The Brooklyn Daily Eagle; d—New York Tribune

Chicago, Boston

The Armory Show of New York was then itinerated to The Art Institute of Chicago (AIC), 24 March-16 April. Four Brancusi works were included in this exhibition. A demonstration was organized in Chicago against this event. Students instigated by conservatories, the heads of The Law and Order League, went down the streets and intended burning the effigy portraits of Henri Matisse, Brancusi, and Walter Pach (American organizer of the exhibition) that were considered as the most dangerous artists of decadent vanguard (Figs. 111a, b)[189][190][191]. *The Armory Show* was then itinerated to the Copley Society in Boston, 23 April-14 May.

Figs. 111a, b. Chicago Daily Tribune, 1913: a—17 February; b—17 April

Paris, Voulangis

He participated with three works to the 29th exhibition of the Independent Artists' Society (*Société des artistes indépendants/29ᵉ Exposition*), 19 March-18 May, Quai d'Orsay, Pont de l'Alma. When the exhibition ended, his friend, Edward Steichen purchased the *Maiastra* (bronze) which had remained unsold. He helped to install the sculpture in the garden of the Blue Bird Villa in Voulangis[192]. The artist carved a high-wood pedestal in order to integrate his sculpture in natural ambient which he made a high wooden pedestal for (Fig. 112).

Fig. 112. *Maiastra* in Ed. Steichen's garden, Voulangis

Upon the medical examination made in view of his sending to the front for the second Balkan war Brancusi was dismissed, being found tuberculous.

He received from V.G. Mortun, Minister for Civil Works, the order for a monument of Spiru Haret, former Minister of Cults and Public Instruction in Romania.

Bucharest

Brancusi participated to the *12th Painting and Sculpture Exhibition of the "Artistic Youth" Society Under the High Patronage of HRH Princess Maria of Romania* (31 March-21 April) with *Maiastra* (blue colored gypsum, 1908-1909). The exhibition included 45 artists with 299 works. Brancusi brought the sculpture to the country especially for this event and it was exhibited there for the first and last time.

Brancusi's sculpture produced a shock to the conservatory artistic mentality of Romanian art critics and artists. This statement is sustained by the ill-favored plastic chronicles of the main publications in the country[193]. Later on, Brancusi himself confessed to Ionel Jianu that "Spaethe was against me. But J. Steriadi and Fritz Storck shouldered me."[194]

On 28 April, the newspaper Seara owned by Alexandru Bogdan-Pitesti printed a caricature portrait of Brancusi by Camil Ressu (Fig. 113).

Munich

The 11th international art exhibition (*XI. Internationale Kunstausstellung*) was organized from 1 June to October 1913 in the Königlischer Glaspalast by the Münchener Künstlergenossenschaft and Münchener Secession organizations, the Romanian government's delegate and Romania's special commissar being Karl Arnold von Gunther, General Consul in Munich and Professor Alexandru Tzigara-Samurcas. Brancusi represented Romania next to Grigorescu, Luchian, F. Storck, Steriadi, G.D. Mirea, I. Strambu, Spaethe, S. Popescu and many others. Art historian W. Hausenstein considered Brancusi "one of the most interesting spirits of the new sculpture"[195].

Fig. 113. *Brancusi* by C. Ressu, Bucharest, 1913

London

In July he participated to *The London Salon of the Allied Artists' Exhibition, Ltd. Sixth Year* at the Royal Albert Hall, where he displayed three works. Art critic Roger Fry appreciated Brancusi's sculptures as this: "His 3 heads are the most remarkable works of sculpture at the Albert Hall"[196]. It was then he met Henri Gaudier-Brzeska.

The second event took place in October, this being the *Post-Impressionism and Futurism Exhibition* organized at Dore Galleries. The exhibition included one *head*, sculpture that had remained unsold at the previous event from Royal Albert Hall.

1914-1915

Prague

The 45th modern art exhibition (*Moderni Umeni, SVU Mánes*) was organized by Alexandre Mercereau under the aegis of the Mánes Union of Beaux Arts (February-March). Next to Mondrian, Delaunay, Rivera, Bruce, Lhote, Dufy, Kisling, Friesz, de La Fresnaye, Villon, Metzinger, Marcoussis, Duchamp-Villon, Archipenko, Gonzáles and a group of Czech, Swedish, Polish and Dutch artists Brancusi exhibited five works remarked in the media (Fig. 114).

Fig. 114. Zlatá Praha, Prague, 13 March 1914

Paris

At the beginning of 1914, Guillaume Apollinaire published the epitaph on Henri Rousseau le Douanier's funerary stone, reminding it was engraved in 1913 by sculptor Brancusi and painter Ortiz de Zarate (Figs. 115a, b)[197].

Figs. 115a, b. Guillaume Apollinaire's epitaph written at the death of H. Rousseau (a) engraved in 1913 by Brancusi and O. de Zarate on the tomb stone (b)

During World War I (1914-1918) some Parisian artists were mobilized (Léger, Villon, Poiret, Braque, Derain, Doucet), others volunteered for the front (Apollinaire, Gaudier-Brzeska, Zadkine), while others were medically rejected (Matisse, Modigliani, Rivera, Duchamp), and a few took refuge abroad (Rodin, Steichen, M. de Zayas). Brancusi moved into an isolated blind alley and began working wood intensely, especially oak from the girders of demolished houses, which he appreciated for patina (Fig. 116).

Fig. 116. Brancusi working to the *Gate,* Paris, 1915

New York

The following year Brancusi's first personal exhibition (*An Exhibition of Original Sculpture, in Bronze, Marble, and Wood by Constantine Brancusi, of Paris*) took place from 12 March to 1 April, organized by Edward Steichen and Alfred Stieglitz at his gallery entitled Little Galleries of the Photo-Secession, familiar name 291 (Fig. 117)[198], being sponsored by Agnes & Eugene Meyer and exhibiting eight sculptures. This aroused enormous sensation (Figs. 118a, b)[199] [200] and American collectors John Quinn, Arthur B. Davies, Alfred Stieglitz, and Agnes & Eugene Meyer purchased almost all the works included in the exhibition, thus providing Brancusi with the revenues necessary for his later artistic creation and a better life. Brancusi was dissatisfied with the photographs and decided to take the photos of his sculptures himself from then on.

Fig. 117. 291 Gallery, New York, before 1913

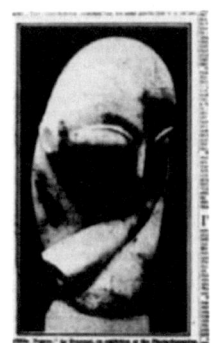

Figs. 118a, b. New York, March 1914: a—The Brooklyn Daily Eagle; b—The Sun

Bucharest, Buzau

The *14th Painting and Sculpture Exhibition of the "Artistic Youth" Society Under the High Patronage of HRH Princess Maria of Romania* (30 March-30 May) was organized, which Brancusi attended with six works, including *Prayer* and *The Bust of Petre Stanescu* (bronze, 1910).

Tudor Arghezi published three articles about Brancusi's creation in Seara newspaper (*Artistic Youth Exhibition*, 28 April 1914; *Pictural Chronicle of*

Artistic Youth, 3 May 1914; *Tabula rasa—Art and art*, 23 June 1914), stating he was fascinated by the *Sleeping Muse* and *Danaide*. Arghezi was among the first ones that saw the innovative and universal character of Brancusi's creation and considered the artist "a pioneer, if not absolutely the first beginner. In all cases he is a new man"[201]. Writing about Brancusi's attendance in the exhibitions of the *Artistic Youth* Society, Arghezi noticed that in 1914 as well the artist exhibited "fully admirable works" but nevertheless "both the state and private collectors ignored him," because artistic creation was not cherished in the country and only a few "organ players and greengrocers of art" were fashionable and fully supported to succeed, while talented artists were asked for "sacrifice and exhaustion"[202].

When he placed the *Prayer* and *Bust of Petre Stanescu* in Dumbrava Cemetery from Buzau (Fig. 119), on 17 June Brancusi left the country deeply afflicted because V.G. Mortun did not accept Spiru Haret's monument they had agreed upon in Paris (*The Fountain of Haret*). He would keep the work in his studio under the name *The Fountain of Narcissus* (Fig. 120). In 1939, the artist remembered his defeat and recounted his affliction once more when he saw Spiru Haret "soldierly aligned in a statue parade—quite an architectonic and plastic horror"[203].

Fig. 119. The funerary ensemble in Dumbrava Cemetery, Buzau

Fig. 120. Fountain of Narcissus in Brancusi's studio, Paris

Paris

Beginning with 1914, the New York lawyer and collector John Quinn started purchasing Brancusi sculptures, reaching 27 by 1923, of which two were gifts from the artist. Quinn invested $21,000 in these works. Brancusi exchanged letters with John Quinn for a long time, first through Walter Pach, then directly with Quinn. He received most orders by means of photographs. The collector had asked pre-emption rights for important sculptures[204].

Brancusi met Marius de Zayas in Paris who, together with Paul Haviland and Francis Picabia, had decided to establish a new gallery—Modern Gallery—in New York, financed by Agnes E. Meyer[205].

During 1915, he sculpted the *Caryatid* and *Prodigal Son* in oak wood. The latter was carved months after the artist's trip to Hobita following a few years' absence.

On 28 December he participated next to Gabrielle Reval, Paul Fort, Georgette Agutte, Maximilien Luce, Bourdelle, Rouault, a.o.[206,207,208] to the tombola exhibition opened in the Bernheim-Jeune Gallery, which was organized to the benefit of Polish artists, victims of the war.

Chicago

Arthur Jerome Eddy published *Cubists and Post-Impressionism* with A.C. McClurg Publisher, one of the first studies referring to Brancusi (Fig. 121); the 2nd edition in 1919.

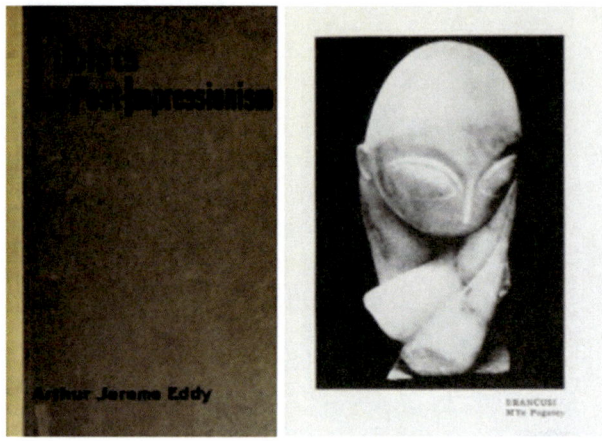

Fig. 121. *Cubists and Post-Impressionism* by A.J. Eddy, Chicago, 1914

To the Peaks of Glory

1916

London

In March, he participated with two sculptures to *The London Salon of the Allied Artists' Association, Ltd. Eighth Year* organized at Grafton Galleries.

New York

From 11 March to 22 April, Marius de Zayas organized the exhibition *Modern Sculpture by Mrs. A. Roosevelt, Mrs. Alice Morgan Wright, Adolf Wolff, Modigliani and Brancusi* at Modern Gallery (Fig. 122). Brancusi attended with two works[209]. Marius de Zayas wrote in his memory book about the success of this exhibition[210].

Fig. 122. View from the Modern Gallery window toward
The New York Public Library

Paris

On 1 January he moved to 8 Impasse Ronsin, 125 m long 8 m wide blind alley (Fig. 123a), where he benefited of three studios lighted with gas lamps and one bedroom upstairs, but he also kept the studio at 54 Montparnasse Street until 10 October. The studios in that area were not solid since they had been built foundation-less of half-timber walls from the remains of the 1889 Universal Exhibition. Alfred Boucher had built them for his workers, and then some were rented. The place belonged to the French state (Public Assistance). There the artist would photograph his sculptures and the arranged space. By October Brancusi rented another studio at 23 Odessa Street (Fig. 123b).

Figs. 123a, b. Paris at the beginning of the 20th century: a—Impasse Ronsin; b—Odessa Street

Upon request of Princess Marie Bonaparte (Fig. 124a), great-grandniece of Emperor Napoleon I, psychoanalyst appreciated by the Psychoanalytic Society of Paris and author of three volumes published by outstanding printers, Brancusi drew several portrait sketches. One older figurative sculpture entitled *Woman Looking in the Mirror* (1909) underwent repeated stylizing in order to reach the essence of things in the future portrait *Princess X* (polished bronze, 1915-1916, Fig. 124b). Martha Bibescu acknowledged to V.G. Paleolog that Marie Bonaparte was the model of *Princess X* as she insisted much to Brancusi and got the drawing *Study for Princess X* and a version of the sculpture.

Figs. 124a, b. Marie Bonaparte—a; *Princesse X*—b

André Salmon organized the modern art in France (*L'art moderne en France*) exhibition, 16-31 July, at Antin Salon. Brancusi submitted the marble *Princess X* to be exhibited, but it was not accepted.

Brancusi made the *Sculpture for the Blind* (veined marble), initially meant for the touch.

Henri-Pierre Roché remembered an exhibition where this sculpture was displayed in a sort of sack with two sleeves visitors could introduce their arms into, being considered "revelation for the hands"[211].

On 27 August, Romania declared war to Austro-Hungary and Romanians were called up for military service. At the end of the year, Brancusi, seen by the military medical commission, got exempted from military duties until 15 October 1917 for poor health reasons. During World War I, the cultural liberalism and internationalism of Montparnasse was replaced by xenophobia and the imposition of French culture, modernism turning into subversive current and attitude. Neutrality was also construed according to various interests, therefore when Romania joined the allied forces in the war, Brancusi told Walter Pach he was happy[212].

New York

The quarterly Camera Work, edited by Alfred Stieglitz, in issue 48 of October (Fig. 125) published Stieglitz' photos taken during the 1914 personal exhibition of Brancusi, organized at 291 gallery, as well as some excerpts from the New York press on that event.

The artist's second personal exhibition was organized by Marius de Zayas (*Sculpture by Brancusi*) from 23 October to 11 November at Modern Gallery, where he exhibited eight sculptures (Fig.126)[213].

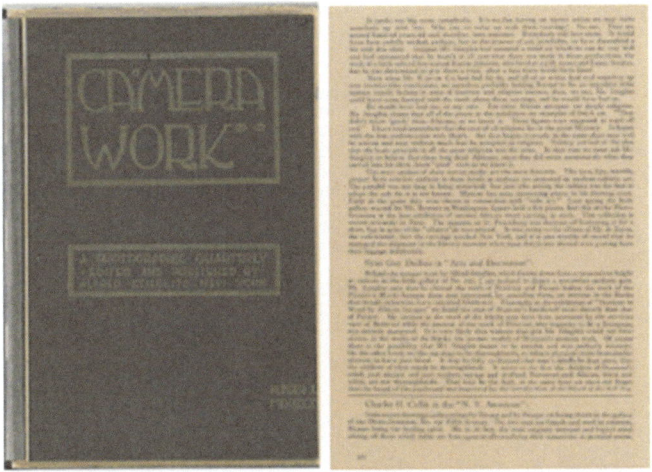

Fig. 125. Camera Work, New York, October 1916

Fig. 126. The Sun, New York, 5 November 1916

On 29 December, the American painter, Walter Pach, who intermediated the connection between the sculptor and collector John Quinn, acknowledged this one received in good conditions the sculptures *Gate* and *Bench* (oak wood,

1914-1916, Figs. 127a, b), *Caryatid* and *Kiss* and mentioned the last two sculptures were highly appreciated[214].

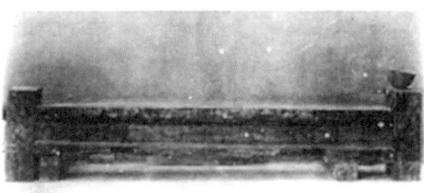

Figs. 127a, b. Wood sculptures in Brancusi's studio, Paris, 1914-1916:
a—*Gate;* b—*Bench*

1917

New York

The Society of Independent Artists had the initiative of organizing *The Society of Independent Artists / First Annual Exhibition* at Grand Central Palace from 10 April to 6 May[215]. Exhibited artists were Brancusi, Braque, Davidson, Delaunay, Derain, Katherine S. Dreier, Duchamp, Duchamp-Villon, Gris, Hopper, Matisse, Pach, Picabia, Picasso, Man Ray, Severini, Stieglitz, Strand, a.o. *Princess X* was not noticed in the exhibition, but scandal was aroused by Duchamp's *Fountain*, an upturned urinal.

Paris

The first *Column* was made using one wooden girder sawed on the side, with three full modules and half modules at both ends. The work belonged to a *mobile group* entitled *Child in the World* (Fig. 128).

Fig. 128. *Child in the World*, mobile group in Brancusi's studio, Paris

He sculpted *Adam* (oak wood) and *Torso of a Young Man* (1917-1922, using a forked maple tree trunk). He finished the *Column of the Kiss* without capital (gypsum, 1916-1917).

He met Moise Kisling and Blaise Cendrars, who would become faithful friend.

In September, Brancusi supported the establishment of the Art and Liberty (*Art et liberté*) group in order to respond to a xenophobe press campaign, sustained by La Renaissance newspaper against designer Paul Poiret accused of promoting the "Munich style," which was non-patriotic and Germanic[216]. Thus, the artist stated publicly his support for cultural pluralism. The issue was settled on 15 September by both parties, signing a support letter for Poiret (Fig. 129).

On 27 December, he notified John Quinn he had dispatched the *A Muse* bronze with stone pedestal and gave him advice for maintenance. On this occasion he also sent the photographs of new offers to the collector, specifying their size and a price list for: 1. the mobile group *Child in the World*, wood (12,000 FF); 2. *Chimera*, wood (3,000 FF); 3. *Mrs. L.R.*, wood (3,000 FF); 4. *Prometheus,* marble (6,000 FF); 5. *Maiastra* (10,000 FF); 6. *Sleeping Muse* (10,000 FF). He specified there were new items and resumed themes, which were not mere reproductions but different in concept and progress[217]. Quinn had no appreciation for wood and preferred marble and bronze sculptures.

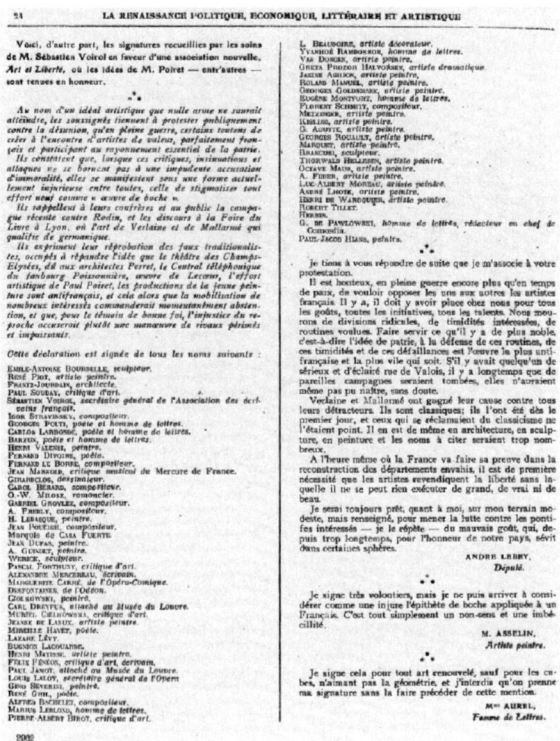

Fig. 129. La Renaissance politique, économique, littéraire et artistique, Paris, 15 September 1917

New York

Allies of Sculpture exhibition was organized for charity from 5 to 25 December 1917 in Ritz Carlton Hotel, to the benefit of the Aid Committee for Art, Belgian Prisoners of War, Wounded Welfare and Volunteers of Motorized Transport (Fig. 130)[218][219]. Exhibited artists were Brancusi (*Miss Pogany*, *Sleeping Muse,* and *Naiad*), Nadelman, Matisse, Bourdelle, Adams, Manship, Fraser, Aitken, Davidson, Evans, French, and Korbell. The Sun of 9 December

1917, wrote about Brancusi's works being at a disadvantage because of the place chosen by the organizers[220].

Fig. 130. Miss Vanderbilt, Miss Payne Thompson and Miss Canfield, members of the organizing committee in the exhibition hall of Ritz Carlton Hotel, New York, 1917

1918

Paris

Following the bombardment of Paris in June, Brancusi accepted the invitation of Odette de Saint-Paul, Léonie Ricou's friend, to go live with her in Chausse (Gard department) and supervise the house restoration. On 8 July, the artist broke his leg in the attic of Odette's house and in August, he was admitted in Alès Hospital, then in September in Necker Hospital of Paris. During recovery he made drawings in his studio and painted in aquarelle and gouache[221].

On 9 November, Apollinaire died because of the Spanish flue epidemics and Brancusi participated to the funeral ceremony of Saint Thomas Aquinas Church.

On 11 November, the armistice was signed. He painfully found out that Gaudier-Brzeska and Souza-Cardoso died as well as many other colleagues from the National School of Beaux Arts. Brancusi turned more and more withdrawn and sulky.

Leiden

De Stijl magazine founded by Theo van Doesburg published an article of painter Vilmos Huszár on Brancusi illustrated by a photo of *Miss Pogany*[222] (Fig. 131).

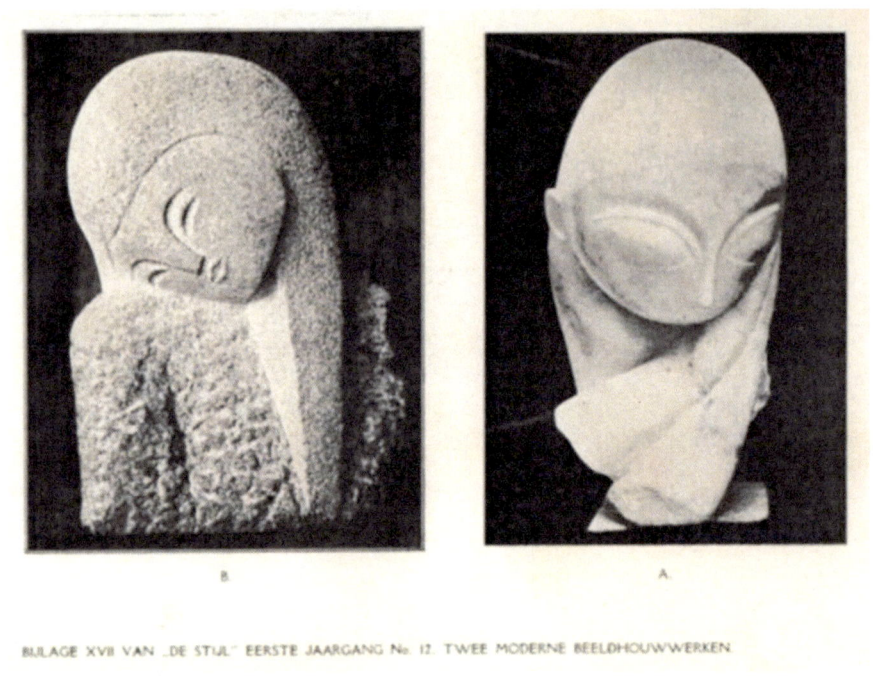

Fig.131. De Stijl, Leiden, 1918, *12*

1919

Paris

In July, Imprimeries A.G. L'Hoir published a volume coordinated by architect Petre Antonescu *La Roumanie en images* [Romania in Pictures], volume 1 (Fig. 132), including Marie Bengescu's study *L'art en Roumanie* [Art in Romania], which also mentioned Brancusi's creation. The text was accompanied by five photos of artist sculptures, among which the *Prayer*[223].

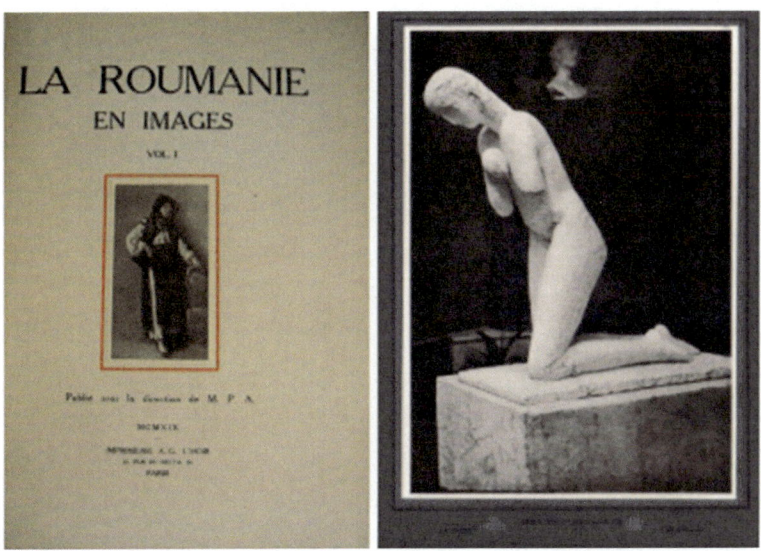

Fig. 132. *La Roumanie en images*, **I**, Paris, 1919

Brancusi met Milita Petrascu through painter Leopold Survage, who had taken him to her studio in Belloni Street. They remained good friends and in 1919-1923[224] she worked in the artist's studio.

Critic and poet André Salmon published *La jeune sculpture française* [Young French Sculpture][225] where he reviewed the national French school, however without mentioning Constantin Brancusi, although the author was an acknowledged supporter of modernism.

He sculpted a *Kiss* with two iron rings in volcanic stone slab, which the artist entitled *Medallion*.

George, Marius de Zayas' brother made a caricature drawing of Brancusi (lithography, Fig. 133), now belonging to the Yale University Art Gallery's collection.

In November, he met Erik Satie through Henri-Pierre Roché.

Later, he found out his mother died in January (Fig. 134). On 23 September, the sculptor would write about this unhappy event to John Quinn: "I have just found out my mother, whom I loved dearly, died and I am very upset."[226] In the Romanian Orthodox Church of Paris, he organized a memorial service for her.

Fig. 133. Brancusi by G. de Zayas, 1919

Fig. 134. Maria Brancusi, Hobita

New York

On 27 December, Marcel Duchamp notified him the decision of Katherine S. Dreier, American painter, art collector and promoter of modernism to purchase the *Little French Girl* with 6,000 FF[227] (Fig. 135). This belonged to the *mobile group* refused by John Quinn.

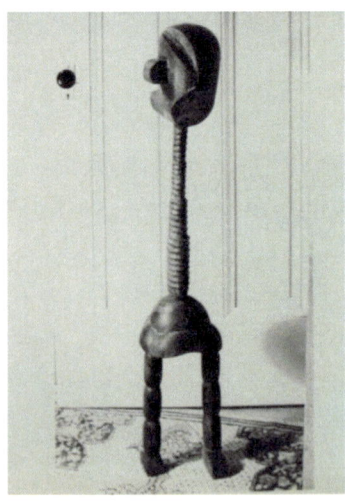

Fig. 135. *Little French Girl* in Katherine S. Dreier's West Redding home (CT), 1941

Amsterdam

Theo van Doesburg in his volume *Drie Voordrachten over de Nieuwe Beeldende Kunst* [Three Lessons on Visual Arts] (Fig. 136) points out that only in the 20th century Archipenko, Boccioni and Brancusi created an "aesthetic solution whereby volumes lead indeed to an artistic concept as such not as body (muscle) volume"[228].

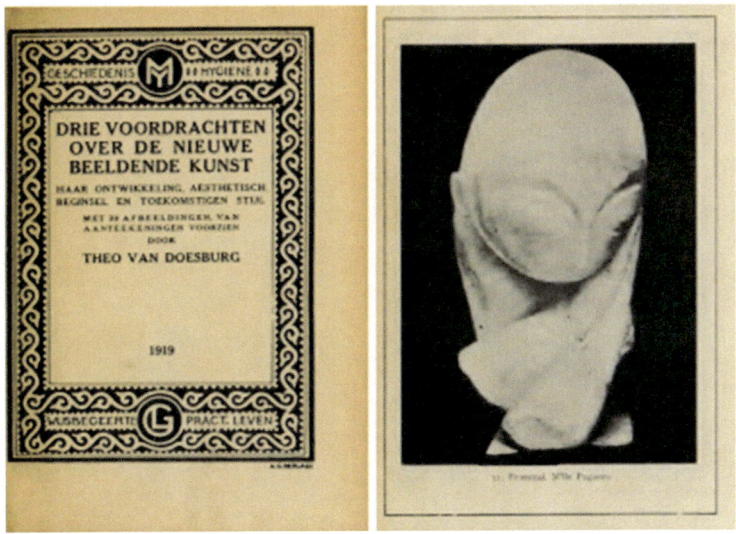

Fig. 136. *Drie Voordrachten over de Nieuwe Beeldende Kunst* by Th. van Doesburg, Amsterdam, 1919

1920

Paris

The 31th exhibition of the Independent Artists' Society (*Société des artistes indépendants/31ᵉ Exposition*), 28 January-29 February, was organized at the Grand Palace of Champs-Élysées and Brancusi participated with *Princess X* (bronze, 1919). On 29 January, he was obliged to provisionally withdraw sculpture from the exhibition before the visit of Raymond Poincaré, president of France, because the police considered it porn sculpture and consequently offensive for public decency. Vasile G. Paleolog believed that Paul Signac, chair of the Salon des Indépendants, was behind this[229].

Brancusi explained journalist Roger Devigne everything was owed to the general misunderstanding of his artistic philosophy based on simplification and form essence [230]. *Princess X* originated in a sculpture known as *Woman Looking in the Mirror*, the refining process of which led eventually to the phallic shape. There are some opinions the reason for such measure was the sculptor's affinity with the vanguard circles that severely criticized the censorship salons imposed on them, which led to the harsh response of the Society's managerial team.

The protest entitled *Pour l'indépendance de l'art* [For the Independence of Art] (Fig. 137)[231] was issued, which was signed by more than seventy personalities, artists and intellectuals, some of whom were close to Brancusi, such as V.G. Paleolog, Erik Satie, Mrs. Curie (Milita Petrascu—A/N), Francis Picabia, Jean Cocteau, Pablo Picasso, Fernand Léger, a.o. They demonstrated against the censorship practiced in art, so the work was brought back to the exhibition.

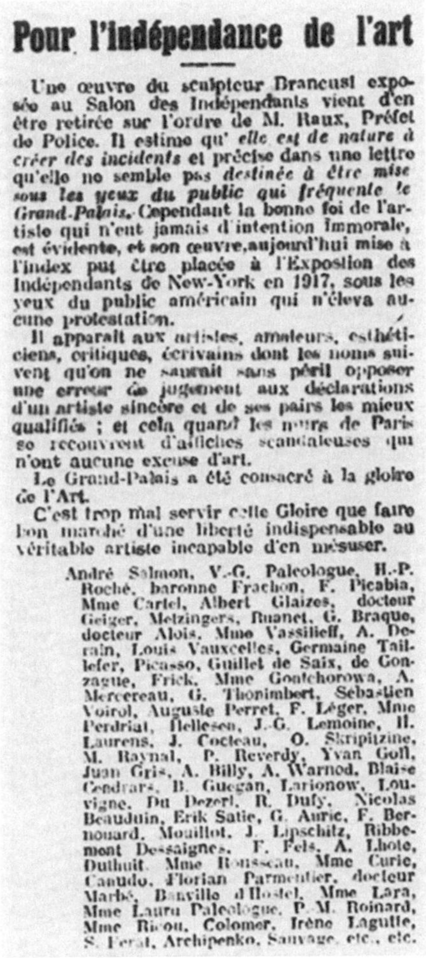

Pour l'indépendance de l'art

Une œuvre du sculpteur Brancusi exposée au Salon des Indépendants vient d'en être retirée sur l'ordre de M. Raux, Préfet de Police. Il estime qu' *elle est de nature à créer des incidents* et précise dans une lettre qu'elle ne semble pas *destinée à être mise sous les yeux du public qui fréquente le Grand-Palais.* Cependant la bonne foi de l'artiste qui n'eut jamais d'intention immorale, est évidente, et son œuvre, aujourd'hui mise à l'index put être placée à l'Exposition des Indépendants de New-York en 1917, sous les yeux du public américain qui n'éleva aucune protestation.

Il apparait aux artistes, amateurs, esthéticiens, critiques, écrivains dont les noms suivent qu'on ne saurait sans péril opposer une erreur de jugement aux déclarations d'un artiste sincère et de ses pairs les mieux qualifiés ; et cela quand les murs de Paris se recouvrent d'affiches scandaleuses qui n'ont aucune excuse d'art.

Le Grand-Palais a été consacré à la gloire de l'Art.

C'est trop mal servir cette Gloire que faire bon marché d'une liberté indispensable au véritable artiste incapable d'en mésuser.

André Salmon, V.-G. Paleologue, H.-P. Roché, baronne Frachon, F. Picabia, Mme Cartel, Albert Glaizes, docteur Geiger, Metzingers, Ruanet, G. Braque, docteur Alois, Mme Vassilieff, A. Derain, Louis Vauxcelles, Germaine Taillefer, Picasso, Guillet de Saix, de Gonzague, Frick, Mme Gontchorowa, A. Mercereau, G. Thonimbert, Sébastien Voirol, Auguste Perret, F. Léger, Mme Perdriat, Helleseu, J.-G. Lemoine, H. Laurens, J. Cocteau, O. Skripitzine, M. Raynal, P. Reverdy, Yvan Goll, Juan Gris, A. Billy, A. Warnod, Blaise Cendrars, B. Guegan, Larionow, Louvigne, Du Dezert, R. Dufy, Nicolas Beauduin, Erik Satie, G. Auric, F. Bernouard, Mouillot, J. Lipschitz, Ribbemont Dessaignes, F. Fels, A. Lhote, Duthuit, Mme Rousseau, Mme Curie, Canudo, Florian Parmentier, docteur Marbé, Banville d'Hostel, Mme Lara, Mme Laura Paleologue, P.-M. Roinard, Mme Ricou, Colomer, Irène Lagutte, S. Férat, Archipenko, Sauvage, etc., etc.

Fig. 137. Le Journal du peuple, Paris, 25 February 1920

He participated to the second exhibition of the Golden Section (*La Section d'Or*) group at Boétie Gallery (3-16 March).

In 1920-1921, he attended several troublesome dada events and his dada friends used to crowd his studio. On 27 March 1920, he attended the launching of the Dada Cannibal Manifesto (*Manifeste cannibale dada*) by Picabia, which André Breton read at the Théâtre de la Maison de l'Œuvre[232] (Fig. 138). On 26 May, he participated to the Dada Festival (*Festival dada*) at Gaveau Hall (Figs. 139a, b), next to André Gide, Paul Valéry and Fernand Léger and signed

Against Cubism, Against Dadaism (*Contre cubisme, Contre dadaïsme*) manifesto.[233] [234]

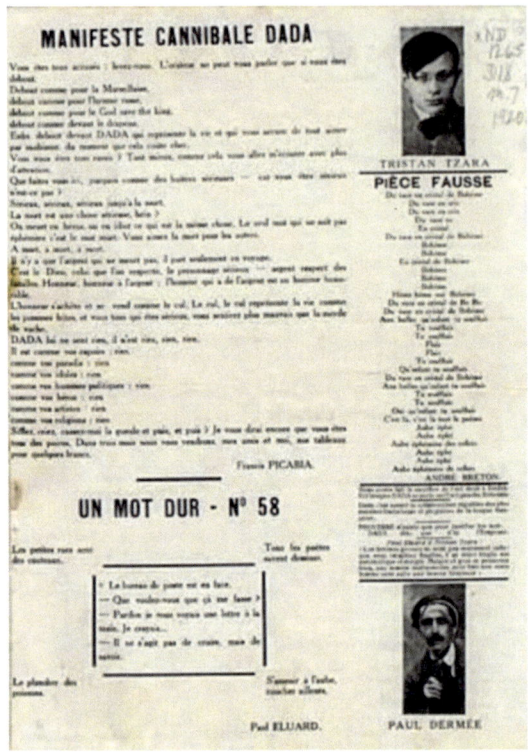

Fig. 138. Poster of the *Manifeste cannibal dada* by Fr. Picabia, Paris, 27 March 1920

Figs. 139a, b. *Festival dada*,
Paris, 26 May 1920: a—poster; b—Gaveau Hall

Tarsila do Amaral, Brazilian painter and leader of South-American modernism settled in Paris and began studying with Émile Renard. In 1922 she began working in the studios of Lhote, Léger and Gleizes. Poet Blaise Cendrars introduced her in his circle of friends from Parisian vanguard, among whom Brancusi, Picasso, Cocteau, Modigliani, Satie, a.o.[235]

Bucharest

Brancusi went to the country upon Camil Ressu's invitation and participated to the *3rd Exhibition of "Romanian Art" Society* (21 March-1 May), and came into conflict with the decision-makers of the *Artistic Youth Society*.

New York

From 30 April to 15 June, an *inaugural exhibition* was organized at the Galleries of the Société Anonyme on the occasion of this society's establishment to promote modern art[236]. From 2 August to 11 September 1920, the same gallery hosted the *Third Exhibition / Works Lent by Walter Arensberg*.

Paris

He sculpted *A Hand* (yellow marble, 1920, Fig. 140) that Sidney Geist considered reminiscence from *A Muse* or *Miss Pogany*, as contrast to Rodin's *Hands*[237]. This sculpture, quite seldom met in the publications dedicated to the artist, can be described as propeller blade, possible related to the cooperation between scientist Henri Coanda and Brancusi, revealed by shapes and components specific to aeronautics then translated into sculpture[238].

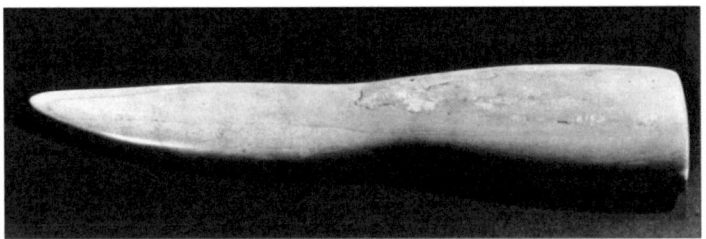

Fig. 140. *A Hand*

Brancusi met Peggy Guggenheim (Fig. 141), niece of Solomon Guggenheim; she was famous American collector who at 21 had inherited a small fortune that she invested in art. That year she settled in Paris, where she became friends with vanguard writers and artists, among whom Brancusi[239].

Fig. 141. Mina Loy and Peggy Guggenheim, Paris, 1920

He sculpted *Leda* (marble) and finished the *Golden Bird* (polished bronze, 1919-1920). He received many orders and devised many projects, as indicated by the materials he brought in the studio.

In 1920, he dispatched four sculptures to Quinn—*Miss Pogany* (marble and bronze versions), *Yellow Bird* (marble) and *Golden Bird* (bronze)—amounting to 50,000 FF as jointly agreed, which the collector had already sent 1,000 FF as a down payment. The artist gave him directions to disassemble and exhibit the sculptures. He also gave as gifts to Quinn a *Miss Pogany* drawing, a *Cup* and yellow marble *Hand*, and again a marble *Torso* for 12,000 FF[240]. The collector was thrilled about the sculptures.

After 1920, Katherine S. Dreier commuted between America and Europe alone or accompanied by Marcel Duchamp, managing to get a network of famous dealers and artists. At that time, Katherine frequented Brancusi's studio (Fig. 142), becoming a close friend of the artist, as some of her memoirist documents recorded. In time, she would acquire the marble *Maiastra, Yellow Bird*, *Leda* (Figs. 143a, b) and *Fish*.

Fig. 142. Brancusi in front of his studio, Paris, 1920s

Figs. 143a, b. *Yellow Bird* (a, photo of 1941) and *Leda* (b, photo of 1948) in Katherine S. Dreier's West Redding home (CT)

1921

New York

The April issue of the New York Dada review edited by Man Ray and Marcel Duchamp printed photos of Brancusi sculptures taken by the artist.

Under the strong impression created by Brancusi's sculpture, the American vanguard composer George Antheil composed *The Golden Bird "After Brancusi"* for the piano (Fig. 144).

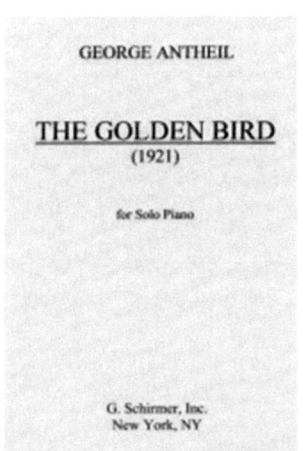

Fig. 144. *The Golden Bird "After Brancusi"* by G. Antheil, New York, 1921

Paris

On 14 April, he participated to the event organized under Dada Excursions and Visits (*Excursions et visites dada*), 1st visit—Saint Julien the Poor Church, Thursday 14 April at 3 h (Fig. 145).

Fig. 145. Poster of the *Excursions et vsites dada*, Paris, 14 April 1921

1920 had brought Brancusi quite a lot of pain—the scandal of *Princess X* taken out of the exhibition and the death of his friend Amedeo Modigliani—to which was added the memory of his beloved mother who died in 1919 without his seeing her. Brancusi began a long voyage in order to get rid of this mood inadequate for artistic creation. The visas in his passport provide the following route—Milan (25 May), Naples (27 May), he entered Romania in Constanta (3 June) and exited at Halmeu, continuing his travel to Prague (20 June) and Brussels (21 June)[241].

Brancusi met Man Ray and Ezra Pound. Ray later settled in Paris and began to guide Brancusi in photography[242].

In June, Quinn paid him a visit together with his friend, poetess and journalist Jeanne Robert Foster (Figs. 146a, b). The meeting was mediated by Henri-Pierre Roché [243] [244].

In 1921-1923, the American sculptress Mariette Mills worked in Brancusi's studio. She had her own studio in Montparnasse and lived with her husband Heyworth Mills in the country, at Clairefontaine near Rambouillet, where they received their friends, American artists and others, among whom Brancusi was present[245]. The Mills gave a Polaire puppy to the artist (Fig. 147).

He sculpted *Eve* in chestnut wood, and *Adam* (oak wood, 1917) became its pedestal.

Berenice Abbott moved to Paris, and her friends Man Ray and Marcel Duchamp took her to Brancusi's studio and introduced the artist. Until 1923, Berenice studied sculpture with Bourdelle and Brancusi[246] [247].

Figs. 146a, b. Brancusi together with Jeanne Robert Foster (a) and J. Quinn (b), Paris, 1921

Fig. 147. Brancusi in his studio, Paris, 1921

Chicago

Lorado Taft published a series of lectures delivered at AIC in 1917 in a *Modern Tendencies in Sculpture* (Fig. 148) volume. In the *Recent French Sculpture* chapter Taft ironically examined the sculpture of Matisse, which he considered caricatural and also found Matisse was not the only French artist displaying such trends as Archipenko, but most of all Brancusi, went in the same direction: "Brancusi was the author of the far-famed *Miss Pogany*, which, we are assured, is *not a servile reproduction of features*, but an interpretation of the soul. Perhaps its companion is *Miss Pogany*'s brother's soul, although it has been called *The Mislaid Egg*."[248]

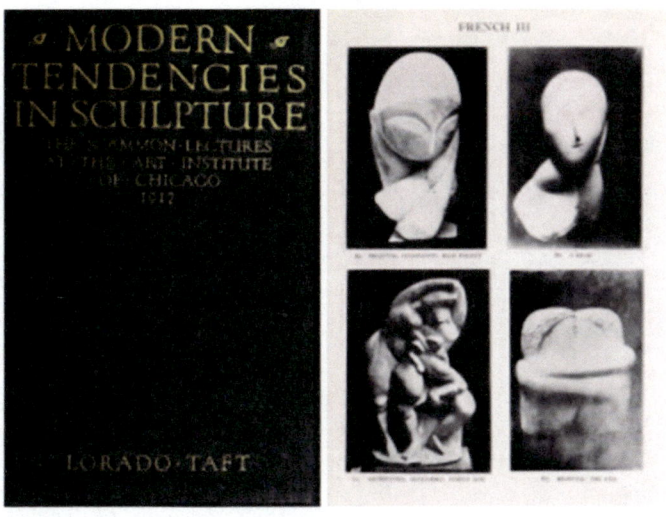

Fig. 148. *Modern Tendencies in Sculpture* by L. Taft, Chicago, 1921

Cambridge (Massachusetts)

To Chandler Rathfon Post in *A History of European and American Sculpture: From the Early Christian Period to the Present Day*, volume II, chapter *Modern Sculpture. Post-Impressionism*, Brancusi represents an "eminent representative" of the artistic current, his sculptures being processed by eliminating some parts while exaggerating and intensifying others, the artist eventually managing "to accentuate the mental and spiritual content of his themes." Post considers "the bust of *Miss Pogany* is the portrait of such another esoteric woman."[249] (Fig. 149)

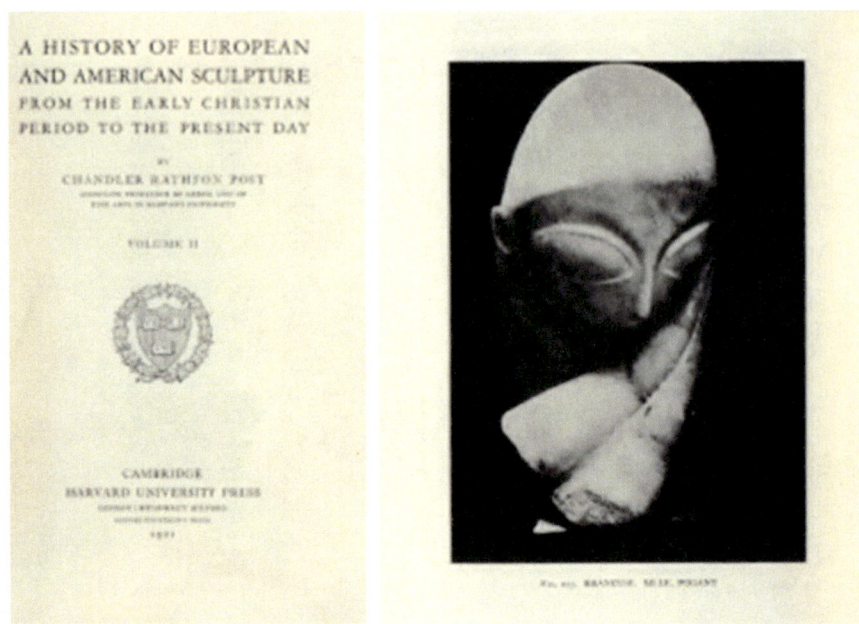

Fig. 149. *A History of European and American Sculpture: From the Early Christian Period to the Present Day* by C. A. Post, **II**, Cambridge (MA), 1921

New York

The Little Review, art and literature publication printed in September the first consistent study dedicated to Brancusi, written by Ezra Pound, and including 24 photos of the artist's works (Fig. 150). In this study, Pound examined Brancusi's successful experiment, in his opinion represented by the ovoid "pure form free from all terrestrial gravitation"[250]. Brancusi's friend, Margaret Anderson (Fig. 151) was founder, editor and publicist with The Little Review, one of the most influential in 1914-1929.

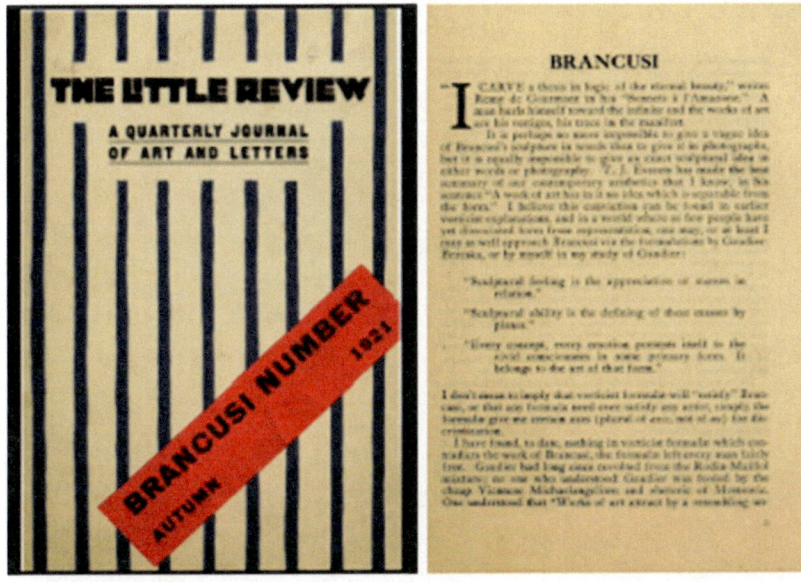

Fig. 150. The Little Review, New York, September 1921

Fig. 151. Brancusi, Maja Chrusecz, Mina Loy, Jane Heap and Margaret Anderson in the sculptor's studio, Paris, 1921

Paris

Francis Picabia and Marthe Chenal organized New Year Cacodylate (*Réveillon cacodylate*) in the Courcelles Street soprano house (Fig. 152a), where Brancusi was invited to participate with Picasso, Vollard, Cocteau, Radiguet, Auric, Morand and many other personalities, artists and famous writers of Paris[251]. On this occasion, Picabia made The Cacodylate Eye (*L'Œil cacodylate*) collage of signatures (Fig. 152b) that will cause a great scandal at the Autumn Salon next year. Brancusi's signature is not on this card.

 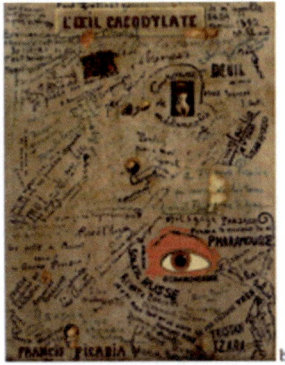

Figs. 152a, b. Paris: a—*Réveillon cacodylate* participants, 31 December 1921; b— *L'Œil cacodylate* collage

1922

Paris

On 10-24 January Brancusi and writer Raymond Radiguet traveled to Corsica.

On 17 February, the artist attended the Paris Congress at Closerie des Lilas, an assembly convened to protest against the attitude of André Breton, *father* of surrealism who opposed Tristan Tzara, Brancusi's fellow countryman. He signed a resolution together with Arp, Zadkine, Kisling, Éluard, Man Ray, Metzinger, van Doesburg, Satie, Radiguet, Cocteau, Survage, a.o. where he added "En art il n'y a pas d'étrangers" [There are no strangers in art][252].

Potsdam

In 1922, German art critic Paul Westheim published the article *Bildhauer in Frankreich* [Sculptors in France], with three photos of Brancusi sculptures and describing the artist as creator of monumental art, which influenced his contemporaries and he named German Wilhelm Lehmbruck, who was influenced by the *Prayer* when making his big *die Kniende* [The Kneeling]. Westheim considered that "a decided impulse to monumentality acts..." in Brancusi and some of his creations "seem conceived as parts of imaginary architecture." The critic indicated the ovoid as fundamental form in the artist's "plastic and psychic perception"[253]. The critic Paul Westheim's article on Brancusi was well commented on by Romanian publications[254].

New York

The *Exhibition of Contemporary French Art* was organized at The Sculptor's Gallery, 24 March-10 April.

Brancusi participated with 16 sculptures from Quinn's collection and one from Walter Arensberg, next to Bourdelle, Degas, Duchamp-Villon, Lehmbruck, Maillol, Manola, Matisse, Picasso, Poupelet, Rodin, Braque, Derain, Dufy, de La Fresnaye, Laurencin, Rouault, Rousseau, de Segonzac, and Seurat. Art critic Henry McBride considered Brancusi "the hero of this event" as he was acknowledged "the most brilliant sculptor of the day" and "the impressions given by Brancusi cannot be rendered in words" (Fig. 153a)[255].

Jeanne Robert Foster would visit him any time she could, being drawn by his personal charm and by his studio. In an article she published in 1922, Jeanne accounted a visit at Brancusi's, describing her impressions and the talks she had with him. She states that even though Brancusi was dressed simply as he worked in the studio, he would "astonish by flashes of wit and knowledge" in any circumstance (Fig. 153b)[256].

Figs. 153a, b. New York, 1922: a—The New York Herald, 26 March; b—Vanity Fair, May

Paris

Sisters Irina and Lizica Codreanu met the artist in 1922, in a small district theater on Gaîté Street (Fig. 154), which the artist went to until World War II[257]. Irina, an important feminine character of Romanian modern art, began her studies in the Beaux Arts School of Bucharest. In 1919, she settled in Paris and continued studying at the Grande Chaumière Academy. She was apprentice of both Bourdelle and Brancusi.

Fig. 154. Gaîté Street, Paris

Lizica Codreanu danced "easily and expressively" as recorded by art chroniclers[258]. She was part of Sergey Diaghilev's Russian ballet team, which in 1922 prepared the *Gymnopaedies* on Erik Satie's music (Fig. 155). Brancusi, watching Lizica dancing to the rhythm of the music got the idea of a stage costume for her, which he cut and stitched himself, thus proving that he had talent fit for the vocation of fashion designer. Upon her next visit, Lizica Codreanu tried the pinned-up dress and the artist took several photographs of her while she danced (Fig. 156a)[259]. One can notice her head structure was inspired from the *Sorceress* (wood, 1916, Fig. 156b), a composition made up of several well-fitted geometrical shapes of visible cubist influence, sculpted from a portion of wooden trunk with three branches.

Fig. 155. Erik Satie in Brancusi's studio, Paris, 1922

Figs. 156a, b. Brancusi's studio: a—Lizica Codreanu dancing, 1922; b—*Sorceress*

In summer the artist received the pianist and writer Cella Delavrancea. Seeing she was greatly impressed by the different shapes exhibited in the studio, the artist explained why his works were so alive. "I polish them for months on end with my own hands, until they turn alive." He showed her *Miss*

Pogany, pressing her finger on the "simplified drawing of an exophthalmic eye," and then Brancusi wanted to hear her discuss the *Cock*. Cella Delavrancea told him that looking at it she could hear the distant cry: "Cock-a-doodle-doo," and then Brancusi exclaimed happily: "Bravo! Nobody else has sensed before this brass is singing. So I was not wrong. You prove me I succeeded. Thank you..."[260]

Edith Taylor arrived in Paris in 1922, after a love set-back and began frequenting fashionable salons, becoming close friend of Natalie Barney, Gertrude Stein, Djuna Barnes, Jane Heap, Man Ray, and Marcel Duchamp. Edith Taylor met Brancusi where they would spend quite some time together. She was the one that introduced the Romanian sculptor to the mystical Armenian philosopher pedagogue choreographer and composer Gurdjieff[261]. Edith Taylor's archives contain a valuable document: the ideogram of *the Kiss* given by Brancusi to her in 1924, drawn on the poetry volume of Edna St. Vincent Millay, 1923 (Fig. 157a)[262] [263].

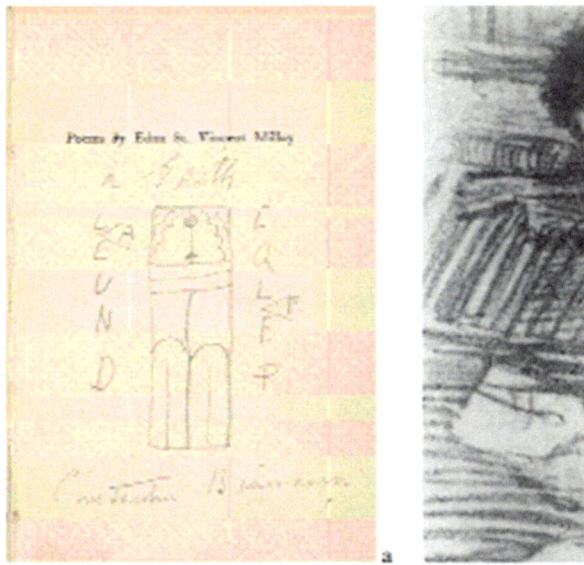

Figs. 157a, b. Drawings by Brancusi: a—ideogram of the *Kiss* with dedication for Edith Taylor; b—*Dimitrie Cuclin*

Brancusi drew the portrait of composer Dimitrie Cuclin (Fig. 157b), whom he met in Paris during his studies. Cuclin married painter Zoe Damian, widow of his school colleague from Bucharest, Emil Damian. The drawing was introduced much later in a book dedicated to the musicologist[264].

Bucharest

On 22 June, the legal heirs of Alexandru Bogdan-Pitesti offered to the Romanian state the entire artistic inventory, according to his testament. Owing to bad reports and to the refusal of prime minister Ion I.C. Bratianu, the execution of documents necessary for the Romanian state to get the collection was procrastinated until the legacy was dissipated, as provided also in Lucia Dem. Balacescu's article (Fig. 158)[265]. Among the disappeared items are also Brancusi's *Kiss* (gypsum, 1907), *Child Head* (marble, 1907-1908), *Kiss* (stone, 1907)[266], *Sleeping Muse* (bronze, 1910)[267].

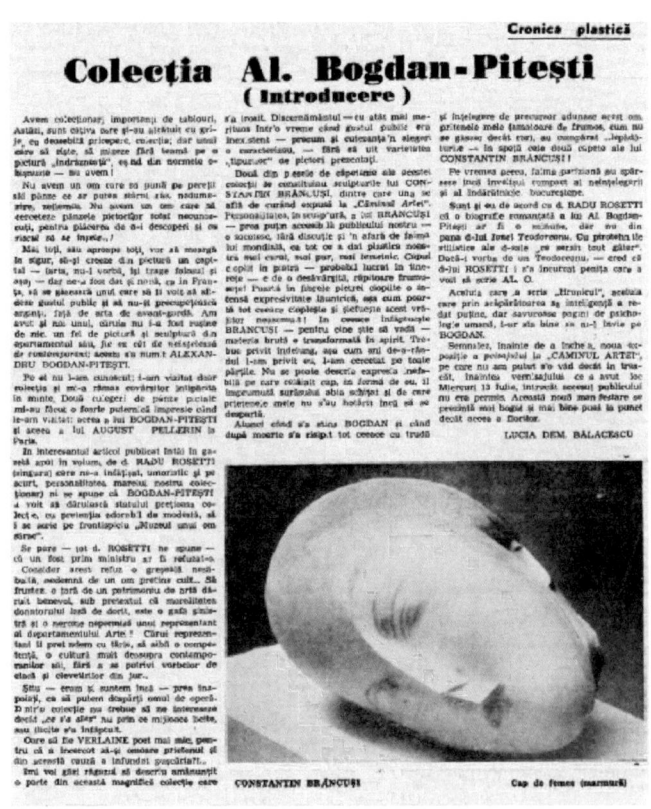

Fig. 158. Universul literar, Bucharest, 1942, *29*

Paris, Sinaia, Ramnicu Valcea, Targu-Jiu, Pestisani, Hobita

Through Irina Codreanu Brancusi met Eileen Lane, American of Irish origin, and was impressed by her beauty and grace, according to Milita Petrascu's memories[268]. To help her forget a sad love affair Brancusi invited Eileen to accompany him in Romania and told her not to be embarrassed by their age difference, because he would introduce her as his daughter[269]. The age issue thus solved, from 11 September to 7 October, the artist and Eileen spent a few days in Bucharest and Sinaia (Fig. 159a), passed by Ramnicu Valcea, where they stayed at the Archiepiscopate of Ramnic and Nou Severin (Fig. 159b), and Targu-Jiu, and then went to Pestisani, where Brancusi wished to make a monument[270].

In Pestisani Eileen stayed in the house of Mihail Tabacu, childhood friend of the sculptor, and he, in the house of Father Vasile Brancusi, nephew from his cousin, and to others relations. Priest Vasile Brancusi and other villagers asked Brancusi whether he intended to do something for his village Pestisani. They had been striving for a long time to erect a monument to the memory of Romanian soldiers killed in WWI.

Fig. 159a, b. Caraiman Hotel, Sinaia—a; Cathedral and Episcopal Palace, Ramnicu Valcea—b

A relative from Pestisani, merchant Gheorghe Nicolcioiu, recounted that Brancusi came accompanied by "a poetess," who wasted no time and got dressed in Oltenia's popular costume (Fig. 160a). Brancusi showed Eileen his childhood places, he introduced his relatives and acquaintances from Franceni and Brosteni and they went together to Tismana Monastery[271].

 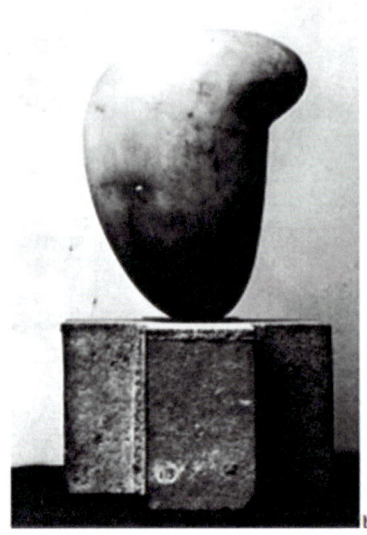

Figs. 160a, b. Eileen Lane: a—in the popular costume of Gorj, Hobita, 1922; b—
Eileen

When they returned to Paris, via Rome and Marseille[272], nothing more was ever heard of Eileen Lane. She went back to the United States and got married, while Brancusi no longer intended to look for her. Nevertheless, Brancusi did not forget her and in 1923 he sculpted her portrait in white onyx (Fig. 160b). Milita Petrascu was right when she said: "She was too fantastically beautiful to acquire habitude."[273]

Chicago

From 19 September to 22 October, the *Exhibition of Paintings from the Collection of the Late Arthur Jerome Eddy* was organized at the AIC.

Paris

In 1922, Jeanne Robert Foster and John Quinn returned to Paris and visited the artist. They were both drawn by the magnetism of Brancusi's studio. Together with their friends Erik Satie and Henri-Pierre Roché spend wonderful days as Jeanne wrote on the back of a photo: "What a gorgeous day!"[274] (Fig. 161). Jean Cocteau would describe why the studio impressed its visitors: "Brancusi's studio resembles a prehistorical landscape: tree trunks, stone blocks, an oven where the house master, primitive man, grills works of meat stuck on a metal rod. In all four corners the Brontosaurus had laid eggs, and shiny statues draw beautiful American ladies like butterflies. Satie liked this landscape very much."[275]

Fig. 161. Satie, Quinn, Brancusi, and Roché on the golf course of Fontainebleau, Paris, 1922

The letter dated 27 October was sent from Paris to his brother, Dumitru and was shown to Petru Comarnescu by Dumitru's son Nicolae; we learn from it that: "I will soon send all details for the monument"[276]. The monument that Brancusi intended to build in Pestisani was never achieved because of the traditional indifference and political misunderstanding.

He sculpted the *Fish* (marble, Fig. 162).

Fig. 162. *Fish*

New York

Mina Loy impressed with Brancusi's art, would write the poetry *Brancusi's Gold Bird*[277][278] (Fig. 163) inspired by the *Golden Bird* of John Quinn's collection.

Carl Sandburg published the poetry *Brancusi*, in *Slabs of the Sunburnt West*[279] (Fig. 164).

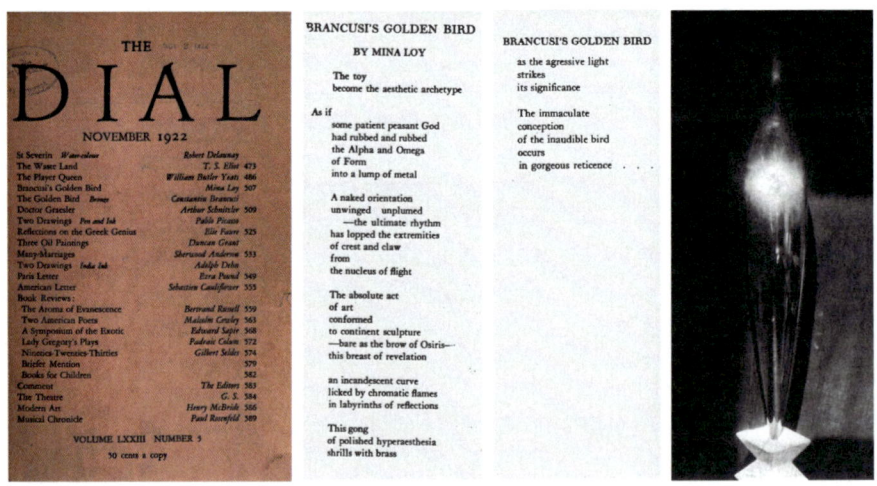

Fig. 163. *Brancusi's Golden Bird* by Mina Loy, The Dial, New York, November 1922

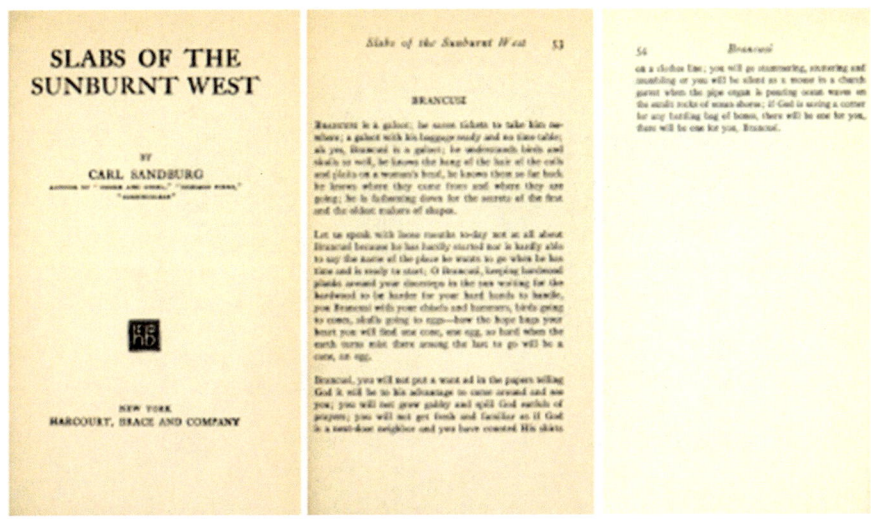

Fig. 164. *Brancusi*, in *Slabs of the Sunburnt West* by C. Sandburg, New York, 1922

1923

Bucharest

By the decree published in the Official Gazette no. 218 of January 4th, King Ferdinand I appointed Brancusi a member of the Order of the *Crown of Romania* in the rank of Officer.

Berlin

Albert Dreyfus in Der Querschnitt magazine published an article dedicated to Brancusi's creation and influence on other great artists: "Brancusi is a loner. He has no students, but the effect on new art is already considerable." In this issue of the magazine are five photographs of Brancusi with his works, as well as a self-portrait (Fig. 165)[280].

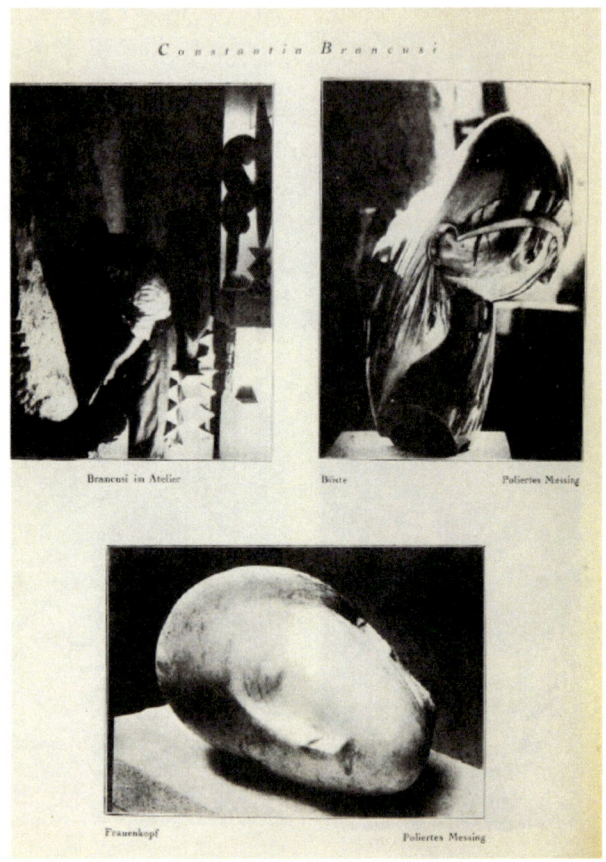

Fig. 165. Der Querschnitt, Berlin, 1923, *3-4*

New York

Brancusi participated with one sculpture to the *Spring Salon* organized at the Galleries of the American Art Association in cooperation with the American Museum of Natural History, the Art and Science Institute of Brooklyn and renowned collectors, from 21 May to 9 June.

In July, The Arts review (Fig. 166) published a referential article in Brancusiology, entitled *Constantin Brancusi: A Summary of Many Conversations* signed by M.M., with 10 photographs of Brancusi works and studio, of which four photographs were taken by Charles Sheeler. This article summarized several talks with the artist who described his artistic philosophy: "Matter itself must suggest a subject and form; both must come from within matter and not be forced upon it from without"[281].

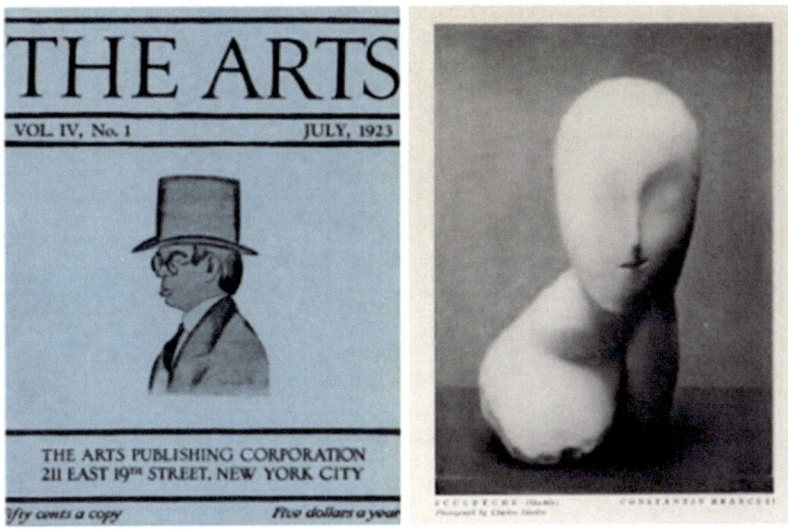

Fig. 166. The Arts, New York, July 1923

Writer Angus Wilson published in New York Times Book Review and Magazine of 19 August, his impressions after visiting Brancusi's studio. A. Wilson saw a *Bird in Space* providing the "thin configuration of the purest form, a thread attached to diminished pedestal," actually the result of "six months of work and twenty years of knowledge" gathered from one model to another. Brancusi explained him it was an attempt to solve the most difficult problem, that of obtaining "all forms into one form"[282].

Paris

This year he finished two referential marble sculptures *Bird in Space* and the *White Negress* (Figs. 167a, b). Brancusi worked very much but he did not neglect relaxing with his friends (Fig. 168).

Figs. 167a, b. Brancusi's studio, Paris, 1923: a—*Bird in Space*; b—*White Negress*

Fig. 168. Outdoor party around Paris attended among others by Léger, Lizica Codreanu and Brancusi

Brancusi's studio was visited by many Americans—Robert McAlmon, Man Ray, Margaret Anderson, and W.C. Williams—who later on would record their impressions in memoirist writings. From 19 September until the end of October, John Quinn with Jeanne Robert Foster visited Paris and Brancusi as well, and then the three devised a joint schedule (Fig. 169).

Fig. 169. Brancusi on the golf course of Chantilly with Roché, Jeanne R. Foster and Satie, Paris, 1923

Fig. 170. Swedish Ballet at Champs-Élysées Theatre, Paris, 1923

Fernand Léger invited him on 25 October to the opening night of the classic ballet *La creation du monde* [The World Creation] at Champs-Élysées Theater[283] (Fig. 170). Jean Börlin was the show choreographer and Darius Milhaud, the composer to a scenario by Blaise Cendrars, décor by Fernand Léger for the Swedish Ballets.

Brancusi was invited to the great French-Scandinavian exhibition (*L'Exposition Franco-scandinave*), also known as exhibition of the French-Scandinavians and its guests (*L'Exposition des francoscandinaves et ses invités*) organized by the Association of Scandinavian Artists, opening on 17 November 1923 in Paris, with 113 participating artists[284].

On 13 December, Brancusi next to Picasso, Cocteau, a.o. attended the funeral of his friend Raymond Radiguet at Père Lachaise Cemetery.

On 17 December, Brancusi wrote to the collector John Quinn he would send the marble *Bird* (first version of the *Bird in Space*—A/N) with guidelines for maintenance[285].

In December, Nancy Cunard (Fig. 171a) met Tristan Tzara and Man Ray and, through them, Brancusi. The occasion was a reception at La Rotonde Restaurant in Montparnasse, where the sculptor was also invited. Nancy, the only child of legendary Sir Bache Cunard, owner of the maritime *Cunard*

Lines, stood out by her political writings and activities, being a fierce fighter against racism and fascism. Once divorced of her first husband Nancy settled in Paris in 1920, becoming the muse of dada and surrealist poets and Maecenas of vanguard artists[286].

Figs. 171a, b. Nancy Cunard, 1924—a; *Sophisticated Young Lady*—b

In 1925-1927, the artist sculpted Nancy Cunard's portrait in wood, entitled *Sophisticated Young Lady* (Fig. 171b); it represents vertical ovoid, ending in a centrally bulging curly bun, supported on one leg. Brancusi adored long-haired women wearing their locks assembled in buns. In the following years, this portrait was cast in gypsum and bronze. Brancusi said about Nancy Cunard's behavior, "she showed herself to be truly sophisticated for her age"[287].

1924

Paris

In 1924, Brancusi attended two important philanthropic events organized by the Union of Russian Artists in Paris: Banal Ball (*Bal Banal*) at Bullier Hall on 14 March (Figs. 172a, b), in order to provide financial support to the Union's Mutual Aid House; vignettes were made by Picasso, Brancusi, Terechkovitch, Berline, Krémègne, Feder, Indenbaum, Braque, Fargue, Volovick, Lébédeff, Lhote, Larionov, Izdebsky; and Olympic Ball Dedicated to Apollo, God of Olympus and the Great Olympiad of Colombes (*Bal Olympique consacré à Apollon, Dieu de l'Olympe et à la grande Olympiade de Colombes*) at the Olympia Tavern on 11 July (Figs. 173a, b), he being one of the fifty artists that decorated the hall next to Chagall, Diaghilev, Friesz, Galanis, Natalia Goncharova, and Lizica Codreanu who also danced.

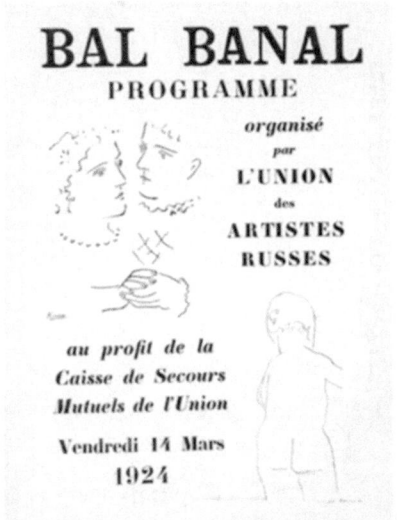

Figs. 172a, b. Bal Banal, Paris, 14 March 1924: a—poster by A. Brodovitch with drawings by Picasso and Brancusi; b—Bullier Hall

Figs. 173a, b. Bal Olympique, Paris, 11 July 1924: a—program; b—façade of the Olympia Tavern

Berlin

Der Queschnitt magazine announced that soprano Georgette Leblanc-Maerterlinck accompanied by his girlfriend Margaret Anderson arrived in Paris from the United States of America and visited Brancusi, James Joyce and Jean Cocteau, with a photo of the artist along with Léger and puppy Polaire in the sculptor's studio (Fig.174)[288].

Fig. 174. Georgette Leblanc, Léger and Polaire in Brancusi's studio, Paris, 1924

Bucharest

The April issue of Contimporanul magazine reproduced a photography of Brancusi sculpture entitled *Woman Head* (*Miss Pogany*—A/N) on the cover (Fig. 175).

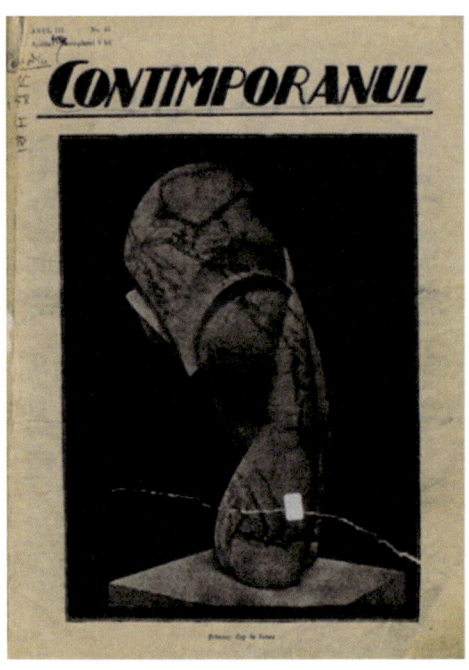

Fig. 175. Contimporanul, Bucharest, 1924, *45*

From 1924 to 1926, Max H. Maxy, János Mattis-Teutsch, and Marcel Iancu, Brancusi's friends, outstanding vanguard representatives in Romania, drew several caricatured portraits of the artist, which they published in Bucharest reviews (Figs. 176a, b).

Figs. 176a, b. *Brancusi* by M.H. Maxy (a) and J. Mattis-Teutsch (b)

Paris

On 15 June, at a Paris Evening (*Soirée de Paris*) organized by Count Étienne de Beaumont at Cigale Theater from Montmartre Brancusi, who participated next to countess Anna de Noailles-Brancoveanu, Tristan Tzara, Paul Morand and wife, Princess Elena Sutu, Marcel Mihalovici, a.o. to Sergey Diaghilev's *Mercure* ballet, music by Erik Satie, décor and costumes by P. Picasso, conductor Roger Désormière, choreography Léonide Massine[289].

The Transatlantic Review of June published five Brancusi drawings, next to works by Picasso, John Storrs, and Nina Hamnett. Texts were signed by Georges Ribemont-Dessaignes, Gertrude Stein, and Nathan Asch (Fig. 177a).

Emmanuel Bénézit included Brancusi's name in the dictionary of painters, sculptors, designers and engravers of all times and in all countries (*Dictionnaire Critique et Documentaire des Peintres, Sculpteurs, Dessinateurs et Graveurs de tous les temps et de tous les pays*), **I**, edited by Ernest Gründ (Fig. 177b).

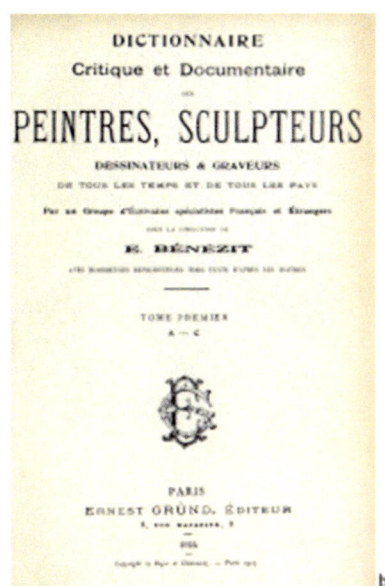

Figs. 177a, b. Paris, 1924: a—The Transatlantic Review, 6; b—*Dictionnaire Critique et Documentaire des Peintres, Sculpteurs, Dessinateurs et Graveurs de tous les temps et de tous les pays* coordinated by E. Bénézit

A good connoisseur of Parisian artistic environments and drawn by the expressivity and talent of dancer Serge Lifar, he took him as model for the *Beginning of the World* (marble, 1924)[290] (Figs. 178a, b).

Romanian sculptors Gheorghe Anghel, Mac Constantinescu and Romul Ladea were each one in turn Brancusi's apprentice for a short while. Sculptress Irina Codreanu became Brancusi's student then his coworker. She worked in the artist's studio until 1928 and, in parallel, in her personal studio of Montparnasse.

He sculpted the first version of the *Cock* (cherry wood, Fig. 179a) and he installed a fireplace in his studio and regulated the stack draft himself. In certain 1924 and 1925 photos (Fig. 179b) Brancusi appeared as cutting a column by saw and hatchet. He carved a column with nine full modules and two halves at the ends (over 5 m high).

Figs. 178a, b. Paris: a—ballet dancer S. Lifar; b—*The Beginning of the World*

Figs. 179a, b. Brancusi's studio, Paris, 1924: a—*Cock*; b—the sculptor carving a *Column*

Saint-Raphaël

In August, Brancusi made a so-called *Crocodile Temple* on the Saint-Raphaël beach, which he would bring to his studio (Figs. 180a, b) in memory of certain terrible moments he experienced when, taken away by high waters he was saved from drowning by clinging desperately to drift wood. The artist had been strongly marked by this, proof being his sending four *temple* photographs to H.P. Roché and his narrating the story to the directors of The Little Review[291].

Figs. 180a, b. *Temple of the Crocodile*, 1924: a—on the Saint-Raphaël beach; b—in the studio, Paris

Venice

Brancusi participated with two sculptures in the Romanian section of the 14th international art exhibition of Venice (*XIVe Esposizione internazionale d'arte della Città di Venezia*) organized in April-October at the Exhibition Palace.

New York

On 28 July, John Quinn died at 54. After the great collector's death, Jeanne Robert Foster dealt with his correspondence that would constitute the *John Quinn Memorial* in the Public Library of New York. His important collection comprising 27 sculptures, two drawings and six pedestals by Brancusi could have negative impact on the art market. Consequently, in 1926 they printed the collection catalogue, and Joseph Brummer [292] was entrusted with the transactions.

Bucharest

The *First International Plastic Arts Exhibition Organized by Contimporanul Magazine* took place in the Beaux Arts' Union Hall of Bucharest, 30 November-30 December. Max H. Maxy was exhibition commissar. Contimporanul issue 49 of November announced the readers about this important artistic event where paintings, engraving and sculptures, as well as work of the best modern art representatives from Belgium, Italy, Germany, Russia, Poland, Czech-Slovakia, Yugoslavia, and Hungary. Brancusi accepted the proposal of Ion Vinea and Marcel Iancu to participate in the exhibition upon Milita Petrascu's and Marcel Mihalovici's insistent pleas. Brancusi's works were from his "Fr. Storck's collection"[293] that remained unsold when the exhibition closed.

The comments of Tudor Vianu, O.W. Cisek, Lucian Blaga, and Scarlat Callimachi stood out among the accounts of this event, which scandalized the art world of Bucharest.

Chicago

The October issue of Poetry—A Magazine of Verse, founded by Harriet Monroe in 1912, included a chapter entitled *Brancusi and others* as well as poem *Brancusi* of the Irish poet Ernest Walsh, editor of This Quarter (Fig. 181). The poet called the artist "the Niagara of the ages" that changes materials—marble, stone and bronze—according to his own will[294].

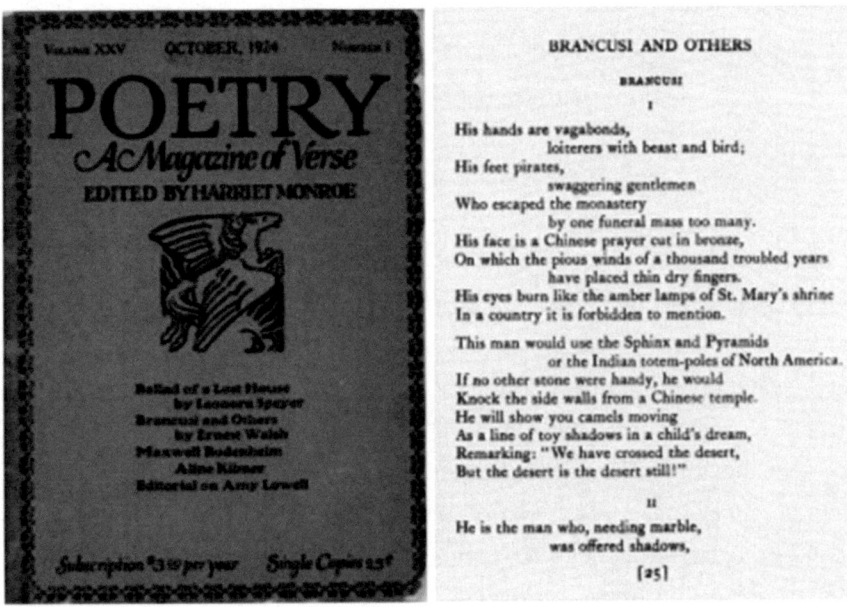

Fig. 181. *Brancusi* by E. Walsh, Poetry—A Magazine of Verse, Chicago, October 1924

1925

Bucharest

Contimporanul magazine dedicated to Brancusi issue 52 of January (Fig. 182). The cover reproduced an image from the artist's Parisian studio, and inside articles on the sculptor were published, authored by M. Iancu, I. Vinea, Milita Petrascu and three photos of Brancusi's works.

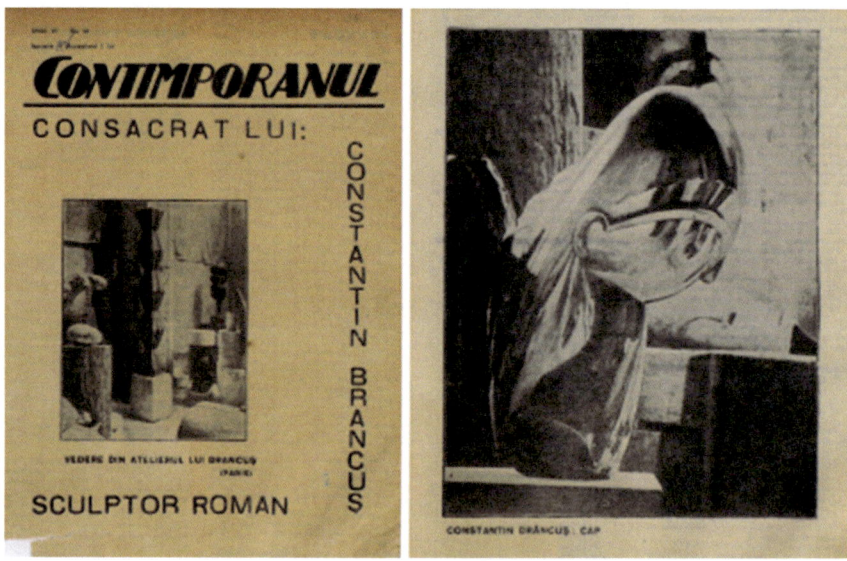

Fig. 182. Contimporanul, Bucharest, 1925, *1*

On 1 April, the second issue of the monthly Integral review, subtitled modern synthesis magazine, organ of the Romanian and foreign modernist movement, published Ion Minulescu's literary medallion with five photos of Brancusi sculptures (*Cock, Princess X, Eve, Blond Negress* and *Danaide*), one from the Parisian studio and the artist's portrait by M.H. Maxy (Fig. 183)[295]. That year the Integral review published the photos of *Narcisse* and *Torso*[296], drawings *Child* and *Dance,* sculptures *Portrait* (marble, 1909) and *Socrates* (wood, 1923), together with *Brigands' Story* and *Aphorisms*[297], *Sorceress* and the *Kiss* of Montparnasse Cemetery[298].

Paris

On 19 February, he celebrated his birthday in La Rotonde restaurant next to close friends (Fig. 184).

He participated to the French, British, and American painting and sculpture exhibition (*Exposition tri-nationale d'œuvres de peintres et sculpteurs français, anglais et américain*), 28 May-25 June, organized by Marius de Zayas at Durand-Ruel Gallery, which then moved to London and New York. Brancusi exhibited three sculptures and five drawings.

Ethel Moorhead, suffragette and painter from England, together with American poet Ernst Walsh edited This Quarter, one of the best art magazines of the time. The first issue of this quarterly review was printed in May (Fig. 185) and was dedicated to Ezra Pound. The art supplement provided Brancusi's photographic self-portrait, 40 photos of Brancusi sculptures, five drawings, *Brigands' Story* and a number of aphorisms of the artist, everything tended by Irina Codreanu[299].

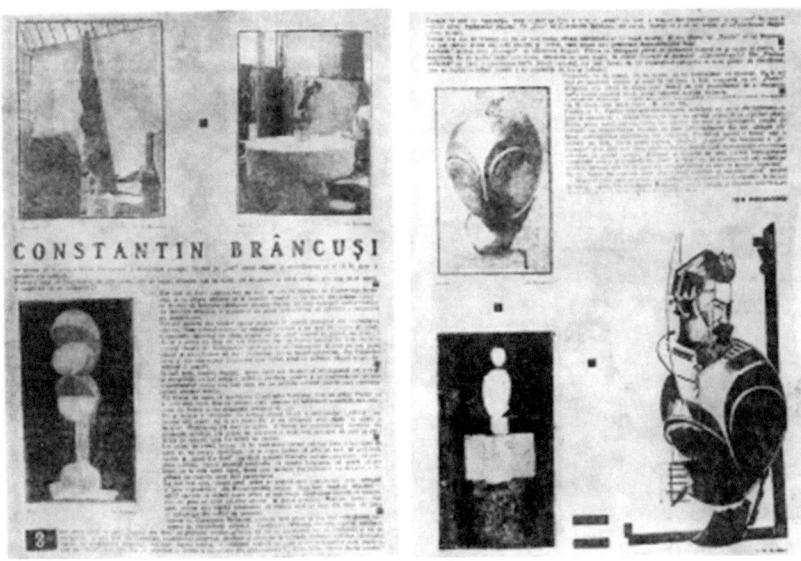

Fig. 183. Integral, Bucharest, 1925, *2*

Fig. 184. Brancusi at the celebration of his birthday in the Rotonde, Paris, 19 February 1925. From left to right: M. Mihalovici, L. Delarue-Mardrus, Dr. Mardrus, O. Cosmuta, G. Bölöni, Th. Aladar

Fig. 185. This Quarter, Paris, May 1925

In summer, the artist endured another painful event since his Polaire dog was crushed by a truck before his very eyes. Brancusi was deeply touched and buried her in the canine cemetery Asnières-sur Seine. Marcel Mihalovici remembered the artist intended to make a funerary monument to his dog, he began to but never completed it[300]. In his memoirs, Mihalovici noted that Brancusi proposed to Marcel Mihalovici to write his biography based on his memories dictated to the composer[301].

Erik Satie died on 1 July and his friends, Princess Edmond de Polignac and Count Étienne de Beaumont, did their best to raise funds in order to have his funerary monument built by Brancusi. The project was not achieved because funds could not be gathered.

During her European tour, Dorothy Adlow went to Brancusi's studio of 8 Impasse Ronsin, being impressed by the bright intelligence and physical attraction of the artist over his collocutors, as well as by his good French.

Margareta Cosaceanu-Lavrillier, recently settled in Paris after marrying medal maker André Lavrillier, would sometimes work in Brancusi's studio[302].

Vidra de Sus (Alba County)

In August Nicolae Pralea, after a four-day visit to Motilor Land on the occasion of a hundred years since Avram Iancu's birth, wrote to Vidra de Sus in need of a monument for the revolution man, made by "one of our great artists," Paciurea or Brancusi[303].

London

Brancusi traveled to London to attend the opening of the exhibition itinerated from Paris and organized at New Chenil Galleries as *Exhibition of Tri-National Art: French, British, American*, 30 September-10 October, as well as other artistic events of the city (Fig. 186). Brancusi exhibited four sculptures and five drawings.

Fig. 186. Augustus John, Brancusi and F.O. Dobson at the National Portrait Gallery, London, 1925

Berlin

The October issue of Sturm magazine published three full-page photos of Brancusi's sculptures *Torso of Young Man*, *White Negress*, and *Bird* (Fig. 187).

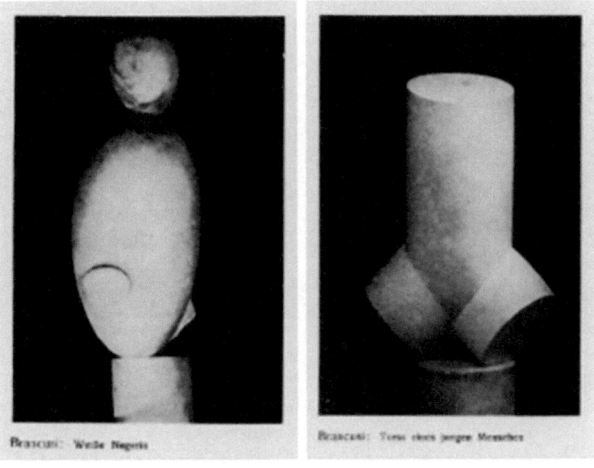

Fig. 187. Sturm, Berlin, October 1925

Paris

The Curiosity and Fine Arts Trade Union Chamber organized the international art exhibition (*L'art d'aujourd'hui*), December 1st and 12th, in which Brâncuși participated with three sculptures. They also exhibited Arp, Delaunay, Gleizes, Léger, Lipchitz, Laurens, Mondrian, Ozenfant, Picasso and others.

1926

New York

The Art Center of New York hosted the *Memorial Exhibition of Representative Works Selected from the John Quinn Collection*, 7-30 January, showing 27 sculptures from such collection. In April, a catalogue was edited in a hurry after this exhibition.

On 20 January, Brancusi got on board the luxury boat France (Compagnie Générale Transatlantique)[304] in Le Havre harbor, making his first trip to New York[305] (Fig. 188a) on the occasion of the Wildenstein Galleries exhibitions. From 28 January to 22 March, Brancusi was in New York and he stayed at Brevoort Hotel (Fig. 189). The impression of the metropolis was overwhelming for him when entering the harbor. The artist later confessed that he could see his "large-scale" studio and that he could not have "built this city any better"[306].

Figs. 188a, b. Cruise ships: a—France; b—De Grasse

Fig. 189. Brevoort Hotel, New York

The London *Exhibition of Tri-National Art: French, British, American* was itinerated to New York, from 26 January to 17 February at Wildenstein Galleries. Brancusi participated there with four works. On the occasion of this exhibition the artist met the Arensberg collectors through Beatrice Wood, and also William Lescaze, American architect born in Switzerland, one of the promoters of modernism in American architecture[307]. From 18 February to 3 March, the New York public could admire eight Brancusi sculptures at his third personal *Exhibition of Sculpture by Brancusi*, organized at Wildenstein Galleries before the artist.

He was invited to celebrate his 50th birthday in the family of lawyer and collector Maurice J. Speiser[308]. There he knew better Louise and Walter Arensberg, future great collectors of his works.

In New York on 27 February, Brancusi was the honorary guest of the Penguin Club, which had given its annual ball (Firemen's Gala, Fig. 190)[309], event remaining in history through the caricature painting of Alexander Calder *Firemen's Dinner for Brancusi* (oil on canvas, 1926, Fig. 191).

Fig. 190. Invitation to the Firemen's Gala, New York, 27 February 1926

Fig. 191. *Firemen's Dinner for Brancusi* by A. Calder, New York, 1926

On 22 March Brancusi left New York and on 31 March he descended in Le Havre, after the voyage back on De Grasse cruise ship (Compagnie Générale Transatlantique)[310] (Fig. 188b).

Bucharest

The January issue of Contimporanul magazine published the article *At Brancusi* by Marcel Iancu, which included an interview and the portrait of the artist made by the author (Fig. 192)[311]. Iancu made this year another portrait of Brancusi (Fig. 193).

Fig. 192. Contimporanul, Bucharest, 1926, *1*

Fig. 193. *Brancusi* by M. Iancu

In the first 1926 issue of the Gandirea, Lucian Blaga published the poetry *Pasarea sfanta* [Saint Bird] and in 1929 he would introduce it in the volume *Lauda somnului* [Praise to Sleep] after some stylization to provide the philosophic concept of the idea-bird.

In his volume entitled *Romania in chipuri si vederi* [Romania in Faces and Images], Nicolae Iorga considered the "true Romanian art" was painting, which began with Aman and Grigorescu and had no representatives in sculpture and architecture[312]. Speaking of sculpture, the scholar slighted what he called "Brancusi's daring attempts of the unreal," but also the works of F. Storck, A. Severin, I. Jalea and O. Han. At the *Early Art* section, he introduced the photos of Brancusi's *Prayer*, and of four more works in the *Modern Art* section: *Study of a Child's Head, Head Carved from a Pebble,* and two *Portraits* (Fig. 194a). In 1922, the first version of this volume was published by Imprimerie A.G. L'Hoir, Paris (Fig. 194b).

Paris, Voulangis

From 20 March to 2 May the 37th exhibition of the Independent Artists' Society (*37ᵉ Exposition de la Société des artistes indépendants*) was organized at the Bois Palace of Paris, where Brancusi exhibited a *sleeping muse*.

In May, Brancusi erected his first *Column* (7.17 m high, poplar wood, Figs. 195a, b)[313] in the garden of Edward Steichen's Blue Bird Villa from Voulangis.

Anvers

On 8-15 May, Brancusi traveled to Belgium. The French modern art exhibition (*Exposition de l'art moderne français*) was organized at the Anvers City Hall Events, 15 May-20 June; Brancusi displayed six sculptures and also attended the opening day.

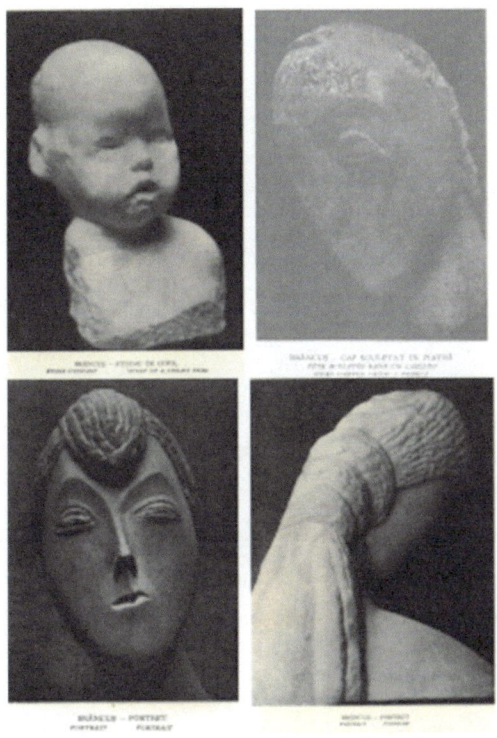

Figs. 194a, b. *Romania in chipuri si vederi*, Bucharest, 1926 with photos of Brancusi's woks—a; *La Roumanie en images*, **I**, Paris, 1922—b

Figs. 195a, b. Brancusi erected the *Column* in Ed. Steichen's garden, Voulangis, 1926

Paris

In June he exhibited two sculptures at the *Tuileries Salon* organized at the Palace de Bois of Paris.

On 19 June, he attended the first night of the Mechanical Ballet (*Ballet mécanique*) opera for percussions and plane propeller at Champs-Élysées Theater, a joint project of composer George Antheil living in Paris, cinema man Dudley Murphy and painter Fernand Léger[314].

He finished polishing two bronze sculptures: *Leda*, which he fastened to a rotating disk and the *Blond Negress*.

Marthe Lebherz, daughter of a doctor from Geneva, came to Paris in 1925 to study classical dance. She belonged to Nijinski's team and became Brancusi's secretary and lover (Fig. 196). His relationship with Marthe from 1926 to 1928 stands out by intensity of sentiments, the artist thinking even of marrying her, despite their age difference. He planned publishing a volume of love letters illustrated by him, and he named the history *Tonton and Tantan*, their endearment names[315]. In the end, nothing was achieved, their paths in life continuing separately.

Fig. 196. Brancusi, Marthe Lebherz and sisters Codreanu, Paris, 1926-1927(?)

The quick devaluation of the French Franc occasioned the appeal of Marechal Joffre, while Paris-Midi newspaper organized the *Salon du Franc* (*L'art français au service du Franc*) [Salon of the Franc (French art serving the Franc)] at Galliera Museum, 22-31 October. Such exhibition gathered

159 pictures and sculptures of foreign artists living in Paris and, in token of gratitude for the country that hosted them they offered their works to be auctioned. Brancusi attended with sculpture *Newborn* (marble, 1919-1921). Meetings took place during the event, people shouted *Boo Brancusi!* and the police interfered by taking protesters out[316][317]. Swedish collector Rolf de Mare, who had established in 1920 the Swedish Ballets Co. in Paris, purchased the *Newborn* with 7,000 FF.

Berlin, Bern

In July-August the painting exhibition by young artists from Germany, England, France and the United States (*Ausstellung von Gemälden jüngerer Künstler aus Deutschland, England, Frankreich und den Vereinigten Staaten*) was organized in the Nationalgalerie from Berlin, which was then itinerated to Kunsthalle of Bern (5-25 September), where Brancusi exhibited as well.

Prague

In August Pásmo, international modern magazine, published the photograph of one Brancusi's sculpture (*Little French Girl*) from his studio (Fig. 197).

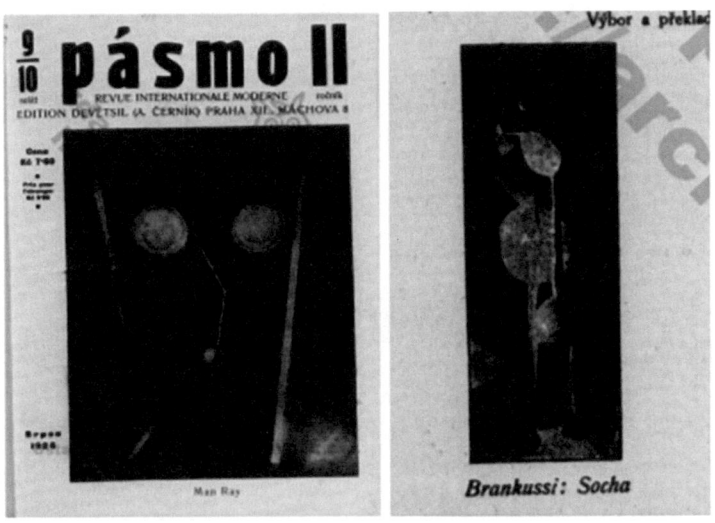

Fig. 197. Pásmo, Prague, 1926, *9-10*

Le Havre, New York

Joseph Brummer offered to arrange him a new personal exhibition in New York to highlight the sculptures from Quinn's collection after his death in 1924. Brummer asked Brancusi to come from Paris to discuss it. On 23 September Brancusi and Ed. Steichen embarked on board to Paris steam ship (Compagnie Générale Transatlantique) in Le Havre harbor, this being the artist's second trip to New York (Figs. 198a, b) and made his second travel to New York. He intended to restore the sculptures remaining from Quinn and wanted to participate in the opening of his fourth personal exhibition at Brummer Gallery[318].

Marcel Duchamp went on board the ship in Le Havre harbor on 13 October and got to New York by 20 October with boxes containing twenty Brancusi sculptures. Through the care Quinn artwork was exempt of taxation when entering the United States, according to the Tariff Act of 1922. Notwithstanding all these on 21 October the customs of New York State charged 40% duties from the amount of the "objects" in the boxes, but they allowed entry on American territory for the Brummer Gallery exhibition.

This is the reason why in 1926, a court trial was instituted against the American customs for the *Bird in Space* (polished bronze, 1925, Fig. 199) bought by Steichen from Brancusi and brought by him in October. The customs of New York State deemed the *Bird in Space* should be classified under *Kitchen Utensils and Hospital Supplies*, taxable 40% from its value of "object"[319].

Figs. 198a, b. Paris cruise ship—a; Brancusi and Ed. Steichen's dog on the deck of the cruise ship—b

Fig. 199. *Bird in Space* for which court trial was opened with the American customs

Brancusi participated at the opening of his fourth personal *Brancusi/Exhibition/The Brummer Gallery* scheduled from 17 November to 15 December, curator being Marcel Duchamp. The illustrated exhibition catalogue comprised 70 works, of which 32 were shown full page, most of them after Brancusi's photographs. Paul Morand signed the foreword while the contents provided press excerpts, Brancusi aphorisms, and texts by Jacques Doucet, Ezra Pound, Clive Bell, John Quinn, Forbes Watson, Henry McBride, Paul Westheim, André Salmon, Albert Dreyfus, Angus Wilson, Ralph Flint, Flora Merrill, Walter Pach, Carl Sandburg, Mina Loy, and Jeanne Robert Foster.

The American press wrote about the success of the exhibition, and Brancusi's presence in New York was noticed by journalists of famous dailies, whom the artist astonished with comments such as "he did not like the statues of public squares and parks" in the city, although he found out "several very attractive architectural structures" there[320].

During the time spent in New York, Brancusi visited the city with architect William Lescaze, they devised installing some large-scale *Endless Column* in the city.

He went to the Meyers' summer residence in Mount Kisco, where he visited until his departure to Washington, D.C. In a discussion with Flora Merrill, the sculptor told her about his much dreamed of project—to build a column in Central Park "three times higher than your obelisk in Washington," with apartments arranged in each pyramid inhabited by people, and "my bird poised on the top" of it[321].

Brancusi paid a visit to Marie Romany, Romanian born near Tecuci and settled in New York, also named Queen of Grenwich Village, Montparnasse of the metropolis[322] [323]. He had met Marie in Paris at a party organized by Fernand Léger and Henri Matisse. In New York she owned a well-known pub frequented by artists, poets and writers (Figs. 200a, b). Marie was also famous for her fortune telling using coffee, and Brancusi proposed to make the drawings for a book on this subject written by Marie Romany[324].

Figs. 200a, b. Marie Romany (a) and her famous tavern of Greenwich Village (b), New York

From 19 November 1926 to 1 January 1927 Katherine S. Dreier, chairwoman of Société Anonyme, and Marcel Duchamp organized the most important international modern art exhibition after the Armory Show, entitled

International Exhibition of Modern Art Assembled by Société Anonyme, at Brooklyn Museum in New York. Works were exhibited by artists of 14 countries, among whom Arp, Brancusi, Braque, Duchamp, Duchamp-Villon, Léger, Moholy-Nagy, Mondrian, Picabia, Picasso, Schwitters, and Stieglitz. The brochure Katherine S. Dreier wrote contained one page dedicated to Brancusi, "The most brilliant of modern sculptors, acclaimed by them all" (Fig. 201). The following year, the exhibition was itinerated at Albright Art Gallery, Buffalo, which purchased *Miss Pogany* (bronze, 1920), and at the Art Gallery of Ontario from Toronto.

In the Yale University Library, Beinecke Digital Collections there is a photograph of Brancusi by Alfred Stieglitz, undated and localized (Fig. 202), which after clothing and traits was made in fall in November 1926, in New York.

At the end of November, he left the United States.

On 3 December Brancusi, on board the cruise ship Rochambeau (Compagnie Générale Transatlantique) arrived in Le Havre harbor[325] (Fig. 203). Marcel Duchamp would keep him posted about the American customs, the exhibition success and the refusal of people from Los Angeles and Denver to host the exhibition from Brummer Gallery. On 31 December, Marcel Duchamp specified that painter Yasuo Kuniyoshi will take photos at the Chicago exhibition. Mary Rumsey firmly ordered the *Bird* (bronze, 1,500 $) and the *Torso* (onyx, 800 $). To avoid New York customs, Duchamp recommended dispatch in other custom points—Baltimore or Philadelphia[326].

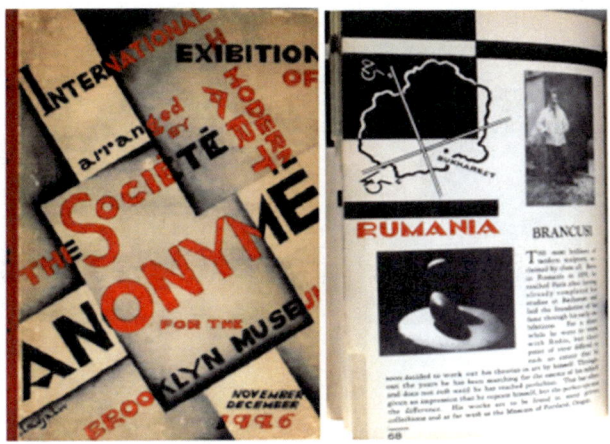

Fig. 201. Brochure by Katherine S. Dreier, New York, 1926

Fig. 202. Brancusi, New York, 1926

Fig. 203. Rochambeau cruise ship

London

Roger Fry in his volume entitled *Transformations: Critical and Speculative Essays on Art* (Fig. 204) expresses his opinion that there are many cases when Chinese art has influenced modern Western art, and one instance was the trend of his contemporary sculptors to use ovoidal elements, among whom "Brancusi is, of course, the most striking example."[327]

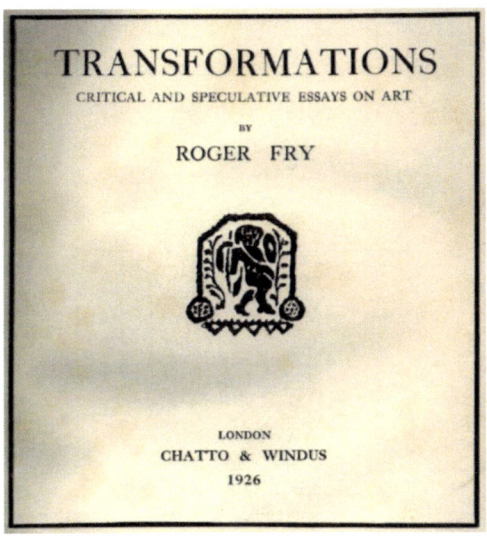

Fig. 204. *Transformations: Critical and Speculative Essays on Art* by R. Fry, London, 1926

New Haven (Connecticut)

The University of Michigan Professor DeWitt H. Parker in his *The Analysis of Art* volume compares the sculpture *Bacchante* of MacMonnies with *Miss Pogany* of Brancusi, considering the former gives the impression it is alive thus pointing out the artist's talent, "But equally, when we look at Brancusi's *Miss Pogany*, for all the geometrization of the head, we get a feeling of reality" (Fig. 205)[328].

Paris

On the occasion of her marriage to Oswaldo de Andrade Brancusi offered to Tarsila do Amaral (Fig. 206), as token of appreciation the kiss ideogram drawn on the catalogue cover of the Brummer Gallery exhibition in New York[329] and a bronze sculpture, *Prometheus* of 1911 (Figs. 207a, b).

Hyères

In the autumn he thought about the possible achievement of 3 m high *Bird in Space* for the Villa Noailles, property of Charles and Marie-Laure de Noailles. Together with engineer-architect Jean Prouvé the artist selected stainless steel, a better metal than bronze in case of air exposure, but he was dissatisfied with the polish quality and this project failed as well[330]. Eventually a bronze *Sleeping Muse* was installed in the garden of the Noailles villa[331] (Figs. 208a, b).

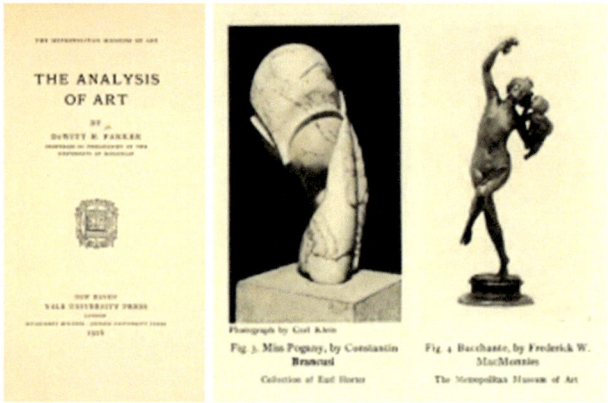

Fig. 205. *The Analysis of Art* by D.H. Parker, New Haven, 1926

Fig. 206. Oswaldo de Andrade, Tarsila do Amaral, Yvette Farkou, F. Léger, Brancusi and M. Gauthier, Paris, 1926

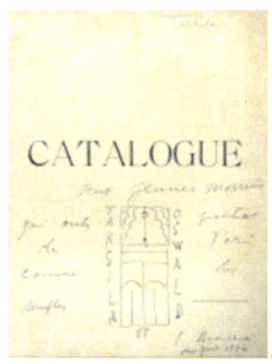

Figs. 207a, b. Brancusi's gifts at Tarsila's wedding, Paris, 1926: a—ideogram of the *Kiss*; b—view of Tarsila's living room with *Prometheus* on the table, São Paulo, 1929

Figs. 208a, b. Hyères: a—Villa Noailles, 1929; b—*Sleeping Muse* in the garden of the villa

Chicago

From 21 December 1926 to 24 January 1927, the *Some Modern Paintings* exhibition took place in the AIC. Brancusi was represented with a *Marble Head*.

Bucharest

Integral magazine in the December issue published *IV. Fluture (Cantece si jocuri)* [Butterfly, the 4th part of the "Songs and Dances" suite] composed by

Marcel Mihalovici and dedicated to Brancusi on 19 September 1924, on the occasion of the artist's arrival in Bucharest (Fig. 209)[332].

Fig. 209. Integral, Bucharest, 1926, *9*

1927

Chicago

With Alice Roullier's help the personal Brancusi exhibition from Brummer Gallery in New York was itinerated to The Arts Club of Chicago from 4 to 18 January, entitled *An Exhibition of Sculpture by Brancusi*, with Marcel Duchamp organizer[333]. Similarly to the show displayed in New York, the exhibition was highly successful. Artist and art critic Walter Pach delivered two conferences on the Romanian sculptor's work. The Arts Club of Chicago purchased *Bird in Space* (bronze, 1919-1920) that had belonged to John Quinn.

New York

Writer Dorothy Dudley Harvey paid a visit to Brancusi's studio of which she would write in 1927, in The Dial magazine, an article illustrated with two photos of his sculptures. Dorothy Dudley Harvey found out that he "was an inventor, a constructor, a worker on many plans." He was fascinated by verticality and height and that was the reason why he "stands among things and uplifts them in his own plan"[334].

London

Another American art critic, Dorothy Adlow, published in Drawings and Design an essay dedicated to Brancusi, where the artist spoke with her about art and what it represents for a creator, and why one should never mistake nature's reproduction for creation. To Brancusi, a body of nature represented with members, facial traits, clothing means nothing else but *biftek*. He admitted it was not simple to render "tangible form" to what is "purely mental," though artists choose the easiest way to transmit their message, "They proceed to exult in the grandeur of draperies, in exaggerated movement, in sentimentality, *biftek*"[335].

Paris

Isamu Noguchi, Japanese born American sculptor arrived in Paris on 30 March and in April paid a visit to Brancusi's studio together with the American writer Robert McAlmon. Despite there existing a language barrier between the two, Noguchi and Brancusi would spend several months together[336]. Noguchi and Juana Müller are the only students of Brancusi whom he offered the privilege to practice polishing, under the careful supervision of the artist. When Noguchi was about to leave for New York Brancusi recommended him to visit Marie Romany's coffee shop in Greenwich Village, which the young sculptor did[337].

In April-June, he participated in the *5th Salon des Tuileries* from the Palais de Bois. In his artistic chronicle the art critic Louis Vauxcelles noted: "this hermetical Brancusi (so solemn, so serious however but whose *Bird*, sparkling with reflections and placed on a gypsum hat box, remains in my opinion a highly troubling enigma)."[338]

Brancusi, upon Braque's advice, purchased a plot of land with house ruins on it at 18 Sauvageot Street, very close to Impasse Ronsin. He devised himself the house plans and of the future studio. The artist executed himself the plans for his future studio et residence (two stories) and a construction demand was registered in the Paris City's Official Municipal Bulletin of 10 February 1928, page 888. However, we do not know very well why he abandoned such plan.

After a violent storm the studio of 8 Impasse Ronsin was flooded as water seeped underneath and soaked the soft half-timber walls. The studio was about to collapse and on 1 July, the sculptor was forced to move out with all his pieces, pedestals and materials to the studio of no. 11 which he had already rented. Little by little, the studio became a place of exhibition and presentation of the sculptures, an art gallery. The impression of sacred space was imprinted to visitors and many have confessed it. The brickwork, the peasant stove, all the arrangements were made by Brancusi.

The bed had been carved from a huge tree trunk. The chairs and benches were carved in wood and stone. He had planted trees and flowers around the studio, which allured the wild birds. Brancusi had good relations with the artists of the other studios as he was reliable friend, discrete and kind. This was the studio where he received the visits of fellow countrymen, great personalities of the arts, great cultured people, politicians, and simple people.

Cahiers d'Art founded by Christian Zervos published an article by Albert Dreyfus dedicated to Brancusi with nine photos of Brancusi works (Fig. 210)[339].

Hamburg

In July, he participated to the European contemporary art (*Europäische Kunst der Gegenwart*) exhibition from Kunstverein Hamburg.

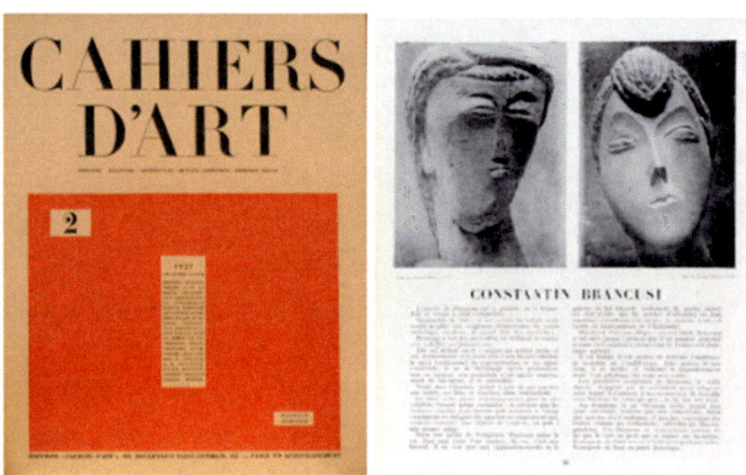

Fig. 210. Cahiers d'Art, Paris, 1927, *2*

Bucharest

On the occasion of the Latin Press Congress, the *Romanian Art Exhibition* was organized in the Pavilion of the Garden House (30 September-10 October) where three Brancusi sculptures were exhibited. Stefan I. Nenitescu signed the catalogue foreword and wrote that Brancusi was the greatest Romanian sculptor who, concerned especially with the material, "joins the handicraftsman's joy and the constructive impetus of the visionary"[340].

Museum conservatory, Tache Soroceanu wrote an article about the State Art Gallery, providing also the manner in which the Romanian art exhibition was organized: "the organizers went in a hurry to the collectors." Soroceanu bitterly recounted that, despite the many foreign tourists visiting Romania to get to know us better, Romania had no national art museum, which would be highly interesting for all visitors. Brancusi to him was "a voluptuous of form," concerned with organizing space and seemingly "competing with God" when his small size pieces acquired "monumental dimensions" once you understood them. Soroceanu recalled that, despite Brancusi's worldwide fame, the Romanian state received only two of his youth sculptures (*Bust of Painter Nicolae Darascu* and *Child Head*, both of gypsum—A/N) (Fig. 211)[341].

Prague

The modern culture magazine ReD published the article *Taneční masky primitivů* [Dancing masks of primitive people] by J. Honzl, presenting several photos of works by great artists, of which the *Sleeping Muse* by Brancusi (Fig. 212)[342].

Voulangis

When Steichen left France at the end of October, beginning in November, Brancusi disassembled the *Column* of Voulangis with Man Ray's help (Figs. 213a, b). The sculptor cut it in two in order to introduce it in his studio.

The inferior part would be exhibited at the Brummer Gallery in 1933-1934, and would be entitled *Endless Column*.

Fig. 211. *Bust of Painter Nicolae Darascu* exhibited in the State Art Gallery, Bucharest

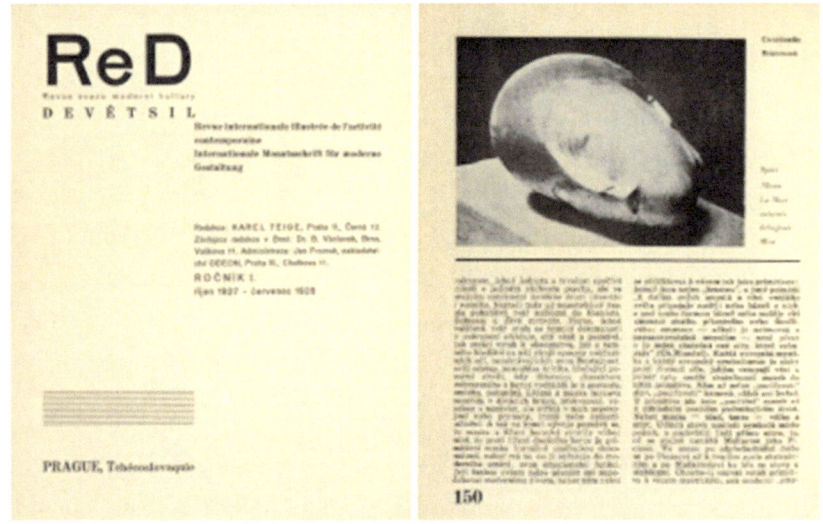

Fig. 212. ReD, Prague, October 1927-July 1928

Figs. 213a, b. Edward Steichen's garden, Voulangis, 1927: a—Man Ray and Brancusi; b—Brancusi disassembling the *Column*

New York

On 21 October the Customs Tribunal was approached by Brancusi that protested against the wrong application of taxes to his *Bird in Space* sculpture, which the custom officials considered a "manufactured object." A strong team would deal with Brancusi's court trial against the customs of New York State, the sculptor being represented by the Philadelphia lawyer Maurice Speiser. Statements for Brancusi were recorded from Edward Steichen, Jacob Epstein, Frank Crowninshield, Forbes Watson, Henry McBride, W.H. Fox and the editors of The Arts and Vanity Fair. An important part of the press supported Brancusi in his lawsuit, but there were also opposing opinions (Fig. 214)[343]. On 12 December, The Gallery of Living Art opened at New York University by *The A.E. Gallatin Collection*.

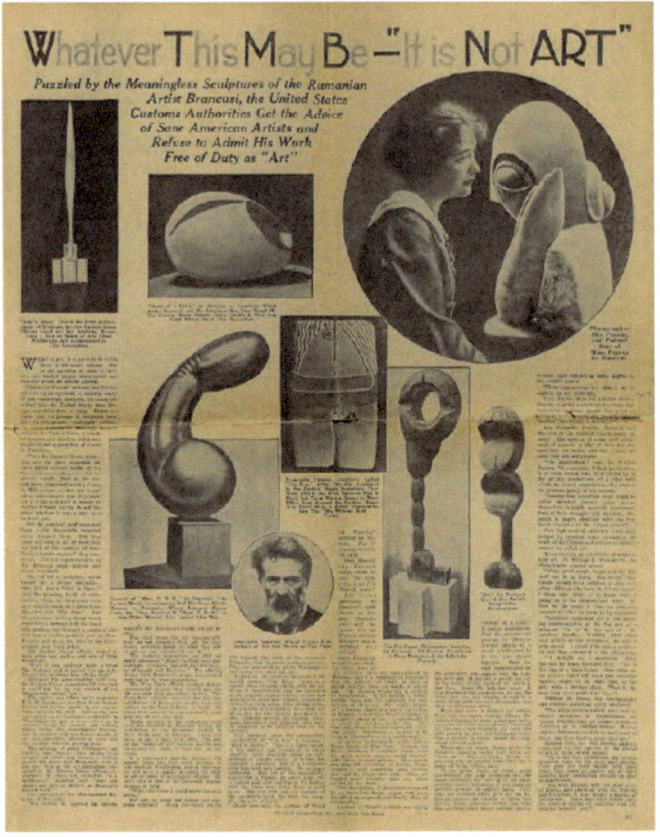

Fig. 214. American Weekly (Chicago Herald-Examiner), 13 March 1927

Nancy

Brancusi met engineer-architect Jean Prouvé in 1927 and at the end of November he went to Nancy to work in this studio (foundry) the *Newborn* polish, made there of stainless steel (Fig. 215). The sculpture was placed on more than 80 cm high pedestal of patina oak wood. Their good cooperation can be also proved by the dispatch of a Vega 2 stainless steel bar by Jean Prouvé to the artist in view of extracting its artistic features[344].

Fig. 215. *Newborn*

Paris

On 9 December, Jim Ede, deputy director of Tate Gallery in London, who had been to Brancusi's studio brought by Henri-Pierre Roché, wrote the artist he wanted to buy the bronze *Fish*, but he was embarrassed to bargain for it. On 28 December Ede acknowledged he received the piece, which he considered wonderful[345].

The 1st annual exhibition of a group of sculptors (*1re Exposition annuelle d'un Groupe de sculpteurs*) was organized by E. Tériade at the Jacques Bernheim Gallery of Paris (1-15 December). Exhibited works were made by Brancusi, Despiau, Laurens, Gargallo and Zadkine.

Leiden

Theo van Doesburg published the article *Brancusi* in the jubilee issue of De Stijl magazine (Fig. 216)[346].

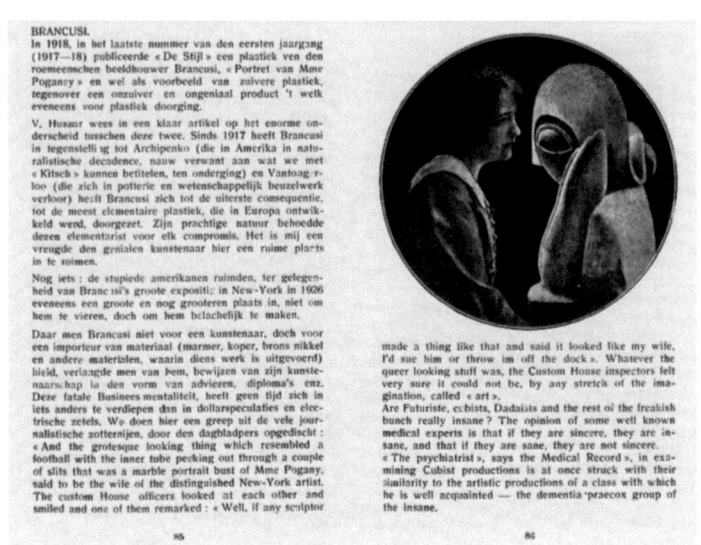

Fig. 216. De Stijl, Leiden, 1927, Jubileum Serie **XIV**, *79-84*

1928

Paris, Nice

On 1 January, Brancusi became officially the dweller of 11 Impasse Ronsin, where he would stay until death. In time, this studio proved too small for the exhibition of sculptures and for work, therefore he would rent other studios as well on 1 April 1928, 11 February 1930, 1 October 1936 and in 1941, inter-connecting all of them. In 1929, Brancusi would write to Margaret Anderson: "Just pass by and see me in my three barracks."

Beginning with January 1928 until 14 March 1929, Brancusi exchanged letters with the Initiative Committee of Caracal about a monument in memory of playwright Haralamb Lecca, which was not achieved.

At the end of February, Brancusi and Marthe Lebherz spent a few days in Nice in order to have a rest (Figs. 217a, b).

Figs. 217a, b. Brancusi and Marthe Lebherz on the beach of Nice, 1928

Bucharest

The *8th Painting and Sculpture Exhibition of the "Romanian Art" Society* was organized in Bucharest, 18 March-April, in the Romanian Book Exhibition Hall. Brancusi, M. Bunescu, H. Catargi, T. Pallady, I. Theodorescu-Sion, I. Iser, C. Michailescu, D. Paciurea, I. Jalea, C. Medrea participated. The event was reluctantly received in certain influential media, which cooled the enthusiasm of exhibiting participants and that was the last exhibition of the *Romanian Art* Society. Brancusi participated with three pieces.

Sasa Pana, vanguard poet and writer, published his *Manifesto* on the cover of the first issue of Unu magazine in April, mentioning Brancusi among the famous vanguard representatives of Europe: "marinetti / breton / vinea / tzara / ribemont-dessaignes / arghezi / brincus / theo van doesburg / hurraaaay / hurraaaaaay / hurraaaaaaaay […]" (Fig. 218).

Fig. 218. Unu, Bucharest, April 1928

In Universul literar Camil Petrescu published the *Sculptor* essay where he examined Brancusi's creations [347] (Fig. 219). Starting from the celebrity acquired by Brancusi abroad, C. Petrescu recalled the public's ignorance regarding Brancusi's work. Such misunderstanding relies on his "often so strange creation" devoid of any prejudice. Petrescu considered the artist's creation had "absolutely ideal purity" conferred by his attempt to stubbornly capture an "idea in [its] absolute sense," and by such attempt Brancusi has become representative for a "new aspect of the Romanian heart."

Thus, Brancusi has become a referential model when defining Romania's "national specificity" focused on the "profound reality" of his work, which was guided by "infinite possibilities." This essay was not to the liking of the magazine owners and Camil Petrescu had to resign from the editorial team. In the same issue painter and writer Corneliu Michailescu expressed slightly different opinions on the sculptor. He sensed a sentiment of "religiousness" in the artist's uninterrupted modest labor, thus he "creates under the same fatality that constituted the universe," and he pointed out that Brancusi's creation provides a "trend toward shape spirituality up to metaphor." Michailescu recalled the respect paid to the artist abroad in comparison with the misunderstanding of his fellow countrymen, but nevertheless he remained unchanged[348].

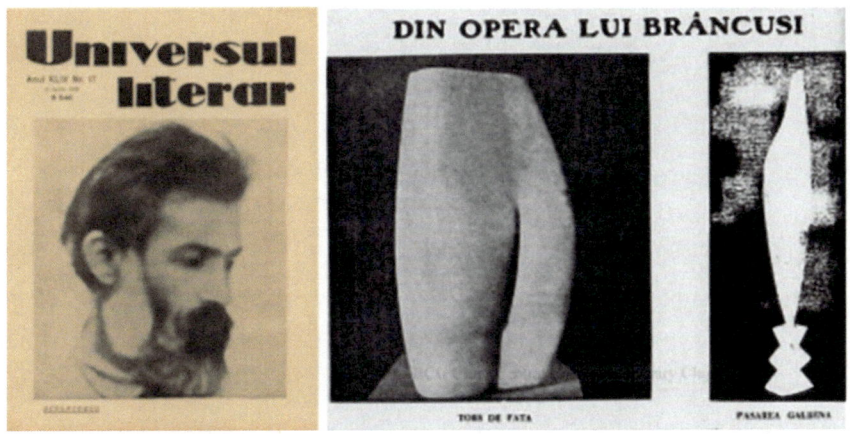

Fig. 219. Universul literar, Bucharest, 1928, *17*

As far back as 1928 Brancusi thought of realizing in Bucharest, a city without monuments, a large-scale *Column*; during one of his country visits, he met Mayor Dem I. Dobrescu where they both agreed to imitate a grandiose project for either a monumental *Column*[349], or a huge *Maiastra Bird*[350]. The Brancusi-Dobrescu agreement and was canceled when elections were lost. The government changed and Dobrescu was replaced with A.G. Donescu who had no interest in furthering his predecessor's civil projects.

Sibiu

Brancusi was invited to attend a contest for a Monument of all Romanians' Union under King Ferdinand I. The contest was to be organized upon an initiative of Generals Constantin Gavanescu and Ioan P. Daschevici, Corps 7 Army of Sibiu. Having already got experience with the military when he achieved the *Bust of General Doctor Carol Davila* back in 1903, the sculptor declined the invitation saying his liberty of creation was limited.

Philadelphia

In April, an inaugural exhibition at the new building of the Museum of Art (*The inaugural exhibition of the New Museum of Art, Fairmount. European and American Sections*) was organized[351].

Paris

In May-June, the *Tuileries Salon* opened in the Palais de Bois and presented the *Bird in Space* (polished bronze). Maurice Raynal considered "Brancusi's *Bird*, elegant piece of metal where the artist intends to simplify the subject up to its pure plastic and material expression"[352]. Philosopher Lucian Blaga also went to the exhibition and admired Brancusi's sculpture, to which he had already dedicated his "Saint Bird" poetry published in 1926.

At the beginning of August, Brancusi received Gabrielle Buffet-Picabia and Jean Arp, then Carola Giedion-Welcker in his studio, the latter becoming a very good friend until his death. He also received American collectors Sidney and Harriet Janis, the German sculptors Arno Breker and Karl Hartung, and James Joyce, who was introduced to him by Ezra Pound[353]. Joyce and Brancusi would become good friends.

Nadia-Alexandra Polizu-Micsunesti, Romanian sculptress married to French writer Joseph Kessel, died prematurely of tuberculosis. Brancusi carved the stone on her tomb in Montparnasse Cemetery and intended placing a sculpture on the slab, but this was not achieved. Marcel Mihalovici saw the artist working and remembered the sculptress' tomb of Montparnasse Cemetery was "just simple slab—Brancusi carved a sort of border all around and, simply, her name SANDA"[354].

A new column (3.60 m high) was made of poplar wood consisting of five whole modules and semi-modules at both ends; it would be exhibited in the Brummer Gallery in 1933-1934.

Still in 1928, Margaret Anderson and Jane Heap organized an international exhibition at the review gallery of New York, on the occasion of their last issue of The Little Review (Spring Number, May 1929). Brancusi agreed to participate and signed the exhibition poster next to the other artists (Fig. 220).

Moscow, Leningrad

In September-October, the *Contemporary French Art Exhibition* was organized in the State Museum of Contemporary Art from Moscow. The special exhibition committee included art critic A.V. Lunacearski, people commissar for culture, revered worldwide for his opinions. Several French artists exhibited 262 works, namely—Derain, Vlaminck, Valloton, de Waroquier, Fauconnier, Gromaire, van Dongen, Campigli, Severini, Foujita, Ernst, Modigliani, Seurat, Utrillo, Marquèt, Ozenfant, Despiau, Natalia Goncharova, Anenkov, Larianov, Lipschitz, Channa Orlova, Iacovlev, Chagall, Epstein, Zak, and Zadkine. Brancusi sent four sculptures and a drawing. In the catalogue A.V. Lunacearski characterized Brancusi as a devoted follower of the "plastic purity principle"[355], and before the exhibition opening, he had also authored another article on Parisian art in general, referring to the top position held by Brancusi[356]. The exhibition moved to Leningrad on 13 October.

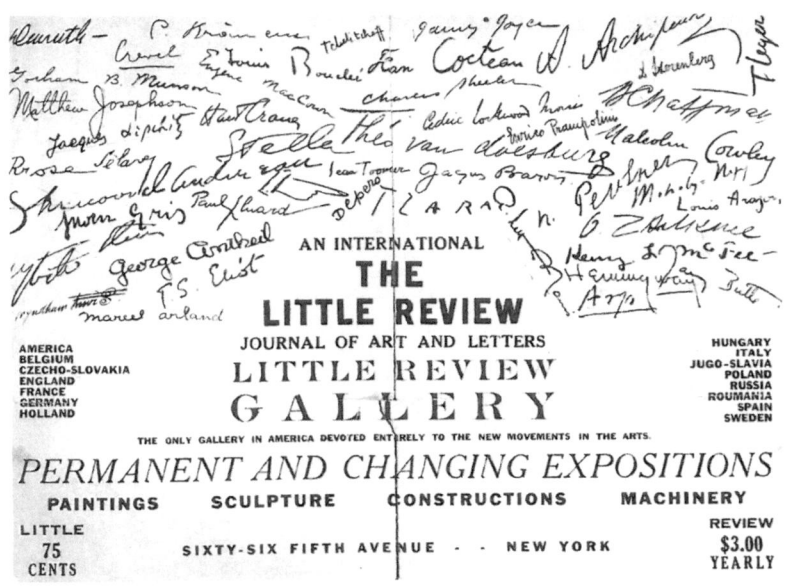

Fig. 220. Poster of the international exhibition at the Little Review Gallery, New York, 1928

Bucharest

From 26 October to November, the *Jubilee Exhibition of the Artistic Youth Society* was organized in the Art Pavilion, under the high patronage of Queen

Maria of Romania. Brancusi was represented with sculptures from the collection of Frederic Storck and Cecilia Cutescu-Storck. On this occasion, the *Maiastra* was exhibited for the last time in Romania during Brancusi's life.

Paris

Brancusi completed the sculpture *White Negress* II (marble, 1928), which was purchased by Helena Rubinstein. At first it was exhibited in her flat of Raspail Boulevard (Fig. 221a), but later it would be displayed in one beauty parlor (Fig. 221b) next to pieces made by other artists. According to Helena Rubinstein's view, the beauty parlor should have been a sort of museum[357] where works of art played double role: to draw as many clients as possible and at the same time charm them by providing inner joy—a form of therapy by art and equally very good management.

Figs. 221a, b. *White Negress* II exhibited in Helena Rubinstein's house, Paris: a—apartment on Raspail Blvd, 1930s; b—beauty parlor, 1950s

André Kertész made several photographic portraits of Brancusi (Fig. 222).

Fig. 222. Brancusi, Paris, 1928

New York

On 23 March, debates of the court trial with the American customs resumed by hearing the academic American sculptors Robert Ingersoll Aitken and Thomas H. Jones, claimant's witnesses that stated Brancusi's sculptures were not works of art[358]. The summary of evidence was submitted and on 26 November, the Supreme Court of Justice, including William Howard Taft, a former president of the United States (Fig. 223), pronounced the case in favor of Brancusi, stating the *Bird in Space* was the "original production of a professional sculptor" and "a piece of sculpture and a work of art" by beauty, proportions, execution[359].

Fig. 223. U.S. Supreme Court Justices that judged the trial of the *Bird in Space*, New York, 1928

1929

Cambridge (Massachusetts)

From 20 March to 12 April, the *Exhibition of the School of Paris 1910-1918* was organized at the Harvard Society for Contemporary Art.

Paris, Villefranche-sur-Mer

In 1929, Brancusi had met Marcel Duchamp, Man Ray, André Breton, Djuna Barnes, Peggy Guggenheim, Paul Éluard, Mina Loy, James Joyce, Jean Cocteau, Samuel Beckett and many others in Mary Reynolds' residence of 14 Hallé Street, which was open for friends almost every night, to dine together and then rest in the superb garden around the house[360]. Her Villefranche-sur-Mer villa was also the place where Brancusi liked to spend his holiday[361][362] (Fig. 224).

Fig. 224. Duchamp, Mary Reynolds and Brancusi, Villefranche-sur-Mer, 1929

Harry and Caresse Crosby, owners of the Black Sun Press of Paris, asked the artist to draw James Joyce's portrait for his volume *Tales Told of Shem and Shaun*, Brancusi made six drawings (three fronts and three profiles) in figurative style, which did not please the editors. Finally to the satisfaction of those placing the order he drew a more *spiritualized* portrait, a spiral called the *Portrait of James Joyce* (Fig. 225).

In May, Jean Arp wrote the poetry Endless Column (*Colonne sans Fin*).

In May-June, Brancusi participated to the *Salon des Tuileries* from the Exhibition Palace.

He arranged a small photographic laboratory and purchased a good 16 mm camera.

Transition, An International Quarterly for Creative Experiment, edited by Eugene Jolas, in issues 16-17 (Fig. 226) provided two photos of Brancusi's works (photos of *Chief* and of his studio). The publication also included texts by Gertrude Stein, Henri Michaux, Samuel Beckett, Michel Leiris, Philippe Soupault, Roger Vitrac, a.o.

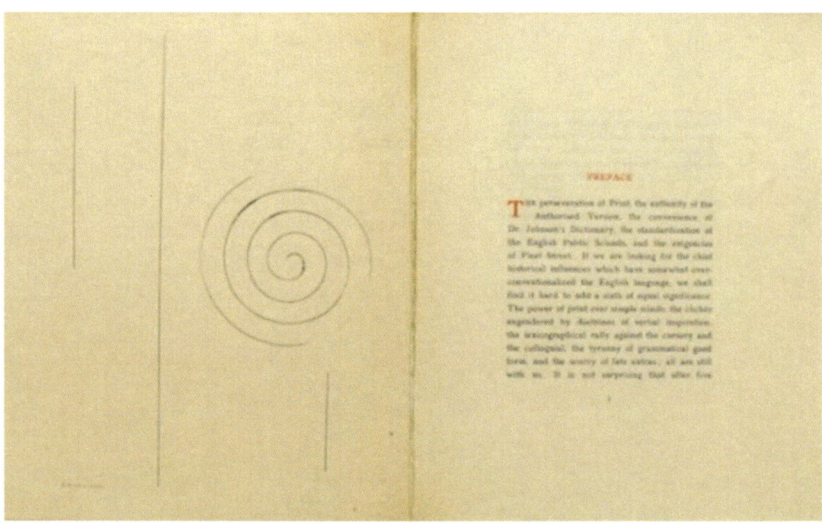

Fig. 225. *Portrait of James Joyce* by Brancusi, in *Tales Told of Shem and Shaun* by J. Joyce, Paris, 1929

Fig. 226. Transition, Paris, 1929, *16-17*

Two essays on Brancusi were published in Paris—one signed by Roger Vitrac, containing 15 photos and a few aphorisms in Cahiers d'Art (Fig. 227)[363], and the second one authored by Benjamin Fondane in Cahiers de l'Étoile (Fig. 228) providing two photos of Brancusi works[364].

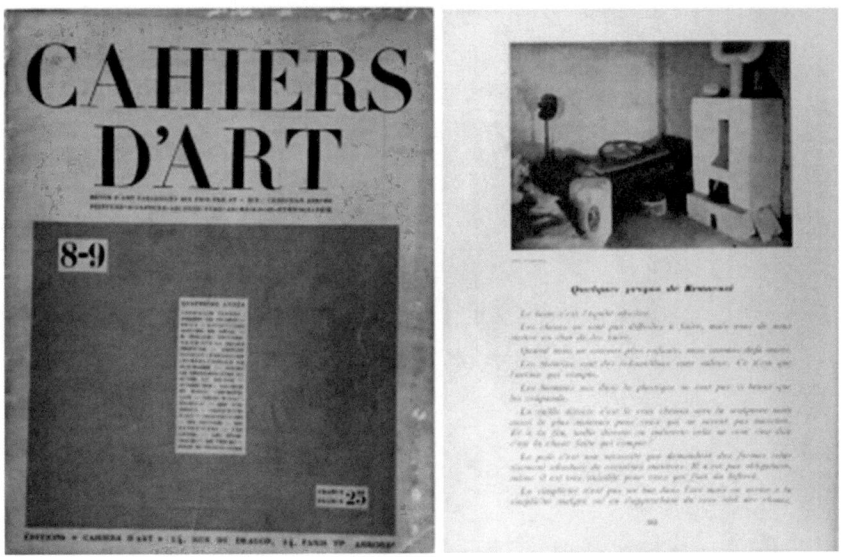

Fig. 227. Cahiers d'Art, Paris, 1929, *8-9*.

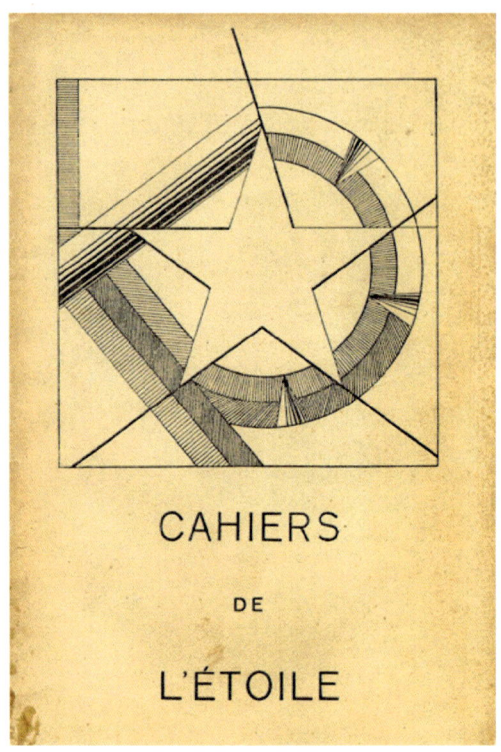

Fig. 228. Cahiers de l'Étoile, Paris, 1929, *11*

Vera Mukhina visited his studio. Later, the Soviet sculptress would state unequivocally about Brancusi's sculpture: "his fine artistic sense is extraordinary," and "his bronze utilization is entirely new"[365].

Brancusi polished Sergey Diaghilev's mortuary mask (Fig. 229)[366] and made three drawings (*Snail and Birds*, *Horned Cattle* and *Shapes*), which would illustrate a poetry volume *Plante si animale: terase* [Plants and Animals: Terraces] by Ilarie Voronca (Figs. 230)[367].

Fig. 229. Death mask of S. Diaghilev polished by Brancusi, Paris, 1929

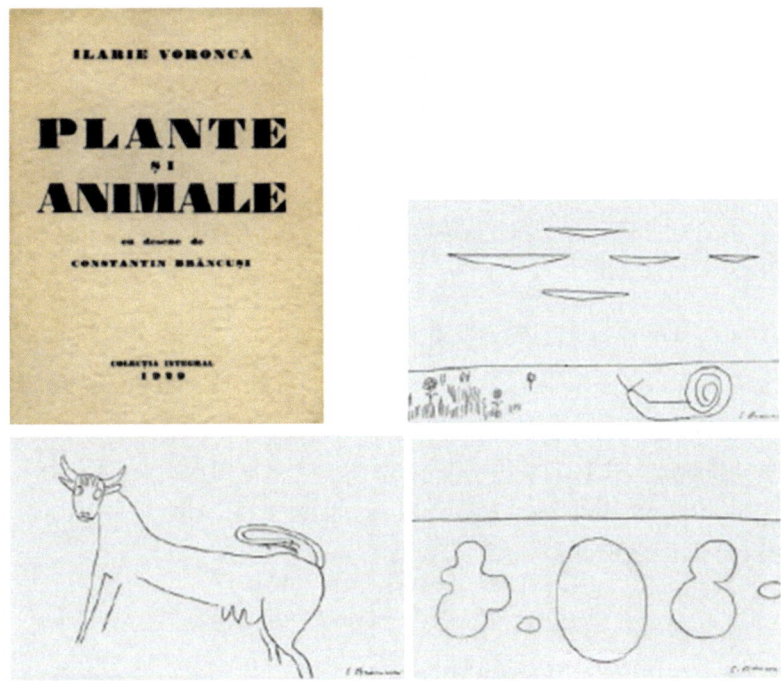

Fig. 230. Brancusi drawings, in *Plante si animale: terase* by I. Voronca, Paris, 1929

Fashion designer and collector Jacques Doucet purchased one *Danaide* (bronze, 1913), which he would exhibit on the staircase of his home at 33 Saint-James Street, Neuilly-sur-Seine, as can be seen in the 1929 photo taken after the completion of the works by Joseph Csáky (Fig. 231)[368].

Fig. 231. *Danaide* exhibited in J. Doucet's house, Neuilly-sur-Seine, 1929

Cologne, Munich, Berlin

A bis Z magazine included sculptor F.W. Seiwert's article illustrated with four photographs[369].

László Moholy-Nagy published his book *Von Material zu Architektur* [From Material to Architecture] comprising several pages on Brancusi and seven photos of his sculptures[370] (Fig. 232).

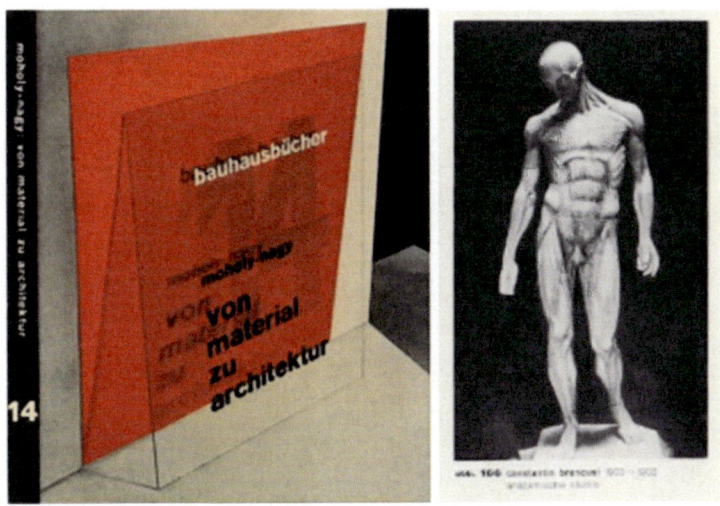

Fig. 232. *Von Material zu Architektur* by L. Moholy-Nagy, Munich, 1929

Aldous Huxley's article published in Der Querschnitt, illustrated with studio photos and one showing Brancusi with Polaire[371] (Fig. 233).

Fig. 233. Der Querschnitt, Berlin, 1929, *12*

Zurich

The abstract and surrealist painting and sculpture (*Ausstellung Abstrakte und Surrealistische Malerei und Plastik*) exhibition organized in the Kunsthaus Zurich, 6 October-3 November, and was attended by the most representative artists of the fore-mentioned currents. Brancusi too invited though he claimed his artistic independence.

Bucharest

The *"White & Black" Drawing and Engraving Salon* open in November at the Art Ministry exhibited in the Art Pavilion two pen drawings which Ilarie Voronca let be displayed at the Salon.

Berlin

The since Cézanne in Paris (*Seit Cézanne in Paris*) exhibition, 23 November-24 December, opened at Alfred Flechtheim Gallery. 500 graphics, sculpture and painting works were exhibited.

Paris

On 3-18 December Brancusi participated to the international sculpture (*Exposition de sculpture internationale*) exhibition organized by art critic E. Tériade at the Georges Bernheim Gallery[372][373].

An exhibition of sculptor drawings and gouaches (*Dessins et gouaches de sculpteur*) was organized for six leading sculptors: Brancusi, Despiau, Gargallo, Lipchitz, Laurens, Maillol at the Gallery of France, 5 to 20 December[374].

1930

Hague, Amsterdam, Brussels

He provided three sculptures to the Romanian art (*Tentoonstelling van Roemeensche Kunst*) exhibition of the Hague, at the Municipal Museum of Modern Art (Gemeente Museum voor Moderne Kunst) from 3 May to 9 June, Amsterdam, at the Municipal Museum (Stedelijk Museum), 14 June to 10 July and Brussels, where it was called *Exposition d'art roumain moderne à l'occasion du centenaire de l'indépendance belge* [Exhibition of Modern Romanian Art on the Occasion of the Centenary of Belgian Independence], at the Giroux Gallery, 20 July to 10 August.

Paris, Villefranche-sur-Mer

In 1930, Victor Brauner (Fig. 234) worked for a while in Brancusi's studio and the artist initiated him in photography, giving him one of his cameras and advising to go out to the street and take a picture of anything that would catch his eye[375]. The same year Brancusi received Julius Bissier, Juan Miró and Darius Milhaud in his studio. Benjamin Fondane introduced Jacques Hérold, who would later work in Brancusi's studio until 1931[376].

Fig. 234. Brancusi together with Margit and V. Brauner, Impasse Ronsin, Paris, 1930

Writer Marguerite Vessereau paid a visit to Brancusi's studio, and then she dedicated to the artist a chapter entitled *Le rythme essentiel* [Essential Rhythm] in her volume *Roumanie terre du dor* [Romania, Country of Longing]. During her visit the sculptor spoke to her about his architectural vision of the *Bird in Space*, which he could see from afar "filling up the sky vault"[377].

Brancusi began working the monumental variants of the *Cock*, in a series of increasing size from the two pieces of 1930 up to the version achieved in the '40s. Such dimensions required his return to plaster, which he had abandoned since youth.

In August Brancusi spent his holiday together with his friends Mary Reynolds and Marcel Duchamp in Villa Marguerite from Vifranche-sur-Mer.

Bucharest, Hobita

From 26 September to 12 October, Brancusi was in Romania. He went to Hobita for one day in order to settle the issue of his niece Ioana, daughter of his brother Grigore, who the parents could no longer sustain after high school for want of means. The girl wrote to her uncle in Paris and consequently he immediately went to Bucharest, then to Hobita by car. He had convincing talks with his brother Grigore and the artist returned to Bucharest with Ioana whom he took to lodge with Milita Petrascu. Brancusi stayed at the Grand Hotel du Boulevard, Elisabeta Blvd (Fig. 235). He explained to his niece why he could not take her with him to Paris. He had no time to take care of her, and his studio was not the proper place for study. Ioana Brancusi graduated the Chemistry-Physics College.

Fig. 235. Grand Hotel du Boulevard, Bucharest

Brancusi's relationships with his three step brothers and with his good brother Grigore were not so close. They were all small traders prone on getting rich and their cupidity turned their relations cold in time. And what more proof they did not keep in touch with Brancusi than his delayed knowledge about his mother's and brothers' deaths? In exchange, he was very attached to his sister Frusina (Eufrosina).

Poet Ion Minulescu printed the *Partenza* poetry dedicated to Constantin Brancusi in his poetry volume *Strofe pentru toata lumea* [Stanzas for Everyone] (Fig. 236)[378].

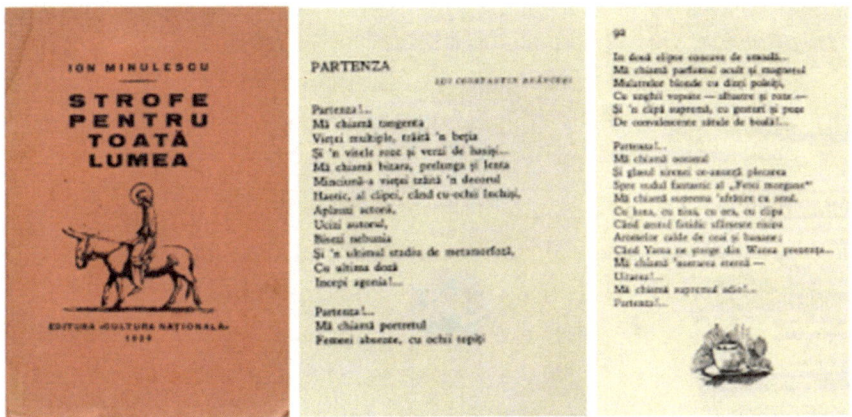

Fig. 236. *Partenza*, in *Strofe pentru toata lumea* by I. Minulescu, Bucharest, 1930

Brancusi gave an interview to journalist Apriliana Medianu where he confessed his intention of making an *Endless Column* in Bucharest. When the journalist asked about the masters that guided him, Brancusi promptly answered: "None. Everything came out from me." To him, artistic currents were "a sort of universal bedlam," and in his opinion only the creation "by philosophy and religion" meant "happiness, light, [and] liberty"[379].

Philadelphia

The *Contemporary French Drawings in Black and White and Color* exhibition (10-27 November) organized at The Print Club of Philadelphia.

Paris

Brancusi met Vera Moore (Fig. 237a) in 1930 through a mutual friend, art collector Jim Ede that invited him to the artist's concert[380][381]. Vera Moore's talent and charm conquered Brancusi, being himself a great music lover. At that time Brancusi had close relations with American galleries and art collectors, so he addressed Vera Moore for various secretariat services (translations, correspondence, keeping invoices, etc.). The artist performed devotedly all these activities not for want of money, since she gained very well from her concerts, but for respect at first, then out of love. There were quite a few bibliographic records about their relationship; 15 years ago, Vera Moore was still known in Romania as Brancusi's secretary for his English correspondence. In time, the relation became passionate, as seen in their correspondence which had been kept secret for so long.

Oskar Kokoschka, a great admirer of Brancusi, painted him a picture (Fig. 237b), which the sculptor did not like according to Marcel Mihalovici's memories[382].

On 22 October, in a small circle including Charles and Marie-Laure de Noailles, Brancusi participated in the première of the *Âge d'or* [Golden Age] movie, Luis Buñuel's surrealist comedy at the Cinema of the Pantheon[383].

From 1930 to 1933, Brancusi executed Agnes E. Meyer's portrait of black marble. In her letter of 18 May 1933, she asked the artist to let her know if she were beautiful in this portrait[384].

Figs. 237a, b. Vera Moore—a; *Brancusi* by O. Kokoschka, Paris, —b

Bucharest

The Cultura Nationala Publishers published in 1930 B. Fundoianu's book *Privelisti/poeme/cu un portret inedit de C. Brancusi* [Sights/Poems/With Unknown Portrait by C. Brancusi] (Fig. 238).

Two issues of the political, social, cultural review Vremea published a few writings of Brancusi, French-Romanian translation by Dan Botta: *Poveste cu haiduci* [Brigands' Story][385] and *Aforisme despre artă* [Aphorisms on Art][386].

Fig. 238. *Portrait of B. Fundoianu* by Brancusi, in *Privelisti / poeme* by B. Fundoianu

Bucharest

In 1930 the Adeverul newspaper published two interesting articles by the ideas taken from the analysis made by art critics Lucian Boz and Henri Blazian. Boz considered that "Brancusi found the formula to impose the purity of the hard crystalline material of the earth," the artist providing "his beings with Edenic clearness"[387], and for Blazian "the character of Brancusi's sculpture is spatiality: he has wide far off vision, and he unites his works into a whole, leaving details aside," [...] "his art is not that of the gallery but of an elite thirsting for spirituality"[388]. The articles were added the artist portrait made by Marcel Iancu (Figs. 239a, b).

Warsaw

The modern architecture magazine Praesens, highly influential then, included Brancusi next to the world's great architects and other great vanguard artists, in its 2nd issue (Fig. 240).

New York

In the book *My Thirty Years' War* (Fig. 241) Margaret Caroline Anderson left us a relishing description of a party with and by Brancusi, which as usual began in the evening and ended the next day. The artist was surrounded by friends whom he organized as he liked: he played Romanian popular songs on the violin for them, danced "wildly" with his heavy sabots on the stone floor, and at midnight, arranged for his guests a group photo, where only his camera setting took one hour. Then he invited all for a stroll in Paris, by night. He stopped in every place where there was music and danced in the middle of the room, he talked to everyone and was not drunk at all, just happy. Toward seven in the morning, he led his friends in Bois de Boulogne, where he lied on the grass by the lake, intending to catch a duck to later take home and cook. He then proposed a boat trip on the Seine to Rouen, but upon their refusal he resigned taking them to the Paris Halls for onion soup[389].

Figs. 239a, b. Adeverul, Bucharest, 1930: a—4 July; b—9 October

Fig. 240. Praesens, Warsaw, 1930, *2*

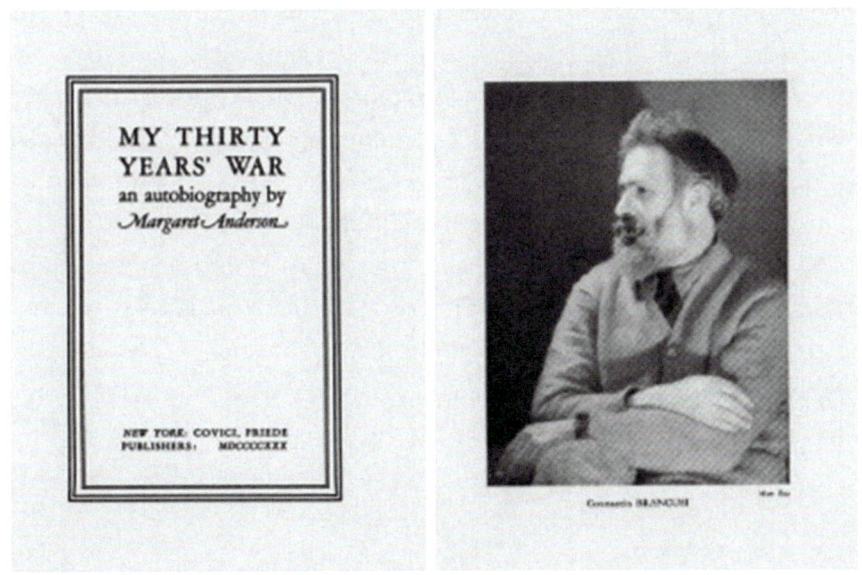

Fig. 241. *My Thirty Years' War: An Autobiography by Margaret Anderson*, New York, 1930

1931

Buffalo (New York)

From 18 February to 20 March *International Exhibition Illustrating the Most Recent Development in Abstract Art*, presented by the Société Anonyme opened at the Albright Art Gallery.

Ploiesti

Brancusi wanted to make a public monument dedicated to writer I.L. Caragiale. Clear evidence is the letter sent by the artist to Toma G. Tomescu, the former colleague in the School of Beaux Arts (Fig. 242)[390].

An attempted recovery of this story follows, in 1931 an initiative committee gathered in the staff room of Peter and Paul High School on the issue of I.L. Caragiale's monument; it included painter Toma G. Tomescu, a drawing teacher and musicologist Ion Croitoru, a music teacher, his attic neighbor in Bucharest. The committee also included lawyer Gheorghe Nicodinescu as committee secretary. It was unanimously agreed on by all members to entrust Brancusi with the monument. The artist gladly accepted and stated: "provided I am granted full freedom and enough time," considering it his duty as he greatly admired Caragiale. Nevertheless, he imposed a few conditions, as shown in his letter of 16 February.

The next year G. Nicodinescu went to Brancusi in Paris and the artist told him he had the mental concept of the project that consisted of an archaic fountain similar to the idea of Spiru Haret's statue—it would be "an outstanding work." Nicodinescu did not understand what all was about and left in dismay, having decided to stop the project. This happened precisely[391].

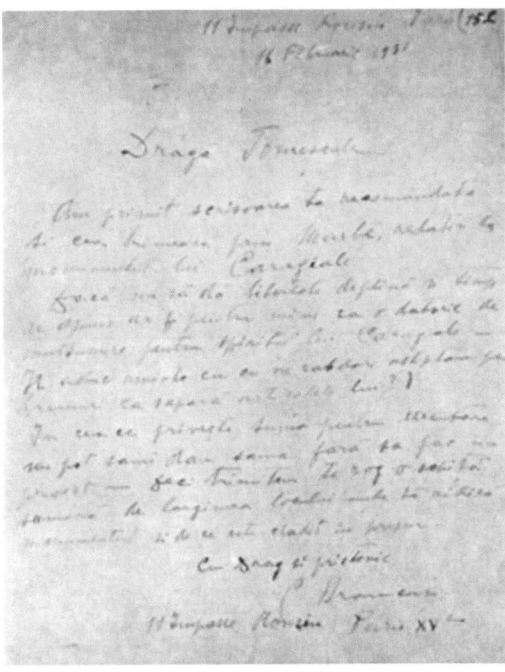

Fig. 242. Letter to T.G. Tomescu, Paris, 16 February 1931

Paris

Brancusi offered *Prometheus* (gypsum, 1911) to Zoe Cuclin, wife of musicologist Dimitrie Cuclin, in memory of her first husband Emil Damian, school colleague of Brancusi, deceased in 1918.

Petru Comarnescu visited Brancusi in 1931, but the artist was not in Paris. Returning to the country, the art historian published a description of the place whence Brancusi renewed sculpture, being astonished by the "desolating air of the dwellings" as if after cataclysm. "The thin tall trees" only were alive in that place, providing an air of "poverty and improvisation"[392].

In 1931, Maharajah Raj Rajeshwar Sawai Shri Yeshwant Rao II Holkar XIV Bahadur from Indore (Fig. 243), an eccentric individual and great art lover was brought by Henri-Pierre Roché to Brancusi's studio[393]. He purchased one polished bronze *Bird in Space* (1927-1931, Fig. 244a) and ordered the artist to create two more to be made of marble, one white and one black that he would purchase in May 1936 (Figs. 244b, c). He proposed the artist to come to India and build a mausoleum and a *Temple of Deliverance* where the *Birds* were to be placed.

 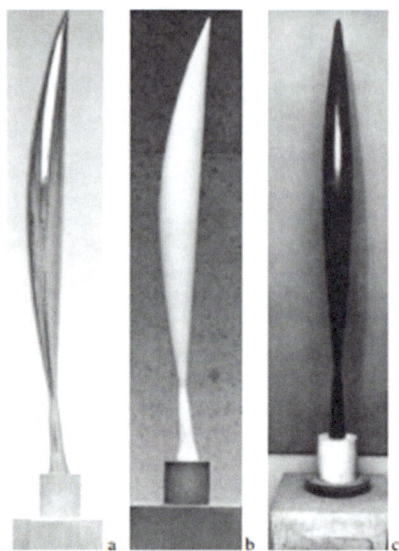

Fig. 243. Maharajah of Indore and his wife, Cannes, 1930

Figs. 244a-c. Birds in Space of the maharajah of Indore: a—bronze; b, c—marble

Villefranche-sur-Mer

Upon the invitation of his friends Mary Reynolds and Marcel Duchamp Brancusi spent a few days with them at their Villa Marguerite (Fig. 245).

Philadelphia

A modern art exhibition *Living Artists* from the United States, Mexico, Italy France, Germany, the Scandinavian countries and the UK was organized at Pennsylvania Museum of Art (20 November 1931-1 January 1932).

Fig. 245. Brancusi on the terrace of the Villa Marguerite, Villefranche-sur-Mer, 1931

Chicago

From 22 December 1931 to 17 January 1932 the *Exhibition of The Arthur Jerome Eddy Collection of Modern Paintings and Sculpture* was organized at the AIC. Brancusi's *Sleeping Muse* (bronze, 1910) was exhibited, which Eddy had purchased in 1913.

1932

Bucharest

The last issue of the Contimporanul magazine of January 1932 announced that essay writer Dan Botta intended to print a volume called *Constantin Brancusi, studiu monografic* [Constantin Brancusi, Monograph Study], though it never happened. Alternatively, the manuscript may have been lost too.

Paris

The 1932 visit to Brancusi's and the discussions with the sculptor deeply marked Barbara Hepworth, and constituted a crossroad moment in her artistic development. Barbara would write later in her memoirs that after the visit she remained with an impression of "the balance between the form to be and the finished sculptures, the humanity animating them, the full unity between form and matter"[394].

Art critic James Johnson Sweeney, curator with MoMA, paid him a visit.

The young beautiful ballet dancer and photographer Florence Meyer, one of Agnes Meyer's daughters, frequented Brancusi's studio hoping to overcome a difficult moment in her life after some love affair. Her beauty and grace inspired the sculptor making the *Miracle* also known as *Seal* (marble, 1930-1932, Figs. 246a, b). Despite their age difference—Brancusi was 57, a sincere love story unfolded before them and was revealed in the rich correspondence. This was the end of a 28 July 1933 letter: "Send me a word, dear Florence and tell me what to do. Loving hugs and many kisses, Brancusi," accompanied by the immortal *Kiss* drawing (Fig. 247)[395].

From 1933 to 1947 there was a love story between Brancusi and Florence Meyer. In a letter Brancusi wrote to Florence, "I have thought and am thinking of you all the time...I love you from the bottom of my heart and wait your arrival with utmost affection" (7 August 1938). "My very, very dear Florence, I am thinking of you very much and I would like to be near you and cuddle you. I embrace you in spirit and send you my love" (21 December 1938), signed Morice, the conspiracy name chosen by Brancusi[396].

The April issue of Formes magazine reproduced a *Portrait of Brancusi* by Lilly Steiner made in 1929[397] (Fig. 248).

Figs. 246a, b. Brancusi's studio, Paris, 1932: a—Florence Meyer; b—*Miracle*

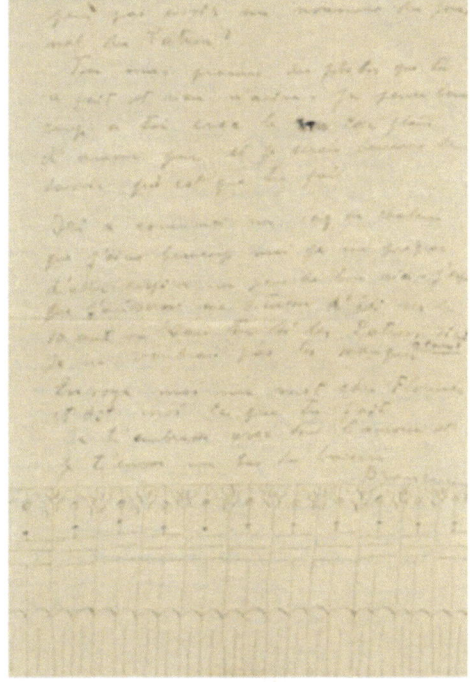

Fig. 247. Brancusi's letter to Florence Meyer, Paris, 28 July 1933

Fig. 248. *Portrait of Brancusi* by Lilly Steiner, 1929

New York

In chap. IX *Past and Present / Michael Angelo and Donatello—Rodin—Brancusi—Modigliani—Maillol—Gaudier-Brzeska—Henry Moore* of the volume *The Sculptor Speaks: Jacob Epstein to Arnold L. Haskell, a Series of Conversations on Art*, Epstein noticed that Brancusi had "an enormous influence not merely on art, but on commercial crafts as well. Certain of his ideas have been translated into an elegant formula. His vision is intensely personal so that he is difficult to follow successfully." The artist focused on the idea of flight, of swimming, being "a sculptor of movement and his figures are simplified so as to give that sensation." Epstein found that, since Brancusi was "working with real individuality and entirely justified in his method," in the United States of America he succeeded having "more imitators" than any other American sculptor[398].

In the book *The Meaning of Modern Sculpture*, Reginald H. Wilenski described Brancusi as "the pioneer experiments and researches" of the 20th century because "Brancusi started to explore geometry, the science which deals with relations of magnitude" and "He turned his back completely upon naturalism" because he says, "Je ne veux pas faire de bifteck."[399]

1933

Paris

In the January issue, Vogue magazine presents the architectural concept of Bruno Elkouken, a French architect of Polish origin, who worked on the arrangement of Helena Rubinstein's apartment, installing the *Bird in Space* (bronze, 1927) in the music salon, on the piano (Fig. 249)[400].

Fig. 249. *Bird in Space* in the music salon of Helena Rubinstein's apartment, Paris, 1933

Pablo Picasso made several drawings entitled *The Sculptor's Studio*. After the scandal of *Princess X* Brancusi was at odds with Picasso. However, by drawing the ideal sculptor Picasso imagined him with Brancusi's traits holding a sleeping model in his arms, one hand pointing to some sculpture resembling the portrait of *Princess X* placed on a pedestal (Fig. 250)[401] [402].

Fig. 250. *Sculptor at Rest, Reclining Model, and Sculpture* by Picasso, Paris, March 1933

New York

The *Sculptors' Drawings* exhibition was organized in the MoMA, 27 March to 3 May.

Paris

In April, Barbara Hepworth returned to Paris with Ben Nicholson and they visited Brancusi to ask for some advice. She was again impressed by the "artist's simplicity and dignity."

São Paulo

The first modern art exhibition (*1ª Exposição de Arte Moderna da SPAM*) was organized by Lasar Segall, Mário de Andrade, Paulo Mendes de Almeida and Paulo Prado, members of the Sociedade Pró-Arte Moderna (SPAM)[403], at the Guatapará Gallery, 28 April throughout May. The exhibition is considered one of the most important events dedicated to modern art in the '30s, where Brancusi participated by two works.

Philadelphia

The *Exhibition of Contemporary Sculpture* was organized by Henri Gabriel Marceau at the Pennsylvania Museum of Art (16 May-16 September).

Paris

He participated to the *11th Salon des Tuileries* opened at Néo-Parnassus (20 May-9 July).

The exhibition of candidates to the grand prize for sculpture (*Grand Prix de la Sculpture*) was organized in the new halls of the French Federation of Artists from 152, Haussmann Blvd, 15-30 June. The list of candidates printed in the press included Brancusi as well[404][405].

Chicago

From 1 June to 1 November, *A Century of Progress. Exhibition of Paintings and Sculpture* was organized at the AIC.

Saint-Jean-de-Luz

In September, Brancusi was invited by Marina Chaliapin and Florence Meyer to spend a few days in the holiday house of the bass singer Feodor Chaliapin (Fig. 251).

Fig. 251. Beach of Saint-Jean-de-Luz

Philadelphia

From 4 November to 6 December, the *Loan Exhibition of Contemporary Painting and Sculpture from the Collections of Miss Anna Warren Ingersoll and Mr. and Mrs. R. Sturgis Ingersoll* opened at the Pennsylvania Museum of Art.

Bucharest

Emanoil Bucuta requested the Romanian Academy to consider establishing an artistic section: "Brancusi, Petrascu, and Pallady are waiting."[406]

Ethno-musicologist Constantin Brailoiu offered Magister Brancusi "with great love" the registration of the "Dragus Complaint," the subject of his latest volume entitled *Despre bocetul dela Dragus, judetul Fagaras—Note sur la plainte funèbre du village de Dragus, district de Fagaras, Roumanie* [About the Dragus Complaint, Fagaras County—Note on the Funeral Complaint from the Village of Dragus, Fagaras County, Romania]. The sculptor was great lover of authentic folk music, most of his records with Romanian music being C. Brailoiu's gifts.

New York

Under the coordination of A.E. Gallatin, a catalogue of The Gallery of Living Art was published where paintings and drawings of famous artists, including Brancusi, or recently deceased, were exhibited.

Upon Joseph Brummer's suggestion, Brancusi agreed with organizing his fifth personal exhibition at the Brummer Gallery from 17 November 1933 to 13 January 1934. In November Marcel Duchamp, the exhibition curator, arrived in New York with the sculptures in order to prepare the exhibition. He attempted to recreate the atmosphere of Brancusi's studio using wood columns, gypsum pieces, stools, studies, and photographs. A number of 70 pieces were exhibited (37 sculptures, 5 pedestals, a painting and 27 studies). During the exhibition Brancusi asked to have the photo of his *Écorché* displayed on one wall because it was the way he could prove to critics how his sculptural shapes developed normally, according to his in-depth knowledge of the human body.

The exchange of messages between Duchamp and Brancusi shows us the exhibition was highly successful, the gallery was always full of visitors, and all New York spoke of nothing else but this; one day 500 persons entered. Mrs. Mary H. Rumsey purchased the marble *Sleeping Muse* and provided the Armory Show gypsum in exchange, and Mr. Samuel N. Behrman bought the *Chief*. Agnes Meyer sent a congratulation telegram for the exceptional exhibition[407].

Paris

Paul Fierens published the *Sculpteurs d'aujourd'hui* [Today's sculptors] study on Rudolf Belling, Jacob Epstein, Henry Moore, Oscar Jespers, John B. Flannagan, Gaston Lachaise, Constantin Brancusi, Charles Despiau, Pablo Gargallo, Henri Laurens, Jacques Lipchitz, Aristide Maillol, Ossip Zadkine, Hildo Krop, Arturo Martini (Fig. 252). Fierens describes Brancusi as the one who "spiritualized matter or, which is the same thing, gives consistency and configuration to the utmost elevated spirit most detached from earth"[408].

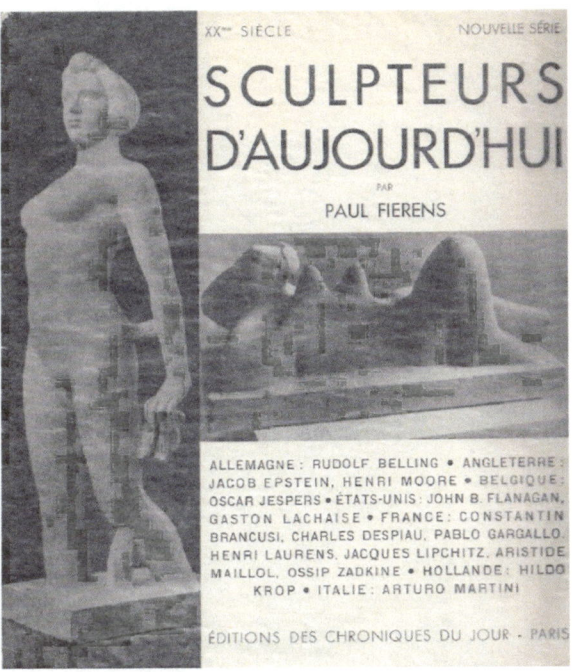

Fig. 252. *Sculpteurs d'aujourd'hui* by P. Fierens, Paris, 1933

Minotaure magazine published Maurice Raynal's article containing four photographs from Brancusi's studio (Fig. 253)[409].

Fig. 253. Minotaure, Paris, 1933, *3-4*

The artist sculpted the *King of Kings* (oak wood, 1930-1933, Fig. 254), later named *Spirit of Buddha* when he would think placing it in the Indore temple.

Fig. 254. *King of Kings* in Brancusi's studio, Paris

London

Sculptor and Professor Herbert Maryon in his volume *Modern Sculpture* with 354 illustrations, considers that "Brancusi is able to suggest character and emotion without any attempt to reproduce natural form. He is certainly amusing and we are glad to meet a sense of humor," and his remark is enhanced by photo of *Miss Pogany* (Fig. 255)[410]. The artist had indeed an inherited sense of humor, specific to his native region Oltenia where people barely remembered their own name as all were known by their nicknames, talks were full of irony and multiple meanings and a serious discussion would be on serious issues. It is only an Englishman that could notice the subtle irony hidden in a sculpture by Brancusi.

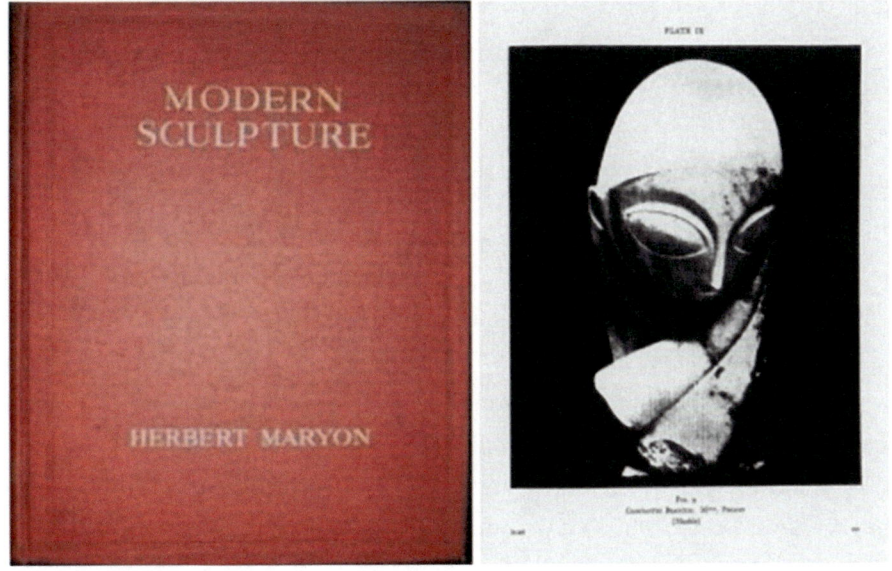

Fig. 255. *Modern Sculpture* by H. Maryon, London, 1933

1934

Philadelphia

From 17 February to 14 March, the *Earl Horter Collection* was open at the Pennsylvania Museum of Art. The exhibition was moved to The Arts Club of Chicago (3-26 April).

Brussels

Poet E.L.T. Mesens and Albert Skira publishers organized the Minotaur (*Minotaure*) exhibition from 12 May to 3 June at the Beaux-Arts Palace. It was the first international surrealist exhibition with 119 pieces[411].

Chicago

From 20 June to 20 August, *A Selection of Works by Twentieth Century Artists* was organized by J.J. Sweeney in the Renaissance Society from University of Chicago.

New York

From 13 August to 13 September, the *New Acquisition: Brancusi, Bird in Space* exhibition was open at the MoMA.

Paris

Brancusi met and knew well Anne Harvey and her mother, writer Dorothy Dudley Harvey, in 1926 when he traveled two times to the United States on the occasion of his personal exhibitions from Wildenstein and Brummer Galleries. In 1934, the two of them came to Paris so that Anne can study painting and at 18 she stunned the Parisian artistic world with her talent. One proof is the oil painting representing Brancusi in his studio (collection The Pierre and Tana Matisse Foundation, Fig. 256a). The artist appreciated her talent and therefore he encouraged her to continue. He took several photos of her when she came to his studio and a portrait—drawing in pencil and pastel on cardboard (Figs. 257a, b), and Anne Harvey made ink drawings on paper (Fig. 256b)[412]. Anne, as written in Sidney Geist's notes, was the happy owner of three *Kiss* ideograms offered by Brancusi[413].

Christian Zervos published *Reflexions sur Brancusi* [Thoughts on Brancusi] in Cahiers d'Art, with three photos made by Brancusi (Fig. 258)[414].

The Abstraction création art non figuratif [Abstract creation, non-figurative art] magazine of the group of artists including Arp, Gleizes, Hélion, Herbin, Kupka, Tutundjian, Valmier, and Vantongerloo reproduced the photograph of two sculptures by Brancusi: *Cock* and *Sleeping Muse* (Fig. 259)[415].

Surrealist Publishers issued René Char's surrealist poetry volume *Le marteau sans maître* [Hammer Without Master], who on March 22, 1935 gave a copy to Brancusi with "master of the hammer" dedication.

Quincy Voisins

Brancusi made for art critic Maurice Raynal a fireplace of stone resembling his own in the studio, at his home of Quincy Voisins (Fig. 260)[416].

Targu-Jiu

Arethia Tatarescu, president of the Women's League of Gorj County and wife of the prime minister G.

Tatarescu had the initiative to build in Targu-Jiu a monument dedicated to the memory of Gorj men killed in WWI. She addressed sculptress Milita Petrascu whom she had met and had already organized in Targu-Jiu a cenotaph for Ecaterina Teodoroiu, but the sculptress denied her saying the work should be better entrusted to the worldwide famed sculptor and son of Gorj County Constantin Brancusi. In winter the Tatarescus visited Brancusi in his studio and ordered the art monument. After some insistency the sculptor accepted even without being paid.

Figs. 256a, b. *Brancusi* by Anne Harvey, Paris, 1934

Figs. 257a, b. *Anne Harvey* by Brancusi, Paris, 1934

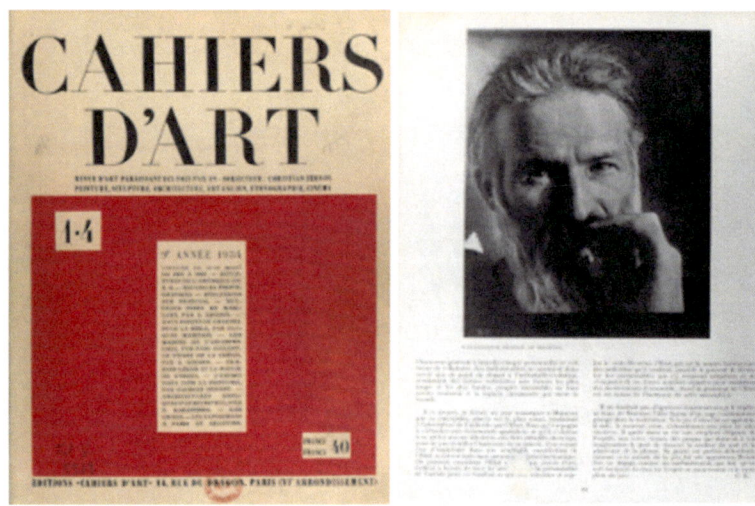

Fig. 258. Cahiers d'Art, Paris, 1934, *1-4*

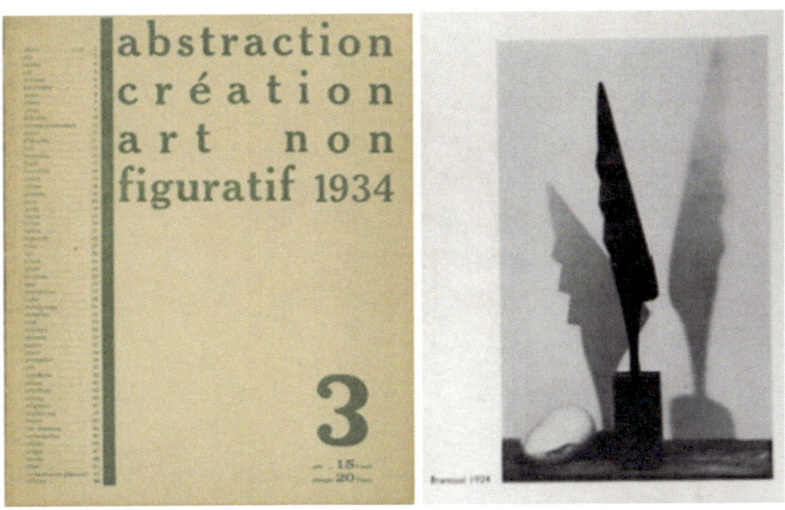

Fig. 259. Abstraction création art non figuratif, Paris, 1934, *3*

Fig. 260. Stone fireplace made by Brancusi in M. Raynal's house, Quincy Voisins

London

On 15 September John was born, son of Brancusi and of Vera Moore, whom the artist refused to meet and recognize. All their life, Brancusi and Vera were discrete about their relationship and especially about their child, even after their break-up in 1935.

New York

From 19 November 1934 to 20 January 1935, the *Modern Works of Art. Fifth Anniversary Exhibition* was organized at the MoMA.

The Romanian Dream

1935

Paris

On 7 January, Stefan Georgescu-Gorjan visited Brancusi, who told him about his talks with Arethia Tatarescu. The sculptor showed him the project of the monumental ensemble "in the main […], insisting on the Endless Column…"[417] and they agreed the technical concept for the *Endless Column*.

Brancusi accepted the proposal of the Women's League of Gorj County to build a monument in honor of the Gorj heroes from WWI. Brancusi's answer was sent on 11 February through Milita Petrascu who had asked him to accept the work: "I cannot express how happy I will be to do something in our country. Thank you and I also thank Mrs. Tatarescu for the privilege she offered to me. At present all the things that had been initiated so long ago are almost completed and I am like an apprentice on the eve of his becoming journeyman, so this proposal could not have found a better time."[418]

From 3 April to 3 May, the 4th didactical exhibition of the International Chamber of Art Experts (*4ᵉ Exposition didactique de la Chambre internationale des experts d'art: Comparaisons—Trois synthèses artistiques*) was open.

New York

The *Museum Collection and a Private Collection on Loan* exhibition was organized at the MoMA, 4 June-24 September.

London

Axis, a quarterly review of contemporary abstract painting and sculpture, edited by the writer Myfanwy Evans, dedicated its third issue to contemporary sculpture and its representatives, Brancusi, Moore, Barbara Hepworth, and Calder (Fig. 261). The article on Brancusi is accompanied by five photos of works by the artist[419].

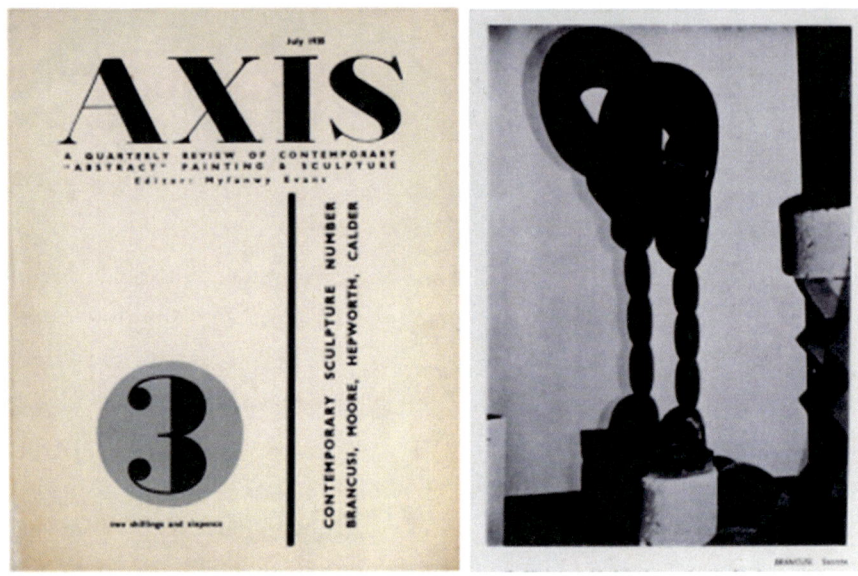

Fig. 261. Axis, London, 1935, *3*

1936

Buffalo (New York)

On 3-31 January, the *Art of Today. An Exhibition of Contemporary Pictures and Sculpture* arranged and sponsored by the Women's Advisory Committee of the Albright Art Gallery, where Brancusi exhibited next to Giacometti, Calder, and Lipchitz. Paintings and sculptures were exhibited made by 118 artists from the vanguard current after World War II. The Romanian artist was named "the greatest modernist" in the exhibition catalogue.

New York

The *Cubism and Abstract Art* exhibition that specific criticism considered one of the most complete cubist exhibitions opened in the MoMA (2 March-19 April). Works made by painters, sculptors, architects, designers etc. were selected from collections of the USA and abroad. The exhibition catalogue made by A.H. Barr Jr. had a chapter dedicated by the author to Brancusi[420]. In 1936, this exhibition moved to San Francisco Museum of Modern Art (27 July-27 August), to the Cincinnati Art Museum and Minneapolis Institute of Arts, and in 1937—to the Cleveland Museum of Art, where only two Brancusi sculptures were exhibited, then to the Baltimore Museum of Art, to Rhode Island School of Design and to the Grand Rapids Art Gallery.

In her volume *Time Has No Shadow*, Dodd, Mead & Company Publishers, Katherine Garrison Chapin published *Bird in Space / Brancusi* poetry (Fig. 262).

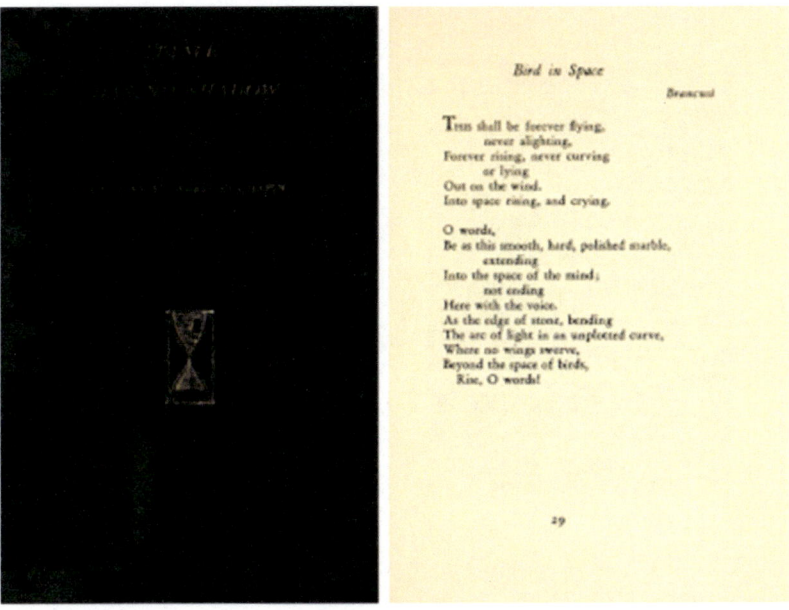

Fig. 262. *Bird in Space/Brancusi*, in *Time Has No Shadow* by Katherine Garrison Chapin, New York, 1922

London

International Surrealist Exhibition opened from 11 June to 4 July to the New Burlington Galleries, where two Brancusi sculptures were displayed.

Paris

He visited Margareta Cosaceanu-Lavrillier's studio and noticed the model for a monument dedicated to Tudor Vladimirescu which interested him also in his youth, as proven by the sketch notebook offered to Ion Croitoru, so he recommended her to Arethia Tatarescu who wanted a monument dedicated to this great historical personality from Gorj[421].

The June issue of Minotaure magazine published an article by Émile Tériade about surrealist painting, illustrated with 31 photos of works by famous artists, of which *Chimera* by Brancusi (Fig. 263)[422], and the 25 issue of Transition magazine (Fig. 264) included a few images of Brancusi, under The Eye entry.

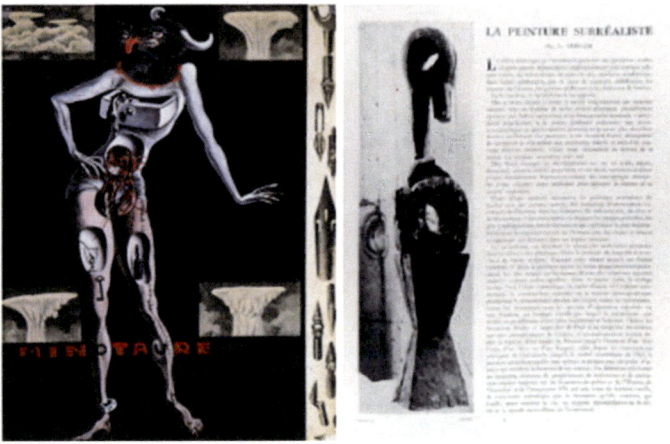

Fig. 263. Minotaure, Paris, 1936, *8*

Fig. 264. Transition, Paris, 1936, *25*

Poiana (Gorj County)

In June, Brancusi arrived in Romania to submit to Arethia Tatarescu his plans for the monument of Targu-Jiu. Sanda Tatarescu, Arethia's daughter, waited for him in the railroad station Filiasi, providing information about the sculptor's stay in Poiana (Fig. 265) and the preparatory talks for the practical achievement of the monumental ensemble of Targu-Jiu[423].

Fig. 265. Tatarescus' manor house from Poiana

Bucharest

He discussed with architect Octav Doicescu (Fig. 266) about the meditation temple project he intended making in India for the Indore maharaja.

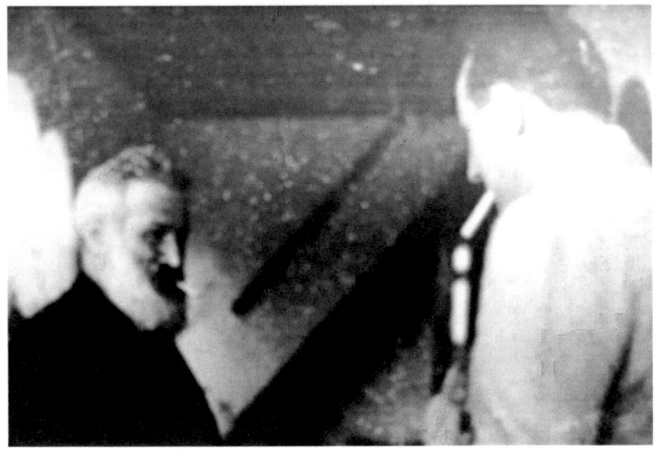

Fig. 266. Brancusi and architect O. Doicescu, Bucharest, 1936

In the '30s—the exact year is unknown—Milita Petrascu was supposed to have achieved Brancusi's portrait of terracotta (Fig. 267)[424].

Fig. 267. *Brancusi* by Milita Petrascu, Bucharest

1937

New York

The illustrated catalogue *Museum of Living Art, New York University, A.E. Gallatin Collection* was published and included two works by Brancusi: *Mademoiselle Pogany* (pencil, 1912) and *Torso of a Young Girl* (onyx, 1922, Fig. 268).

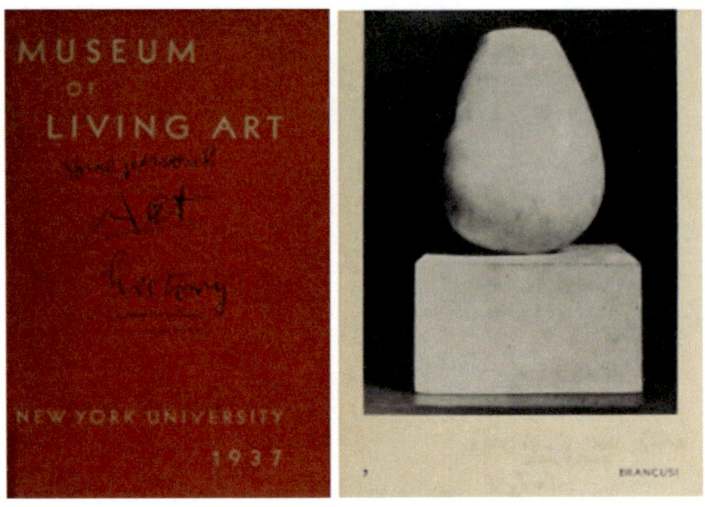

Fig. 268. Catalogue *Museum of Living Art, New York University, A.E. Gallatin Collection*, New York, 1937

Paris

On 1 May, André Dézarrois wrote and invited Brancusi to join Marie Cuttoli, Braque, Cassou, Éluard, Laugier, Léger, Marcoussis, Raynal, Rivière, Zervos and Dézarrois in the jury where the Helena Rubinstein Prize would be granted[425]. The sculptor turned down the offer and said he was unable to participate.

The Universal Exhibition of Paris opened from 25 May to 25 November, where Romania's Pavilion was outstanding (architect Duiliu Marcu, Fig. 269a). The allocated financial sources were sized to put in operation this grandiose project. Brancusi participated with only one sculpture to this exhibition, although a Brancusi Hall was designed initially. Officials headed by Professor Dimitrie Gusti, exhibition commissioner (Fig. 269b), apologized that such an initial agreement could not be observed for want of money. Brancusi fully understood and provided an exhibit matching their explanations: the *Little Bird* (bronze, 1928)[426].

Brancusi met Maria Tanase, called "Edith Piaf" of Romania, when she sang at the Universal Exhibition in Paris for the public entering the Romanian pavilion. The two had a flashing love affair during two years.

During the Universal Exhibition the Origins and Development of the International Independent Art (*Origines et développempement de l'art international indépendant*) exhibition was organized from 30 July to 31.

October in the Jeu de Paume Museum. Brancusi was present with a work from Helena Rubinstein's collection. An unsigned article from Cahiers d'Art included the "Romanian Brancusi" among the artists unaligned to any current or trend in art that broke the promise he made to Dezarois to fully contribute to the exhibition, where he "withdrew for no reason, as he accustomed us"[427].

In 1937, Chilean sculptress, Juana Müller[428] began working in Brancusi's studio (Fig. 270).

Figs. 269a, b. Universal Exhibition, Paris, 1937: a—Romania's Pavilion; b—Romania's representatives among whom Brancusi, Th. Pallady, D. Gusti, Elena Vacarescu

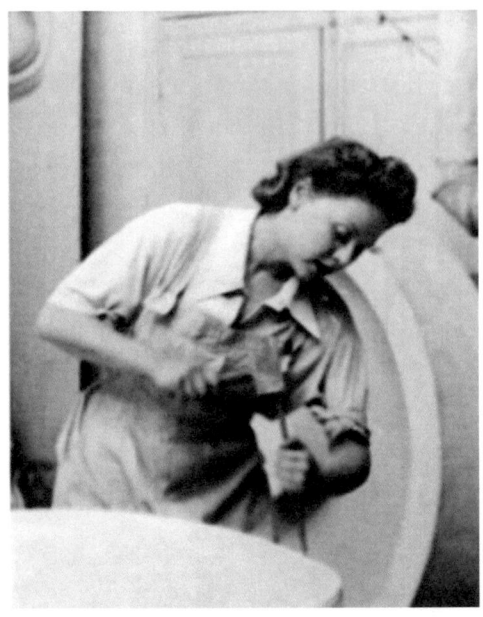

Fig. 270. Juana Müller working in Brancusi's studio, Paris, 1937

Zurich

In her volume *Moderne Plastik/ Elemente der Wirklichkeit, Masse und Auflockerung* [Modern Plastic Art:

Elements of Reality, Volume and Disintegration] (Fig. 271), Carola Giedion-Welcker considered Brancusi "the greatest sculptor alive"[429].

Bucharest

In June the sculptor went in the country and discussed financial and organizational issues with the governing team of Petrosani Society, director general being engineer Ion Bujoiu; the decision was taken to have engineer Stefan Georgescu-Gorjan dealing with the technical aspects of the *Column*.

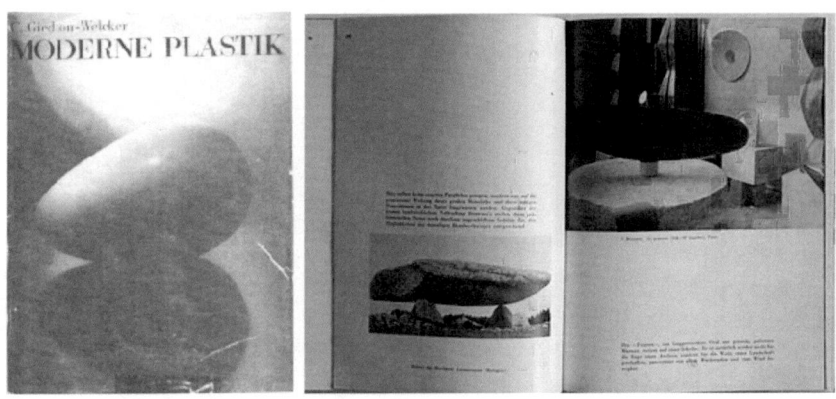

Fig. 271. *Moderne Plastik* by Carola Giedion-Welcker, Zurich, 1937

Poiana, Targu-Jiu

From Bucharest Brancusi went to Poiana, to the Tatarescus. He visited Targu-Jiu with Arethia Tatarescu in order to select the location of the monument. The artist chose the Outside market, warning Arethia: "Don't you make a park all round!"[430]

Vasile G. Paleolog accounted Brancusi came to Romania in June intending to make one single piece. He submitted a photograph at a meeting of the League's Committee in the Poiana house of the Tatarescus (Fig. 272), saying: "In Paris, I decided the monument to be an endless column. Here it is!"

Fig. 272. Brancusi with Irina Codreanu and Milita Petrascu (first row), Arethia Tatarescu (second row, middle) and two other members of the Women's League of Gorj County, Poiana, 1937

London

The Circle: International Survey of Constructive Art magazine, editors J.L. Martin, Ben Nicholson and N. Gabo, had a chapter dedicated to sculptors that published three photos of works by Brancusi (Fig. 273), Calder, Gabo, Giacometti, Hepworth, Holding, Meduniezky, Moore, Pevsner, Tatlin[431].

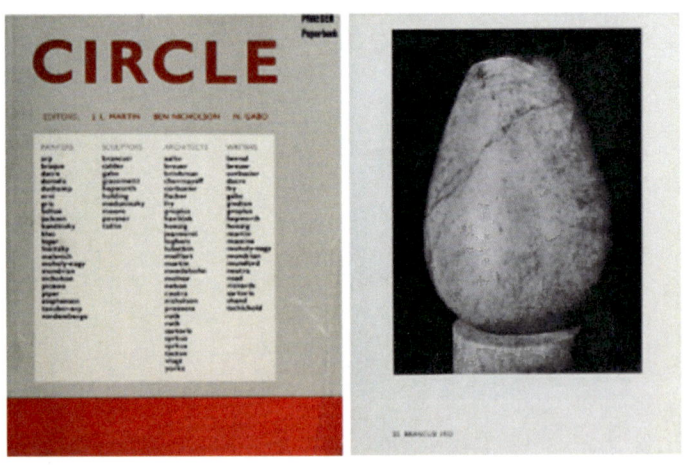

Fig. 273. Circle, London, 1937

Craiova

Vasile G. Paleolog published the first monographic study dedicated to Brancusi, including several photographs of the sculptor's pieces and aspects from his Parisian studio (Fig. 274). The author defined in this study the artist's universality and singularity, as he "no longer belongs to our country, or any other for that matter" but to the times to come[432].

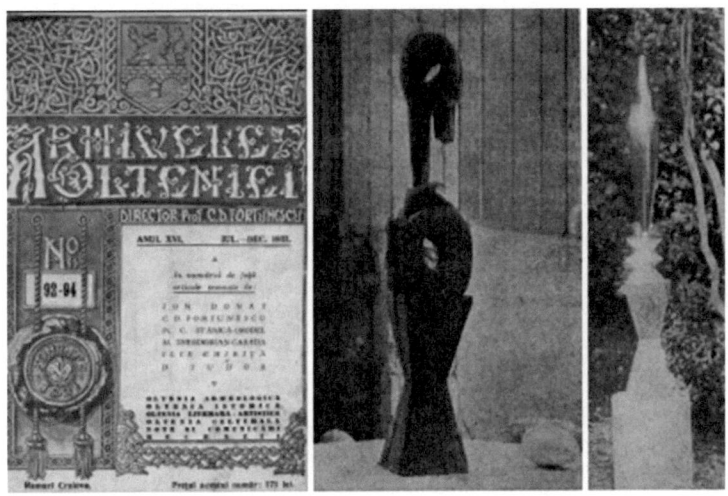

Fig. 274. Arhivele Olteniei, Craiova, July-December 1937

Targu-Jiu, Petrosani

At the end of July, Brancusi and engineer Stefan Georgescu-Gorjan met in Targu-Jiu and went together to the place the artist selected, by joint agreement with Arethia Tatarescu, in order to locate the *Column*[433][434]. Engineer Georgescu-Gorjan took a photo of this place and the artist would sketch on it a *Column* with 12 modules and architectural-decorative elements around (Fig. 275a, b).

Figs. 275a, b. Targu-Jiu, 1937: a—outside market; b—sketch of the *Column* and of the architectural-decorative elements, drawing by Brancusi

During his stay in Targu-Jiu, 1937-1938, besides the hotel (Fig. 276a), Brancusi also stayed in Ganescu's house (Fig. 276b) where he arranged a provisional studio in the courtyard. There he gathered several stones from the surroundings, with shapes near his sculptures. He worked on the others, providing them with the form and arrangement he desired (Figs. 277a, b and 278).

Figs. 276a, b. Brancusi's accommodation places in Targu-Jiu, 1937-1938: a—Royal Hotel; b—Ganescu house

Figs. 277a, b. Stones arranged by Brancusi in the Ganescu courtyard, Targu-Jiu: a—mill stones; b—river stone

Fig. 278. Stones arranged by Brancusi in the manor house garden of the Tatarescus, Poiana, 1937

Brancusi worked to complete the *Endless Column*. The realization of the monument began at the end of July, in Petrosani (Fig. 279a) and ended in November, in Targu-Jiu. Brancusi selected iron as working material instead of bronze, for the possible "coating" of this dark gray material.

Stefan Georgescu-Gorjan recorded that from 26 July onward Brancusi stayed for more than one month in Petrosani, in his house of 2 Closca Street (Fig. 279b)[435]. There the artist carved one side of the lime wood module as model for workers hired, which was used to make the mold (Fig. 280a). Engineer Georgescu-Gorjan accounted in his writings there was one difference between the sculptor-approved initial module and the ones cast in iron, as regards their form: "the first had a pronouncedly convex surface, while the surface of the cast elements had a barely perceptible curvature." (Fig. 280b).

Brancusi went to the quarries of Pietroasa, Banpotoc, Baciu, and Ruschita to select the stone of which he would sculpt the *Gate of Kiss*.

During his stay in Romania he had the idea to make a table, so the first table of river boulders was made at the Poiana house of the Tatarescus, and another one in Targu-Jiu, in the Ganescu house. The first variant for the *Table of Silence* was made in July—the Campulung stone.

In August/, Arethia Tatarescu convinced her husband, prime minister Gheorghe Tatarescu, to get the necessary funds in order to extend Grigore Saftoiu Street between the Outside market and C.A. Rosetti Blvd, which bordered the town's public garden. The plan for such straight street had been approved back in 1900, but it had not been achieved[436].

Bucharest, Paris

On 2 September Brancusi left Bucharest for Paris where he was supposed to meet the Indore maharajah in view of discussing the *Temple of Deliverance*. The latter did not keep the appointment date, so on 15 October Brancusi.

Figs. 279a, b. Petrosani, 1937: a—Central Workshops; b—2 Closca Street

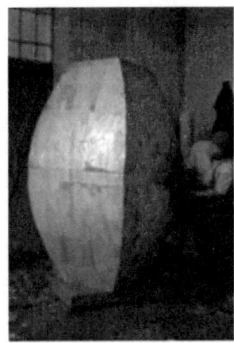 

Figs. 280a, b. Central Workshops of Petrosani, 1937: a—wood module for the mold; b—assembling the *Column* for integration tests

Targu-Jiu

On 13 September, the town mayor submitted the Heroes' Road plan to the local council (Figs. 281 and 282a, b): "The entire project consists of an alley which, starting from the Jiu River dike—the evocation place for Gorj's men heroic facts—would pass under a portal which would also indicate the entrance into the public garden so that, continuing to the church under renovation it can end at the point of the gratitude monument embodied in 29 m high column going unendingly up, the same way our gratitude should be for the heroes that founded modern day Romania; this monument will be located in the middle of a park to be developed on the location of the cattle fair and this avenue will be entitled the Heroes' Road."[437]

The development of the new park around the *Column* began on 1 October and was completed on 26 August next year. In accordance with Brancusi's plans, 300 pyramidal poplar trees were to be planted there as well as 2,000 kg of wild flowers[438].

On 20 October, Arethia Tatarescu sent a letter to the mayor of Targu-Jiu (Fig. 283) notifying him the decision taken by the Women's League of Gorj County to donate to the Municipality the Sculptural ensemble comprising "a column and a stone portal, achievements of the great sculptor Constantin Brancusi, who thus shows his gratitude to his native County."[439]

In October, the *Gate of Kiss* of Banpotoc travertine blocks selected by Brancusi was assembled, and the following year it should be sculpted. The two alleys ("rounds" as Brancusi called them) surrounding the *Gate* and re-joining again on the axial line of the sculptural ensemble were made upon the artist's request. 20 pyramidal poplar trees were planted on the borders of the alley made in the garden[440].

Beginning with 2 November, the landscape architect Frederic Rebhuhn re-arranged the town's public garden—the alley connecting the *Table of Silence* to the *Gate of Kiss* was traced in the extension of the Heroes' Road and the former Outside market where the *Endless Column* stood. Before leaving Targu-Jiu Brancusi gave "indications about the manner in which main alleys should inter-connect" in the public garden, "in relation to the ensemble of the work…"[441]

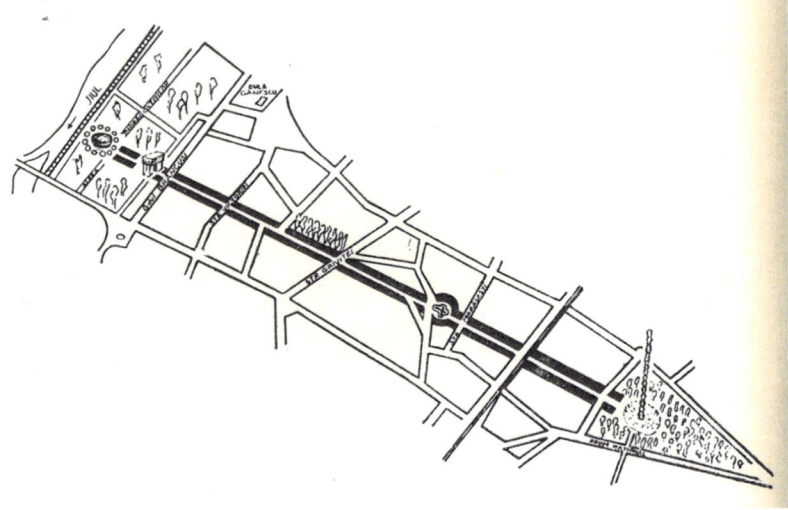

Fig. 281. Plan of Targu-Jiu town indicating the monuments (drawing by T. Paleolog)

Figs. 282a, b. Heroes' Road Street after urban planning, Targu-Jiu

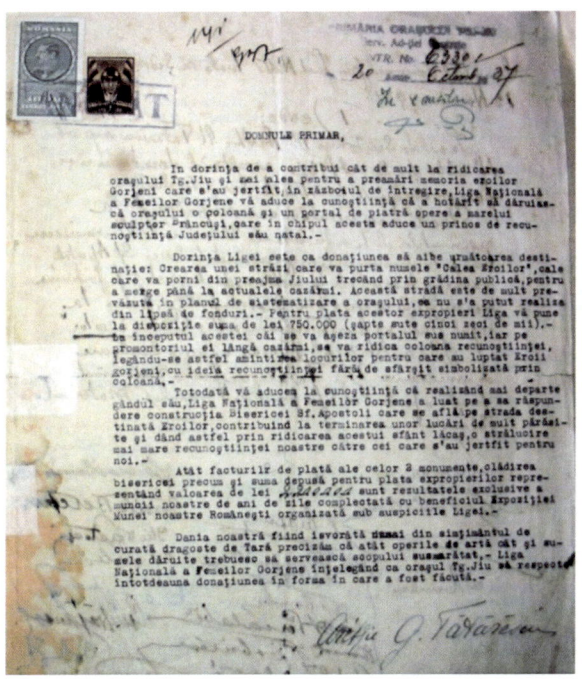

Fig. 283. Donation deed to the Targu-Jiu Town Hall by the Women's League, 20 October 1937

An official document of November recorded a transport of limestone slabs "for paving and steps to the platform near the Jiu River dike"[442]. Such stairs were not executed, the same way the stairs meant to go to the *Column* failed to be executed according to Brancusi's sketch, reconstituted by stone cutter Ion Alexandrescu and Tretie Paleolog[443] (Figs. 284a, b).

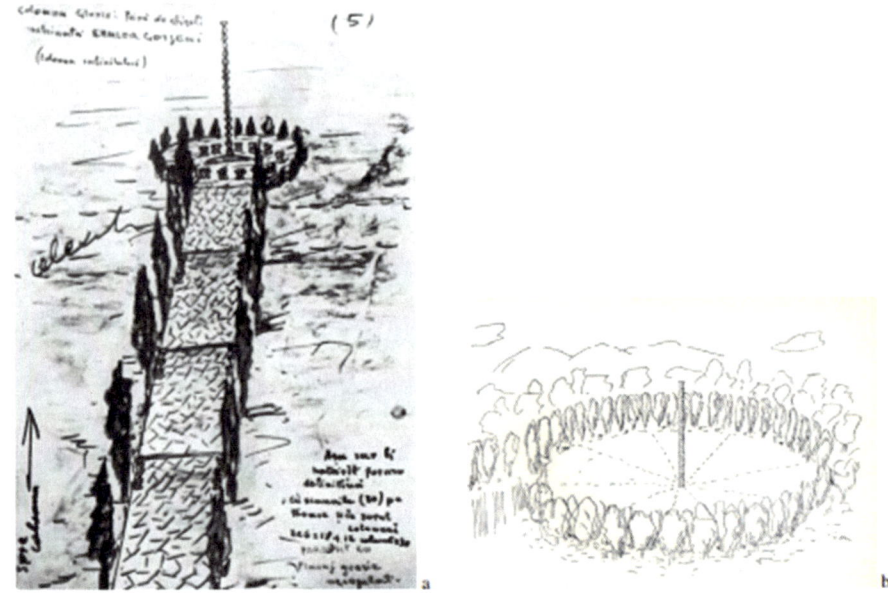

Figs. 284a, b. Targu-Jiu: a—access stairs to the *Endless Column* (reconstitution by I. Alexandrescu); b—the square project with the zodiac around the *Endless Column* (reconstitution by T. Paleolog)—b

Cleveland

From 4 November to 5 December the *Sculpture of Our Time* exhibition was opened at the Cleveland Museum of Art.

Bucharest, Targu-Jiu

Claudia Millian, poetess and publicist from Bucharest, differentiated herself from the other publicists when she expressed the idea of the Romanian spirit embodied in each component of the Targu-Jiu ensemble achieved by Brancusi, insisting on the "harmony of perfect proportions" and the simple drawing outline wherefrom "synthesis grows in purity" and "a spirit rises over the forms." She paid particular attention to the *Gate of Kiss*, with rhythm consisting of "unity" and "feeling;" she collected herself in front of Brancusi's creation, which she deemed "symbolic and primordial" (Fig. 285)[444].
Brancusi came to Romania at the beginning of November for a short time. In Targu-Jiu he inspected the stone portal (*Gate of Kiss*) and the *Endless Column* (Fig. 286) and participated to the inauguration of St. Apostles Peter and Paul

Church on 8 November before Patriarch Miron Cristea, Prime Minister G. Tatarescu and his wife Arethia (Figs. 287a-c).

He returned to Bucharest where he stayed a few days (9-14 November), being accommodated in Ambassador Hotel (Fig. 288), then he traveled to Paris.

At the meeting of the Communal Council of Targu-Jiu on 12 November in the "conclusion no. 151," they acknowledged the letter from the Women's League of Gorj County and approved calling the new route the *Heroes' Road*[445].

On 28 December, the government Tatarescu ended, having started on 5 January 1934.

Fig. 285. Adeverul, Bucharest, 4 November 1937

Fig. 286. Brancusi supervising the *Column* work, Targu-Jiu, November 1937

Fig. 287a-c. Patriarch Miron Cristea, Prime Minister G. Tatarescu and his wife Arethia (a, b), and Brancusi (c) participating to the inauguration of St. Apostles' Church, Targu-Jiu, 8 November 1937

Fig. 288. Ambassador Hotel, Bucharest

Paris, Bombay, Indore

In December, Brancusi traveled to India in order to study the location and finish the plans of the funerary monument. From Paris Brancusi went to Genoa, wherefrom on 18 December, he went on board the Conte Biancamano (Lloyd Triestino) cruise ship to Bombay and arrived there on 30 December.

1938

Indore, Cairo, Paris

Brancusi liked the stone samples the maharajah had sent and was glad to work with Indian masons. In the artist's vision recounted by Carola Giedion-Welcker[446], H.P. Roché[447], Penelope Curtis[448], Florence M. Hetzler[449], and others, the Indore temple was devised as a doorless windowless cube, pierced by two cylinders intersecting as a Grecian cross. Inside the temple was shaped as a cube of 12 m side, with three niches sheltering the three *Birds in Space* (white, black marble, and polished bronze) that the maharajah had bought, as well as the wood sculpture *King of Kings*, named in this context *Spirit of Bouddha*. The sculptures were placed on each side of a rectangular water basin placed in the middle, and they were meant to get mirrored in the water. At a certain time of the day the sun light gets in through a ceiling aperture and shines on the polished bronze *Bird*, turning it golden.

Walls were covered with frescoes showing flying birds as white triangles on blue backgrounds (according to the drawing and gouache in his studio). The exterior of the temple was the double capital of the *Column of Kiss* with relief and semi-relief forms (Fig. 289). Temple access was designed underground for one person at a time, who would have to cover a certain distance to obtain access. Everything was created so as to provide peace, recollection, and meditation.

Fig. 289. Column with double capital (1930-1933)—model of the *Temple of Deliverance* from Indore, Paris

However the maharajah could not receive the artist because of his health, but in exchange, the sculptor met there the German vanguard architect Eckart Muthesius who designed the Manik Bagh Palace in 1930 (Fig. 290a), residence of the maharajah, considered then the world's third fortune[450][451], where he stayed during his visit of India. The artist selected the temple location on the ground in front of the Palace, but the onset of World War II and the political and social circumstances did not enable him to execute this project[452], and the models remained in his studio.

During the time spent in Indore, Brancusi polished the three birds of marble and bronze (Fig. 290b) and took tours in the region, which profoundly impacted him as there he found fundamental elements of what he called "his forefathers' doctrine" or the "philosophy of eternal naturalness," this being the reason why he said "I feel at home in India…"⁴⁵³ (Fig. 291a).

On 27 January, Brancusi left Bombay. Vasile G. Paleolog, Petre Pandrea, H.P. Roché, and Florence Hetzler provide Brancusi's impressions after his travel to India in January 1938 (Fig. 291b).

Returning from India, the artist stayed for two days in Egypt, went to Cairo and saw the pyramids (Figs. 292a, b), which, despite their huge appearance, "[were] so perfect they [did] not overwhelm".⁴⁵⁴

Figs. 290a, b. Indore: a—Manik Bagh Palace; b—*Birds in Space* of marble in the palace, 1968

Figs. 291a, b. Brancusi in India, January 1938—a; book edited by Florence M. Hetzler, New York, 1992—b

Figs. 292a, b. Brancusi in Egypt, 1938

On 8 February, Brancusi returned to Paris via Genoa, with the Conte Biancamano cruise ship (Figs. 293a, b). He then visited the Netherlands.

Figs. 293a, b. Conte Biancamano cruise ship—a; Brancusi on board, February 1938—b

Amsterdam

From 2 to 24 April, the abstract art exhibition (*Tentoonstelling Abstracte Kunst*) was organized at the Stedelijk Museum, where Brancusi exhibited four sculptures.

London

From 8 April to 2 May, the *Contemporary Sculpture: Brancusi, Laurens, Pevsner, Henry Moore, Duchamp—Villon, Hans Arp, Calder, Taeuber-Arp* exhibition opened at the Gallery Guggenheim Jeune. Brancusi participated with three sculptures.

Bucharest

In June, Brancusi returned in Romania to complete the *Gate of Kiss*. He met Arethia and Gheorghe Tatarescu in their house on 19 Polona Street (Fig. 294); he also met Dimitrie Gusti, Marcel Mihalovici, Ionel Jianu, Petru Comarnescu, a.o. He stayed at the Ambassador Hotel.

Fig. 294. Residence of the Tatarescus, Bucharest

Targu-Jiu

He went every day to the building site opened in the public garden on the Jiu River bank (Fig. 295a), where he supervised the sculpting to the *Gate of Kiss* according to his approx. 1:1 drawings. Early in the morning, the sculptor would trace the guidelines and decided the working schedule of the current day. He made the first cuts to the stone (Fig. 295b) following which stone cutter Ion Alexandrescu continued the sculpture helped by the other artisans. Brancusi, whom everyone called "Mr. Engineer," coordinated the work from the ground (Figs. 296a-c).

Figs. 295a, b. Targu-Jiu, 1938: a—building site organized in the public garden; b—Brancusi cutting the stone by saw mill

Figs. 296a-c. *Gate of Kiss*, Targu-Jiu, 1938:
a—before sculpting; b—during work; c—after the work

On the days when work raised no particular problems requiring his permanent attendance, the sculptor walked around through markets and fairs, went to the villages of Gorj County and to other picturesque places, taking photographs and sketching everything that drew his attention, talking to peasants, watching them working and celebrating[455] (Figs. 297a, b).

Figs. 297a, b. Gorj County in the 1930s: a—women washing their laundry in the Jiu River, Targu-Jiu; b—wood carpenters

In accordance with Brancusi's drawing on 9 July they ordered the Deva Workshop of the Pietroasa Co. Bucharest 30 tubular chairs of square seat dedicated to the 10 recesses of the main alley (three in each recess), as well as 12 tubular chairs of round seat meant to be placed around the round stone table (Fig. 298). On 1 August, the order was achieved and the execution was "according to the given model".[456]

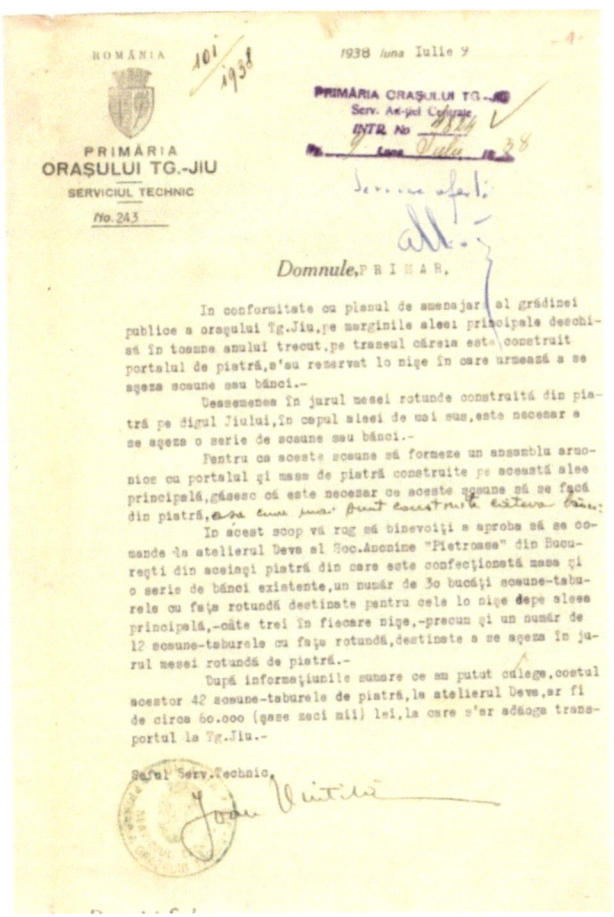

Fig. 298. Document of the Targu-Jiu Town Hall, 9 July 1938

The banks bordering the portal are of granite, but carved wood banks were placed in the first stage (Fig. 299). Chisel traces can be noticed on the surface of stone benches according to the sculptor's recommendations—one should see "the man's hand, the piece was not cast".[457] The work to the stone banks is completed on 20 July (Figs. 300a, b).

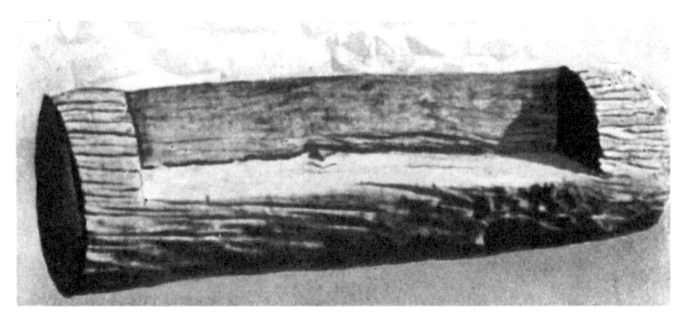

Fig. 299. A bank carved from tree trunk, provisionally located in the public garden, Targu-Jiu

Figs. 300a, b. Targu-Jiu, 1938: a—Brancusi carving a stone bank; b—stone bank and chairs

From June to 25 July, the *Endless Column* was metal-coated "using pure brass wire in fusion applied as high pressure jet projected by means of special pistol" (Fig. 301).

On 23 August, Targu-Jiu Town Hall approved under Decision 5742 "procuring from Deva Workshop two pieces of round stone" necessary to install a table in the end of the main alley from the public garden, on the Jiu River dike, against 26,000 Lei[458]. The Town Hall justified its achievement as follows, "in order to create harmonious ensemble with the monument portal […] and to provide a most aesthetical aspect as possible to the fore-mentioned monument and to the entire park."

This new order of stone for the table on the Jiu River dike was owed to the artist's dissatisfaction with the size and texture of the material in the first variant, which did not comply with his architectural vision. In the end, the

Table of Silence (Fig. 302a) resulted from overlapping the newly cut plate of Banpotoc stone on the plate of the first table variant.

The *Lonely Table* was an attempt that the sculptor declined eventually, resulting from overlapping the legs of two tables. For a while it stayed in the public garden, then it was taken away. This was the *Column* park upon gardener Jacob Esperschildt's initiative (Fig. 302b)[459].

New York

The overseas foreign press did not delay the echoing articles about the sculptural-architectural urbanist ensemble from Targu-Jiu during its construction. The Partisan Review published George L.K. Morris' article about a lesser-known side of Brancusi, the architectural one[460] accompanied by photos of the models used by Brancusi to make the *Gate of Kiss* (Fig. 303).

Fig. 301. Brancusi taking the photograph of the *Column*, Targu-Jiu, 1938

Figs. 302a, b. Targu-Jiu, 1938: a—*Table of Silence*; b—*Lonely Table*

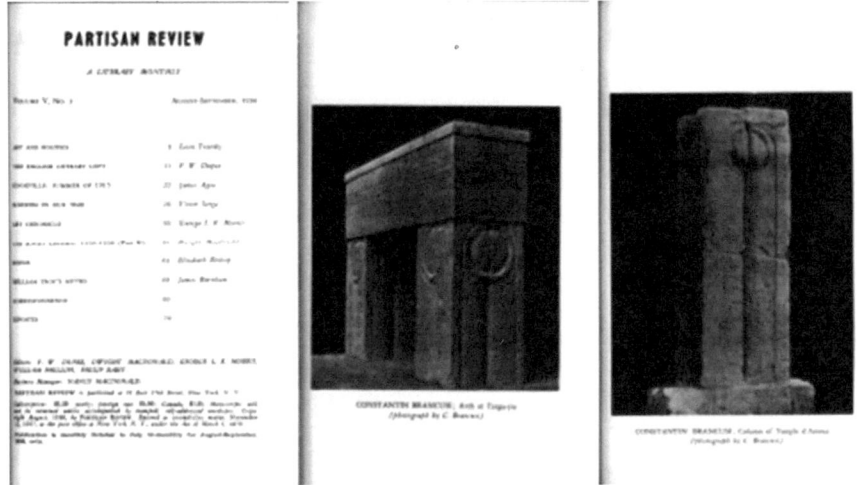

Fig. 303. Partisan Review, New York, 1938, *3*

Targu-Jiu

The festivities on the occasion of final handing over of Brancusian masterpieces to the Targu-Jiu Town Hall by the Women's League of Gorj County took place on 27 October: "The Women's League of Gorj County handed over the monuments dedicated to heroes to the Town Hall and also wrote down the sums spent to achieve them—St Apostles' Peter and Paul Church: 666,462 Lei; Expropriation to open the Heroes' Road: 746,000 Lei; The stone portal of the Public Garden: 683,198 Lei; Column to the memory of heroes: 340,615 Lei. We are kindly asking you to preserve these monuments in order to remind us of the Heroes who sacrificed their lives to their country" (Fig. 304)[461].

Nothing was recorded about the *Table* and the *Alley of the Chairs*. According to some Brancusiologists, the fault stays with the bad organization of the respective festivities, which were devised in such a manner, that they simply ignored the component of the masterpiece near the water. More exactly "[…] the multitude of people in grandiose procession, priests in front' walked from the *Column* (that was consecrated by 16 priests) to St. Apostles Church, then *on the heroes* path to the portal where another brief religious service was held" (Figs. 305a, b). Later on the procession was guided on C.A. Rosetti Blvd to the Jiu River Bridge, when actually the dead heroes of 1916 should have been evocated "on the dike, around the *Table of Silence*".[462]

Perhaps the *Table* elimination was deliberately done by the Targu-Jiu Town Hall, because it intended to keep it in silence owing to the frequent critical articles in the Bucharest press, stating the Town Hall spent the state funds on some "useless works": the *Column*, the *Portal* and the *Heroes' Road*.

Brancusi did not participate to the ceremonies because on 20 September, he went to Bucharest, angry with the criticism of journalists, the hostile attitude of the new team installed after elections in the Targu-Jiu Town Hall, as well as because of some work remaining unfinished.

In 1938, architect George Matei Cantacuzino together with Milita Petrascu, Arethia Tatarescu and her daughter Sanda paid a visit to Brancusi's monumental ensemble of Targu-Jiu, which caused him great emotion, which he confessed in a letter of 21 August 1938.[463] Sanda Tatarescu would account later how much G.M. Cantacuzino was overwhelmed by the beauty and infinity of the *Column*.[464]

Ciucea (Cluj County)

Brancusi had great respect and a particular friendship for great poet Octavian Goga (d. 1938), therefore he immediately accepted Veturia Goga, the poet widow's proposal to make a monument in Ciucea, where O. Goga wanted to be brought for his final repose. Being in Romania, Brancusi went to Ciucea (Fig. 306a) to study the location of the future funerary monument. While thinking of Goga as great national poet, he proposed Veturia to bring some stone boulders from the mountains to adjust and arrange them in the shape of a fountain. Here thirsty ones could drink and thank the departed man, and nearby a sort of chimney flowing a perpetual smoke that should linger along the Cris River valley and be carried by air drafts into the wide world (Fig. 306b[465]).

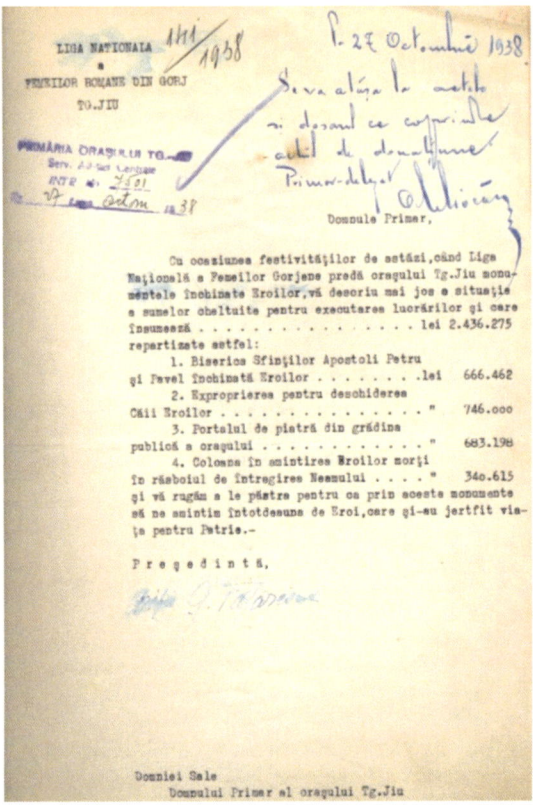

Fig. 304. Letter of the Women's League, Targu-Jiu, 27 October 1938

Figs. 305a, b. Aspects from the inauguration of the sculptural ensemble of Targu-Jiu, 1938

Figs. 306a, b. Ciucea: a—Octavian Goga's Castle; b—funerary monument in Brancusi's vision (reconstituted by P. Comarnescu)

In a letter published by historian G. Bodea, Veturia Goga recounted that the artist wanted to build the poet's monument and so she took him to Ciucea in the summer of 1938. Veturia was dissatisfied with the term Brancusi offered and asked for the sketch of the monument to have it done by domestic masters, but he refused by saying he did not work by sketches but took the "hammer and chisel in hand" and stopped only when he finished. At that, Veturia required the services of architect George Matei Cantacuzino.[466] In the end, she confessed the simple truth, which was that she gave up Brancusi's project because she deemed it "foolish".[467] "Even if polished by Brancusi, they are still boulders!"[468]

Bucharest

In autumn Brancusi stayed at the Athenaeum Palace Hotel on Episcopiei Street (Fig. 307).

Fig. 307. Athenaeum Palace Hotel, Bucharest

During this time he posed for a portrait made by Milita Petrascu and interfered during work.[469] He gave interviews to Ioana Giroiu and to writer Radu Boureanu.[470] [471] Upon Ioana's question about his favorite piece the sculptor answered: "The Maiastra! I have been working to it since 1908 and haven't finished yet."

Brancusi found time to visit doctor Dimitrie Gerota at his manor house of Saftica, near Bucharest (Figs. 308a, b).

Figs. 308a, b. Saftica, near Bucharest, 1938: a—Brancusi and the Gerotas at their manor house; b—Brancusi in Gerota's garden

Craiova

Vasile G. Paleolog published on his own account the first volume on Brancusi with Ramuri Printing House (Fig. 309). The volume comprised his essay written in 1937, its abstract in French, the beginning of Brancusi bibliography and one note.

Fig. 309. *C. Brancusi* by V.G. Paleolog, Craiova, 1938

Brancusi visited his good friend V.G. Paleolog at his manor house of Corlate, near Craiova (Fig. 310). They had separated on bad terms in 1921 and on that occasion, they talked for two nights. On this occasion the sculptor told Paleolog his vision on the sculptural memorial of Targu-Jiu, calling the stone portal *Heroes' Gate*. He used to say that: "Heroism itself is an act of love." They would part again at odds and would never see each other again.

Fig. 310. Manor house of V.G. Paleolog from Corlate

Senior Years

1939

Paris, Le Havre

Yvonne Zervos organized an exhibition with works by Brancusi, Arp, González, Klee, and Laurens at MAI (Furniture/Architecture/Installation) Galleries, recently inaugurated in Bonaparte Street.

On 21 April, he went on board the Champlain cruise ship (Compagnie Générale Transatlantique, Fig. 311a) in Le Havre harbor, going to New York.[472] At first, this trip was meant to be on board the cruiser Paris, but it was destroyed by fire on 18 April and it changed his plans, which was recorded by the media (Fig. 311b). It was his last voyage to the United States in order to participate to a few historical events.

Figs. 311a, b. Le Havre, 1939: a—Champlain cruise ship; b—Le Petit Havre, 21 April

New York

In 1939, Romania participated in the World Fair from New York (30 April-1 October), exhibiting two particularly imposing edifices, the Pavilion and the House of Romania, both luxurious, marble plated, and of Romanian styled architecture (architect Octav Doicescu's project). Professor Dimitrie Gusti, commissioner of Romania's Pavilion, had devised a "special Brancusi Hall" but nevertheless, he could not achieve it, so he had to inform the artist that "considering the events, your exhibition becomes impossible with our budget".[473] Notwithstanding all that, on 5 May Brancusi attended the official opening of Romania's Pavilion (Figs. 312a, b).

Figs. 312a, b. World's Fair New York, 1939: Suzana Doicescu, Brancusi and Maria Tanase (a) at the opening of the Romanian Pavilion (b)

Brancusi participated as the Romanian art representative to the inauguration of the *Art in Our Time* exhibition at the MoMA. This event occurred during the New York World's Fair (10 May-30 September), on the occasion of 10 years from MoMA's establishment and the inauguration of a new location. The exhibition had several sections, the sculpture one providing for 20th century artists. Two pieces were exhibited by him: *Miracle* (marble) and *Bird in Space* (bronze). In the exhibition catalogue, Brancusi was introduced as "the great sculptor of abstract shapes," which stand out more by their own beauty than "representations of nature".[474] Brancusi was happy to meet Alfred Barr Jr., Museum Director, Isamu Noguchi, Pierre Matisse, Pierre Bourdelle and many other friends.

The MoMA exhibition attracted great personalities of the whole world, the art loving or just curious public, the people interested in advertising for themselves or to assess the trends. Fashion designer Elsa Schiaparelli did not miss the opportunity to display her own designs. Thus a photograph remains made by Louise Dahl-Wolfe of a leading model dressed up in Elsa Schiaparelli clothes, perfectly framed between the two sculptures by Brancusi exhibited at the MoMA (Fig. 313). Looking at this photo, we can understand why the Italian fashion designer was considered too modern for her time.

Brancusi was invited to spend a few days in Locust Valley of Long Island, at Marion Willard's, owner of an art gallery, together with the Giedions and architect Alvaro Aalto[475][476] (Figs. 314a, b); they all called on architect Wallace K. Harrison, coordinator of the World Fair project from New York, as Sigfried Giedion remembered.[477]

Listening to Brancusi's account of the Indore project, Aalto exclaimed: "I see now, Brancusi! You stand at the crossroad of Asia and Europe!"[478] Carola Giedion-Welcker agreed with classifying Brancusi's art at the "crossroad of the Orient and the Occident," given the "double essence of Brancusi's work".[479] Indeed, the creation of Brancusi relies on elements from the traditional popular art, where the artist contributed his working technique and philosophy, which are added to the refinement of Western creation.

Chicago, Philadelphia, Washington D.C., New York

In May, on the occasion of his stay in the United States Brancusi went to Chicago, Philadelphia and Washington, D.C. In Chicago, while talking with city counselors and journalists, the artist mentioned the Targu-Jiu ensemble and his desire, dating as far back as 1935 to build a stainless steel *Endless Column* as tall as a sky-scraper in an American city. Called forth again in 1956, this project of an inhabitable gigantic Column in Chicago was never achieved.

Fig. 313. Elsa Schiaparelli's model between Brancusi's sculptures, MoMA, New York, 1939

Figs. 314a, b. Brancusi in Long Island, 1939 together with: a—Marion Willard and architect A. Aalto in architect W.K. Harrison's garden; b—S. Giedion and Marion Willard

In Philadelphia, Brancusi was a guest of Martha and Maurice Speiser.[480] There as well they talked about a gigantic *Column*. Isamu Noguchi testified about this project and acknowledged that Ingersoll had approached Budd Company of Philadelphia to execute an endless column of welded stainless steel, but Brancusi did not agree with welding of the modules since he could not consider it to be sculpture, it was something against his beliefs.[481] When Barbu Brezianu accompanied Noguchi in his documentation tour to Hobita and Targu-Jiu in 1981 (Figs. 315a, b) he heard from him about this Brancusi project and the reasons why the sculptor could not achieve it.[482]

Figs. 315a, b. Isamu Noguchi in Gorj County, 1981: a—near the *Endless Column* of Targu-Jiu; b—in front of the gate from the memorial house of Hobita

In Washington, Brancusi spent a few days with Agnes and Eugene Meyer. Returning to New York, he stayed at St. Moritz Hotel (Fig. 316) until his departure to France on board the Champlain cruiser.

Fig. 316. St. Moritz Hotel, New York

In New York, Malvina Hoffman published the volume *Sculpture: Inside and Out* where she recorded what Brancusi said about his works, because everybody knew the artist did not like talking about himself and his work. Malvina Hoffman saw in his studio the models for the Targu-Jiu ensemble in a time period before construction. The column was the result of many years of "searching," and its repetitive shape of the same size bottom up made "a pedestal or plinth unnecessary for support, the wind cannot destroy it, being sustained by its own strength." The idea of the *Gate of Kiss* was taken from the "group of two embraced beings," were then thought of "a gate to pass beyond".[483] The volume included 5 photos of Brancusi's works, of which some from Targu-Jiu (Fig. 317).

Fig. 317. *Sculpture: Inside and Out* by Malvina Hoffman, New York, 1939

The Museum of Living Art, The A.E. Gallatin Collection exhibition opened in January at The Museum of Living Art, New York University.

In September, World War II began.

1940-1941

Paris

From 1940 to 1945 during World War II, Brancusi kept to himself in Impasse Ronsin and dignifiedly endured the war's hardships until Paris was freed. Nevertheless, he would attend collective exhibitions during this time, particularly in the United States, and a few of his friends from the artistic world would remember him.

In 1940, the *Maiastra* was purchased after liquidation of Paul Poiret's collection (Fig. 318). Peggy Guggenheim tried for a long time to buy some sculptures from Brancusi, at a good price based on her personal relations with the artist, but she failed. In an interview taken by Mircea Deac, Peggy

Guggenheim told him the story of her purchasing the two sculptures—*Maiastra* and *Bird in Space*—from her own collection, and how much she wanted to have "a bronze by Brancusi" because she would grow much of the fame from her collection, however the price was high even for her.

In 1940, in the height of war, Peggy Guggenheim paid a visit to Brancusi's studio to purchase a polished bronze *Bird in Space*, and that time the two of them struck a bargain. Before giving her the sculpture, Brancusi polished it for several weeks, because there was nobody like him in polishing the works.[484]

In her biographical volumes, Peggy Guggenheim described honestly each artist she met with fine irony. She wrote of Brancusi that "He was half astute peasant and half real god. He made you very happy to be with him. It was a privilege to know him." The artist's dear name for her was Peghitza. "He loved me very much…"[485]

Fig. 318. Peggy Guggenheim and *Maiastra* on the terrace of her Parisian house, 1940

New York

From 26 January to 24 March 1940, the *Modern Masters from European and American Collections* exhibition organized at the MoMA.

Jacob Epstein in his autobiographic volume *Let There Be Sculpture* published by Putnam's Sons accounted how he met Brancusi and the visits to his studio while in Paris, working to the funerary monument at the tomb of Oscar Wilde from Père Lachaise graveyard. Some testimonies of the Romanian artist have been also published as well as some comments about the lawsuit with the American customs, when Epstein was among the American artists that pleaded for Brancusi's art, an episode he mentions as "one of the most amusing." From among all modern sculptors, Epstein has considered Brancusi "the man who brought the greatest individual touch into sculpture," whose work "was strongly influenced by Negro art, and also by Cycladic sculpture," concluding that "in our own period of tortured and realistic work his highly sophisticated art seems fresh and strange—a paradox".[486]

Chicago

From 25 April to 26 May 1940, *The Nineteenth International Exhibition of Water Colors* opened at the AIC.

Philadelphia

From 18 May to 1 October, 1940 the *International Sculpture* exhibition took place in the PMA.

New York

From 23 October 1940 to 12 January 1941, the *Painting and Sculpture from the Museum Collection* exhibition opened in the MoMA and from 30 December 1940 to 26 January 1941, the *Landmarks in Modern Art* exhibition opened at the Pierre Matisse Gallery.

From Rodin to Brancusi, European Sculpture of the Twentieth Century exhibition, 11 February-8 March 1941, opened at the Buchholtz Galler. The *Animals in Art* exhibition organized at the MoMA, 1-15 July 1941.

1942

Toronto

In January, the *Ideas and Sculpture* exhibition opened at the Art Gallery of Toronto.

Paris

On 7 January, Brancusi sent a letter to the Association of Henri Rousseau le Douanier's Friends, in which he unequivocally opposed the transfer of the painter's bones from Bagneux graveyard (Paris) to Laval (Bretagne area), his native place. Brancusi considered that "such [an] act would be sacrilege" because Henri Rousseau as an artist "was born in Paris," and "would have achieved nothing"[487] had he stayed home. Brancusi understood only too well the situation of his departed friend, since he as well could have been a failed artist if he had stayed home.

Sculptor Niculae Agarbiceanu, son of writer Ion Agarbiceanu, settling in Paris, began frequenting Brancusi's studio introduced by his aunt, painter Rhea-Silvia Radu. Agarbiceanu would write an article *In the Master's Studio*[488] about the time he spent at Brancusi's.

Bucharest

Oscar W. Cisek published an article in Dacia Rediviva magazine (Fig. 319), where he examined the situation of arts in Romania and found out "it was difficult for new sculpture to find an activity field" in the 19th century, until the next century when Brancusi became the "father of new sculpture." The art critic noticed the artist started from simple wood-carved forms characteristic of popular creation and from Thracian cultural elements to discover the road to the new sculpture, as ascertained by Paul Westheim as well.[489] Although O.W. Cisek appreciated the "synthesis of spatial form" in Brancusi's creation, he considered the artist turned "too anti-sculptural and abstract" in the last years.[490]

From 17 October to 15 November, the *Portrait in Contemporary Romanian Art* exhibition was organized at the House of Art Gallery (Kretulescu Galleries), where Brancusi's *Girl Head* (*Danaide*—A/N, stone, 1908, Fig. 320) was exhibited to be sold, though no buyer could be found.

Fig. 319. Dacia rediviva, Bucharest, 1942, 6

Fig. 320. *Danaide*

New York

Three exhibitions including Brancusi's works were organized: *20th Century Sculpture and Constructions*, at the MoMA, 2-26 October, *Homage to Rodin. European Sculpture of Our Time*, at the Buchholz Gallery, from 10 November to 5 December, and *20th Century Portraits*, at the MoMA, from 9 December 1942 to 24 January 1943.

In 1942, Alfred H. Barr Jr. published the illustrated catalogue *Painting and Sculpture in the Museum of Modern Art* with paintings and sculptures from the MoMA collections (Fig. 321a), including Brancusi's *Bird in Space* (bronze, 1919). In 1948, Alfred H. Barr Jr. re-edited this catalogue (Fig. 321b) including text about Brancusi and his sculptures, accompanied by the photos of the *Bird in Space* (bronze, 1919) and *Newborn* (bronze, 1915).

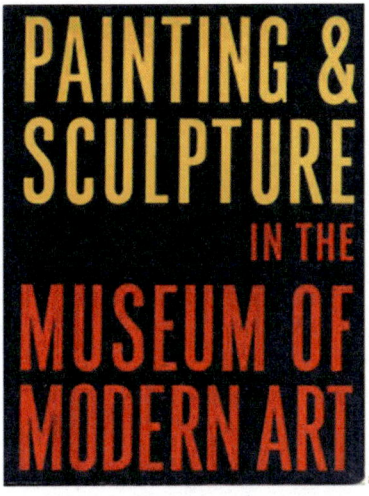 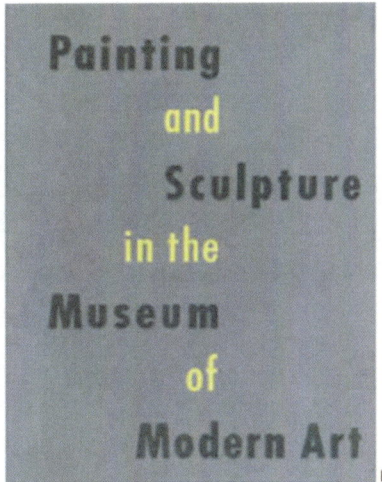

Figs. 321a, b. Catalogue of the MoMA by A.H. Barr Jr., New York: a—1942 edition; b—1948 edition

1943

New York

In May the *Museum of Living Art: Mirror of Our Time, The Gallatin Collection* exhibition opened at the MoMA. 168 pieces were exhibited: sculptures, paintings and other works on paper.

Zurich

From 23 March to 18 April, the Romanian contemporary painting and sculpture (*Rumänische Kunst der Gegenwart: Malerei und Plastik*) exhibition was organized at the Kunsthaus Zurich. Although Brancusi was not included in the exhibition, the catalogue provided O.W. Cisek's text *Constantin Brancusi* (pp. 14-15), which was taken from Dacia Rediviva magazine of June 1942.

Craiova

Meridian magazine dedicated issues 17-18-19 (Fig. 322a) to sculptor Brancusi and included four photos of his sculptures; Vasile G. Paleolog published *Cartea a doua despre C. Brancusi* [Second Book on C. Brancusi] with C. Radulescu-Motru's foreword, still with Ramuri Printing House (Fig. 322b).

 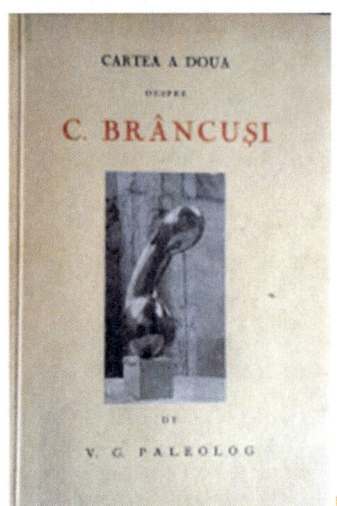

Figs. 322a, b. Craiova, 1943: a—Meridian, *17-18-19*;
b—*Cartea a doua despre C. Brancusi* by V.G. Paleolog

Constantin S. Nicolaescu-Plopsor, Victor N. Popp, V.G. Paleolog and C.D. Fortunescu organized the Oltenia Week exhibition, during wartime, 24-31 October, at Jean Mihail Palace (Fig. 323) and the Romanian plastic art stands exhibited three Brancusi sculptures from Popp's collection. King Mihai provided patronage to this exhibition, on which occasion Jean Mihail Palace was open to the public for the first time.

Paris

He was concerned all his life with flight and speed, as far back as his childhood, and thus introduced forms that preserve or increase the energy potential of objects in his creation, for which reason it is not by mere chance his archive included photographs of railroad car or plane components and prototypes, manufactured in order to travel through space on the horizontal or on the vertical. Such photos were sent him by his friend, architect William Lescaze when he taught industrial design with Pratt Institute [491] [492] (Figs. 324a, b).

Fig. 323. Jean Mihail Palace, Craiova

Figs. 324a, b. Terrestrial and air means of transport manufactured by US companies, 1943-1945

Brancusi sculpted the *Seal* (gray-bluish veined marble) and installed it next to sculptures with various shapes and complexities that suggest motion making a "kinetic" corner in the studio (Fig. 325).

Fig. 325. "Kinetic" corner in Brancusi's studio, Paris, 1943

1944

New York

The *Modern Drawings* exhibition including two drawings by Brancusi was organized at the MoMA, 16 February to 10 May.

Cincinnati

From 18 March to 16 April, the *Pictures for Peace: A Retrospective Exhibition Organized from the Armory Show of 1913* opened at the Cincinnati Art Museum.

Basel

From 18 March to 16 April, the concrete art (*Konkrete Kunst*) exhibition opened at the Kunsthalle.

New York

The *Modern Paintings: The Lee Ault Collection* exhibition was organized to the benefit of The American Field Service at the Valentine Gallery, 10-29 April.

The *Art in Progress: 15th Anniversary Exhibitions: Painting, Sculpture, Prints* of the MoMA was organized to celebrate the establishment's 15 years (24 May-15 October) and comprised two sculptures by Brancusi. The festive agenda included an exhibition about the relation between function, technology and form in design, *Art in Progress: 15th Anniversary Exhibitions: Design for Use,* with one sculpture of the artist displayed.

Philadelphia

From 1 July to 1 November, the *History of an American: Alfred Stieglitz: "291" and After* exhibition opened at the Philadelphia Museum of Art, which also included the Brancusi sculptures from the Stieglitz collection.

Paris

He finished the *Flying Turtle* (marble, 1943-1944).

Bucharest

Besides V.G. Paleolog, Petru Comarnescu also proved to be devoted admirer and good connoisseur of Brancusi's creation, philosophy, sources of inspiration, and working techniques. The art historian used to say about the sculptor he represented the "genial expression of absolute Romanian naturism," and his genius greatly influenced the "aged cultures" of the whole world, bringing them back to primordial sources. Comarnescu wrote about Brancusi's influence over other great contemporary artists such as W. Lehmbruck, who was inspired from the *Prayer* when he sculpted his kneeling woman (*Die Kniende*). The German sculptor paid a visit to Brancusi and was profoundly marked by the manner in which suffering was made when one loses someone dear, which the gypsum woman kneeling in the studio endured dignifiedly and transcendentally.[493]

Revista Fundatiilor Regale [The Review of Royal Foundations] of December 1944 published Petru Comarnescu's article on Brancusi accompanied by several studio and sculpture photos, of which also the *Prayer* from Dumbrava Cemetery in Buzau, and *Torso* were included, further enabling readers to know more about his work (Fig. 326). [494] Mentioning the photographs taken of Brancusi's works printed in various publications P. Comarnescu noticed their important pedagogic and artistic contribution with respect to knowing his creation.[495]

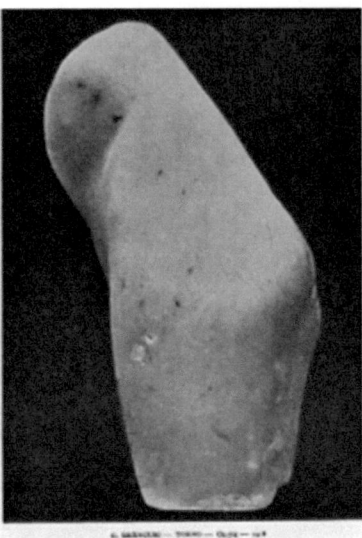

Fig. 326. Revista Fundatiilor Regale, Bucharest, 1944, *12*

1945

New York

The *Recent Acquisitions* exhibition was organized with a view to show the latest procurements of MoMA to the public, which also included the *Newborn* (bronze, 1920) by Brancusi, 15 February to 18 March. *The Museum Collection of Painting and Sculpture* exhibition opened at the MoMA from 20 June 1945 to 13 January 1946, including two sculptures by Brancusi exhibited in the *New Forms* section.

Paris

Herbert Read together with Henry Moore paid him a visit to his studio as they were concerned with preparing the exhibition of contemporary English art, with the support of the British Council (Fig. 327).

Fig. 327. Brancusi, H. Moore, F. McEwen (British Council), H. Read, and P. Eluard at the British Council Gallery, Paris, 1945

He sculpted *Milestone* (stone, 1945, Fig. 328). This sculpture can be considered the artist's message transmitted to his fellow humans: it was the landmark between two worlds, the old one in which he believed, created and felt at ease and the new one, where he could no longer find his place, being profoundly marked by the war that just ended and by the new world division. Thus we can better understand why Brancusi allowed his photo to be taken in the frame of his sculpted wood gate set in the studio (Fig. 329a). He was 70 and was concerned about his departure from this world. How? By means of a symbolic gate (a virtual portal). The artist was and would remain interested in the philosophic aspect of the gate in a person's life or in that of the community (Fig. 329b), component of the Romanian peasant's philosophy.

Fig. 328. *Milestone* in Brancusi's studio, Paris

Figs. 329a, b. Brancusi in his studio gate frame, Paris, 1946—a; young Gorj peasants at the house gate, at the beginning of the 20th century—b

Bucharest

Petre Pandrea published the volume *Portrete si controverse* [Portraits and Controversies] (Fig. 330) with a chapter dedicated to Brancusi, whose portrait relied on his origin from the geographical ethno-cultural space of Oltenia—an "energy reservoir" for Romania. This topic would be resumed in an essay about the Oltenian spirit, included in the *Atitudini si controverse* [Attitudes and Controversies] volume issued by Minerva Publishers in 1982. Pandrea provided an interesting sociologist review, classifying the Oltenia-born inhabitants in the dual type, somewhere in-between the person walking on foot to town with *cobilita* and "the man with Brancusi's Maiastra".[496]

Fig. 330. *Portrete si controverse* by P. Pandrea, **I**, Bucharest, 1945

1946

Detroit, Saint Louis (Missouri)

The *Origins of Modern Sculpture* exhibition (22 January-3 March) was organized at the Detroit Institute of Arts. Four Brancusi sculptures were exhibited in the abstract art gallery (section of new techniques and symbols). An exhibition under the same title was organized at the City Art Museum of Saint Louis (30 March-1 May). The exhibition dealt with sculpture from prehistorical antique times until the modern age (the beginning of the 20th century).

New York

The Museum Collection of Sculpture was organized at the MoMA (19 February-5 May). This year, the MoMA opened the *Paintings, Sculpture, and Graphic Arts from the Museum Collection* exhibition, 2 July 1946 to 12 September 1954, which included paintings, sculptures and drawings installed in the permanent galleries under the coordination of Alfred H. Barr Jr., Director of Research for Painting and Sculpture.

New Haven (Connecticut)

From 4 April to 6 May, the *Plastic Experience in the 20th Century, Contemporary Sculpture: Objects, Constructions* exhibition opened at the Yale University Art Gallery.

Cincinnati (Ohio)

Four Modern Sculptors: Brancusi, Calder, Lipchitz, Moore exhibition opened at the Cincinnati Art Museum (1 October-15 November).

New York

On 16 October-6 November, the *1910-1912. The Climatic Years in Cubism* exhibition opened at the Jacques Seligmann & Co. Gallery. Brancusi participated with a sculpture.

Newark (New Jersey)

From 24 October to 1 December, the *Owned in New Jersey: Paintings and Decorative Arts from New Jersey Homes* exhibition opened at the Newark Museum. It included 186 paintings of the 18th, 19th and 20th centuries, pieces of furniture, textiles and carpets from Europe, glass, ceramic and porcelain items, etc.

Paris

A few testimonies are kept about the artist in the first years after WWII, among which a photograph by Tristan Tzara and an unknown person (Fig. 331).

In November, the French state purchased for the first time sculptures from Brancusi for the National Modern Art Museum-*Cock* (1935), and *Seal* (1943).

He met Doctor Pascu Atanasiu, stipend holder of the French state working with the Pasteur Institute who would become close friend and take care of his health, becoming also his testament executor at his death.

Fig. 331. Brancusi, T. Tzara and an unknown person, Paris, 1946

1947

New York

The *Alfred Stieglitz Exhibition: His Collection* exhibition, 10 June to 31 August at the MoMA, included sculptures, paintings, drawings, graphics and publications from the Stieglitz collection. The collection included two sculptures by Brancusi displayed in 1914 to the artist's personal exhibition organized by the famous photographer at the 291 Gallery.

Avignon

Upon René Char's initiative, the contemporary painting and sculpture exhibition (*Exposition de peintures et sculptures contemporaines*) was organized by Yvonne Zervos, René Girard, and Jacques Charpier at the Grand Chapel of Popes' Palace from Avignon, 27 June-30 September. 150 pieces were exhibited.

Paris

Under the patronage of the Romanian ambassador Simion Stoilov, a French artist aiding Romanian children (*L'art français au secours des enfants roumains*) exhibition was organized to help the children affected by the 1946-1947 drought, on 1-4 July at the Chaillot Club. Tristan Tzara and Jean Cassou signed the catalogue's foreword. Brancusi participated with a sculpture and a drawing. When the exhibition ended, the pieces were donated to achieve the goal of the event.

Although the artist did not agree with the political changes in Romania, he stayed in touch with Romanians, as proven by his participation in various events organized by the Romanian Legation of Paris. In the historical movie, Of 56 Seconds,[497] Brancusi was seen next to George Enescu (Fig. 332), his friend from his youth.

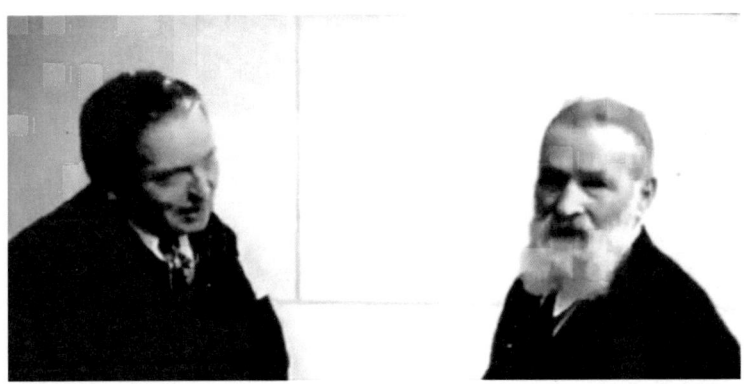

Fig. 332. Brancusi and Enescu at Romania's Legation (screen capture), Paris, 1947

Sculptor Constantin Antonovici (Fig. 333a) became Brancusi's apprentice until 1951. He was the only student whom the artist wrote a recommending certificate to[498] (Fig. 333b). After settling in the USA Antonovici would sculpt several pieces representing Brancusi as he had known him during his apprenticeship in Paris (Fig. 334).

Berlin

The French sculpture from Rodin to the present days (*La sculpture française de Rodin à nos jours*) exhibition opened in the Zeughaus from 12 July to 5 August under the auspices of the French Group Control Council, Division of Education and Cultural Affairs.[499]

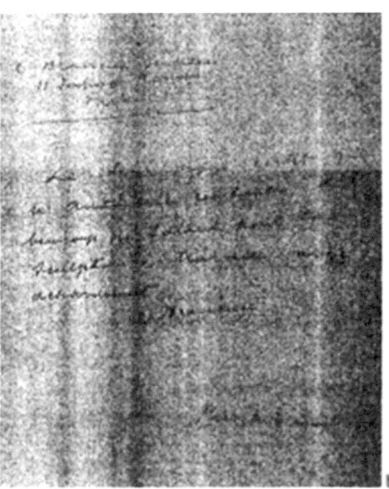

Figs. 333a, b. Paris: a—sculptor C. Antonovici and painter A. Istrati in the Brancusi's studio, 1947; b—recommending certification given to C. Antonovici by Brancusi, 9 May 1951

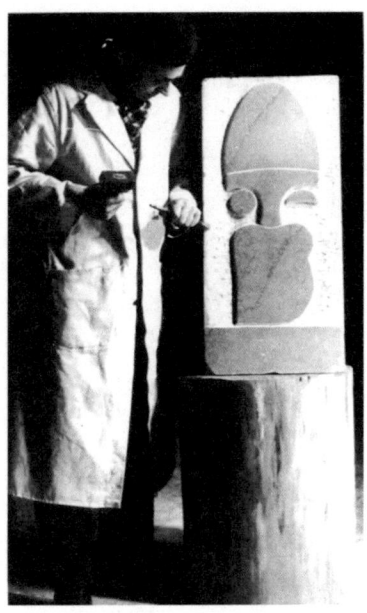

Fig. 334. *Brancusi* by C. Antonovici

Brno

The *From Rodin to Our Days* exhibition was organized from 20 November to 20 December. Brancusi provided two sculptures.

Bucharest

In 1947, V.G. Paleolog published *Constantin Brancusi*, a 58 page book in French (Fig. 335)[500] and 27 black and white photos reproduced from Aurel Bauh studio. It was the first and only monograph printed during the artist's life, with his tacit approval, and a successful one as well. The work was appreciated by authors Ezra Pound and Carola Giedion-Welcker. The same year V.G. Paleolog also published the study *Brancusi, valeur internationale* [Brancusi, International Brand], in the first issue of Arcades, with 16 photos of the artist's works[501] (Fig. 336).

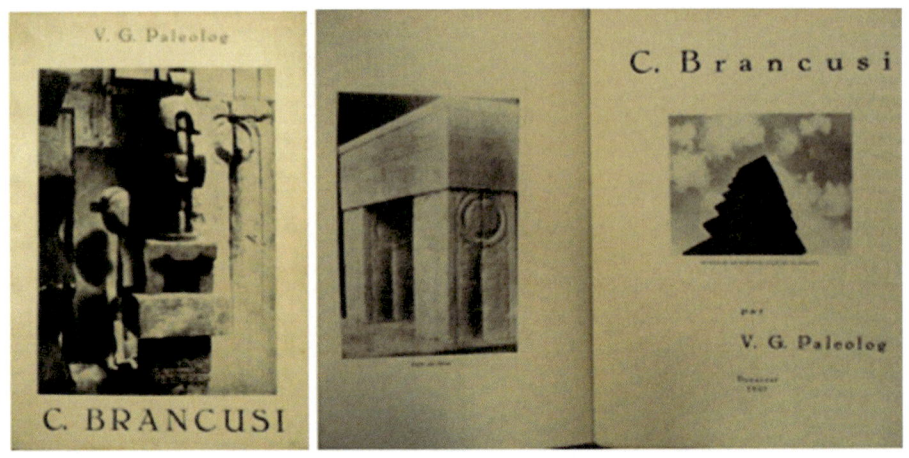

Fig. 335. *C. Brancusi* by V.G. Paleolog, Bucharest, 1947

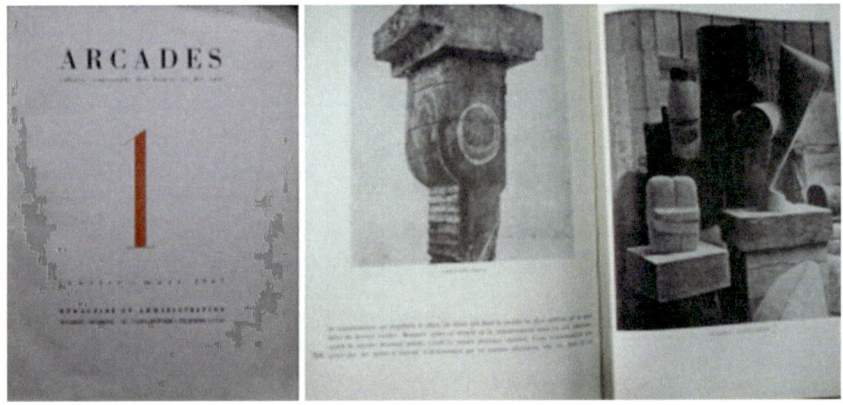

Fig. 336. Arcades, Bucharest, 1947, *1*

1948

Paris

Beginning with January, the Romanian painters Natalia Dumitrescu and Alexandru Istrati were visiting him again and again, making themselves useful. They came to Paris on a scholarship granted by the French state. The artist installed them nearby at No. 4 and provided them with material support, advice, and liaisons to artistic personalities. Brancusi would designate the Istratis as his legatees, entrusting them with his entire fortune.

London

The Institute of Contemporary Arts (ICA) organized the *40 Years of Modern Art 1907-1947: A Selection from British Collection* exhibition at the Academy Hall, 10 February to 6 March. At the end of years, from 20 December 1948 to 29 January 1949, ICA organized the *40 000 Years of Modern Art. A Comparison of Primitive and Modern* exhibition at the Academy Hall. One Brancusi piece was exhibited.

Chicago

The *Collection of The Works of James Joyce* exhibition was organized at The Newberry Library, 1-26 March, and included the volume *Tales Told of Shem and Shaun* (1929) as well for which Harry and Caresse Crosby, owners of The Black Sun Press in Paris, asked the artist to draw the writer's portrait. Brancusi drew a spiritualized portrait entitled *Portrait of James Joyce*.

Baltimore

From 15 April to 23 May, the *Themes and Variations in Painting and Sculpture* exhibition opened at the Baltimore Museum of Modern Art. Brancusi participated with one sculpture.

Venice

The 24th Biennial of Venice (*XXIV Biennale di Venezia*) opened from May to September. A pavilion dedicated to the collection of Peggy Guggenheim exhibited the two Brancusi sculptures, *Maiastra* and the *Bird in Space*.

Paris

Alicia Penalba, Argentinian sculptress, settled in Paris with stipend from the French government to study engraving in the Beaux Arts School. Working in Zadkine's studio Alicia discovered Arp, Brancusi and Giacometti of whom she got close and influenced her creation.[502]

Marta Pan paid a visit to Brancusi and such an encounter marked her entire artistic life, according to her own testimony. She was greatly impressed by the turning sculpture *Newborn*, which was moved by impulse from Brancusi. The artist told her that was how he imagined how "the beginning of the world should have been". [503]

Chilean sculptress Marta Colvin frequented for a while Brancusi's studio.[504] Sculptor François-Xavier Lalanne, one of Brancusi's neighbors, also frequented the artist (Fig. 337).[505]

New York

The *New York Private Collections* exhibition opened at the MoMA, 20 July-12 September, and included one sculpture by Brancusi. In October the *Twentieth Century Masters* exhibition was organized at the Pierre Matisse Gallery and included one sculpture by Brancusi. From 16 November 1948 to 23 January 1949, the *Timeless Aspects of Modern Art* exhibition opened at the MoMA, where one sculpture by Brancusi was exhibited.

Amsterdam

From 26 November 1948 to 1 February 1949 the 13 sculptors of Paris (*13 Beeldhouwers uit Parijs*) exhibition opened at the Stedelijk Museum. Duchamp-Villon, Brancusi, González, Gargallo, Laurens, Arp, Chauvin, Zadkine, Lipchitz, Giacometti, Richier, Couturier, and Auricoste exhibited there.

Fig. 337. Brancusi and F.X. Lalanne in front of the studio, Paris, 1948

1949

New Haven (Connecticut)

From 14 January to 13 February, the *Sculpture since Rodin* exhibition opened at the Yale University Art Gallery.

Minneapolis

The *Masterpieces of Sculpture* exhibition was organized at the Minneapolis Institute of Arts in February.

Florence

From 19 February to 10 March the *Collection Peggy Guggenheim* exhibition opened at Strozzi Palace. After opening in Venice, the exhibition was the first event organized by Peggy Guggenheim to introduce her modern art collection, which aroused fiery debates.[506][507] The Italian painter Pietro Annigoni was quite outraged that such "sad farce" occurred in the very heart of Venice.

Paris

An exhibition about the first masters of abstract art (*Les premiers maîtres de l'art abstrait*) was organized at the Maeght Gallery of Paris, in two stages: I: *Préliminaires à l'art abstrait* [Preliminaries of Abstract Art], 30 April-23 May and II: *Épanouissement de l'art abstrait* [Full Development of Abstract Art], 27 May-30 June. Brancusi provided four sculptures. Michel Seuphor considered that "Mondrian's cross and Brancusi's ovoid" were "essential signs and primary shapes" that took art into a new era.[508]

He modeled the large gypsum *Cock* with metallic fitting, 4.80 m high (Fig. 338). Later Brancusi wanted to cast it in stainless steel and approached an art collector that also had a foundry in Pittsburgh, but his health did not enable him to travel to the USA and supervise the sculpture casting.

Fig. 338. The *Cock* IV in Brancusi's studio, Paris

Simone Boisecq and her husband, Karl-Jean Longuet, upon the invitation of the writer Henri-Pierre Roché, called on Brancusi in his studio in 1949.[509] Like all those that crossed the threshold of his studio, the two artists would profoundly change their artistic direction, Simone becoming a successful non-figurative sculptress.

Bucharest

On June 29, the newspaper Scanteia, the official organ of the ruling Romanian Workers' Party, published the statement of the Professor Traian Savulescu, President of the Academy of the Romanian People's Republic, in which Brancusi was harshly criticized, considering him "fallen into the sin of the so-called art for art, which, without a doubt, he cannot understand it either, of the art sublimated to the absurd and paradox, of the art valued in dollars by the overseas billionaires." For Professor Savulescu, who was ecstatic about the works of Soviet artists, Brancusi's art "has nothing in common with the specifics of his country" and therefore "agonizes and falls apart in the distinction of a few snobs."

Venice

In September, the contemporary sculpture (*Mostra di scultura contemporanea*) exhibition was organized by Peggy Guggenheim at Venier dei Leoni Palace. This was the first exhibition at the new residence. Peggy took care to photograph the two polished bronze sculptures she bought from Brancusi, *Maiastra* and *Bird in Space*, in the garden of her palace and these photographs can be found in the 1979 catalogue Peggy Guggenheim Collection Venice (Figs. 339a, b).

Figs. 339a, b. *Maiastra* (a) and *Bird in Space* (b) in the garden of Venier dei Leoni Palace, Venice

New York

From 26 September to 14 October, the *Sculpture* exhibition opened at the Buchholz Gallery, Curt Valentin.

To Honor Henry McBride. An Exhibition of Paintings, Drawings and Water Colors opened at the M. Knoedler & Co., Inc Galleries from

29 November to 17 December. The exhibition included works appreciated by the art critic while he was an active critic.

Chicago

From 20 October to 18 December, the *20th Century Art from the Louise and Walter Arensberg Collection* exhibition opened at the AIC, where 19 Brancusi sculptures were displayed. The exhibition showed art works of the most important 20th century artists from the Louise and Walter Arensberg collections, but "The most artists most fully represented are Marcel Duchamp and Constantin Brancusi".[510]

1950

New York

From 31 January to 7 May, the *Recent Acquisitions* exhibition opened at the MoMA.

Philadelphia

On 4 February, the *S.S. White Collection* exhibition opened at the PMA and on 20 May the *Masterpieces of Philadelphia Private Collections* exhibition.

Providence (Rhode Island)

The *A Century of Sculpture, 1850-1950* exhibition was organized at the Museum of Art from Rhode Island School of Design, 30 March-18 May, including one Brancusi sculpture from the Harvard Art Museum collection.

Bucharest

The National Gallery opened on 20 May, the first section of the Art Museum of Romania placed at the disposal of the public, where two Brancusi pieces were displayed from the former Simu Museum.

Pomona (Los Angeles County)

From 15 September to 1 October, *Masters of Art from 1790 to 1950* exhibition organized at the Art Building by Los Angeles County Fair Association and included 50 paintings and 25 sculptures.

New York

From 26 September to 14 October, the *Contemporary Drawings* exhibition opened at the Buchholz Gallery, Curt Valentin.

On the occasion of the PMA diamond jubilee, from 6 December 1950 to 6 January 1951, *The Heritage of August Rodin* exhibition was organized at the Buchholz Gallery, Curt Valentin. 80 works by 27 European and American modern artists were exhibited.

New Haven (Connecticut)

Yale University Art Gallery published an illustrated catalogue *Collection of the Société Anonyme: Museum of Modern Art 1920* (Fig. 340). John Marshall Phillips signed the catalogue foreword, texts by Katherine S. Dreier, Marcel Duchamp, George Heard Hamilton, a.o. This in turn provided G.H. Hamilton the ability to write a brief biography and bibliography on Brancusi, where he introduced a photograph Brancusi's *Yellow Bird*.

Philadelphia

An event of the American artistic world took place on 27 December, when the collectors Louise and Walter Conrad Arensberg donated more than one hundred objects to the PMA, of which twenty-two were sculptures by Brancusi.[511]

Paris

National Museum Publishers published *Musée national d'art moderne: catalogue—guide* [National Modern Art Museum: Catalogue—Guide] (Fig. 341) with texts by Jean Cassou, Bernard Dorival, Geneviève Homolle; the catalogue included Brancusi's sculptures: *Cock*, and *Seal*.

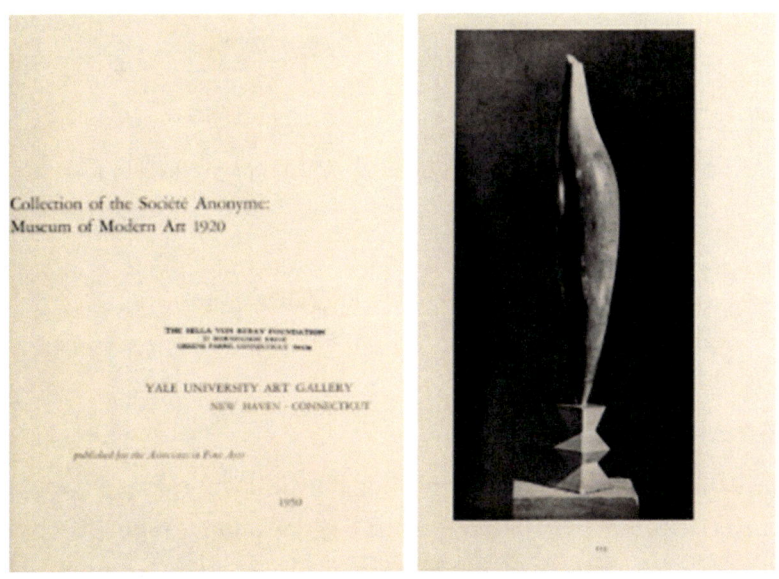

Fig. 340. *Collection of the Société Anonyme: Museum of Modern Art 1920*, New Haven, 1950

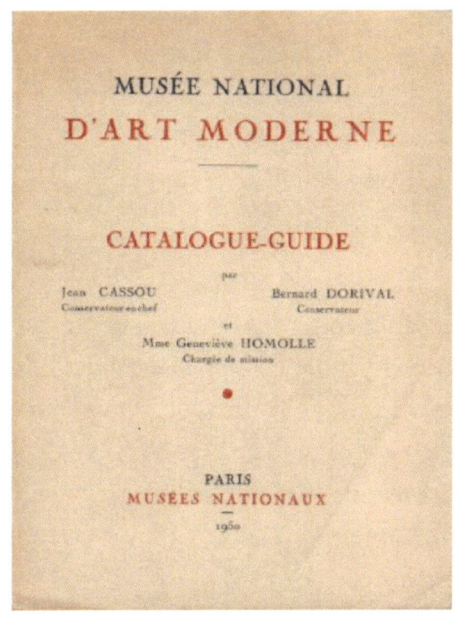

Fig. 341. *Musée national d'art moderne: catalogue—guide*, Paris, 1950

Preparing for the Final Voyage

1951

Amsterdam, Brussels, Zurich

The Surrealism + Abstraction. Choice of the Collection Peggy Guggenheim (*Surrealism + Abstractie. Keuze uit de verzameling Peggy Guggenheim*) exhibition opened at the Stedelijk Museum of Amsterdam from 19 January to 26 February. The exhibition was itinerated to Brussels entitled *Surréalisme + Abstraction, choix de la Collection Peggy Guggenheim*, 3-28 March, at the Beaux Arts Palace, then to Zurich entitled *Moderne Kunst aus der Sammlung Peggy Guggenheim*, April-May, at the Kunsthaus.

De Stijl exhibition of the Stedelijk Museum in Amsterdam opened from 6 July to 25 September. It dealt with bringing back the spirit that animated the De Stijl movement as promoted in the magazine of the same title, based on the documents from Stedelijk Museum.

Bucharest

At the 28 February meeting of the Language Science, Literature and Art Section from the Academy of the People's Republic of Romania they debated the creation of sculptor Constantin Brancusi. On 7 March was organized the second meeting on Brancusi's works (Fig. 342).[512] Alexandru Toma, favorite poet of the communist regime, chaired the meeting attended among others by academicians George Oprescu, Victor Eftimiu, George Calinescu, Camil Petrescu, Krikor Zambaccian, Alexandru Graur, Geo Bogza, George Murnu, Iorgu Iordan, Alexandru Rosetti, Gala Galaction, and Ion Jalea. Alexandru Toma in his speech considered Brancusi "reactionary and enemy of the regime."

Professor G. Oprescu accused him of "insincerity" because, in his opinion, the artist does nothing else but speculates "by bizarre means the morbid tastes of bourgeois society." In G. Calinescu's opinion Brancusi "cannot be considered creator of sculpture because he does not use the expressive means of this art." Ion Jalea, Camil Petrescu and Geo Bogza provided accounts favorable to the artist and Victor Eftimiu pointed out the national and international value of Brancusi. Academician Mihail Sadoveanu chaired this section and he had previously had his say about Brancusi's creation, which he did not appreciate.

Targu-Jiu

Archive documents recorded two attempts to destroy the *Endless Column*, because it had neither artistic value nor public utility for local officials. The purpose of *Column* knocking down was to recover the metal it was made of. Consequently on 7 March the Popular Council of Targu-Jiu sent a letter to the Communal Management and Local Industry Department requesting their approval to demolish the *Column*: "Taking into account this Column, with the materials resulting from demolishing, could be used for other civil works highly necessary in our town we are kindly asking you to provide us with the due approval to put it down;" the letter was sent for approval to the specific commission of the Academy of the People's Republic of Romania (Fig. 343a).[513]

This attempt was not finalized because, after some correspondence between local and central officials, a letter was sent to the Academy of the People's Republic of Romania on 5 January 1952 by the Art Committee from the Council of Ministers, Beaux Arts Section stating: "the conclusion was arrived at that such structure can be considered decorative work inspired from the forms of popular art in the region, so it can be maintained as it is." The Academy acquired this point of view. Nevertheless, the *Column* was left unattended until 1966 (Fig. 343b).

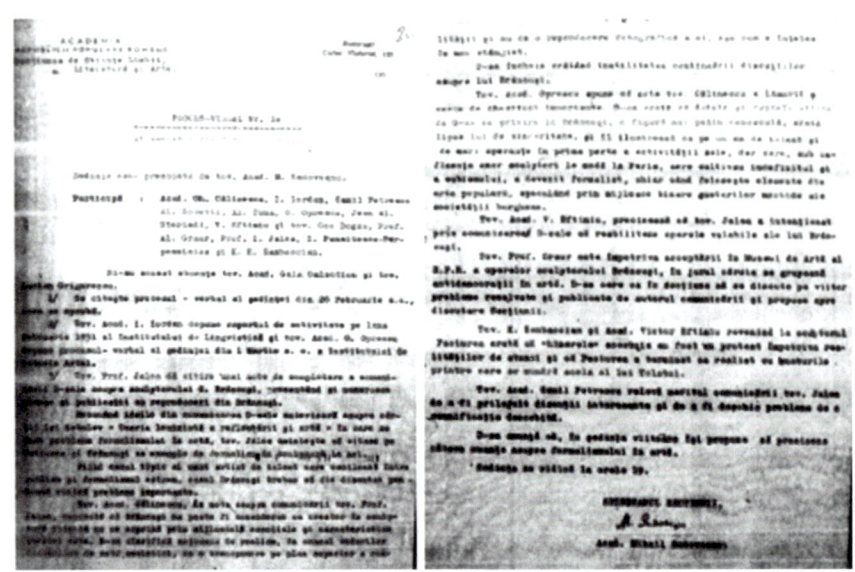

Fig. 342. Minutes of the 7 March 1951 session of the Language Science, Literature, and Art Section from the Academy of the People's Republic of Romania, Bucharest

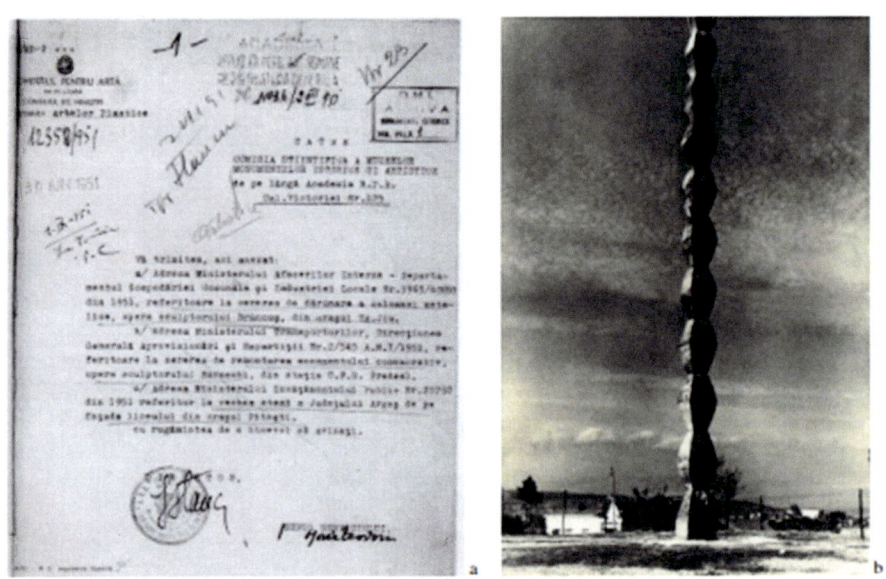

Figs. 343a, b. Request for approval to demolish the *Endless Column*, Bucharest, 30 June 1951—a; *Column* in the 1950s—b

New York

From the Alfred Stieglitz Collection: An Extended Loan from the Metropolitan Museum of Art exhibition was organized at the MoMA, 22 May-12 August and included works of the Alfred Stieglitz collection borrowed from the Metropolitan Museum of Art. MoMA organized the *Selections from 5 New York Private Collections* exhibition, 26 June-9 September, which included 87 works selected and installed by Andrew Carnduff Ritchie, Director of the Painting and Sculpture Department. Two sculptures by Brancusi were exhibited.

Paris

On 1 August, after the proletarian stigmatization from the Academy of the Romanian People's Republic, Brancusi deposed his Romanian passport to the Embassy of Romania, and asked for the French citizenship that would be granted him under the naturalization decree of 13 June 1952 published in the Official Gazette of France, 15 June 1952, p. 5998.

New York

From 17 September to 27 October, the *Brancusi to Duchamp* exhibition opened at the Sidney Janis Gallery.

In the book *The Arts and Their Interrelations* published by The Liberal Art Press (Fig. 344), art historian Thomas Munro studied the art influence brought about by Brancusi's court trial with the American customs, reaching to the conclusion that "The case well illustrates how problems of philosophic theory can take on practical importance, and how the conduct of affairs—here legal and commercial—can be impeded by vague, confused thinking or by the conflicting views of supposed experts. It brings in several different ideas about the nature of art".[514]

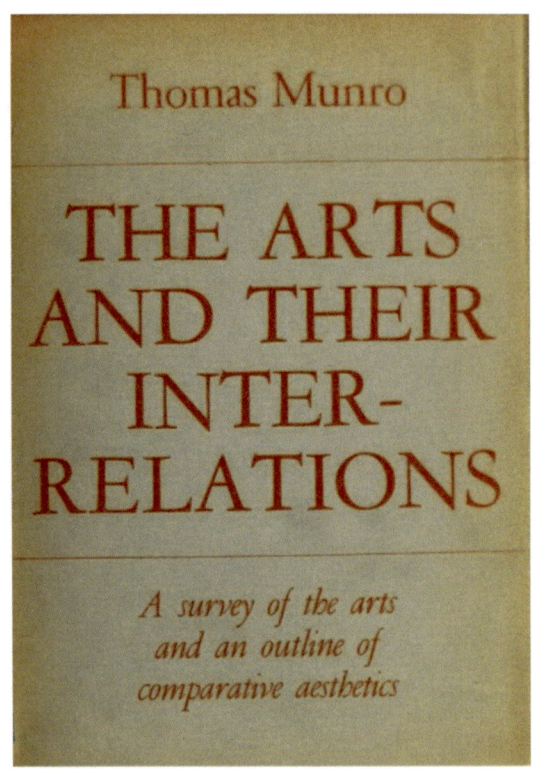

Fig. 344. *The Arts and Their Interrelations* by Th. Munro, New York, 1951

Scottsdale (Arizona)

In December the *Sculpture from Rodin to Today* exhibition opened at the Desert School of Art.

1952

Melbourne

In February sculptures by Brancusi were exhibited at the National Gallery of Victoria.

Paris, London

The painting and sculpture works of 20th century (*L'Œuvre du XXe siècle. Peintures—sculptures*) exhibition was organized by Jean Cassou in May-June at the MNAM in Paris and included paintings and sculptures of the 20th century. The exhibition from the MNAM reopened from 15 July to 17 August at the Tate Britain from London, entitled *20th Century Masterpieces. An Exhibition of Paintings and Sculptures*, and J.J. Sweeney was commissioner. 125 pieces were exhibited.

On 28 May, Brancusi was summoned to vacate his studio, as the quarter was included in a vast urban modernization plan. The artist resorted to donating to the MNAM, so he asked Marcel Duchamp and Henri-Pierre Roché to find a proper place where his studio could be moved and put to value when he would be dead. Marcel Duchamp thought two to three museum halls could be obtained but he did not dare act, as he knew how exacting the artist was.

Brancusi participated with seven sculptures to the 4th Salon of young sculpture (*Quatrième Salon de la jeune sculpture*), 11 June-14 July, Museum Rodin garden, dedicated to Rodin and he wrote *Homage to Rodin* published in the exhibition's illustrated catalogue.[515]

New York

The Museum of Modern Art published Andrew Carnduff Ritchie's volume *Sculpture of the Twentieth Century* (Fig. 345) with a chapter dedicated to Brancusi: *The Object Purified: Brancusi and Organic Abstraction*.

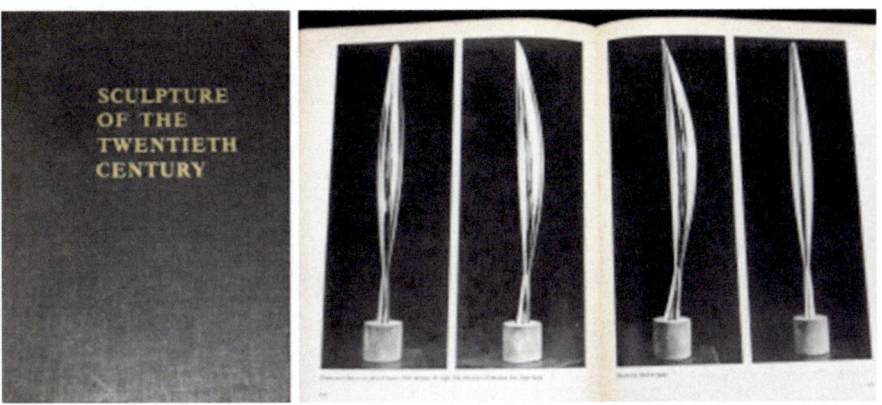

Fig. 345. *Sculpture of the Twentieth Century* by A. C. Ritchie, New York, 1952

Reinhold Publishing Company published the *Art in Modern Architecture* by Eleanor Bittermann, which examines the works of several artists that displayed architectural vision in their creation, as well as those of architects following the modernist movement. Brancusi is represented by *Miss Pogany* named "Wall Niche Figure," a sculpture of the Arensberg collection installed in his Hollywood home (Fig. 346).

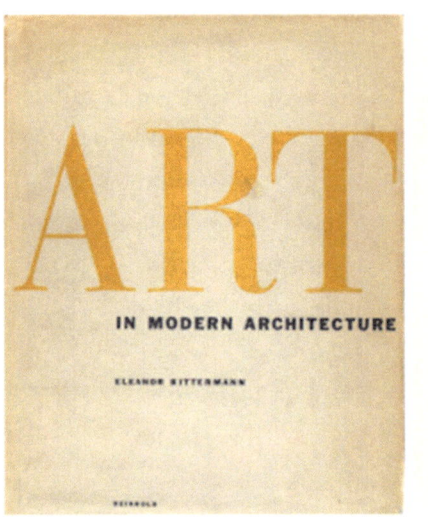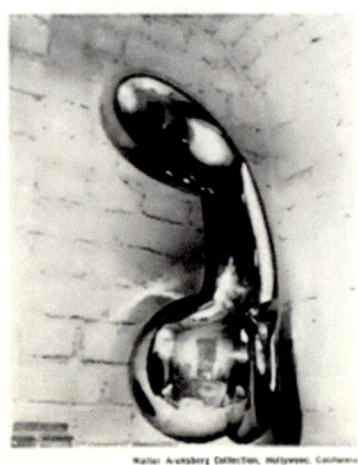

Fig. 346. *Art in Modern Architecture* by Eleonor Bittermann, New York, 1952

Philadelphia

From 11 October to 7 December, the *Sculpture of the Twentieth Century* exhibition opened at the PMA, which included five sculptures by Brancusi. In 1953 the exhibition was itinerated to the AIC, 22 January to 8 March, then to the MoMA of New York, 28 April to 7 September.

New Haven (Connecticut)

In memoriam of Katherine S. Dreier, 1877-1952: Her Own Collection of Modern Art exhibition opened from 15

December 1952 to 1 February 1953, at the Yale University Art Gallery. Three Brancusi sculptures were exhibited.

One of Katherine S. Dreier's last photos before dying was with parrot Coco and Brancusi's *Leda* (Fig. 347).

Fig. 347. Katherine S. Dreier with Coco, and *Leda*, West Redding (CT), 1952

1953

New York

From 19 January on February, the *French Masters* exhibition opened at the Sidney Janis Gallery and from 11 February to 15 March the *New Acquisitions* exhibition organized at the MoMA, included 36 newly procured works made by 31 artists, of which one sculpture by Brancusi as well.

Her memoirs published The *Passionate Years* (Fig. 348), Caresse Crosby tell us how visits took place in Brancusi's studio, his charming hospitality and, naturally, the original lunches provided by the artist on his working table, where he would place "a white sheet of crispest tissue paper to serve as tablecloth," as well as "one of his chiseled marble gems" in the middle. "A plump pullet" was placed on the grill, and "Rosé from the Midi" would be poured at table, dessert consisting of "strawberry jam and hearts of cream." The impression about the artist was that of an adorable man who "cut up the pullet with a sculpting knife". [516]

Fig. 348. *The Passionate Years* by Caresse Crosby, New York, 1953

Paris

From 30 January to 9 April, the cubism 1907-1914 (*Le Cubisme 1907-1914*) exhibition opened at the MNAM where Brancusi attended with two pieces.

The new director of the Solomon Guggenheim Museum, James Johnson Sweeney, got in touch with the sculptor to organize the first retrospective exhibition of his creation. The negotiations took some time and his son Sean's memories, reproduced by Florence Hetzler, introduce us in the atmosphere of such debates.

Targu-Jiu

The second attempt to destroy the *Endless Column* took place, on the occasion of the 4th World Festival of Youth and Students organized in Bucharest (July-August). Important funds were necessary for the sites opened in order to organize this event. Scrap iron being revenue item, they raised again the issue of demolishing the *Column*. The art monument underwent pulling with a tractor chained to it, but such attempted failed lamentably.

Anvers

The 2nd Biennial of sculpture (*2e Biennale voor Beeldhouwkunst*) exhibition from 20 June to 30 September was organized in Middelheim Park.

New York

The *New Acquisitions; Recent American Prints, 1947-1953; Katherine S. Dreier Bequest; Kuniyoshi and Spencer; Expressionism in Germany; Varieties of Realism* exhibition, 23 June-4 October, included paintings, sculptures, drawings and stampas from the MoMA collections, selected and installed by Alfred H. Barr Jr. and Dorothy C. Miller in cooperation with William S. Lieberman, including the *Maiastra* (marble, 1912), donation by Katherinei S. Dreier's testament.

Houston

The *Seventy-Five Years of Sculpture in Houston* exhibition was organized at the Museum of Beaux Arts (6 November-6 December), sponsored by the Allied Arts Association.

São Paulo

The 2nd Biennial in São Paulo (*II Bienal de São Paulo*) exhibition from December 1953 to February 1954 was organized at the Modern Art Museum, where Brancusi was represented by one sculpture.

New York

From 22 December 1953 to 24 January 1954, the *Sculpture and Sculptors Drawings* exhibition opened at the Curt Valentin Gallery with 75 works.

1954

New York

From 7 July to 15 August, the *Sculpture by Constantin Brancusi* exhibition opened at The MoMA. It is the sixth personal exhibition of Brancusi in the United States of America, which included six works of the artist from the museum collection.

Yverdon, Zurich

The seven pioneers of modern sculpture (*Sept pionniers de la sculpture moderne*) exhibition opened at the Ville Hotel (18 July-28 September). Brancusi participated with three sculptures and one drawing next to Arp, Chauvin, González, Laurens, Pevsner, Duchamp-Villon.

The Yverdon exhibition reopened from 27 November to 31 December at the Kunsthaus Zurich entitled *Begründer der Modernen Plastik: Arp, Brancusi, Chauvin, Duchamp-Villon, González, Laurens, Lipchitz, Pevsner* [Fathers of Modern Sculpture: Arp, Brancusi, Chauvin, Duchamp-Villon, González, Laurens, Lipchitz, Pevsner]; Brancusi increased his participation with three more sculptures.

Craiova

An important event took place in Craiova, in September, when writer Eugen Schileru, employee of the Art Museum of Romania, searched in the storehouses of the Regional Museum and found the bust of *Vitellius*, which was authenticated together with V.G. Paleolog and Professor C.S. Nicolaescu-Plopsor.[517]

Philadelphia

On 16 October, they inaugurated the *Louise and Walter Arensberg Collection* that was permanently included for exhibition in the Philadelphia Museum of Art. Brancusi and Duchamp were the sensation of this exhibition.

The catalogue *A.E. Gallatin Collection* was published by PMA in the format of 1940. Texts were authored by A.E. Gallatin, Jean Hélion and J.J. Sweeney, with critical notes by George L.K. Morris (reprinted from earlier editions of the catalogue published by New York University), and artists' biographies.

1955

Bloomfield Hills (Michigan)

From 12 January to 6 March, the *Levin Collection* exhibition opened at the Cranbrook Academy of Art Galleries. Brancusi attended with one sculpture.

Paris

From April to May, upon the invitation of the French government the MoMA New York organized the *50 Years of Art in the United States: Collection of the Museum of Modern Art of New York / 50 Ans d'Art aux États-Unis. Collections du Museum of Modern Art de New York* at the MNAM.

New York

On June, the *Closing Exhibition: Sculpture, Paintings and Drawings* opened at the Curt Valentin Gallery and included 179 sculptures, pictures and drawings in the gallery collections at time of dissolution.

Bucharest

The *Endless Column* of Targu-Jiu was protected by being included in the list of cultural monuments from the People's Republic of Romania, attached to Decision 1160 of June 23, 1955 of the Council of Ministers.

Ann Arbor (Michigan)

From 30 October to 27 November, the *Twentieth Century Painting and Sculpture from the Collection of Mr. and Mrs. Harry L. Winston* exhibition opened at the Museum of Art from the University of Michigan. The exhibition included 71 paintings and sculptures, including one sculpture by Brancusi.

Paris

The Cahiers d'Art magazine (Fig. 349), in 1955 and issued in 1956 dedicated several articles to Brancusi.[518]

Fig. 349. Cahiers d'Art, Paris, 1955, *30*

New York

In 1955 architect Phyllis Barbara Lambert came to Paris to discuss with Brancusi[519] about the possible installation of a monumental *Cock* in front of the Seagram Building;[520] Phyllis elaborated the plans together with architect Ludwig Mies van der Rohe, in cooperation with architect Philip Johnson. They thought of a stainless steel *Cock*, however the sculptor was meant to decide on the material. Brancusi had also to be consulted on the fountain and water jets around this *Cock*. The project did not begin because Phyllis had some doubts about how the sculpture's artistic integrity could be maintained with such great size.[521]

From 26 October 1955 to 8 January 1956, the great retrospective *Constantin Brancusi* (seventh personal) exhibition was organized by James Johnson Sweeney, director of Solomon R. Guggenheim Museum in New York, including 59 sculptures and 10 drawings and gouache. The exhibition was itinerated to Philadelphia in 1956. Such major event was much commented by art critics and journalists. Dore Ashton published an encomiastic article in Arts and Architecture (New York), and Dorothy Adlow in the Christian Science Monitor (Boston) wrote about the first powerful achievements of modern art on behalf of Brancusi, and the artist's contribution was revealed when cubism and abstraction began being defined.[522] James Johnson Sweeney wrote about the significance of such exhibition for the appreciation of Brancusi's genius[523] in the museum's press release.

Before the exhibition opening, Brancusi looked back at his life and stated for New York Times magazine that Americans helped him achieve everything he left behind, in order to bring joy to those that see and understand.[524]

Life magazine in the 5 December issue dedicated several pages to Brancusi, an artist for whom success and Western life did not change (Fig. 350): "The old man lives as modestly as when he was a peasant's son in Romania." The article contained several sculpture photos by Brancusi (*Miss Pogany*, bronze, *Torment*, bronze, *Prometheus*, gypsum, *Archaic Figure*, stone), as well as photos taken in the artist's studio, all by Bernhard Moosbrugger.[525]

Fig. 350. Life, New York, 5 December 1955

1956

Paris

On 6 January, the sculptor broke his leg and this accident gave him pain until the end of his life; he spent 5 months (11 January to 3 May) in the Foch Hospital of Suresnes.

Philadelphia

The retrospective exhibition of Guggenheim Museum reopened at the Philadelphia Museum of Art (Fig. 351) from 27 January to 26 February.

Fig. 351. *King of Kings* in "dialogue" with a fan, PMA, 1956

Paris

In the artist's last years, painter Sonia Delaunay was one of his closest friends and had a great influence over the old and ill artist. In the end, she persuaded him to leave a testament clearing up who and how they would take care of his sculptures and studio, as Doctor Pascu Atanasiu, executor, had also testified.[526]

On 12 April, Brancusi left by testament to the French state all his pieces and studio items consisting of 144 sculptures and sketches, more than 80 pedestals and furniture items, about 20 molds, 35 drawings and gouache; two paintings, a valuable photo archive of 1250 photographs of various size and exposures as well as 560 negatives, most on glass, a library and disk collection of folk, ethnographic and jazz music, provided his studio was accurately reconstituted.[527][528]

As regards Brancusi's testament Pascu Atanasiu explained in his last interview that the notary appointed to record the testament was Alexandru Istrati's friend and while writing the document he invited the witnesses—Pascu Atanasiu, laboratory head at Pasteur Institute and his wife Irène, Jean Cassou, director of MNAM and Gabrielle Vienne, art historian—to leave the studio. This means the testament was executed while the testamentary executor and witnesses were absent.

When they were allowed to re-enter the room, Brancusi embraced Atanasiu and told him: "You are going to have the greatest headaches in your entire life. I have designated you as testamentary executor," which he already knew. In her interview Irene Atanasiu completed her husband's testimony by providing an important detail, namely that the notary introduced by Istrati "could not write accurately the names of the involved people. He never even asked the right manner to write them down".[529] Afterwards the people present to this significant event found out severe irregularities but nobody contested the legal deed's inaccuracy at that time.

In May, Brancusi has purchased his resting place in the Montparnasse Cemetery. As true Oltenia inhabitant he was preparing to leave this world and left nothing to chance; this was the reason why it is difficult explaining what had happened during the testament writing.

In Paris two exhibitions were organized, where Brancusi was represented by sculptures. From 5 to 27 May, the 12th Salon of May (*XIIe Salon de mai*) opened at the Modern Art Museum of the City (Musée d'Art Moderne de la ville Paris). In June Rodin Museum organized the international contemporary sculpture (*Exposition internationale de sculpture contemporaine*) exhibition, which included 151 works authored by 151 artists from 19 countries (Argentina, Austria, Belgium, Czecho-Slovakia, Denmark, Egypt, Switzerland, France, Germany, Greece, Israel, Italy, Great Britain, Norway, The Netherlands, Poland, United States of America and Sweden).

Craiova

The homage exhibition for Brancusi's anniversary (*Expoziția omagială pentru aniversarea sculptorului C. Brancusi*) was organized in the Art Museum Craiova, in the Mirror Hall, July-August. On this occasion, five sculptures, photos, books and Romanian and foreign studies were exhibited. The event was well attended by the public and included notable speakers such as V.G. Paleolog, among others. A delegation from the Ministry of Education and Culture including Marin Mihalache, Eugen Schileru, and Pavel Tugui participated to the opening. On this occasion, the ministry's request was submitted to the Regional Popular Council of Oltenia in order to borrow Brancusi's sculptures from Craiova for the homage exhibition of Bucharest.[530]

Bucharest, Paris, Chicago

Brancusi's friends, fans, and admirers from Romania made particular efforts to draw the responsible people of the communist regime near the Romanian artist in Paris. During that summer, upon the proposal of Constanta Craciun—the Romanian minister of Culture, the artists Marietta Sadova and Dida Solomon with her husband, journalist Scarlat Callimachi and director W. Siegfried called on Brancusi and told him about the Romanian authorities' intentions to celebrate the artist's 80th birthday by an exhibition in the Art Museum of Craiova and a retrospective one in Romania's Art Museum of Bucharest. Upon Brancusi's question about the pieces of the sculptural ensemble in Targu-Jiu, Marietta Sadova told him she had been there in 1955 and the sculptures were legally protected. Returning to the country, they wrote their impressions after visiting the sculptor's studio.

A citizen committee of Chicago, led by lawyer and collector Barnet Hodes, had the initiative of installing an inhabitable *Endless Column* on the banks of Lake Michigan. On 5 December, Brancusi wrote to Hodes that, if it were of "polished stainless steel, it would be one of the world's wonders".[531] The correspondence of Brancusi with B. Hodes (letter of 26 June) revealed the artist would have liked building about 122 m tall column.[532]

His health again prevented Brancusi going across the ocean to select the place of the monument, and when he died B. Hodes wrote to one of his friends "his disappearance is a great loss, not only for art but for the whole world in general".[533]

In October, the artist received Florica and Eugen Jebeleanu. Although suffering from a broken leg, he received the couple in his studio several times and discussed with them a possible trip to Romania in order to participate to the varnishing day of the homage exhibition, as accounted by those involved in this event, among whom Mircea Balanescu as well, plenipotentiary minister in the Romanian Legation of Paris.[534] During her visit, Florica Cordescu Jebeleanu made several drawings of the ill artist, of which one became the cover of the Tanarul Scriitor [Young Writer's] magazine issued on 11 November (Figs. 352a, b).[535]

Hamburg

Critic of architecture Sigfried Giedion published *Architektur und Gemeinschaft* (Fig. 353a) in the German Encyclopedia Rowohlt series, the

English version of which would be issued in 1958 (Fig. 353b). Giedion expressed his astonishment examining *Bird in Space*, a work which he considered to be a "clastic vertical" characterized by "magnificent simplicity" and, notwithstanding all that, it managed to "claim possession of all space." Giedion considered the consecration of artists like Le Corbusier, Mondrian, or Brancusi to restore confidence in a "brighter era".[536]

Figs. 352a, b. *Brancusi* by Florica Cordescu Jebeleanu, Paris, 1956—a; cover of the Tanarul Scriitor magazine, Bucharest, November 1956—b

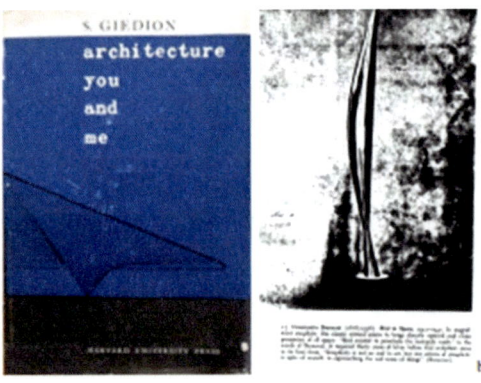

Figs. 353a, b. Sigfried Giedion: a—*Architektur und Gemeinschaft,* Hamburg, 1956; b—*Architecture. You and Me*, Cambridge (MA), 1958

New York

The *Rodin to Lipchitz, Part II* exhibition was organized to the Beaux Arts Associates Gallery, 9 October-3 November.

The *Recent European Acquisitions* exhibition was put up at the MoMA, 28 November 1956-20 January 1957, including works recently purchased by the museum from the creation of several European artists, of whom Brancusi. The same year at MoMA, the Italian actress Silvana Mangano made a group of photographs with Brancusi's sculptures from the museum collection, borrowing the attitude and hair style of *Miss Pogany* (Fig. 354).

Fig. 354. Silvana Mangano at the MoMA, New York, 1956

London

The Art of Sculpture was published by Faber and Faber (Fig. 355) and author Herbert Read noticed the manner in which Brancusi uses light to the maximum through his polished shapes whose mirroring surface confers the "illusion of movement" to the sculpture. *Miss Pogany* made of different materials also provided different sensations: "The marble is the more tactile, the brass the more visual form." Art critic and historian Read found that a succession of plans with contrasting surfaces systematically organized provided the sculpture *Adam and Eve* with an "architectonic unit".[537] The volume included six pages with photographs of *Miss Pogany*, *Bird in Space* and *Adam and Eve*.

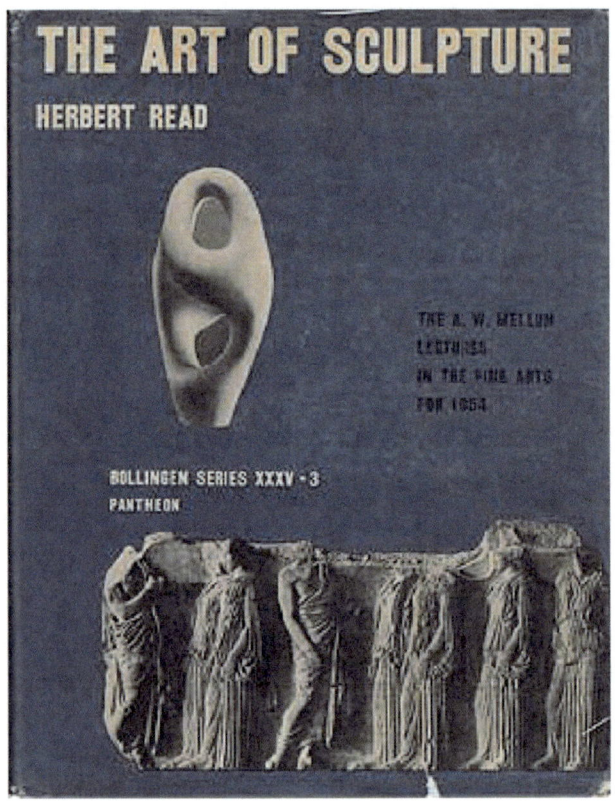

Fig. 355. *The Art of Sculpture* by H. Read, London, 1956

Bucharest

The Brancusi homage exhibition on the occasion of his 80th anniversary (*Expozitie omagiala Brancusi cu ocazia aniversarii de 80 de ani*) was organized on the ground floor of the Art Museum of Romania, 22 December 1956-1 March 1957, his first personal exhibition of Europe. On 20 January, painter Camil Ressu sent him a letter announcing the organization of Brancusi exhibition in the country and inviting him to attend this event.[538] The following sculptures were exhibited: four from the Art Museum of Romania in Bucharest, one from Professor G. Oprescu's collection; two from the Frederic Storck and Cecilia Cutescu-Storck Museum, three from the Art Museum Craiova, and one from the Plastic Art Institute Nicolae Grigorescu.

The Ministry of Education and Culture purchased the *Prayer, Wisdom of the Earth* and the *Model of the "Gate of Kiss" Pole* from the owners for the

Art Museum of Romania, exhibiting the pieces to the public. The sketchbook that Brancusi gave to Ion Croitoru in 1904, upon leaving the country, was also exhibited for the first time. Sculptress Milita Petrascu agreed to exhibit her *Bust of Brancusi* modeled before WWII, with the sculptor's corrective intervention. On this occasion they cast the bronze after the bust made by the artist (Fig. 356).

This event attracted a great public and aroused vivid interest; newspapers and magazines allocated large printing space to it.[539] Pavel Tugui noted of the event: "a great cultural artistic battle was won." Due to strong guild solidarity and respect for Brancusi, the "phenomenon," they succeeded organizing in Bucharest the first Constantin Brancusi personal exhibition from Europe. According to M.H. Maxy's and Eugen Schileru's accounts too, it follows that the "number of visitors exceeded 10,000".[540]

Fig. 356. *Brancusi* by Milita Petrascu, Bucharest, 1956

Departure

1957

New York, Palm Beach (Florida)

From 14 January to 2 February, the *Paintings and Sculpture from the Minneapolis Institute of Arts; A Loan Exhibition* opened at the M. Knoedler & Co. Gallery, New York and then at the Society of the Four Arts, Palm Beach, 15 February-10 March.

From 22 January to 23 February, *The Struggle for New Form: Loan Exhibition for the Benefit of Just One Break* opened at the World House Galleries.

Expoziţia *Drawings Recently Acquired for the Museum Collection* organizată la MoMA, 29 ianuarie-24 februarie, including 50 drawings by 43 artists, recently procured by the museum, organizer being Dorothy C. Miller, curator of MoMA collections.

Philadelphia

From 8 February to 28 April, the exhibition *T. Edward Hanley Collection* was organized at the PMA.

Cluj

In a chronicle about the personal exhibition Brancusi opened in December 1956 at the Art Museum of the People's Republic of Romania, published in the review of the Writers' Union from the People's Republic of Romania, Steaua (Fig. 357), the art critic Ion Frunzetti considered the artist is known in Romania through "the fame acquired by the great echo of his art abroad," noticing "however the thought Brancusi is a value is slowly turning into a natural thought." Frunzetti proves thus being tributary to the opinions of his great forerunner, Alexandru Tzigara-Samurcas, former professor of the artist, by considering that "without his folklore roots, which give Brancusi his basic grounds," his creation "would become either untransmissible artistic play, or willful confusion disguising the snobbish imitator's absence of interior substance, desiring to acquire stolen success as any other epigone".[541]

Paris, Bucharest

On 16 March, 2 a.m., Constantin Brancusi died in his bed in his own studio (Fig. 358), having turned down the doctor's advice to be admitted to a hospital: "I will wait for the Good God at home in my studio".[542] A week before that, he confessed and received the Eucharist from Archbishop Teofil Ionescu of the Romanian Orthodox Church in Paris, whom he shared his heartache and wish to die away from his country and decay in foreign earth, far from his beloved mother.[543]

Brancusi's death surprised many of his close friends, as well as those who had come to his place during this time. He was ill but he seemed mastering the illness, as could see also director W. Siegfried: "When I saw Brancusi for the last time, last year in Paris, nobody could believe his suffering which seemed temporary, that much he was vital, would defeat him."[544]

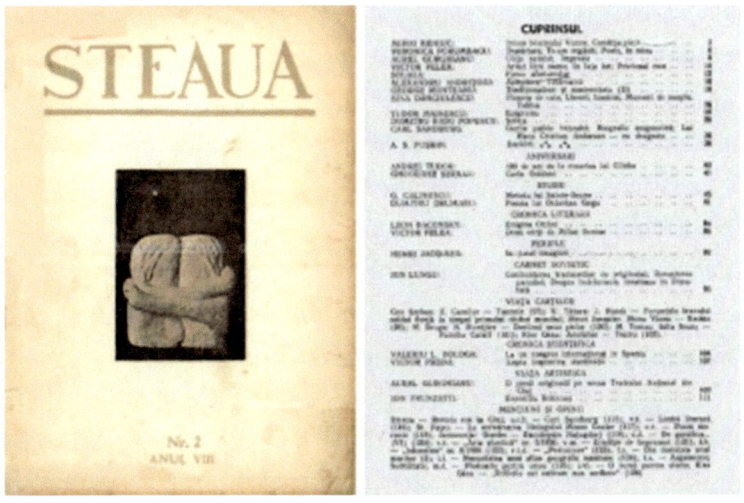

Fig. 357. Steaua, Cluj, 1957, *2*

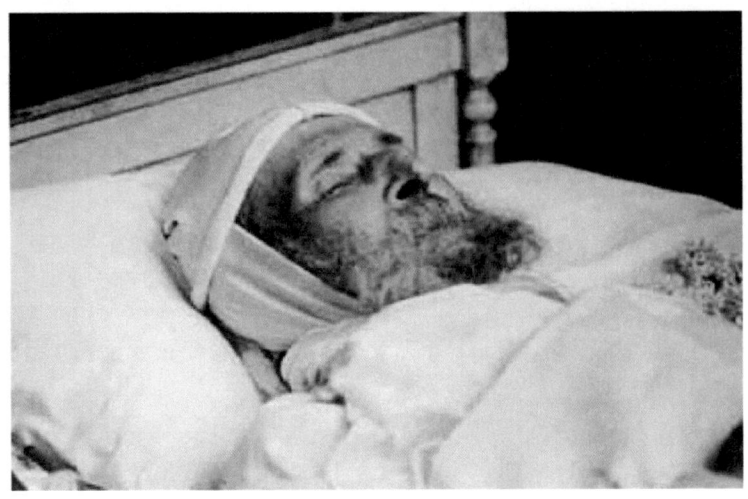

Fig. 358. Lifeless body of Brancusi in his studio, Paris

What moved was the misery inflicted on the artist by the Istratis, his testamentary heirs. Ambassador Mircea Balanescu recalled what he had found when he paid him a visit: "He was wearing a shirt that was white once upon a time..." [545] and poet Eugen Jebeleanu wrote indignantly how Brancusi looked, being in the 'care' of his heirs whose single concern was his fortune. What happened to Brancusi and the cause of his surprising death we can find in the late 1994 testimony of Dr. Pascu Atanasiu, his close friend and caring doctor, which was overlooked although it is thrilling: "I can tell you how he got in the coma—one Monday when I went to see him he was already in the coma. They gave him Dubonnet wine. As he drank the whole bottle he got in the coma he never came to of. I knew him to be a very strong man. But this astonished me. It was fatal to him. He could have lived on for many more years. He was afraid of alcohol; he was very brave and highly willful in keeping a life discipline."[546]

On Tuesday 19 March, Bucharest dailies printed in a black box reported that the sculptor Constantin Brancusi had died in Paris at the age of 81.[547] On 19 March, the burial service was performed at the Romanian Orthodox Church of Jean de Beauvais Street, on which occasion speeches were delivered by Jean Cassou, director of the MNAM in Paris, Georges Salles, director of French museums, and Basile Munteanu, director of the Romanian School from Fontenay-aux-Roses. He was buried in Montparnasse Cemetery according to his own will. In the graveyard in "splendid spring weather" *coliva* was offered—"noble Romanian recipe of boiled wheat", [548] "something so intimate, of so unexpected flavor that strongly brought the impression of Brancusi"[549]

On 19 March, Jana Brancusi, the niece's sculptor, whom Brancusi had helped finance her studies to become a chemical engineer, arrived at the Montparnasse Cemetery in order to attend his funeral. At the time, according to Minister Mircea Balanescu's testimony, the legatees did not allow her to enter her uncle's studio, which she had very much wished to visit in the past.[550]

Brancusi's funeral was disturbed by the improper behavior of his heirs that hooted and threatened the Romanian embassy's representative for his adherence to the communist politics, the most violent being Alexandru Istrati. Man Ray, Brancusi's friend, was strongly affected by what he had seen and decided on the spot to never again participate to such events; and Ambassador Mircea Balanescu was utterly surprised by Istrati's behavior since he had known him while still living in Romania as being a devoted member of the communist party.[551]

At Constantin Brancusi's death, homage texts were written by A. Auricoste, M. Berger, G. Bogza, J. Cassou, G. Calinescu, D. Chevalier, P. Comarnescu, R. Couturier, Carola Giedion-Welcker, E. Giglioli, P. Guéguen, Claire Gilles Guilbert, É. Hajdu, Luce Hoctin, A. Kesser, D. Lewis, M. Lipsi, N. Margineanu, B. Munteanu, H.P. Roché, G. Salles, G. di San Lazzaro, G. Schiff, E. Schileru, M. Pedrazo, Milita Petrascu, V. Posteuca, H. Read, R. Sollier, B. Urbanowicz, G. Veronesi, A. Vogt, O. Zadkine and many others. The artistic world was in mourning.

New York

On 28 March-20 April, the *4 Masters Exhibition: Sculptures by Rodin, Gouaches and Drawings by Brancusi, Drawings by Gauguin, Sculptures and Drawings by Calder* opened at the World House Galleries. After Brancusi's death this was the first exhibition that included his works.

Life magazine in its 1 April issue paid the last homage to the great departed in the article entitled *The Death of a Pioneer* (Fig. 359).

Fig. 359. Life, New York, 1 April 1957

Saint-Étienne

The first exhibition of France that included works by the sculptor was dedicated to the first generations of abstract artists (*Art abstrait: les premières générations 1910-1939*) organized at the Museum of Art and Industry, 7 April to 26 May.

Zurich

The Neue Zürcher Zeitung dedicated the April issue to the memory of Constantin Brancusi. Texts were signed by Carola Giedion-Welcker, Heinz Keller, Armin Kesser, A.G. Vogt and René Wehrli.

Paris

From April to May, the exhibition Homage of Sculpture to Brancusi and Émile de Coninck Prize (*Hommage de la sculpture à Brancusi et Prix Émile de Coninck*) was organized at the Suzanne de Coninck Gallery. The exhibition included works by young sculptors.

The architects of the UNESCO Palace in Paris—Bernard Zehrfuss, Pier Luigi Nervi and Marcel Breuer—planned making an *Endless Column* of stainless steel before the building from Place Fontenoy, which remained unachieved. Luce Hoctin sustained this project in Art magazine, 16 April.

L'Œil magazine, issue 29 from 15 May (Fig. 360) published paper *Souvenirs sur Brancusi* [Memories on Brancusi] by H.P. Roché.

From 5 June to 14 August, the Galliera Museum organized the exhibition on splendors and scenery of Parisian life from 1909 to 1929 (*Paris 09-29. Fastes et décors de la vie parisienne de 1909 à 1929*).

Fig. 360. L'Œil, Paris, 1957, *29*

Milan

From 27 June to 4 November, the 11th Triennial of Milan (*XI Triennial di Milano*) opened at the Palazzo dell'Arte al Parco. The Romanian pavilion organized an exhibition in memory of Brancusi with three sculptures of artist. On this occasion All'Insegna del Pesce D'Oro Publishers reprinted Ezra Pound's study translated in Italian by Mary de Rachewiltz, his daughter (Fig. 361), which was issued in 1921, in The Little Review.

Paris

In October, Christian Zervos printed a homage volume *Constantin Brancusi, sculptures, peintures, fresques, dessins* [Constantin Brancusi: Sculptures, Paintings, Frescoes, Drawings] (Fig. 362) with Cahiers d'Art Publishers. The text with 89 photos had been already printed in 1956. The volume had the introduction signed by C. Zervos and homage texts by U. Apollonio, G.C. Argan, J. Arp, P.G. Bruguière, A. Calder, L. Degand, G. Duthuit, P. Fierens, Carola Giedion-Welcker, W. Grohmann, Peggy Guggenheim, W. Haftmann, É. Hajdu, Valentine Hugo, H.L.C. Jaffé, G. Marchiori, H. Read, G. Richier, F. Roh, J. Rothenstein, G. Schmidt, R. Stoll, J.J. Sweeney, Dora Vallier, L. Venturi, and J. Villon.

Fig. 361. *Brancusi* by E. Pound, Milan, 1957

Fig. 362. *Constantin Brancusi, sculptures, peintures, fresques, dessins*, Paris, 1957

London

In 1957, immediately after the artist's death David Lewis published the first western monograph Constantin Brancusi with Alec Tiranti Publishers of London (Fig. 363). The volume could have been printed before but the sculptor did not allow monograph authors to write about him during his life. It contains notes, aphorisms of the artist, a short biography and concise bibliography and illustrations, and represented a synthetic description of Brancusi's creation and not simply an analysis classifying it in contemporaneity and history. D. Lewis noticed that Brancusi was different from the other artists because his creation "[did] not fall under clear-cut stages" and sculptures were difficult to assign dates to. With Brancusi, a series of sculptures could "last almost a lifetime," and the last pieces of the series differed "only by small adjustments" from the first ones. [552]

Detroit

The *Collecting Modern Art: Paintings, Sculpture and Drawings from the Collection of Mr. and Mrs. Harry Lewis Winston* exhibition opened at the Detroit Institute of Arts (27 September-3 November). The exhibition was itinerated by the Institute of Contemporary Art, Boston to the Virginia Museum of Art (Richmond, 13 December 1957-5 January 1958), the SFMOMA (San Francisco, 23 January-13 March 1958), the Milwaukee Art Institute (Milwaukee, 11 April-12 May 1958), and the Walker Art Center (Minneapolis, 15 June-3 August 1958).

Boston

From 10 October to 17 November, the *European Masters of Our Time* exhibition opened at the Museum of Beaux Arts.

Fig. 363. *Brancusi* by D. Lewis, London, 1957

***

Brancusi's death was the beginning of a long and sad time interval of posthumous exploitation of the artist's memory and creation consisting of: law suits instituted by the heirs with the French state's institutions in order not to comply with testamentary provisions and establish an 'industry' of bronze copies of his sculptures; reconstituting his studio in several versions with negative impact over the physical integrity of works and written and photographic documents; distorting the truth about the artist; launching forged works on the market; falsifying the documents or stealing them from archives; changing his tomb into a 'common grave', etc. Brancusi could foresee all this during his lifetime: "When I am gone prey birds will tear me apart"[553].

They Have Met Brancusi...

Teacher Dumitru Pupaza

D. Pupaza, *O mandrie a neamului: sculptorul Brancusi* [One great national pride: sculptor Brancusi], Gorjanul, Targu-Jiu, 1930, **7**, *41-42*, 8-15 November

Undoubtedly we Romanians simply do not know how to appreciate our valuables. To gain glory our works should go into the wide world. This is also what happened to Brancusi, peasant sculptor. To have his work acknowledged and assigned to the rhythm of immortal art he had to go far away, overseas and countries and leave his beloved land—where he dreamily fondled his childhood innocence, the regions of Bradiceni from Gorj County, which deeply imprinted the grandeur of artistic thinking in his heart.

Truly Brancusi is the greatest sculptor of our times. A great labor exhibition took place a few days ago before the royal family, but King Albert of Belgium was mostly impressed by Brancusi's *Maiastra*. Our entire national pride stands before the royal looks, gazing steadily to Brancusi's sculpture. This is where his words come true, namely the "artist is god, emperor and slave alike." Two years ago, the American magazine The World dedicated one issue entirely to the Gorj peasant, sculptor Brancusi—who managed in so grand manner to sanctify stone and wood, achieving what others could not: *thought into sculpture*; not its figure, but its innate idea. In this part of sculpture Brancusi is unique and profound visionary, aspiring to supreme idealness.

Brancusi has never sculpted figures but thoughts, knowing how to reveal the secrets of wood, stone and metal. This is where his artistic superiority resides. But his greatest merit comes from the fact that, although resident in Paris for a long time, far away from us in isolation and in contrasting atmosphere, Brancusi achieves always Romanian thinking, thus ascribing the very triumph of Romanian art in the rhythm of universal progress.

Brancusi loves life and nature with deep wisdom. The total difference of his sculptures can be also found in his everyday life that resembles nobody's. His studio is an extension of nature's laboratory in the middle of which stands, huge, the creator of living art. His table was made up by two mill stones placed one on top of the other, and the chairs are made from chisel-chopped stumps. But among so many stone and marble blocks, carved wood, etc., something which looks even more original—a peasant's hearth stands proudly in one corner, which the sculptor manufactured himself. This is where the master is found every time his thoughts wander to our lands. In the silence and satisfaction of its poverty, all thoughts were nurtured that shine nowadays so strongly in the *Maiastra*, *Narcissus* and the *Cock*.

The work of Master Brancusi is the labor of the faithful monk who dedicated entirely his mind to the elements of matter in order to provide them with piousness, force and heart within the originality specific to our nation.

The triumph of Brancusi's art is the greatest happiness for our Gorj region. If our officials had not encouraged and awarded so many caricature beings, had they granted the national prize to Brancusi we could have had him among us.

We are rejoiced however the beloved spoiled child of Gorj will know to further provide his sculptures with Romanian thinking, as much as Gorj region can provide feeling, love and will-power for the victory of its inhabitants. His hermit's life in Paris is sacrifice and heroism put to the service of Romanian culture's victory.

Director W. Siegfried

W. Siegfried, *Ultima intalnire cu Brancusi* [Last meeting with Brancusi], Informatia Bucurestiului, Bucharest, 1957, **IV**, *1139*, 2 April, p. 2

When I saw Brancusi for the last time, last year in Paris, nobody could believe his suffering which seemed temporary, that much he was vital, would defeat him.

Brancusi lived in Impasse Ronsin between the two studios, separated by long narrow courtyard.

I approached in excitement the places I had seen a long time ago and entered through the door that was left open for me. I got in the studio among gypsum bags, tools, blocks of stone and marble, wood stumps and fantastic shapes, when all of a sudden, I found myself in front of the old master.

He was stretched on a sort of bench and was covered with a fluffy blanket. His eyes looked keenly and youthfully, so youthful that his white thick beard seemed an addition. He wore a small white pique hat with downward brims, which he pulled now to the nape and now suddenly over his eyes. After a few minutes, he could no longer stand the blanket. He had no more patience to lie down. And, angry with his ailing leg, he hit and pointed at it as if it were an enemy forbidding him to work. Turned eighty, Brancusi spoke of his projects like a young man. He told me about his sculptures underway, about music and sunrays and their heat power against altitude; he discussed the structure of materials and their maximum expressivity. He said: "A sculptor who does not carve directly the stone cannot express the idea with vigor and utmost plasticity." The turns of his ideas were fast, unexpected, revealing a universe of thought.

Then he remembered his childhood in the country. He evoked the beauty of the Romanian landscape, the hot summer days when he bathed with the boys and his parents' anxiety, love and care for him. Happy memories followed from the time when he was a student of the Fine Arts School in Bucharest, the students' pranks, but also the affection of their professors.

Old time Bucharest passed before his eyes and he remembered every street, each house. Sometimes he would stop at one corner and asked me: "Isn't it? Now you turn right on Campineanu and get downhill…"

Evening was setting in. The light got sideways through the studio windows. The master stood in the middle of his studio, among his tools, and it was difficult to distinguish this living figure from a statue. He stood there, surrounded by the plastic universe created by him not like direct representation of 3D but as an answer to the exigency of his imagination.

This great artist fastened his work into the deepest sources of inspiration from Romanian art. The creation of the great sculptor, providing so many folklore elements, has constituted the pride of worldwide museums and collections for a long time.

Academician Victor Eftimiu

V. Eftimiu, *Portrete si amintiri* [Portraits and memories], Literature Publishers, Bucharest, 1965, pp. 427-431

Son of peasants from Gorj County of Oltenia province, Constantin Brancusi had difficult childhood and even more difficult youth. Barely out of his teens had he left to deal with the future into the stronghold sheltering the greatest number of painters and sculptors, the city where those intending to immortalize their names on the parchment of ever-changing eternal art are sustaining their confrontations, falls or successes.

Our Brancusi has surpassed his own success dreams. He had ploughed a deep new furrow, had opened untrodden paths, and had imposed to the occidental world the gifts of a nation from the mouths of the Danube River, thus adding his name to the most illustrious sons of our country. He loved his country and his art and served them both until death, in great devotion and dedication of his genius.

The life of Brancusi was a great example of daring reverie and abnegation, of unending sacrifice, eventually crowned with the laurels of immortality.

He arrived in Paris poor and unknown, with no support from anyone. With his blessed hands that back home tempered clay, cut stone and polished metals he washed plates and glasses in restaurant basements or acted as sexton, also sweeping the Romanian chapel from Paris, cleaning the candlesticks of wax and rubbing the silver icon lamps and censers of the church from Jean de Beauvais Street.

To sustain himself and achieve his dreams, Brancusi left from a country that sultan processions and autochthonous exploiters had kept for centuries in bondage and darkness—smothered ideals. […]

Brancusi, whom I have met when he was unknown person with black hair and beard, once showed me in his Parisian studio a series of editions of the same piece, eight or nine variants.

The initial work was incontestable perfection according to all academic rules. But as long as he tempered a new edition in clay, he simplified it, targeting stylization, synthesis and abstraction. Had he remained at the first forms of his creation Brancusi would have been great classical sculptor. But going to the fourth or fifth interpretation of the same model, he was a great modern sculptor.

Having reached to the supreme achievement, which I could understand only by looking at the previous variants, he became the most original statuary of the epoch, unanimously appreciated by the experts of the two hemispheres.

But how much toil, how much scrupulosity until he imposed his originality, his personality! And how many enemies, how much irony he aroused!

A malicious person said the woman who sows, which he modeled eight or nine times until reaching its final expression, represented a kidney or a bean.

The *Child head*, so plastic and expressive at first, reached upon its supreme appearance a simple lump of polished marble where only some detail here and there reminded the suave smile of the model.

There is no need to carve this noble matter which is marble but only polish it: it lives through its own beauty! told me the sculptor, caressing the round shiny stone. Certainly, this is arbitrary paradoxical thinking, but it contained a grain of truth, a departure point.

Then I visited Brancusi much later, when he turned into some white-bearded patriarchal figure, at the peak of his talent and glory. His studio was overcrowded with his own sculptures, old and new which, especially the new ones put me out, obsolete person that I was.

But getting out of that oppressive room gorging of originality, troubling poetry and personality, I could contemplate only indifferently the statues from Parisian parks and boulevards, as they looked dusty, rusty, and harmless to me with their useless tiring scrupulous details and academic uniformity.

Brancusi was the younger contemporary of Rodin, Bourdelle and Maillol.

But he has traced his own route. Detaching himself from material ornamentation, he dashed into spirituality. He targeted the geometrical simplicity, stylizing, suggestion with its immense perspectives beyond classical perfection. Enclosed within its own horizon, perfection hinders imagination.

The spirit of the onlooker cannot add anything to the vision of the creative artist. Giving it all, he deprived the admirer of the possible addition to the work of art from one's own reverie, from the unachieved creation vibrating in each spectator, reader or music listener.

Without such spiritual accompaniment and sensitive tribute, the work of art ceases being poetry, aura or apotheosis.

The art of Brancusi still provides the aura of the past and the millennia of plastic attempts of the people that, in the depth of time and continents, were cutting oak with the axe after their forefathers chiseled by silex the rocks of ancestral caves, painting forest animals on the walls.

Brancusi's art is liberation from everything centuries taught and imposed us, return to the primitive vigor and candor. It is the cooperation between the artist and his mirror—the spectator; it is the fusion of the demiurge with the simple person aiming at becoming demiurge in his turn, if not by constructive genius at least by adorning the work of art with all the beauties he coveted and could not turn alive.

The artist is the interpreter of thousand and thousand aspiring dreams, the nostalgia of those who cannot create themselves…

The dream of anonymous multitudes create the chosen one, the creator, the same way human dreams gave birth to the gods.

Sculptress Irina Codreanu

Irina Codreanu, *Ucenicie la Brancusi* [Apprenticeship with Brancusi], Brancusi Colloquium, Bucharest, 13-15 October 1967

In the end direct contact with the master's work has been overwhelming. We have asked him—the same way we asked Milita Petrascu before—to allow us working with him. At first he refused, in his joking gallant tone telling us that, in case he took apprentices, in the first place he would made certain he could provide, together with the lessons, some physical correction as well; or "such beautiful girls like you I would not dare touch with my fingertip…"

However we insisted and repeatedly asked him to accept us as students, so he found some compromise: he gave us boys' names to enable him being severe with us, "apprentices." He called Sanda Kessel—Peter, Margareta Cosaceanu, who sometimes came also and worked with Brancusi, became Mihalache, and myself—Costica. Thus he could be a little bit harsher with us, when need be. He taught us the "direct cut" technique into stone and wood, the bronze polish. But more than anything it was from our talks with him, our eating at his table—he liked to cook for his friends and he did it extremely well—that we learned very much. He expressed his ideas with simplicity and in plastic terms like the peasants. He formulated his lessons into axioms, he colored them with his rich imagination full of unforeseen improvisation.

Brancusi revealed us the true sense of the stone or marble block, of the wood trunk. That is, he taught us we should observe the shape nature or hazard gave to matter and therefore, starting from this origin, we should find the sculpturally proper structure. He also taught us the balance which can be rendered to bronze by one polished face, but also all the dangers of the polishing art as it made conspicuous all imperfections of a line, of a curve, of some bronze volume thus polished.

He said, a sculpture should first be an object made for eye delight, an object that the onlooker's hand would instinctively want to caress. And he transmitted us all these in his patriarchal speech, full of spirit and wisdom. He shared these with violin sounds, because he could play Romanian songs and dances on the violin. When Mihalovici came with his violin, he would accompany him. Other times he invented dances he performed before us, while Mihalovici improvised violin tunes that pointed out the graceful gestures and curious rhythms of the illustrious dancer.

Sculptor Mac Constantinescu

M. Constantinescu, *Evocari* [Evocations], Brancusi Colloquium, Bucharest, 13-15 October 1967

It was the autumn of 1924, year when they prepared the epoch's International exhibition of decorative arts in Paris, which should provide new impetus to arts and imprint new aspects to everyday life. It was then I crossed the threshold of the studio in Impasse Ronsin. The first impression persists intensely in my memory. The bright face of the master detached itself from among the carved stones, the girders made of hundred year oaks, wood stumps carved by hatchet. With his gentle inquisitive eyes like a child's, hat brim downward, dressed in worn out working clothes—Constantin Brancusi, with nobody's help was cutting with the forester's saw one of the stumps wherefrom some new symbol of his vision was meant to occur: the *Cock*, the *King of Kings*, *Socrates* or perhaps something else. The sculptor seemed the very embodiment of the spirit that dwelled in the stones and woods of his studio.

To him raw matter—stone, bronze, wood became shape with its own life. Before an oak girder originating in the demolition of houses from the Mansard or Puget eras, which by carving would become a new variant of the *Endless Column* conceived eight years before the master was counseling his disciple: "Just think this oak tree before you is the wise talkative grandfather. The speech of your chisel should be respectful and caring. It is the only way you can satisfy it." At that time I did not imagine after 21 years of studies and experiments the *Column* would dominate, by concept and dimensions the ensemble of Targu-Jiu, Romanian symbol of the most beautiful expectations.

Brancusi's studio, the environment the artist spent most of his creator life in and rendered eternal by its reconstitution in the Modern Art Museum of Paris, was situated in a district where people worked much. It provided white empty walls. Table—two mill stones placed on top of each other. Hatchet-carved stumps as chairs; in the background was the hearth, which Brancusi manufactured himself: the habitual hearth of Gorj peasants.

Any time of day Brancusi was working, fighting matter. There was no clay or gypsum in the studio but only final materials waiting to be directly attacked with the sculptor's chisel.

In Paris, where artists are highly disciplined at work, Brancusi could serve of example. There was no clock in the studio. The siren of a nearby factory was regulating the working hours. The tenacity of labor was sustained by his simple sober life. The master spent his moments of leisure in the same studio, among the stones, stumps and bronze items, polished as nobody else knew to bring to perfection.

At that time, around evening, Brancusi would listen to readings from classical Greeks, Plato's dialogues for instance, or worldwide registered folk music.

There were also friends calling on him. The master called forth his friendship with Modigliani, Erik Satie, composer of *Gymnopedes*, Edmond Radiguet, phenomenon of literary precocity and author of *Le diable au corps* that aroused commotion. With Radiguet he made an unforeseen travel to Morocco and the Middle East, which Brancusi remembered with pleasure. From his Romanian friends Panait Istrati and composers Stan Golestan and Marcel Mihailovici, whom the master liked very much, visited him at the time when I frequented his studio. I met sculptor Gheorghe Anghel there and also his co-citizen Sfetcu, both coming from Severin town, as well as sculptor Romul Ladea, who actually introduced me to the master.

Before me, Milita Petrascu and Irina Codreanu worked with Brancusi who the master nurtured fine friendship for. The famous photographer Man Ray and a series of Romanian and foreign people also frequented his studio at that time, among whom the artists and writers grouped around the vanguard magazines Integral and Contimporanul; their style and sensitivity agreed well with the visual and tactile sensations yielded by the unique beauty of Brancusian shapes. Brancusi exhibited four of his sculptures in this group to an international exhibition organized in Bucharest in 1924.

A little bit later, after some personal exhibitions organized in all big artistic centers, and after the happenings with the US customs that mistook his masterpieces for industrial products, when Europe and America had consecrated him as head of modern sculpture, when important magazines had dedicated him special issues and big museums had placed his sculptures in high places, the visits to the artist's studio turned into pilgrimages. Besides the great cultural personalities, important gentlemen wearing medals to their button-holes would make their appearance in the studio; pushed by snobbism they came to look at art they could not understand.

Brancusi showed them everything patiently; he watched on their faces the effect produced by his work and, according to each case, opened some discussion about archaic art, "the only true one" or about the culinary recipes of the famous "bouillabaisse" [fish borsch], which cannot be cooked better than in Marseilles. When the last visitor exited the studio Brancusi, with his good times voice, would tell some intimate friend:

"Have you seen the butterflies? They all left with their clothes spotted by the pollen of my stones."

Going to Bucharest at the beginning of 1930, I had the opportunity to publish homage article dedicated to the great master and his sculptures. The construction of the monumental ensemble of Targu-Jiu in 1937 occasioned new meetings. The master showed enthusiasm for the achievement of one of his old dreams, namely to leave on Romanian ground the bronze and stone substantiation of what he had conceived best for the longest time. The *Endless Column, Gate of Kiss* and *Table of Silence* with its stone chairs finally found their shape and were dedicated to the heroes of WWI.

The last meeting with Brancusi was in 1939 in New York, in front of his *Leda* installed in a specially arranged hall of the recently inaugurated Museum of Modern Art. A mechanical device was imprinting permanent turning to the pedestal and put to value the subtle shape and its various aspects. Turned gray, cigarette in the corner of his mouth, the master looked with satisfaction to the kinetic structure made by the museum, the first attempt of "mobility" in sculpture. I would like to overlap the two images, the first one of 1924, surprised in incipient elaboration stage and the last one, in the euphoric state provided by the satisfaction of achievement.

The roundness of the *Leda* and of the *Fish*, of the *Maiastra* ("I have attempted all my life—said Brancusi—to grasp the essence of flight"), the ovoid of the "beginning of the world" considered as "primary element of sculptural form," have given rise to emulators in all the world while the spread of Brancusian principles took further the "aesthetics of forms" universally known as *industrial design*. In this respect contemporary times remain indebted to such principles. [...]

To conclude I quote Brancusi's own words, who explained his artist attitude before creative work: "In all things there is purpose, which to be attained requires your getting free from you own self."

Lawyer and Philosopher Petre Pandrea

P. Pandrea, *Pravila de la Craiova* [Law Code of Craiova], Vremea Publishers, Bucharest, 2010, pp. 227-237

The language of Constantin Brancusi raises some highly complicated problem. He was French-Romanian in thinking and live speech. He knew German very well from a biographical segment lasting six years.

He never contented himself with habitual materials and canons in the sculptural art inherited from the three Fine Art schools that he attended conscientiously: the School of Crafts in Craiova, Bucharest and Paris. Actually in Paris he was expelled for *age limit*. [...]

Brancusi was *experimenter* until his old age and was concerned with the specific language of materials used in sculpture, as well as with the tongue of verbosity, where he was master. I believe the effervescence, change and utilization of materials with other canons is owed exclusively to his un-country going from Romania to France.

Emigration predestined him to revolution in sculpture.

Emigrants are unmistakable, uncomfortable; they despise canons and double or tenfold their inner forces as well as social energy. As I was saying before, Brancusi provides the case of un-countried, not of un-rooted person.

Emigrants frequently form among themselves commercial groups with specific life style, desires, melancholy and different norms in their value range.

Emigrants are forming compact energy groups with huge role, beyond the measure of their ranks.

Constantin Brancusi expatriated five times—in Hobita (until 12), in Craiova (a decade), in Bucharest (four years), he walked in Germanic countries, then in Paris (1904-1957).

These five biographical stages changed his language and his vision of life and of the world. Brancusi left his basic class, Oltenia-born peasantry with its judgment. It is only in Paris that he *deliberately* returned to the thinking and living manner of Gorj peasants, in order to protect himself against the satanic malefic environment. He would eat raw traditional food and read as the Bible the folklore volumes of G. Dem. Theodorescu and the proverbs of Iuliu Zane (ten volumes). During his Craiova decade he would be tradesman candidate (shop assistant) and skilled handicraftsman in repairing the local French style furniture of local people. His language is that of a tradesman and his *argot*—that of pub owners.

In Bucharest, he discovered cultivated German (Hoch Deutsch). Insistent mention should be made of this biographical stage. It was not something short-lived. He worked four years in the studio of his favorite professor, Vladimir Hegel. He attended also his courses. From 22 to 26 the apprentice's personality is effervescent and in the making. Professor Hegel also had one daughter.

Feverish love and long engagement, German style, lasting for years in order to let them know each other, check and devour one another. Erotic love was in place, just unlike the Romanians where love begins on wedding night. Those were the times. Costache Brancusi had been the fiancé and groom of Hegel's daughter four years. He acquired new language and life style. Style and language are decisive with artists.

Constantin Brancusi, as a *man*, was no *tragedy* character. This is what I have frequently expressed in writing and in speech. I saw him always as a dramatic character, an Ibsenian individual, a man of all great initiatives, of pathetic solitude and un-countried of the 19th century and the first half of my century, the 20th, which was so full of pathetism and sorrow, exacerbated class fights, wars and riots.

Naturally, appalling tragedies did occur during this epoch (his and mine).

Brancusi was not born for tragedy or for comedy. His vocation was for plenitude, harmony, construction and serenity. He lacked nothing to be balanced and happy. Illness, old age, destiny, poverty and two world wars were faced vigorously, energetically, a smile on his face, standing up like old gray fir trees with no fear, full of individual initiatives in his individualist life but harmonized to his fellow beings' up to synchronization, on the platform of the highest decency and stoic moral principles.

However, I have surprised the tragedy of language as effect of un-countried persons. The language is the serious issue of an artist. It is thought in words. Brancusi did no longer think in Romanian like he used to in the 1900s, before his departure from the country, but in German (prolonged engagement to the daughter of his professor and sculptor Vladimir Hegel). This tragedy of verbosity was misinterpreted by a series of his Romanian contemporaries. Words are not essential to the chisel handler, but neither negligible. We are few Romanians left who had known Brancusi and can bring authentic testimonies in this difficult problem of our countryman's language. […]

There is strange discord aroused between Brancusians and Brancusiologists. […]

It was Ionel Jianu who gave the tone, who introduced Brancusi as "Carpathian shepherd," a man lacking superior theoretical culture. Vasile G. Paleolog and partially Petru Comarnescu rallied to this thesis of genuine shepherd and rude peasant.

Jean Cassou resumed the incomprehensible idea of the "shepherd" from Carpathians. Jean Cassou wrote the foreword to Ionel Jianu's monograph. He did not visit and did not "prize" the "peasant," although he lived near him in Paris. I was and still am perplexed by this opinion discrepancy and true controversy.

I could not find this thesis of Brancusi's genial primitive "lack of culture" with Ezra Pound, nor with James Joyce, or with the avalanche of foreign commentators. His refined Western friends considered him their equal both in theoretical culture, in values and in multilateral information.

Professors D. Gusti (in his unknown personal diary) and G. Oprescu (youth and old age texts) are close to such thesis of the Carpathian uncultivated shepherd, with much reticence and many divagations. They did not "prize" him.

I confess that when I was in Paris and met Brancusi I thought him to be aesthetics professor and only rarely talked in our Oltenia sub-dialect or in cultivated Romanian. I noticed he expressed himself difficultly in his mother tongue, with by-passes and blunders. I quickly turned to French, language I could speak pretty well since 11 years of age from monsieur Pierre Grimm, with intense readings in this language until I was 24, plus conversation for three years in Bucharest, in a Romanian family turned French.

To my surprise Brancusi understood perfectly German and could speak it easily. I had come from the University of Berlin. […] I attended there aesthetic courses of Max Dessoir, Arthur Liebert and of the existentialist Catholic monk Romano Guardini. Our first talks were on aesthetics. We ceased speaking in Romanian but in French and German. In 10 years, popular or cultivated Romanian covered only 20% in our meetings, with long disputes.

Vasile G. Paleolog, Petru Comarnescu, Ionel Jianu, G. Oprescu and D. Gusti talked to Brancusi exclusively in Romanian. These intellectuals coined Brancusi, *volens nolens* as totally uncultivated Oltenia-born, a Carpathian shepherd with mentality of stable boy and fair seller (V.G. Paleolog's thesis). This is their dilemma, not mine, Peter Neagoe's, Erik Satie's or Guillaume Apollinaire's. This is how I explain the differences in the interpretation and presentation of the fore-mentioned Romanian exegetes that deprecate him utterly unfair and groundlessly.

Vasile G. Paleolog, P. Comarnescu and Ionel Jianu have got idolatry for Brancusi's work. Idolatry, admiration and ecstasy are not enough. One still needs lucid rational knowledge, disputing and un-tangling the intricate threads of Brancusi's biography full of contradictions and social class clashes, inner doubts and intimate decisions, followed tenaciously among ruins and disasters.

[…] In French with his language, Constantin Brancusi could have rivaled, in my opinion, Nicolae Titulescu, another highly national Franco-Romanian. In aesthetic issues sculptor Brancusi could have stood Titu Maiorescu, but in French not in Romanian. I witnessed the same kind of dialogue with Maiorescu's German exposure and Brancusi's French reply.

***

P. Pandrea, *Brancusi. Amintiri si exegeze* [Brancusi. Memories and exegeses], Meridiane Publishers, Bucharest, 1967, pp. 104-106

Brancusi arrived in New York at the same time with the World Fair, May-June 1939, without exhibiting in the national Gusti—Doicescu pavilion but to the Museum of Modern Art. He brought there the *Seal*, which he caressed like a beloved woman, the *Fish*, and borrowed a version of *Miss Pogany* from a private collection of Chicago.

Romanian officials attempted to set things right. Octav Doicescu and Maria Tanase were in the group, and the latter had not yet her final dispute with D. Gusti.

Dimitrie Gusti also invited Brancusi to the solemn exhibition opening by the American officials in order to point out his belonging to a small people from south-east Europe. It was propaganda. The professor attempted reconciling at any cost.

Brancusi agreed to come to the official opening of Romania's Pavilion, detaching himself from his habitual circle of Franco-American friends from the Museum of Modern Art in New York. Among his friends were Bourdelle's son (specializing in decorative art) and Pierre Matisse, the painter's son, tradesman of paintings on 57 in Fifth Avenues (Madison).

At the opening besides Eleanor Roosevelt, wife of the US President, were also diplomats and officials with top hats, the same as the Romanians, including architect Octav Doicescu, pavilion designer.

Constantin Brancusi came wearing light gray overcoat and felt hat, usually worn by painters and artists. They did not take him amiss, although it was *shocking* at such solemn gathering of diplomats and dignitaries.

When collation began Brancusi took Doicescu's arm and invited him to lunch in the English pavilion: "Do not climb up too high on the ladder. There are plenty of places downstairs, to the bottom. Just a few reach to the top and they are quickly overthrown. Life is down here, on earth." Octav Doicescu replied with some Persian proverb:

One should treat kings, emperors and officials like fire. Too close, one gets burned. Too far, one is freezing.

Very well!

When they arrived in the restaurant of the English pavilion, surrounded by a lawn, the British had nonchalantly thrown their top hats on the grass.

Brancusi threw away his felt hat on the lawn, took off leisurely his light gray overcoat and folded it near the hat. All his other clothes were of the official gentleman's. The felt instead of top hat and the overcoat were just a trick. Doicescu had given up the official lunch, thinking the sculptor could not participate because of his attire. He had the costume. He had hidden it away. Was it practical joking or neglect from Brancusi? Doicescu considered him joker and playful, one side of his character.

Together with Suzana and Octav Doicescu and a few Americans and Frenchmen he began wandering each evening in the "pubs" of New York, small picturesque night clubs in Parisian style.

Architect Octav Doicescu

O. Doicescu, *Brancusi sau arhitectul* [Brancusi or the architect], Brancusi Colloquium, Bucharest, 13-15 October 1967

Brancusi—architect? What can best express Brancusi as ideal architect than the American offers of his time, after the great exhibition of the "Armory Show," which I partially attended, to have the shapes of his sculpture enlarged and developed in view of their construction in the great Central Park of New York; is this not significant gesture for the intuition of the American collective when faced with the time viability and formal validity of Brancusian structures? Near Frank Lloyd Wright, close to Philip Johnson or Mies van der Rohe the American citizen felt the need for the essential structure, total personalization for the architectural clerk.

It means functional rational, thus functional entirely opposing it with human value. And nowadays the sculptural architecture of the opera house in Sydney, of the church built by Lindon in California, of Corbusier's Ronchamp should justify their functional-aesthetic existence with the entire round-shaping system of plastic structures from Brancusi's sculpture. As a matter of fact, Brancusi phenomenon appears essential in the chapter on syntheses and inter-penetration of arts in modern times, like some nodal point wherefrom all existing domains of aesthetics originate and focus.

If *Miss Pogany* represents "fairy grandmother" for abstract sculpture as sculptor Jean Arp was saying, the entire Brancusian system configuring shapes in space can signify all the modern architecture to "ideal" Architecture; I think of that architecture going toward functionalism at human scale supervising the whole Man accommodation in the formal space, idea targeted and only partially achieved by the few true genial architects of our time.

After all, what are Brancusi's sculptures containing? Before all the formal possibilities of plastic expression enabled by our epoch, Brancusi appears today as key backbone for all essential milestones of modern architecture: he brings the symmetrical axis and its balance, in sculpture, as essence of his concerns in a space representing quintessence between the functional space based on cavities of the architect and the nonfunctional one, based on fullness of the sculptor. The new formal structure brought by Brancusi into his sculpture is also generated by extraordinary tri-dimensional mastery over matter, which thus designs the Brancusian ensemble of empty-full, along the most daring trajectories possible which, exceeding the limited statics, will be launched toward absolute unlimited beauty.

Academician George Oprescu

G. Oprescu, *Constantin Brancusi*, in *Amintiri. Evocari* [Memories. Evocations], Literature Publishers, Bucharest, 1968, pp. 83-94.

Since my first visit I have only seen him once more together with Steriadi, his good friend, in the autumn of 1937, in the studio of 11, Impasse Ronsin. The huge wood girders of old days were no more there, Brancusi was then concerned with stone sculpture and polished metal. Such pieces were installed on mobile platforms and turned before us. This mode of presentation quite surprised me but not so good, as it reminded me the women hairdressers' windows in Paris. The *Torso of Young Man*, *Adam and Eve*, some variants of the *Cock*, *Chief*, *Socrates*, as well as the bizarre statues representing the *Sorceress*, *Chimera*, all of wood, which had been made previously, were in the museums or somewhere in the studio, in the shadow.

We ate the food prepared by the artist, as he always did when he received and talked about what we saw, which lasted at least two hours. What stroke me again in Brancusi's personality and had left unforgettable memories from our first meeting was the rustic nobility of his figure, his supple accurate body movements, which had remained strong and youthful. In time, his hair, somewhat hirsute, although his beard was more orderly, showed plenty of white hairs framing the cheeks that seemed carved in ivory. His singularly distinct traits resulted from his almost ascetic life and meditation all day long; since there is no chisel cut into stone or wood which was not well pondered beforehand. His speech was calm, clear, long-devised, the same way our old peasants did. That night seemed to have gathered around him the serenity of an artist that eventually reached to the supreme truth in art.

Regardless whether one agrees with that truth or not you can feel the solemnity of the moment worth recalling. During the calm conversation the artist suddenly turned passionate and violent: "Michelangelo is all flesh," declared he, understanding by it the constant concern of the great Florentine artist for exactness of anatomic muscles. This unexpected description uttered with a bit of spite, even disregard, impressed me, naturally, in bad manner. However, on better judgment it made me think later. Whoever dared speak like this about one of the world's greatest geniuses should feel capable to replace the "flesh" with something equally important for art development, but new and different.

And indeed Brancusi could issue this claim in that particular moment, when most of his work in marble, wood and bronze had been done. As a matter of fact flesh was not always shown in sculpture; it occurred from Renaissance onward. In the case of ancient civilized peoples creating art, like Egyptians for instance, flesh was not present and neither with primitive peoples nor in the popular art anywhere. But as regards the popular art of Brancusi's country of origin, the sculptor was nurtured with it in his childhood and teens; he knew all its implications. It was then only natural for the author of the *Wisdom of the Earth*, of the *Endless Column* and of the *Maiastra* to see the future of sculpture in that direction.

A great part of his inspiration originated in such popular art, as deep sentiment. We have to take into account his attitude toward such topics and toward the materials and execution procedures of the people for hundreds of years in order to understand the profound motives of Brancusi's art. And since we cannot speak about the anonymous artists' absence of sincerity in those peoples that practiced such art, the same way we cannot question Brancusi's sincerity. We can admire or not his art. It is not didactical but intellectual in the first place.

But his example, his beautiful honest life of creative artist is determining and we should be convinced this is the only way to make serious art, able to interest our generation and the future ones, only by absolute sincerity, daily uninterrupted labor, understanding the material we use, the same way true scientists proceed by identifying themselves with the noble aspirations of our time.

Academician Henri Coanda

V. Firoiu, *Din nou acasa… Convorbiri cu Henri Coanda* [Home again… Speaking with Henri Coanda], Tineretului Publishers, Bucharest, 1969, pp. 145-147, 226-229.

However one cannot speak about Rodin, in universality, without a stop for Brancusi.

We attempt only one question:

- **Have you also met Brancusi in person?**
- Brancusi was a great man and genial artist. I became Brancusi's friend in no time drawn by his art, his charm as a person. A good affectionate man he was, great romantic beyond his serious mask hidden in the thick wild beard, beyond his sudden sometimes even rigid gestures, even restrained, too little understood.

But one did not have to understand Brancusi; it was much simpler and easier to perceive him; Brancusi was giving himself to you, he became truly yours, entirely, no restraints, so that in your turn you could remain near him, something of your living soul was kept there for good, unwillingly, without escape in his Montparnasse studio, close to that good playful child that he was, Brancusi.

Personally, I was drawn to Brancusi because he was a sculptor and Romanian; when he found I was also born in Oltenia region, his face flared up, this time with glee across his entire visage and beard and, without being able to refrain his joy according to his nature that could not hide his anger either when it burst, issued:

- Good heavens, bless you, well then, we are one of a kind, are you also Oltenia-born?—Because for Brancusi, strange coincidence, precisely like my own father, although of entirely different culture, training, temperament and education, being born in Oltenia was no regionalism but true nationality. It was our moment of total understanding.

This was the entrance gate, Oltenia style but which made Brancusi's nature glitter the gems of genius, the door to solid friendship that put us together for good, regardless where life and time took us, his clay or my propeller-free wings, a path that never ended no matter how busy I was with my tests in the world of metallic birds, no matter how deep Brancusi sank in his thinking universe including his "Maiastra."

Because, you know—told us engineer Coanda—his sculpture was, as I could also grasp and learn from him and from Rodin, nothing else but philosophy rendered in relief shapes, plunged into clay and gypsum, carved in stone, with outlines true to his cerebral output, some philosophy initiated in clay and completed in stone, the same way it was then offered to humanity, to posterity…

I loved Brancusi—continued my collocutor in a low tone as if he unwounded his memories using cello strings not words, from deep down inside—I loved Brancusi because I understood him. I defined his substance and thus I could cherish it, because he was really what one calls *creator*. He did not imitate and then, consciously or unwillingly by mere inhibition, the way even great artists make mistakes unknowingly and still human and art history retained them, you could perceive Brancusi and he explained himself first of all for his own person, from the very raw material.

You should better understand when I say raw material since the drawing, the clay stayed in the after-plan for Brancusi, as raw material is the thinking where his great creation, authentic and personal, originates.

Speaking of Rodin, I should think of Brancusi; you see in my mind the two of them are inextricably linked, the same way when halting for Brancusi we cannot overlook Rodin.

Like Brancusi I was Rodin's student, his apprentice, the same Rodin who was engulfed by eternity while still alive. Rodin accepted me in his studio, he even considered me his talented student and perhaps I had some of these features or otherwise he would not have got me. Especially that I went to him with nobody's recommendation, with no credentials from any great person of the day but only guided by my faith in beauty and by the sculpture as I understood it then.

Once drawn to this language, as beautiful as that of technique, as large as mathematics, sculpture was a passion to me, if you wish even the accomplishment of vocation. They said I had the talent and skill, and what more is, that I had the *eye* and even the *hand*, attributes and organs of absolute necessity.

I began working with this titan whom not only then, at my beginning but also nowadays with the experience I have gathered in more than half century, I ascribe to the same huge gigantic geometry, considering him a sort of Michelangelo if one needs some artistic comparative gauge.

Well then, I appreciate our Brancusi for his kind of thinking and for the manner in which he rendered such thought, carving it into eternity in his own way, his proper universal mode, more dimensioned than Rodin's, that great Rodin.

And since we still speak sculpture, of Rodin and of Brancusi, let me remind you a cherished disciple of Rodin was a Romanian sculptor, Ion Jalea, student of Bourdelle.

***

- **You have spoken about Brancusi, about your friendship with this titan of art, as you have also mentioned Rodin, great immortal Rodin. Perhaps from your many memories you could share a few with us now, some less known…**
- I have met Brancusi through Rodin. When Brancusi appeared on the threshold of Rodin's studio, I was already a student of the "great Frenchman," as we disciples called him and his friends liked calling also.

Therefore I was old recruit; Brancusi was the freshman with Rodin. But of course our common nationality was the first bridge drawing us close, although deep down inside our friendship emerged from the very beginning based *on our identity of interests, which was then sculpture.* Everything else remained in the detail, mere particulars along the way. It was not the deep thinking of the Gorj born fellow, his honesty, his disinterest in worldly things, which he could not care less for but satisfied in order to observe some minimum self-support (giving what he had to the people around more than he kept for himself) that maintained and grounded our amicable relationships, but art in the first place.

Yes indeed, it was what consolidated and preserved our friendship.

When I realized I could not keep up with Brancusi, when I understood that, beyond Brancusi's personal worth was his true class that I could not reach or attain, nor aspire to because sculpture meant for me only fulfilling my yearning (however a strong one, you know, it mastered me!) while being everything to Brancusi; that technique, scientific research was for me what sculpture was to him: the *reason of one's life*, then I decided to let the brain work willingly in the domain of my scientific creation. I was practicing some imaginative sculpture, more or less faithful to the surrounding world while he, Brancusi, was making conceived matter and provided relief for thought.

And then, not without pain—oh yes, how much I had to struggle to be able to detach myself from that place, from the studio, from the world of sculpture, then to get acquainted with the idea of giving up—so I simply ran away from Brancusi in order to remain myself, to become Henri Coanda in aerodynamics and scientific research, in my positive art…

Naturally I remained a friend to Brancusi, that savage man with a heart of gold and gaze that replaced speech, which smiled the same way it grumbled, yes Brancusi's eyes were grumbling precisely because I stopped sculpting, I did no longer work with him.

Such friendship knew no disputes, no fluctuations of the sentiment, or disagreements. Oh no, with Brancusi I stayed *friend, he a brother to me and I to him*, regardless who was around, no matter what happened in the world or closer to us, near us, among our ranks even. And this because I understood Brancusi and that was *enough*, and he, Brancusi could perceive me, and that was *everything…*

But if you stirred me to re-live those times so precious to me, like a man who departed voluntarily from a beloved world to further love it, I am going to tell you now things too little known of the Rodin—Brancusi relationship, which I recorded mentally more than half century ago but I kept in my memory because I witnessed them, being the only eye and ear witness of such moments, which I lived with the intensity of the person who loved them both, Rodin and Brancusi.

"Go cut your hair," Rodin told Brancusi one day, as he was frequently scolding him, quite ruthlessly sometimes, because Brancusi was so careless about his clothes and his own person; other times Rodin was quite insistently inquiring, with true compassion, whether this peculiar morose Romanian was feeding or sleeping enough!

"You will be deprived of the stamina you need, then wherefrom can you get the energy for the sculptures, what are you going to put in them from you?" tried Rodin to stimulate him, to detach Brancusi from the harsh difficult life, to make him less self-indifferent to the primary needs of his physical existence.

At the beginning Brancusi did not answer. He had no response. He was totally absent from what Rodin was saying. He was feigning not to hear or, truly, he did not understand Rodin was addressing him, but rather thought Rodin spoke for somebody else from among those in the studio.

But one day, the Gorj native stiffened; he listened that indeed Rodin was talking to him, that all those speeches were for him. He answered briefly, curtly, so briefly that he said everything: "I will put what I think in my sculptures; it will be no food or shelter, in any way."

And that ended one more chapter in the Rodin—Brancusi coexistence, since neither Rodin ever talked to Brancusi again about his obligations to his own person nor Brancusi mentioned any longer about the thinking he was carving for posterity, "for whoever he knew he should."

...In the studio, I used to ask explanations from Rodin. He naturally provided it to me, the same way he watched me in silence over my shoulder, almost without my notice and from time to time added some guidance: "Here you should consult with Brancusi. He can indicate a better solution for what you are trying to do, he will show you the best way."

It was not his manner of getting rid of me, of...annihilating me, comfortably and honorably as I thought at first; oh no, he was entirely right. He spoke in the earnest, openly. He really wanted to assist me finding the most appropriate solution for my abilities, my way of thinking back then. He knew that Brancusi could find the solution for me, because in a certain manner and to a certain extent my thinking was closer to Brancusi's than to Rodin's.

And I also knew he sent me to Brancusi because he cherished him in all honesty for his manner of thinking, for his solutions, for his being a master in the world that united and yet separated them: sculpture.

"I am no longer going to the Frenchman," Brancusi told me one day. I thought he was having a fit of anger, those times when the Gorj native forgot everything—sculpture and people alike in order to sort out some confrontation, some imaginary offense, to stay alone with his own self, Brancusi.

Quite amused I asked him:

– Well, what has he done to you?

– Nothing, he has done nothing, he answered in earnest, but I do feel he is doing something without doing it, everyday something, every moment.

Again I told myself this was one of those times when Brancusi talked to himself, for his own self, a day for him to make his accounts out loud, thus revealing troubled waters inside.

It was Brancusi that went on:

– I feel that, as great as he is, all-powerful, he alone master of his art, Rodin is creeping insidiously in me and I will begin thinking through him as well. Well, I do not want it! My sculpture is mine and it springs from here, and Brancusi pointed his head, it comes out of me, and Brancusi put his hand to his chest. The moment I am incapable to do what I see in my mind, but in my own mind, what I feel inside then sculpture will no longer be mine but only his, the one who provided the thinking!

He was speaking serenely, even calmly, with lucidity originating in his reason, but such calm was usually missing from Brancusi.

Well, added engineer Henri Coanda, in this brief stop over the memorized world of sculpture, it is precisely that moment I deem the great Brancusian moment, the crossroad in the artistic life of the one who would become and stay Brancusi in universality.

Art Historian Petru Comarnescu

P. Comarnescu, *Om, natura si Dumnezeu in plastica romaneasca* [Man, nature and God in Romanian fine art], Revista Fundatiilor Regale, Bucharest, 1943, **X**, *1*, 1 January, pp.129-139

To many ignorant people Brancusi is revolutionary still nowadays, far from any tradition. The truth is his sculptural abstraction expresses the Romanians' ancient relation with the stones and rocks, which provide shapes imposed by geological fatality not by man. His contempt for nudes and portraits and, in general, for concrete human shape is in the Grecian Orthodox style, which forbids carved idols and especially humans' idolatry for humans. Concurring natural force and beauty Brancusi harmonized with nature, animating it partly and partially allowing him to be animated by it.

He does nothing else but grinding the stone the same way winds, water and centuries grind it and often times provide perfect forms, suggestive geometries, sensual surfaces, objects we cannot say whether they result from nature or from human activities, the same with the strange object arousing the dialectics of Valéry's dialogue *Eupalinos*. And when he is working in wood the sculptor follows its fiber and dryness the same way with the roadside crucifixes of his native Oltenia region. With metal, he would caress surfaces even better and would achieve geometrical perfection since, next to the peasant, the artisan wakes up in Brancusi, the Romanian handicraftsman so skilled at such technique that does not confront nature but follows its suggestions and procedures. [...]

We have shown here almost without intending it the story of cultivated Romanian art, depending on the trend of ancient popular and Church art in stylizing, with the entire animation and life, found both in them and in the artist himself, the objects and apparitions of nature that our people harmonized with, sometimes submitting to it in Christian manner and other times following its procedures and skills in almost magic mode. The old trends of Romanian popular art found the natural way due to Europe in the 19th century of the landscape. But it was Europe that was itself turning to the same sources which Romanians had lived so far with, and which it was about to forget.

***

P. Comarnescu, *Brancusi. Mit si metamorfoza in sculptura contemporana* [Brancusi. Myth and metamorphosis in contemporary sculpture], Meridiane Publishers, Bucharest, 1972, p. 61

The data about his first experiences are quite vague because he also deprived them of importance. Brancusi liked to narrate, both in the country and in Paris, his life happenings, but usually only those of significance or at least funny. When he talked, he did not speak like a historian providing accurate data, but he dealt with biographical details in legendary mode as bits and fragments from his trials and suffering, which he overcame manly but not without scars. He did not want to remember some more difficult episodes or unpleasant experiences. This explains the difficulty in determining accurate chronology for some stages and facts in his life.

Art Collector Aimé Maeght

T. Balaj, *Autografe pariziene* [Parisian Autographs], Dacia Publishers, Cluj-Napoca, 1972, pp. 34-38

Besides the pieces from the National Modern Art Museum of Paris, France still keeps Brancusi's work also in the prestigious collection of Saint-Paul-de-Vence. The director of this foundation is the well-known art collector, Aimé Maeght.

First time I have met Brancusi a few years after France's liberation—confesses Mr. Maeght. Writer Henri-Pierre Roché, an old friend of the sculptor, took me to his studio of Impasse Ronsin, behind the Montparnasse. Brancusi looked like a patriarch of this city of artists, which has kept for decades its legendary picturesque. The sculptor's studio was itself a true work of art. Brancusi's work, Reconstitution, which can now be seen in the Modern Art Museum, is only a pale image of that fabulous amazing studio where all pieces of furniture and all objects bore the mark of the sculptor's dominating personality.

Brancusi invited us to lunch and had it no other way than to prepare alone the meal.

It was long that I had greatly admired the work of Brancusi. He was to me the only sculptor that managed to stylize and purify the form, to free it from outer appearances without becoming decorative.

Ever since that first meeting, I have understood the secret of his success: what I look for, said Brancusi, is liberty in the first place. By freeing matter from the contortions of fixed forms, beauty reveals itself profusely.

The pride he was so often reproached of was nothing else but the honest expression of his spiritual independence.

His fight against academism? He could not care less.

The only adversary worthy of clarification was to him people's lack of understanding, their short-sightedness in art.

When I asked him why he sometimes gave the impression he was uncommunicative and short-tempered, he answered his irritation was directed only against himself and his own powerlessness.

Besides simplicity, this anxiety haunting him was one of the essential features of his character. He had the simplicity of a wise peasant and mature artisan, the simplicity of intelligence and candor. He confessed needing no exterior means to destroy inside him what culture and excessive civilization sterilized in art. He had remained close to his childhood and his country, keeping intact the gift of freedom and of the candid bewilderment before the world.

I saw Brancusi several times afterwards, especially when once he exhibited one of his masterpieces in my gallery, a *Caryatid*. He has always given me the same pleasure and admiration.

Truly he was a man and artist one of a kind. A great personality that seemed to have descended to us directly from the simple ceremony of his high flights, in order to generously share with us the charms and magic of a world whose secrets he alone knew first...

- **Have you known Romania outside Brancusi?**
- No. Or better said, not...yet. Brancusi however is enough, I believe, to truly draw near his country and to sincerely respect Romania and the Romanians.

Engineer Stefan Georgescu-Gorjan

S. Georgescu-Gorjan, *Amintiri despre Brancusi* [Memories about Brancusi], in *Marturii despre Brancusi* [Testimonies about Brancusi], Targu-Jiu, 1975, pp. 25-35

I have met Brancusi since I was a child, back in 1914-1915, then in 1922 in Craiova. In 1934 and 1937 I visited him in Paris. [...]

One morning in December 1934 I was excited to step into the courtyard packed with artists' studios in 11, Impasse Ronsin in the Montparnasse, the district of Parisian bohemian environment. Someone directed me to the big tall studio. I had shyly pulled the cord of the bell; a short clear joyful tinkling followed and a man with smoky beard, intensely spotted by tobacco stains, appeared in the doorframe. I had not seen Constantin Brancusi since I was a teenager, back in 1922; after a few words he remembered me and in a happy mood invited me in the studio.

When the artist joined me inside the studio I could not conceal my amazement and emotion. His work cannot be completely perceived but in ensemble and in its creation place, in the studio where each stone slab, piece of metal or wood girder suffered slow and uninterrupted transformation.

Overwhelmed with the multitude of impressions I was like numb. I needed some time to recollect so that, out of the throng of sensations and emotions I could express thoughts, judgment, or questions. Brancusi realized what happened and left me look without talking for a long time, then he introduced me the house. The furniture was simple, peasant-like, artistically manufactured by him. A corner was well equipped with sculptor and artisan tools. His sleeping place was an aerial platform over whose banister a velvet cloth was carelessly thrown, making folds. Round tables were there of rough stone. A hearth, a pot, a small stove could be found as well. The famous gramophone with acoustic corn was his own construction, which would play its part on the evening of 7 January 1935, on the occasion of some reunion.

At lunch time, he invited me to the restaurant, apologizing for being unable to treat me with food prepared by him—according to his habit—because it was meatless day. At the restaurant, where he often lunched when the butcher boy did not bring him meat a surprise was prepared for me: he had booked snails for some time and the owner had kept them under a glass cover with holes. Such boiled snails could have been hard to swallow without the vinegar sauce with finely chopped parsley—according to Brancusi's recipe—and without the proper accompanying wine. The sculptor liked this recipe greatly.

When we parted, Brancusi apologized he could not retain me in the afternoon, but he invited me some other time and set himself the date: "Come on 7 January, we shall be together all day long…"

[…] At 10:00 h it was warm in his studio. In the most intimate corner, the inhabited one, barely separated from the studio the celebration took place. I have written before about it in the press and provided our detailed conversation.

Of all Brancusi's creations, the only ones that have reached their final form after few attempts were the "Endless Column" and the "Cock," both resounding deeply in Romanian popular art. Speaking with the artist about the endless column he explained why it cannot have either pedestal or capital, like ancient columns. It has no beginning and no end. The repetition of the identical element of the column provides it, by mathematical analogy, with the same character of certain curves—for instance, those representing trigonometric functions to enable their repetition and extension to both infinite directions. Two opposing sinusoids drawn around a vertical axis have a familiar aspect like the figure of the endless column and represent the strictly mathematical justification of the name Brancusi gave to this sculpture.

When the artist had spoken about sculpture he addressed his second preferred topic—music. With the gramophone he manufactured, provided with special acoustic box and other tailored devices, he made a demonstration of exotic folk music from the Pacific islands, then with Romanian music. The sound effects obtained by changing the normal rhythm of the song, while also changing the speed while the disk was turning constituted extraordinary surprise to me. This musical game lasted for several hours. It ended with a dedication for me, on the first page of the 1926 catalogue of his exhibition at the Brummer Gallery.

Before leaving discussions turned again to the Endless Column, the one the artist was hoping to build in the country. We discussed the modes of achievement of a large-scale *Column*, on which occasion I told him how to solve various constructive issues in technical terms. Highly interested the artist asked me whether I could cooperate with him in building the *Endless Column* of Targu-Jiu. My affirmative answer marked the beginning of our future working cooperation of 1937-1938. […]

We met in Targu-Jiu around 25 July 1937. The artist invited me to walk together on the road of the Jiu River bank, through the public garden on the Heroes' Road up to the Hay Fair, a market where the Endless Column would stand. Great hay stacks were found in that place. We have taken on film the image of the location. The next day in Petrosani, the quickly developed and copied cliché provided us with a small photo, which would constitute the only original sketch of the Endless Column from Targu-Jiu, drawn by the master's hand. The evening I brought the photograph of the Hay Fair from the photo studio into my home on 2, Closca Street, Petrosani, where he stayed for more than a month, Brancusi asked for a pen and sketched in a few moments in ink, with straight lines, the figure of the column in the middle of a round plot, the circular road and its branches.

The endless column of the sketch is shorter than reality with fewer elements, because I had informed him, cautiously, it could not be more than 25 m high. Reaching actually to almost 30 m constituted later a pleasant surprise for the artist. The technical problem raised by the big size column was the agreement of the central metallic core section with the maximum possible height, needed by strength considerations. Once such height settled, the artist was to verify the concord of the element proportions with the resulting height. Unlike habitual metallic structures where the basic section is bigger than the upper one, Brancusi's column with the resistance element in the central steel core of uniform square section provides the disadvantage of having the same section at the base, where the bending hazard is greatest and the top section narrower than the most limited exterior part of the element. […]

The sculptor wanted this fine slender column like its wood model to provide the impression it springs from the earth, from the grass like a stem; I could satisfy his desire by strong underground base embedded in a massive foundation concrete block, calculated to stand the worst upturning strain.

Professor Vasile Blendea

V. Blendea, *Amintiri despre Brancusi* [Memories about Brancusi], in *Marturii despre Brancusi* [Testimonies about Brancusi], Targu-Jiu, 1975, pp. 53-64

In 1905, according to his own confession [Brancusi] had finally settled in Paris. His hard destitute life of serious study in the Capital City of France (at the beginning only with the 25 FF that Doctor Gerota sent him each month) detached him from his family; he did not write so often home and went there even less. His concern for his mother and younger brothers did not end, which can be proved by some of his letters. What did he do in order to live? He washed glasses in a restaurant, swept the Orthodox Church in Paris or sang in the same church. He spoke often of these times but preferred to point out their funny sides.

He did not forget his friends and informed himself about the artistic life in the country. He frequently sent his sculptures to the exhibitions of the Official Salon or of the Artistic Youth. He had friends and admirers but however official people were indifferent to his art. Writers like Tudor Arghezi or Professor Mihail Dragomirescu wrote enthusiastically about the young sculptor in the exhibition chronicles. But most chroniclers ignored or disapproved him. Vlahuta himself showed very little understanding in an article published about the *Wisdom of the Earth* that Brancusi sent for the exhibition in Bucharest.

World War I separated him from his family and country for a while. His mother died in the meantime. Thus his strongest link with the family was broken.

After the war, he came to the country in two consecutive years, 1921 and 1922.

Ioana Brancusi remembered his first visit. She was grazing the cattle in the common and returning home they told her their uncle of Paris was expected, but she was ashamed she was barefoot.

"We-e-ell! Grigore has one more girl!" were the sculptor's words seeing her.

At that time there was a difficult problem in the house of Grigore. His youngest daughter, Ioana, after 1-2 primary school classes was retained home as her father wanted to "liberate" her from school the same way he did for his two older daughters. However, the school wanted her back and they had just received the written summons. The sculptor told the girl: "Niece, you should go to school and if my brother Grigore does not want to let you study further, I will do it!" With such intervention, things were settled. Her father ceased opposing, Ioana went to school and graduated it, then continued in high school and never forgot her uncle's words.

In 1922, Brancusi came to Romania with the beautiful Irish girl Eileen Lane. He took her in his village and in the house of his brothers and relatives. They stayed in Pestisani at a friend's, well-to-do who placed at their disposal some minimum comfort, in the center of the village. He stayed for a longer time there, visited the surroundings, watched the peasant dances, and talked to the villagers. His relatives and acquaintances gave the young lady national costumes, objects made by their own hands, which the foreigner appreciated highly. Brancusi told his relatives she was the daughter of a foreign noble person who wanted to know his country. The brothers took this explanation for granted but in their heart they thought she was his fiancée.

When he came to the village he talked with many peasants. He knew all those of his age: he had played with them; they had bathed in the Bistrita River and together went with cattle in the Gorj Mountains. But many of his former playmates were no longer there—they died in the war. This should have impressed him greatly. The villagers were speaking of a monument to their memory in the village. Such monuments were built in other villages as well at that time.

Brancusi told them: "I'll come do it. Just provide the necessary material and I will come." In time the image of the dead soldiers faded away in the villagers' memory and they gave up the idea of the monument. But this idea remained in the heart of their former mates. And it was embodied 15 years later; not in their village but in the capital town of their county. The Column of infinite gratitude of Brancusi also comprised the icon of his childhood friends […]. And this shows what Brancusi had in his heart and who he thought of when he made the artistic group of Targu-Jiu […].

One episode though brought Brancusi back to the country in 1930, and almost every year afterwards.

I told you about his intervention for the younger daughter of his brother Grigore and the promise he made on that occasion.

Ioana Brancusi took her uncle's advice: she attended primary school in Pestisani then went up to high school. In 1930 she was in her graduation year of high school and her father shrugged his shoulders: "I cannot do more!" She thought of her uncle's promise and wanted to write him everything. But she did not know where to write. The sculptor had not written for a long time, and the scrap of paper with his address was lost.

She wrote me in Bucharest, where I was a student and asked me to find her uncle's address. I remembered I had read an article on Brancusi published by Mac Constantinescu in a Bucharest newspaper and retained the words: "When you go to him in Impasse Ronsin, he would ask: *are you a smoker?* And he gives you his tobacco purse." I thought the article could contain more than what I remembered about the sculptor's address. A colleague helped me, as he was working as night corrector with that newspaper. He brought me the old issue of the journal but, to my regret, there was nothing more. I told Ioana Brancusi everything I could find.

Doubting in her heart, she sent a letter to her uncle at "Impasse Ronsin, Paris." She told him how she took his advice, having graduated high school and could hope for no more help from her parents, but remembered his words, uttered years back. Although with incomplete address the letter reached the sculptor who hastily answered her. He congratulated her for graduating high school and notified in 15-20 days he hoped to be in the country.

At the beginning of September 1930, I prepared my departure to Bucharest to enlist in the following year of study.

One day I found out from some people who had been to Hobita that Brancusi had come to the village by car, fetched Ioana and left with her to Bucharest the same day.

When Ioana was preparing herself for the road, Brancusi went quickly to the coppice of Bistrita River up to the mill, seeing again the places of his childhood games.

After 10-15 days, a carriage stopped at the gate of the student hostel Stanescu of 5 Painter Grigorescu Street—where I lived—and my cousin Ioana came out of it. I barely recognized her! She was dressed in fine new clothes. "Come on, cousin, I came to take you to uncle, as he wants to meet you. I told him about you and he wants to meet you!" What an excitement! I went. He stayed at Boulevard Hotel, above the Academy Library nowadays. It was his free afternoon.

When I got in the room a rather short man with big beard and shiny eyes stood up. That is all I could see!—"Come here, I know you, I can remember you after the traits of your parents!" were his first words, getting near me with his arms stretched forward. He was a happy man, talked a lot, knew a lot and spoke about everything. It was only him that talked; I was numb.

After some time painter Camil Ressu came to him. This is how I met Camil Ressu. The two former colleagues remembered a great many things before us.

- Did you know I exhibited in Russia?
- What? And you could get out of there? answered Ressu half in earnest half-jokingly.
- Well, they exhibited only my sculptures! The Russians came and took everything they could find in my studio.

At this first meeting Brancusi told me: "What could I do? I came here because I owed it to her, I promised it and niece reminded me."

Then he told me what he wanted his niece to study and how she was supposed to live. He wanted her to have a career and be independent from the bourgeois state. He would have liked medical studies. "I want her to be happy. I could endure in joy! Misery was terrible…but I glided onto it being joyful; I was happy and loved life," shared he from his life. Then thinking of the past: "I would like my niece to have the kind of life I wanted to have!"

He enlisted her to college and took her lodging at Milita Petrascu's, his former student of Paris then he saw his friends who celebrated him and also Doctor Gerota and afterwards he went back to France, wherefrom he only dispatched telegrams and regularly sent 6,000 Lei each month. […]

Some people said Brancusi was tight-fisted, a hint about his original life style in Paris. But I told you how he provided for his niece so I do not believe it befits him. Perhaps what someone said at his funeral is more appropriate: he was moderate with his money, the same way his brothers were and our peasants are, in general.

During my talks with Brancusi, he told me about the Bucharest atmosphere with respect to his art and how many hardships he had to confront. "When I went to Vienna I participated to an exhibition, displaying a few pieces. It was on the first floor. My art was not wanted so I do not know how I managed to sell one statue. A lady purchased it. I cannot even tell how I managed to run quickly down the stairs, for fear the buyer would change her mind!"

"In 1905, I settled in Paris," he told me and added, lifting up a finger with pride: "But I still am Romanian citizen!" And his greater shine of the eyes pointed out the pride of this utterance.

He did not expect anything from the country, but he did not forget it. All Romanians passing through Paris know it. [...]

Ever since he took upon himself the support of his brother's daughter he came often to the country, being happy to come. He confessed how satisfied he was when she called him "papa." Some of his friends and admirers noticed he was coming more often to the country and he said: "You should thank my niece for it!"

[...] Brancusi came to the country for the last time in 1940. It was the year when his younger sister, Eufrosina, brought up by his widow mother, herself a widow of WWI, married her daughter and Brancusi gave her 10,000 Lei as dowry.

However, the next war broke Brancusi's links with his country and his niece whom nevertheless he did not forget.

In his last years, he was ailing and stubbornly attempted to overcome the body's incapacity brought about by an accident. In the last days, bad people embittered him even more as they crawled near him and whispered news allegedly about his niece's ingratitude, when he so benevolently helped her. All the letters she sent him were hidden and never reached Brancusi. To this, the French authorities' misunderstanding added, as they always postponed Ioana Brancusi's many applications to go to Paris to look after Brancusi who was ill. It seems they were afraid the niece could have convinced her uncle to come to the country.

Stonecutter Ion Alexandrescu

I. Alexandrescu, *Cu Brancusi la Targu-Jiu* [With Brancusi in Targu-Jiu], in *Omagiu 100 Brancusi* [Homage 100 Brancusi], Targu-Jiu, 1976, pp. 10-13

One day about nine o'clock I came to the hotel together with engineer Doppelraiter, delegated with payments. I had met him in 1937 in Targu-Jiu, for a short while; he was with the stonecutters in the park, where they were saw-cutting the stone and carved it; he was among the workers as everybody expedited the work to the *Heroes' Gate* and the *Endless Column* (or the

"Endless Glory Column" as it was called back then), which engineer Georgescu-Gorjan was dealing with: he was around 35 then. There was a team from Deva "Pietroasa Company" for the stone operations.

The planned work, the *Endless Column* and the *Heroes' Gate* should have been finished by the autumn of 1937 and the remaining stone pieces: the *Table of Silence* (or the family), the chairs, benches and the *Gate* sculpture were scheduled for 1938.

In the spring of 1938, more precisely in May, architect Giurgea recommended me to the Master in Gheorghe Tatarescu's house of Polona Street from Bucharest, where I was working then.

After some professional recommendation and discussion about what I was supposed to do in Targu-Jiu, and after another half hour's talk among themselves the architect came to me and said: leave your work here, take your tools and go with Mr. Brancusi to Targu-Jiu, since you and Bucharest have nothing in common, you are alone and would stay at his disposal as long as he needs you and you will return when you finish; master Boitan will assign two more cutters so you can finish faster.

I was 27 back then and a stone sculptor; perhaps the Master liked me from the beginning because he told me: "Tomorrow you come here again to take an envelope you have to deliver to the address on it (Eng. architect Doppelraiter Iulius) when you get there, and in one or two days, I will also come together with the master for *Column* metal-coating."

I went to Targu-Jiu after two days together with the two cutters. I found the engineer easily since everyone knew him and delivered him the envelope, the contents of which I ignored. Reading it he told me separately: "You and the other two cutters will be accommodated to the White Lamb where you will also eat, and Master Brancusi will stay at the Royal Hotel, which is near the park; you will liaise between us and masters Di Bernando, Gheorghe and Ionucu, whom you will meet and I shall place a scaffold the and required materials at your disposal while the town hall would provide the helping hands, through engineer Vintila Nicolae and the technical department."

The Master arrived after two days and he was met at the station by Eng. Doppelraiter, the vice-chair of the Women's League of Gorj County and a well-dressed peasant with a cart. I took his suitcase and we stopped at the Royal Hotel where the Master had his room reserved. I stayed there and they went on to Poiana, where Mrs. Tatarescu was waiting for them, and I was to meet him when he returned. In the evening, I went to the hotel precisely upon his return and he told me: "How good you have come, I was about to look for you to discuss before beginning the work."

He offered me a chair while he was sitting on the sofa and said: "You and the others—are you satisfied with the accommodation and salaries?"

I answered: "Yes, Master, everything is all right."

"Well then, go upstairs and fetch the woman to come and arrange the room the way I want." We took the carpet out of the room, a few chairs and left there only the wardrobe, a chair with a back, a kitchen stool and the sofa, and the rest was empty space.

He sent me buying white packaging paper to draw on, while also instructing me to come every morning there between 8 and 9 for working instructions, because time is short and work is plenty. The next morning I came and saw he had drawn something on the paper, but I asked him nothing. He dressed up and said: "Now we go to the market." He took a bag and purchased: ¼ kg cheese, ½ kg pears, 1 kg apples as well as a pack of 100 National cigarettes since he was smoking like a Turk, especially when he was drawing or thinking.

The following days we did the same thing in the morning—procurement.

Sometimes, in the evening especially, he dined at the Berbec restaurant (Costica Costachescu); there he liked sitting with peasants in the cigarette smoke, eating grilled sausage and drinking red wine, not to mention brandy. He ordered spit roasted meat, or minced meat in cabbage leaves with polenta and drank red wine.

I noticed he was drawing at night or at dawn, and when I got to him in the morning the drawings were ready; he told me to cut out what was traced in thick outlines and place it on the sofa or in the suitcase and this took place every time.

Then we went to the site, after he had filled his pockets with fruit and cigarette packs. He stopped in front of the *Heroes' Gate* (or the *Gate of Kiss* as they call it today) and always looked from the street, from the Jiu River side. He was thinking, writing something down in his notebook, and after three-four days he told me: "Prepare your tools, make the scaffold and let's begin the work. You will do exactly as I tell you, working directly with me then you direct the others; just listen to me and everything will be all right."

When he began drawing the portal with carbon, he told me to contour the lines with graphite, lest the drawing should erase. I could not understand the drawing but I saw it was very simple for me. He used to direct me from downstairs, standing near the portal, from a distance and from the lateral sides, then he came to the scaffold and told me to carve both the leg and the frontal part of the left side; the other two cutters were planning off downstairs. He only worked for 4-5 hours a day, then he went away and left me working alone.

Sometimes he took me with him and also the camera; we went to the weekly fair where he admired the peasant-made objects, plates, burnt clay pots, sculptures on flutes, pitchfork handles, national costumes; he photographed some of them while asking where they were from and discussed their work; he particularly liked the sculpture of spoon and knife handles.

Other times he went to the fields and looked at the peasants while they worked the land, or sat in the shadow with their ox-pulled cart, or ate; he asked them something and then went into the wheat crop, as it was before harvest; once he set the camera for me to take his photograph, and the wheat was almost as tall as him, he took it in his hand as if caressing it. Other times, I went with him on the Jiu River bank and he admired the washing women beating the cloth with the wooden mallet.

Some days, usually Saturday or Sunday he would leave with one of Peschir's carriages who he asked before leaving: "Have you provided everything for the horse and food for one day?"

Peschir told him: "Yes, Mr. Engineer (they all called him that), everything is ready for departure."

Once, I accompanied him to Tismana, I do not remember what village, but he stopped and looked at the old houses with carved gates and verandas with poles resembling columns; he sketched in some notebook and did not speak anymore, he was just looking. One day at the hotel I saw him using a pocket knife and incising some 20-30 cm long wood sticks of square sides like small poles; he also had a V-shaped chisel that he used.

Outside the working place, especially seeing he cared for me I dared ask him this and that about art and artists and he disagreed with me: "Leave this aside, art is what you have seen at the peasants', this is your art since you can go everywhere with it, even abroad, you will see that later."

Then I understood why we always went to the countryside, why the column resembled the porch poles and the motives on the Portal front resembled those on the gates and dowry boxes from old peasant houses.

In my opinion, the Master had thought for a long time and he took inspiration from the Gorj popular art, which I also noticed in his satisfaction for what he achieved. He said about the chairs of the *Table of Silence* they should look like two joined overlapped pots.

In July 1938 he consulted with engineer Vintila from the Town hall and with the mayor as well in view of placing an order to Pietroasa Co. from Deva for two table slabs and 42 more for the chairs, of which 12 to the *Table of Silence* (family), and 30 were to be placed between the *Heroes' Gate* and the *Table*, in the recesses—3 each.

Engineer Vintila provided technician Meculescu Alexandru and a team of workers to deal with transports and materials and stay at the Master's disposal. The table with the 12 chairs were installed, which represented the most difficult problem since the ox-pulled cart was used for transport from the railroad station, as the slabs weighed 4-5 thousand kg.

We installed the *Family table* together with the master; I was sitting on a chair, he measured, the chairs were near one another in pairs and they were to be fixed to concrete by bolts.

Then we discussed placing the other chairs on the *Heroes' Road* about 10-15 m apart and the alley was to be paved with irregular slabs from the table to the *Column*, and a big tree circle was to be traced around the *Column*; they planted the trees but did not observe the plan.

That was Master Brancusi in Targu-Jiu, who was highly interested in achieving his work unhindered by anyone; he selected his models from the Gorj folklore and felt home all the time, especially when he was among peasants, in the market or at the inn.

He avoided discussing with other personalities of the town. When prime minister Tatarescu was changed and a military prefect was appointed, colonel Leoveanu, he received no more support; he left partly satisfied and partly dissatisfied, because he said: "This is all for now and we will see what to do next year." On 20 September (1938) he went to Bucharest, then to Paris and he never returned. He did not participate to the inauguration because it took place in October and he had rheumatism, avoiding cold and shadows.

I worked with him until 29 September, when he left to Paris. I accompanied him to the station and waited there until the train left.

Ambassador Mircea Balanescu

R. Bogdan, *Despre un fals istoriografic—Constantin Brancusi n-a propus niciodata vreo donatie statului roman* [About a historical-biographical forgery—C. Brancusi never proposed a donation to the Romanian state], Observator Cultural, Bucharest, 2002, *102*, 5 February

Mircea Balanescu: Several of my acquaintances told me that in the recent broadcast of Iosif Sava with baritone Dan Iordachescu, the latter stated something about my relations with Brancusi in Paris. I was surprised because what Iordachescu said, and unfortunately others took for real, is far from reality. Brancusi never made any offer to the Romanian state during the communist regime to provide his sculptures or some of them. I truly wonder where this account came from, namely that when Brancusi, allegedly came to the Legation with his offer while I was out of France, I shed into tears when I returned and found out! It was not like that! Brancusi never came there! There was no refusal of the Romanian state! During the four years and something I spent in Paris there was never an issue about Brancusi desiring to provide anything to the Romanian state or even to his family in the country. I would like to regulate all these statements. I am sorry Iordachescu perhaps cannot remember precisely or maybe he was also misinformed from other sources, but this is the simple truth and nothing can be added to it any more.

Radu Bogdan: Therefore what was stated so firmly, obstinately and still is sustained nowadays with the same force is actually some legend, trivially said some nonsense! MB: Absolutely! Nothing is true! …It is outrageous lie! […]

RB: Are you certain?

MB: Absolutely! This is the beginning of what you are going to find out: Mrs. Lavrillier, sculptress of Romanian origin settled in Paris that I knew very well told me one day: "Would you like to go to Brancusi?"

Yes, of course, I answered, why not? Does Brancusi agree?

"I will talk with him and we will see!" she assured me. After a few days she said: "Let us go to him! Or if you want to go alone…" I went alone.

RB: In 1957?

MB: I believe so, I cannot say precisely! Because you see, from '57 until '97 there is plenty of time. I went to Brancusi at the set time. From the very beginning my impression was disagreeable, because I found a studio full of dust...

RB: But this is how things are with sculptors! It was normal.

MB: Brancusi himself was not so clean...

RB: He could not be, he was working in the dust!

MB: He was wearing a shirt that was white once upon a time...Brancusi immediately told me: "Aaa!—said he—you represent the Bucharest regime, the communists that destroyed the country!" Of course I did not like at all such disrespectful reference to a government, in quarrelsome manner: "Master, I represent the government of Bucharest but I also represent Romania in France. In this capacity I concern myself with our Romanians as well. Some time ago I took a garland of flowers to the tomb of Titulescu, which is in a church of Cannes, south of France."

Brancusi's response: "Yes indeed, but you have destroyed the country!"—and he kept on vehemently. "It is not us who destroyed it—I told him —the war made the destruction and you know who caused the war, we repair it now, and we try to put it right!" But he continued in the same violent manner and I declared: "Master, I do not want to talk like this, I would like to settle some relations but, if you do not agree, all that I can do is take my hat and leave!"...So I took my hat and bade him good day.

RB: He did not answer to that?

MB: He said nothing! This is how our relations, personal so to say, ended. A few months after that Brancusi died. I found it from the French press, which also stated he had left nothing to the Romanian state but to the French one. Legatees were painter Istrati and his wife, a painter as well. The Istratis took everything! What could I do? Brancusi did not leave anything to the Romanian state but to the French one, which also built and arranged his museum subordinated to and managed by the Pompidou Center. However I dispatched the Legation counselor to the funeral, to represent us. His name was Gheorghe Pascu. He went there but he returned, pale faced and trembling, telling me: "I was threatened with punching. I barely escaped!"

I did not ask him who threatened him, because I suspected that. In fact, I knew! A few days later I was notified some niece of Brancusi would come to Paris bearing the same name; she was sent by the minister of Culture in order to see whether—she being a close relative—she could recover something for herself from the sculptor's work or belongings. She arrived in the train station and I sent someone to meet her, because I did not know whether she could speak French or manage around. We accommodated her in the Legation. She was about 30-35, nice woman, chemist engineer, working with a laboratory she did not mention. She asked my guidance and we talked. I told her the posthumous representatives of Brancusi are the Istratis and she should go to them and see what can be done. She went there and returned crying, saying that "Istrati, the husband, chased me away!" I calmed her down and told her she could stay one or two more days in the Legation, if she wanted. She answered this invitation, calmed down and then went to Bucharest.

RB: I want to ask you something. It is something I witnessed therefore I know what I am saying: beginning with 1956, when Brancusi was still alive, the state initiated a close-up policy with him, still shy and hesitant, not without reserve, however it was favorable to him. I was the one who, during the communist regime, wrote the first article on Brancusi, soon followed by others. I went to Gorj County in 1956 in his footsteps, studying the region where he was born and grew up; I saw the famous complex of Targu-Jiu and this was possible precisely because the state began a sort of courtship. My question is: **to what extent you acted in the spirit of this new political attitude to Brancusi?**

MB: Except for my courtesy visit to Brancusi, I ignore whether any more courtship followed from the Romanian state. It is only fair, my visit to Brancusi was the consequence of personal attitude, and I asked no approval from Bucharest for it. It was my attempt to get Brancusi near Romania, which failed. This is life—there is both success and failure in it. But in official terms so to say there was no initiative, no guideline came from Bucharest. It was my manner of working, the way I thought fit. There was no assignment in this respect, it cannot be considered state or party directive. When I got to the country after this period, the atmosphere was favorable to Brancusi and it continued like this. Nobody thought of disregarding the construction of Targu-Jiu, if we exclude the bewildered ones that did not understand it.

RB: Obviously, as you have also shown, Brancusi refused the courtship of the communist regime.

MB: It is impossible to understand how some people still can believe Brancusi could have intended, even for one moment, to offer his studio and sculptures to the Romanian state led by Ana Pauker, Gheorghiu-Dej, Petru Groza or any other character of the same team! All the more so that he had been long "briefed" by Istrati, fierce anti-communist, former party member for opportunistic reasons a few years back in order to exit the country…There were also some other important considerations. Brancusi should have been impacted by the fate of Gheorghe Tatarescu and his wife, as they chaired the achievement of the Targu-Jiu ensemble.

There is no serious argument that can be sustained in favor of the assumption that Brancusi could have been prone at a certain moment to donate something to the Romanian communist state. As you have well pointed out it is only nonsense, absurd statement it is! And I believe this clears up the essential of what we intended to explain.

(Excerpts from the discussion of 22 April 1997 between the art critic and historian Radu Bogdan and Mircea Balanescu, former plenipotentiary minister of Romania in Paris from April 1956 to June 1960—A/N)

Abbreviations

AIC—The Art Institute of Chicago

a.o.—and others

A/N—Author's note

FF—French Franc

HRH—Her Royal Highness

MNAM—The National Museum of Modern Art, Paris

MoMA—The Museum of Modern Art, New York

PMA—The Philadelphia Museum of Art

SFMOMA—The San Francisco Museum of Modern Art, San Francisco

SPAM—The Society Pro-Modern Art, São Paulo

SVU Mánes—The Mánes Association of Fine Artists, Prague

Bibliography

AT (1914), *Cronica picturala. "Tinerimea artistica". Expozitie,* Seara, Bucuresti, 28 April.

Acterian, H. (1978), *Vorbeste Brancusi*, Steaua, Cluj-Napoca, **29**, *8,* August.

Aderca, F. (1929), *De vorba cu Ion Minulescu,* in *Marturia unei generatii*, S. Ciornei Librar—Editor, Bucuresti.

Adlow, Dorothy (1927), *C. Brancusi*, Drawings and Design, London, **II**, February.

Adlow, Dorothy (1955), *Brancusi and Modern Sculpture*, Christian Science Monitor, Boston, 20 October.

Adrian, P.G. (1957), *Constantin Brancusi,* Goya, Madrid, *16*, enero.

Agarbiceanu, N. (1976), *In atelierul mesterului*, Secolul 20, Bucuresti, *189-191.*

Alazard, J. (1937), *L'art roumain à l'exposition de 1937,* Le Journal des Arts, Paris, September.

Alazard, J. (1951), *L'Atelier de Brancusi*, Art d'aujourd'hui, Paris, **II**, *3,* janvier.

Alden Jewell, E. (1933), *Brancusi Exhibition at Brummer Gallery Hard on Realists but Highly Pleasing to the Imaginative*, The New York Times, New York, 18 November.

Alden Jewell, E. (1943), *A. E. Gallatin Art Finds a New Home*, The New York Times, New York, 5 February.

Alden Jewell, E. (1944), *Art and Alfred Stieglitz*, The New York Times, New York, 10 September.

Alexandrescu, I. (1965), *Esentialul: tezaurul si viziunea artistului*, Ramuri, Craiova, *6, iunie.*

Alexandrescu, I. (1965), *Marturiile unui cioplitor*, Ramuri, Craiova, *3*, 23 martie.

Al-George, S. (1981), *Brancusi et l'Inde*, Revue Roumaine d'Histoire de l'Art, série Beaux-Arts, Bucarest, Tome **XVIII**.

Amaral, A.A. (2003), *Tarsila: sua obra e seu tempo*, Editora 34/Editora da Universidade de São Paulo.

Amzallag-Augé, Elizabeth, Curtil, Sophie (1990), *Constantin Brancusi: Le Coq*, Coll. L'Art en jeu, Éd. Centre Pompidou, Paris.

Andrei, N.A. (1976), *Ani de luminta—Istoria liceului "Nicolae Balcescu", Craiova, 1826-1976,* Ed. Scrisul Romanesc, Craiova.

Andrei, N.A. (2005), *Istoria invatamantului din Craiova*, **II**/1864-1918, Ed. ALMA, Craiova.

Andrews, Mary-Elizabeth (2014), *"Memory of the Nation": Making and Re-making German History in the Berlin Zeughaus*, PhD Thesis, The University of Sidney, Andrews_ME_Thesis.pdf.

Andritoiu, A. (1980), *Constantin Brancusi in amintirile unui discipol, Constantin Antonovici*, Flacara, Bucuresti, *26*, 26 iunie.

Anghel, P. (1967), *Brancusi la el acasa—itinerar omagial*, Scanteia, Bucuresti, 21 October.

Anghel, P. (1968), *Arhiva sentimentala*, Ed. pentru Literatura, Bucuresti.

Anghel, P. (1972), *Convorbiri culturale*, Ed. Eminescu, Bucuresti.

Anghel, P. (1975), *Noua arhiva sentimentala*, Ed. Eminescu, Bucuresti.

Anon (1937), *Les expositions: Origines et développement de l'art international indépendant, Musée du Jeu de Paume, Juillet-Novembre 1937,* Cahiers d'art, Paris.

Anonim (1925), *Comment*, This Quarter (supliment), Paris, **I**, *1*.

Antonovici, C. (2001), *Cum l-am cunoscut pe marele Brancusi*, Literatorul, Bucuresti, **XI,** *4-5(358-359)*.

Antonovici, C. (2002), *Brancusi maestrul. Marturii, amintiri, exegeze*, Ed. Semne '94, Bucuresti.

Apollinaire, G. (1912), *Le Salon des Indépendants / Fin de la promenade à travers les Salles du quai d'Orsay*, L'Intransigeant et le Journal de Paris, 3 April.

Apollinaire, G. (1914), *Inscription pour le tombeau du peintre Henri Rousseau le Douanier*, Les Soirées de Paris, **2**, *20-27,* janvier.

Apostolos-Cappadona, Diane, Altshuler, B., eds. (1994), *Essays and conversations*, Harry N. Abrams, Inc. & Isamu Noguchi Foundation, New York.

Argan, G.C. (1968), *Arta lui Brancusi si arta actuala*, in *Colocviul Brancusi—Bucuresti, 13-15 octombrie 1967,* Ed. Meridiane, Bucuresti.

Argan, G.C. (1970), *L'Arte moderna 1770-1970,* Ed. Sansoni, Firenze.

Argatu, C. (2001), *Pace si bucurie cu Brancusi*, Ed. Dacia, Cluj-Napoca.

Arghezi, T. (1912), *Expozitia Salonului Oficial*, Facla, Bucuresti, 2 iunie.

Arghezi, T. (1913), *Cronica artistica. Expozitia Societatii "Tinerimea artistica",* Seara, Bucuresti, 28 April.

Arghezi, T. (1913), *Expozitia "Tinerimii artistice". Vernisajul*, Seara, Bucuresti, 1 April.

Arghezi, T. (1913), *Expozitia Societatii "Tinerimea artistica",* Seara, Bucuresti, 18 April.

Arghezi, T. (1914), *"Tinerimea artistica"*, Seara, Bucuresti, 3 May.

Arghezi, T. (1914), *Tabula rasa. Arta si arta*, Seara, Bucuresti, 23 iunie.

Arghezi, T. (1946), *Din viata lui Stefan Luchian*, Lumina si Coloare, Bucuresti, *1*, mai.

Arghezi, T. (1973), *Pensula si dalta*, Ed. Meridiane, Bucuresti.

Asendorph, C. (1994), *L'helice et l'avantgarde: Léger—Duchamp—Brancusi*, in *Fernand Léger, Le rythme de la vie moderne*, Éd. Flammarion, Paris.

Ashton, Dore (1955), *Brancusi Exhibition at Guggenheim Museum,* Arts and Architecture, New York, December.

Ashton, Dore (1963), *Seven American Decades*, Studio International, London, *165*.

Atanasiu, A.D. (1909), *Expozitia oficiala a Ministerului Instructiunii Publice*, Arta romana, Iasi, iunie.

Aubert, J. (1975), *Joyce & Paris 1902... 1920-1940... 1975*, **I**, Actes du 5e Symposium International James Joyce, Paris 16-20 juin 1975, Éd. du CNRS, Paris.

Auricoste, A. (1957), *Hommage à Brancusi*, Les Lettres françaises, Paris, *664*, 28 mars.

Avon, Alice (1926), *Polishes Like Jeweler. Shakespeare Said It*, New York Telegraph, New York, 7 March.

B.C. (1930), *L'art roumain*, Nation belge, Bruxelles, 20 juillet.

Bach, F.T. (1987), *Constantin Brancusi: Metamorphosen plastischer Form*, DuMont Buchverlag, Köln (reprint 2004).

Bach, F.T. (1991), *Brancusi: Photo Reflexion*, Didier Imbert Fine Art, Paris, 1991.

Bach, F.T., Rowell, Margit, Temkin, Ann (1995), *Constantin Brancusi: 1876-1957*, Éd. Gallimard & Center Pompidou, Paris.

Bachelin, L. (1909), *A VIII Expozitie anuala a Tinerimei artistice (cu 33 reproduceri de pe operile A. S. R. Principesei Maria a Romaniei si a D-lor Aricescu, Artachino, Basarab, Brancusi, D-na Cutescu-Storck, Harlescu, Kimon Loghi, Lukian, Mihailescu, Mirea, Murnu, Patrascu, Spaethe, Steriadi, Storck, Strambu si Vermont)*, Noua Revista Romana, Bucuresti, **5**, *25*, 29 martie.

Bachelin, L. (1910), *Expozitia "Tinerimii artistice"*, Seara, Bucuresti, 16 aprilie.

Bachelin, L. (1913), *La XII-ème Exposition de "Tinerimea artistica"*, La Politique, Bucuresti, 14 avril.

Bachelin, L. (1914), *L'exposition de "Tinerimea artistica". La Sculpture. Le Grand Salon*, La Politique, Bucuresti, 13 avril.

Baillat, C. (2012), *Vera Moore, pianiste, de Dunedin à Jouy-en-Josas*, Collection Univers musical, Éd. L'Harmattan, Paris.

Balacescu Dem., Lucia (1942), *Cronica plastica. Colectia Al. Bogdan-Pitesti (introducere)*, Universul literar, Bucuresti, **LI**, *29*, 18 iulie.

Balas, Edith (1987), *Brancusi and Rumanian Folk Traditions*, Columbia University Press, New York.

Balas, Edith (1996), *Sculptura lui Brancusi in lumina mostenirii lui romanesti*, Brancusi, Targu-Jiu, **II**, *1(5)*, februarie.

Balintescu, A. (1967), *Contributii documentare referitoare la Brancusi*, in *Placheta Brancusi, Muzeul de Arta din Craiova*, Artis, Bucuresti.

Baltazar, A. (1974), *Convorbiri artistice*, Ed. Meridiane, Bucuresti.

Balteanu, G.S. (1935), *Cronica ocazionala*, Gorjanul, Targu-Jiu, *36*.

Barr, A.H., Jr. (1936), *Brancusi*, in *Cubism and Abstract Art*, The Museum of Modern Art, New York.

Barr, A.H., Jr. (1954), *Masters of Modern Art, The Museum of Modern Art, New York,* Simon & Schuster, New York.

Basler, A. (1928), *La sculpture moderne en France*, Éd. G. Crès & C-ie, Paris.

Beekman Taylor, P. (2004), *Gurdjieff's America: Mediating the Miraculous*, Lighthouse Editions Ltd., Cambridge (UK).

Bell, C. (1926), *The Art of Brancusi. The Layman Finds the Very Simplicity of This Sculptor Hard to Understand*, Vogue, New York, *67*, 1 June.

Benedict, S.J. (2011), *Constantin Antonovici (1911-2002)—A Great Brancusi's Disciple / A Brief Biography*, 2 November, http://www.bjt2006.org/SJB_Antonovici_4411.pdf.

Bénézit, E. (1949), *Dictionnaire critique et documentaire des peintres, sculpteurs et graveurs de tous les temps*, **II**, Librairie Gründ, Paris.

Bengescu, Marie (1908), *Les artistes roumains au Salon de la Société Nationale des Beaux-Arts et à celui des artistes français,* L'Indépendance Roumaine, Bucarest, 17 mai.

Bengescu, Marie (1919), *L'Art en Roumanie*, in *La Roumanie en images*, **I**, coord. Petre Antonescu, Imprimeries A.G. L'Hoir, Paris.

Bercus, I.C. (1981), *Legaturile lui Brancusi cu medicii si medicina*, in *Trecut si viitor in medicina*, Ed. Medicala, Bucuresti.

Bergers, M. (1957), *Constantin Brancusi ou le sculpteur des mythes*, Preuves, Paris, *76*, juin.

Berk, N. (1968), *Sculptura-stela la Brancusi*, in *Colocviul Brancusi—Bucuresti, 13-15 octombrie 1967,* Ed. Meridiane, Bucuresti.

Bertin, C. (1982), *Marie Bonaparte: A Life*, Yale University Press, New Haven.

Blaga, L. (1923), *Constantin Brancusi*, Patria, Cluj, **V**, *116*, 3 iunie.

Blaga, L. (1926), *Pasarea sfanta intruchipata in aur de sculptorul Constantin Brancusi*, Gandirea, Bucuresti, **VI**, februarie.

Blaga, L. (1929), *Lauda somnului,* Ed. Cartea Romaneasca, Bucuresti.

Blaga, L. (1944), *Trilogia cunoasterii—Spatiul mioritic*, Fundatia pentru Literatura si Arta, Bucuresti.

Blaga, L. (1968), *Zari si etape*, Ed. pentru Literatura, Bucuresti.

Blazian, H. (1930), *Sculptorul Constantin Brancusi*, Adeverul, Bucuresti, 9 octombrie.

Blazian, H. (1931), *Constantino Brancusi*, Poligono. Rivista mensile d'arte diretta da Raffaello Giolli, Milano, **V**, *2*.

Bodea, G.I. (2010), *INVESNICIREA lui Octavian Goga la Ciucea*, Ed. Vremi, Cluj-Napoca.

Bogdan, R. (1957), *La muzeul din Craiova. Valori clasice ale artei noastre contemporane*, Contemporanul, Bucuresti, **41**, 30 august.

Bogdan, R. (1957), *Omagiu lui Brancusi*, Arta plastica, Bucuresti, *1*.

Bogdan, R. (1997), *Brancusi si avangarda romaneasca a anilor '20*, Brancusi, Targu-Jiu, **III**, *3(11)*.

Bogdan, R. (2001), *Universalitatea operei lui Constantin Brancusi*, Observator Cultural, Bucuresti, *81*, 11-17 septembrie.

Bogdan-Pitesti, A. (1910), *Expozitia Societatii "Tinerimea Artistica", mai 1909—Expozitia oficiala iunie 1909*, Anuarul presei romane si al lumii politice, Bucuresti.

Bogza, G. (1957), *Medalion / Brancusi*, Contemporanul, Bucuresti, **41**, 29 martie.

Bordet-Maugars, Maryse, Rubercy, E. de, Le Buhan, D. (1998), *Brancusi, 1876-1957*, Éd. du Cercle d'Art, Paris.

Botta, D. (1933), *Sculptorul Constantin Brancusi*, Gazeta literara, Bucuresti, **II**, *82*, 30 septembrie.

Botta, D. (1936), *Limite*, Ed. Cartea Romaneasca, Bucuresti.

Boureanu, R. (1938), *Constantin Brancusi. O clipa afara din timp*, Romania, 9 noiembrie (reprint in *Funia de nisip*, Ed. Cartea Romaneasca, Bucuresti, 1972).

Bowness, A. (1977), *Modern European Art*, Thames & Hudson Publishers, London.

Boz, L. (1930), *Brancusi*, Adeverul, Bucuresti, 4 iulie.

Boz, L. (1930), *De vorba cu Const. Brancusi*, Facla, Bucuresti, **IX**, *379*, 13 octombrie.

Brancusi, C. (1925), *Histoire de brigands; Aphorismes*, Integral, Bucuresti, **I**, *4*, iunie.

Brancusi, C. (1925), *Réponse de Brancusi: Aphorismes, Histoire de brigands*, This Quarter, Paris, spring, **I**, *1*.

Brancusi, C. (1956), *Bucuria de a trai*, Tanarul scriitor, Bucuresti, **V**, *11*, noiembrie.

Branisteanu, B. (1910), *Expozitia "Tinerimii artistice" (Salonul de toamna)*, Adeverul, Bucuresti, 18 noiembrie.

Branisteanu, B. (1912), *Salonul oficial 1912*, Adeverul, Bucuresti, 10 mai.

Branisteanu, B. (1913), *Salonul "Tinerimii artistice"*, Adeverul, Bucuresti, 4 aprilie.

Bratu, Ileana (1967), *Cu sculptorul american de origine romana, Constantin Antonovici, despre Brancusi*, Amfiteatru, Bucuresti, II, 10, 22 octombrie.

Brest, J.M. (1955), *Recuerdo de una visita a Constantin Brancusi*, Ver y Estimar. Revista mensual de critica artistica, serie 2, Buenos Aires, *5*, marzo.

Brezianu, B. (1963), *O statuie de Brancusi in Bucuresti*, Gazeta Literara, Bucuresti, 9 aprilie.

Brezianu, B. (1964), *Graficianul,* Luceafarul, Bucuresti, **V**, *18*, 29 august.

Brezianu, B. (1964), *Les débuts de Brancusi,* Revue Roumaine d'Histoire de l'Art, série Beaux-Arts, Bucuresti, Tome **I**.

Brezianu, B. (1964), *Pages inédites de la correspondance de Brancusi*, Revue Roumaine d'Histoire de l'Art, série BeauxArts, Bucuresti, Tome **I**.

Brezianu, B. (1965), *The Beginnings of Brancusi*, Art Journal, New York, **XXV**, *1*.

Brezianu, B. (1966), *Brancusi si Transilvania,* Tribuna, Cluj, 24 februarie.

Brezianu, B. (1967), *Fisa biografica*, Flacara, Bucuresti, *41(645),* 7 octombrie.

Brezianu, B. (1967), *La jeunesse de Brancusi*, Les Lettres françaises, Paris, 13 septembre.

Brezianu, B. (1969), *Brancusi l'artisan,* Revue Roumaine d'Histoire de l'Art, série Beaux-Arts, Bucarest, Tome **VI**.

Brezianu, B. (1969), *Debutul lui Brancusi—Craiova, 1898*, Contemporanul, Bucuresti, **53**, 2 octombrie.

Brezianu, B. (1970), *Prima Expozitie Brancusi pe vechiul continent*, Romania literara, Bucuresti, 4-10 iunie.

Brezianu, B. (1972), *Mihail Sadoveanu si bursierul Brancusi*, Manuscriptum, Bucuresti, **III**, *3,* martie.

Brezianu, B. (1973), *Danaida*, Arta, Bucuresti, 9.

Brezianu, B. (1974), *Opera lui Brancusi in Romania*, Ed. Academiei R.S.R., Bucuresti.

Brezianu, B. (1976), *Anii de internat*, Tribuna, Cluj-Napoca, **20**, *9,* 26 februarie.

Brezianu, B. (1976), *Brancusi in Romania* (2nd edition, issue in english language), Ed. Academiei R.S.R., Bucuresti.

Brezianu, B. (1976), *Cu Isamu Noguchi pe urmele lui Brancusi,* Secolul 20, Bucuresti, *10-12(189-191),* octombrie-decembrie.

Brezianu, B. (1976), *Incununarea unei creatii. Complexul de la Targu-Jiu: Coloana, Poarta, Masa*, Tribuna Romaniei, Bucuresti, **V**, *79*, 15 februarie.

Brezianu, B. (1977), *Brancusi, Voronca si avangarda romaneasca*, Secolul 20, Bucuresti, *10-11-12,* octombrie-decembrie.

Brezianu, B. (1981), *In Search of Brancusi*, Holidays in Romania, Bucuresti, **XXIII**, *119*, November.

Brezianu, B. (1996), *Dada, Tzara, Brancusi*, Caiete critice, Bucuresti, *4-5(101-102)*, aprilie-mai.

Brezianu, B. (1998), *Brancusi in Romania*, Ed. ALL, Bucuresti (reprint in Ed. Allfa, Bucuresti, 2005).

Brezianu, B. (2001), *Brancusi, sapte prilejuri pierdute*, in *Brancusi si Transilvania*, Ed. Grinta, Cluj-Napoca.

Brezianu, B. (2002), *Varii peripetii brancusiene*, Romania literara, Bucuresti, *21*, 29 mai-4 iunie.

Briolle, C., Fuzibet, A., Monnier, G. (1990), *Mallet-Stevens: La villa Noailles*, Éd. Parenthèses, Marseille.

Brion, M. (1956), *L'art abstrait*, Éd. Albin Michel, Paris.

Broche, F. (1989), *Anna de Noailles: Un mistère en plein lumière*—biographie sans masque, R. Laffont, Paris.

Brown, Elizabeth A. (1995), *Brancusi Photographs*, Thames & Hudson Publishers, London.

Brown, I.H. (1924), *Gypsy Fires in America; a Narrative of Life Among the Romanies of the United States and Canada… / with Many Illustrations from Photos*, Harper New York & London.

Brown, M.W. (1988), *The Story of the Armory Show*, Abbeville Press, New York.

Bucuta, E. (1930), *Cronica / Carti, conferinte, congrese, expozitii: Arta romaneasca in straini*, Boabe de Grau, Bucuresti, **I**, *6*, august.

Bucuta, E. (1931), *Muzeul Simu*, Boabe de Grau, Bucuresti, **II**, *1*, ianuarie.

Bucuta, E. (1933), *Cronica / Carti, conferinte, congrese, expozitii: Expozitii de arta*, Boabe de Grau, Bucuresti, **IV**, *10*, octombrie.

Buican, A. (2006), *Brancusi: O biografie*, Ed. Artemis, Bucuresti.

Buley-Uribe, Christina (2013), *Mes sœurs divines—99 femmes de l'entourage de Rodin*, Éd. du Relief, Paris.

Bulliet, C.J. (1927), *Artless Comment on the Seven Arts*, Chicago Evening Post, Chicago, 11 January.

Bulliet, C.J. (1927), *Sculptor's First Big Show at Arts Club*, Chicago Press, Chicago, 4 January.

Bulliet, C.J. (1939), *Brancusi Pays Chicago First Visit*, Chicago Daily News, Chicago, 27 May.

Bunescu, M. (1965), *Insemnarile unui pictor*, Ed. Meridiane, Bucuresti.

Buot, F. (2002), *Tristan Tzara—L'homme qui inventa la révolution Dada*, Éd. Grasset & Fasquelle, Paris.

Burileanu, M. (1912), *Deschiderea "Salonului oficial"*, Epoca, Bucuresti, 8 mai.

Burke, C. (1996), *Becoming Modern / The Life of Mina Loy*, Gregor Rare Books, Abaa, Langley.

Burnham, J. (1969), *Beyond Modern Sculpture*, George Braziller, New York.

Burton, S. (1990), *My Brancusi*, Art in America, New York, March.

Busuioceanu, A. (1930), *Arta romaneasca in Olanda*, Gandirea, Bucuresti, **X**, august-septembrie.

Busuioceanu, A. (1939), *Cronica artei: 1938*, Romania, Bucuresti, **I**, *212*, 1 ianuarie.

Buzila, B. (1965), *Din fresca unei vieti. De vorba cu Cecilia Cutescu-Storck*, Magazin, Bucuresti, 29 mai.

Buzila, B. (1974), *Marturii in amurg*, Ed. Dacia, Cluj-Napoca.

C.V. (1957), *Brancusi*, Les Lettres françaises, Paris, *663*, 21-27 mars.

Caby, R. (1929), *Autour d'un extraordinaire procès, Constantin Brancusi*, Montparnasse, Paris, *55*, avril-mai.

Cairns, H. (1940), *Mr. Epstein's "Thirty Years' War"; His Apologia for Himself and His Work Explaining His Predeliction for Asiatic Types*, The Washington Post, Washington, D.C., 10 November.

Callimachi, S. (1957), *Ultima intalnire cu C. Brancusi*, Flacara, Bucuresti, *8(105)*, 15 aprilie.

Callimachi, S. (1970), *Cu Brancusi la Paris*, Magazin istoric, Bucuresti, *10*, octombrie.

Carles, H.G. (1972), *L'année 1908*, Les Lettres françaises, Paris, 30 août.

Cassou, J. (1946), *Visite à Brancusi*, Cahiers France-Roumanie, Paris, *4*, juin-juillet.

Cassou, J. (1971), *Panorama artelor plastice contemporane*, **I, II**, Ed. Meridiane, Bucuresti.

Cassou, J. (1976), *Miracolul Brancusi*, Romania literara, Bucuresti, *8*, 19-25 februarie.

Cassou, J., Langui, E., Pevsner, N. (1961), *Les sources du vingtième siècle*, Éd. des Deux Mondes, Paris.

Chaudonneret, Marie-Claude (2007), *Les artistes étrangers à Paris, de la fin du Moyen Âge aux années 1920*, Peter Lang Verlag, Bern.

Chelimsky, O. (1958), *A Memoir of Brancusi*, Arts, New York, **32**, *9, June.*

Chelimsky, O. (1958), *In Memoriam*, Dial Press, New York.

Cheney, S. (1933), *A Primer of Modern Art*, Liveright Publishing Corporation, New York.

Cheney, S. (1934), *Expresionism in Art*, Liveright Publishing Corporation, New York.

Cheney, S. (1958), *The Story of Modern Art*, Viking Press, New York.

Cheops (1913), *Expozitiunea a XII-a a "Tinerimii artistice"*, Ilustratiunea nationala, Bucuresti, aprilie.

Chirico, G. de (1945), *Memorie de la mia vita*, Astrolabio, Roma.

Chisholm, Anne (1979), *Nancy Cunard: A Biography*, Alfred A. Knopf, New York.

Cioroianu, Eugenia (2001), *Pasi spre infinit. Istoricul Colegiului Tehnic de Arte si Meserii "Constantin Brancusi"*, **I** (1871-1948), Ed. Aius, Craiova.

Ciotori, D.N. (1957), *Brancusi* (panegiric), La Nation Roumaine, Paris, **X**, *168*, avril.

Cisek, O.W. (1925), *Expozitia internationala a revistei "Contimporanul"*, Gandirea, Bucuresti, **IV**, *7*, 15 ianuarie (reprint in *Suflet romanesc in arta si literatura*, Ed. Dacia, Cluj-Napoca, 1974).

Cisek, O.W. (1925), *Muzeul A. Simu,* Gandirea, Bucuresti, **IV**, 5 decembrie.

Cisek, O.W. (1928), *Arta romana. Cronica plastica*, Gandirea, Bucuresti, **VII**, aprilie-august.

Cisek, O.W. (1942), *Limpeziri / Arta romaneasca*, Dacia Rediviva, Bucuresti, **II**, *6*, iunie.

Ciuca, E. (1964), *Brancusi inedit*, Luceafarul, Bucuresti, **V**, *26*, 19 decembrie.

Ciuca, E. (1964), *Brancusi la Targu-Jiu*, Contemporanul, Bucuresti, **48**, *16*, 17 aprilie.

Ciuca, E. (1965), *The Heroes' Architectural Ensemble*, Romanian Review, Bucuresti, *1*.

Coates, R.M. (1936), *Modern,* The New Yorker, New York, 12 December.

Cocteau, J. (1952), *Eric Satie*, La Revue Musicale, Paris, *214.*

Codreanu, Irina (1968), *Ucenicie la Brancusi*, in *Colocviul Brancusi— Bucuresti, 13-15 octombrie 1967*, Ed. Meridiane, Bucuresti.

Cogniat, R. (1962), *Brancusi et Zadkine ou deux aspects du baroquisme moderne*, Le Figaro, Paris, 12 avril.

Cogniat, R. (1967), *Brancusi,* Le Figaro, Paris, 14 septembre.

Colombier, P. (1951), *Histoire générale de l'art*, **II**, Éd. Flammarion, Paris.

Comarnescu, P. (1938), *Noi intelegeri si viziuni in estetica si stiinta artei*, Revista Fundatiilor Regale, Bucuresti, **V**, *8*, 1 august.

Comarnescu, P. (1943), *Om, natura si Dumnezeu in plastica romaneasca*, Revista Fundatiilor Regale, Bucuresti, **X**, *1*, 1 ianuarie.

Comarnescu, P. (1944), *Ilustratii din opera lui C. Brancusi*, Revista Fundatiilor Regale, Bucuresti, **XI**, *12*, decembrie.

Comarnescu, P. (1944), *Valoarea romaneasca si universala a sculpturii lui C. Brancusi*, Revista Fundatiilor Regale, Bucuresti, **XI**, *6*, iunie.

Comarnescu, P. (1945), *Alte ilustratii dupa opera lui C. Brancusi*, Revista Fundatiilor Regale, Bucuresti, **XII**, *2*, februarie.

Comarnescu, P. (1963), *Insemnari despre "Tinerimea artistica"*, Arta plastica, Bucuresti, *12*.

Comarnescu, P. (1964), *Desene de Brancusi din timpul studiilor in tara*, Tribuna, Cluj, **8**, 29 octombrie.

Comarnescu, P. (1965), *Brancusi. Marturii despre marele sculptor*, Magazin, Bucuresti, 12 iunie.

Comarnescu, P. (1965), *Portile vietii lui Brancusi*, Iasul literar, Iasi, **XVI**, 4 aprilie.

Comarnescu, P. (1966), *Atelierele pariziene ale lui Brancusi*, Tribuna, Cluj, **10**, 29 decembrie.

Comarnescu, P. (1966), *Inceputurile lui Brancusi*, Tribuna, Cluj, **10**, 24 februarie.

Comarnescu, P. (1967), *Aspecte din atelierul lui Brancusi*, Cronica, Iasi, **II**, *25.*

Comarnescu, P. (1967), *Iconografie si biografie brancusiana*, Cronica, Iasi, **II**, *22*, 3 iunie.

Comarnescu, P. (1967), *Monumentele de la Targu-Jiu in cadrul creatiei lui Constantin Brancusi*, Steaua, Cluj, **18**, *3,* martie.

Comarnescu, P. (1972), *Brancusi, mit si metamorfoza in sculptura contemporana* (editie ingrijita de Nina Stanculescu), Ed. Meridiane, Bucuresti.

Comarnescu, P., Eliade, M., Jianu, I. (1967), *Témoignages sur Brancusi*, Arted, Éd. d'Art, Paris.

Comarnescu, P., Eliade, M., Jianu, I., Noica, C. (1982), *Brancusi— Témoignages*, Arted, Éd. d'Art, Paris.

Coninck, Suzanne de (1957), *Hommage de la sculpture à Brancusi et Prix Émile de Coninck*, Éd. de Beaune, Paris.

Constantinescu, M. (1930), *Arta si artisti. Brancusi*, Cuvantul, Bucuresti, **VI**, *1748*, 4 martie.

Constantinescu, V. (1937), *Istoricul si Anuarul Liceului industrial "Regele Ferdinand I"*, Imprimeria Biruinta, Craiova.

Coresp. (1910), *Scrisori din Bucuresti / O noua expozitie a tinerimii artistice / Bucuresti, 12 aprilie*, Tribuna, Arad, **XIV**, *83*, 14-27 aprilie.

Cornel, T. (1907), *Artisti romani la Paris. Despre cativa artisti care expun la "Saloanele" din 1907*, Adeverul, Bucuresti, 16 aprilie.

Cornel, T. (1908), *Expozitia societatii "Tinerimea artistica". Sculptura*, Ordinea, Bucuresti, 12 aprilie.

Cornel, T. (1910), *Discutii. Curentul nou artistic de la noi si critica de arta*, Noua Revista Romana, Bucuresti, **IX**, *7*, 12 decembrie.

Cornel, T. (1910), *Indrumari noi in arta. Cu prilejul expozitiei societatii "Tinerimea artistica"*, Viata sociala, Bucuresti, **1**, *4*, mai.

Cornel, T. (1911), *Figuri contimporane din Romania, Dictionar biografic ilustrat / Figures contemporaines de Roumanie, Dictionnaire biographique illustré*, Tipografia Socec, Bucuresti.

Cosmuta, C. (1964), *Brancusi si prietenii sai*, Inainte, Craiova, 16 martie.

Cosmuta, C. (1965), *Cu Brancusi*, Ramuri, Craiova, *6*, 15 iunie.

Cosmuta, C. (1967), *Album de familie*, Almanahul Ramuri, Craiova.

Cozmuta, Otilia de (1908), *Scrisori din Paris. Saloanele*, Luceafarul, Sibiu, **VII**, *19*, 1 octombrie.

Cozmutza, Otilia de (1908), *Scrisori din Paris*, Luceafarul, Sibiu, **VII**, *3*, 1 februarie.

Courthion, P. (1958), *L'Art indépendant. Panorama international de 1900 à nos jours*, Éd. Albin Michel, Paris.

Couturier, R. (1957), *Hommage à Brancusi*, Les Lettres françaises, Paris, *664*, 28 mars.

Craciunoiu, C., Sandachi, G.P. (2010), *Henri Coanda... si avioanele sale 1910-2010*, Ed. Modelism, Bucuresti.

Cristache, N. (1976), *"Am invatat de la maestrul Brancusi sa nu vorbesc niciodata despre mine sau despre lucrarile mele"—convorbire cu Ion Alexandrescu*, Flacara, Bucuresti, *7*.

Croitoru, I. (1967), *L-am cunoscut...*, Arges, Pitesti, **II**, martie.

Crosby, Caresse (1953), *The Passionate Years*, The Dial Press, New, York.

Cublesan, C. (1996), *Nostalgie dupa Brancusi (la Ciucea lui Goga)*, Brancusi, Targu-Jiu, **II**, *1(5)*, februarie.

Cublesan, C. (2001), *Brancusi si Goga, la Ciucea*, in *Brancusi si Transilvania*, Ed. Grinta, Cluj-Napoca.

Cuciurea, I. (1974), *Brancusi fotograf*, Steaua, Cluj-Napoca, **XXV**, *1*, ianuarie.

Cuclin, D. (1976), *L-am cunoscut pe Brancusi*, Tribuna Romaniei, Bucuresti, **V**, *79*, 15 februarie. Curtis, Penelope (1999), *Sculpture 1900-1945: After Rodin*, Oxford University Press, New York.

Cutescu-Storck, Cecilia (1944), *Fresca unei vieti*, Bucovina, I. E. Toroutiu, Bucuresti.

Cutescu-Storck, Cecilia (1966), *O viata daruita artei*, Ed. Meridiane, Bucuresti.

Dachy, M. (1994), *Dada et les dadaïmes*, Éd. Gallimard, Paris.

David, P.I. (1972), *Constantin Brancusi in cultura romaneasca si arta universala,* Revista Mitropolia Olteniei, Revista Oficiala a Arhiepiscopiei Craiovei si Episcopiei Ramnicului si Argesului, **XXIV**, *11-12*, noiembrie-decembrie.

David, P.I. (1976), *Arta si cultura, coordonatele eternitatii unui popor. Centenarul nasterii lui Constantin Brancusi (1876-1976),* Biserica Ortodoxa Romana, Bucuresti, *3-4,* martie-aprilie.

Davis, Mary E. (2006), *Classic Chic: Music, Fashion, and Modernism*, University of California Press, Berkeley.

Deac, M. (1962), *Brancusi—fragmente monografice*, Arta plastica, Bucuresti, 6.

Deac, M. (1965), *Brancusi. Interviu la Venetia cu Peggy Guggenheim in palatul de pe Canale Grande*, Flacara, Bucuresti, *3,* 16 ianuarie.

Deac, M. (1966), *Brancusi*, Ed. Meridiane, Bucuresti.

Deac, M. (1982), *Brancusi: surse arhetipale*, Ed. Junimea, Iasi.

Deac, M. (1996), *Romanul Brancusi,* Ed. Thausib, Sibiu.

Dearborn, M.V. (2004), *Affairs of the Art: Mistress of Modernism, the Life of Peggy Guggenheim*, Houghton Mifflin, New York.

Degand, L., Arp, J. (1957), *La Collection H. et L. Winston au Musée de Detroit*, Art et architecture, Boulogne, décembre.

Delarue-Mardrus, Lucie (1938), *Mes mémoires*, Éd. Gallimard, Paris.

Delavrancea, Cella (1971), *O vizita in Atelierul lui Brancusi*, Contemporanul, Bucuresti, 19 noiembrie.

Delavrancea, Cella (1976), *L-am cunoscut pe Brancusi*, Tribuna Romaniei, Bucuresti, **V**, *79*, 15 februarie.

Delevoy, R. (1965), *Dimensions du XXe siècle, 1900-1945*, Albert Skira, Genève.

Devigne, Marguerite (1930), *Les Expositions*, Horizon, Bruxelles, 16 août.

Devigne, R. (1920), *L'homme qui rabotte les femmes*, L'Ère nouvelle, Paris, 28 janvier.

Devree, H. (1948), *Modern Art Opens Exhibition Today*, The New York Times, New York, 1 July.

Devree, H. (1951), *20th Century Art in New Exhibition*, The New York Times, New York, 23 May.

Devree, H. (1951), *From Five Collectors*, The New York Times, New York, 1 July.

Devree, H. (1953), *Sculpture Survey*, The New York Times, New York, 3 May.

Devree, H. (1954), *Modern Panorama*, The New York Times, New York, 10 October.

Devree, H. (1955), *Sculpture Gamut*, The New York Times, New York, 30 October.

Devree, H. (1957), *Modern Americans*, The New York Times, New York, 3 February.

Devree, H. (1958), *Modern Masters*, The New York Times, New York, 18 May.

Diaconescu, R. (1970), *Cu V. G. Paleolog despre Brancusi*, Tribuna, Cluj, **14**, *28*.

Diaconescu, R. (1981), *Trebuia sa se nasca Brancusi*, Ed. Cartea Romaneasca, Bucuresti.

Doesburg, T. van (1927), *Brancusi*, De Stijl, Leyda, Jubileum, XIV, *79-84*.

Doicescu, O. (1966), *Brancusi asa cum l-am cunoscut*, Contemporanul, Bucuresti, 18 februarie.

Doicescu, O. (1968), *Brancusi sau arhitectul*, in *Colocviul Brancusi—Bucuresti, 13-15 octombrie 1967*, Ed. Meridiane, Bucuresti.

Doicescu, O. (1976), *L-am cunoscut pe Brancusi*, Tribuna Romaniei, Bucuresti, **V**, *79,* 15 februarie.

Dorfles, G. (1956), *Il segreto di Brancusi*, Domus, Milano, aprile.

Dragomirescu, M. (1907), *Revista critica—Miscarea artistica*, Convorbiri critice, Bucuresti, *8-10*, 15 mai.

Dragu Dimitriu, Victoria (2004), *Povesti ale Doamnelor din Bucuresti,* Ed. Vremea, Bucuresti.

Dragut, V. (1976), *Cei din neamul lui Brancusi. Centenar*, Romania pitoreasca, Bucuresti, **V**, *9*, septembrie.

Dragutescu, E. (1962), *La sase ani de la moartea lui Brancusi. Amintiri si note*, Revista scriitorilor romani, München, *1*.

Dragutescu, E. (1967), *Brancusi—omul*, Gazeta literara, Bucuresti, *42*, 19 octombrie.

Dragutescu, E. (1996), *Patru intalniri cu Brancusi*, Jurnalul literar, Bucuresti, **VII**, *1-4*, aprilie.

Dreier, Katherine, Duchamp, M., eds. (1952), *Collection of the Société Anonyme*, Yale University Library, New Haven.

Dreyfus, A. (1923), *Constantin Brancusi*, Der Querschnitt, Berlin, **III**, *3-4*.

Dreyfus, A. (1927), *Constantin Brancusi*, Cahiers d'art, Paris, *2*.

Duchamp, M. (1996), *Deux interviews new-yorkaises, septembre 1915*, L'Échoppe, Paris.

Dudley Harvey, Dorothy (1927), *Brancusi*, The Dial, New York, **LXXXII,** February.

Dumitrescu, Elena (2013), *Ecorseul Brancusi—Gerota—istoria unei lucrari realizate la Scoala de Belle Arte din Bucuresti*, Ed. UNARTE, Bucuresti.

Duthuit, G. (1954), *Brancusi Revisited and the Arensberg Brancusis,* The Art News, New York, **LIII**, October.

Duthuit, G. (1961), *Le sanctuaire de Brancusi, L'image en souffrance*, Éd. George Fail, Paris.

E.A.J. (1941), *"From Rodin to Brancusi" at Buchholz Gallery—Ehrin and Carl Milles*, The New York Times, New York, 16 February.

Eddy, A. J. (1914), *Cubists and Post-Impressionism*, A.C. McClurg Grant Publishers, Chicago.

Ede, J. (1984), *Kettle's Yard. A Way of Life*, Cambridge University Press, Cambridge (UK).

Edelman, B. (2001), *L'adieu aux arts. 1926: L' affaire Brancusi*, Éd. Aubier Montaigne, Paris.

Édouard-Joseph, R. (1930), *Dictionnaire biographique des artistes contemporains: 1910-1930,* **I-IV** (**I**/1930, Braun et C-ie, Mulhouse-Dornach-Paris, R. Vitrac text and Brancusi aphorisms, pp. 196-198).

Edwards, H., ed. (1956), *Surrealism and its Affinities: The Mary Reynolds Collection*, Art Institute of Chicago, Chicago.

Eftimiu, V. (1966), *Portrete si amintiri*, Ed. pentru Literatura, Bucuresti.

Eftimiu, V. (1968), *Brancusi la Buzau*, Viata Buzaului, Buzau, *22*, septembrie.

Eglington, L. (1933), *Marcel Duchamp, Back in America, Gives Interview*, The Art News, New York, 18 November.

Einstein, C. (1931), *Die Kunst des 20. Jahrhunderts*, Propyläen-Kunstgeschichte, Propyläen-Verlag, Berlin.

Eleancu, C. (1997), *Cazna si izbanda lui Brancusi—eseuri, traduceri, dialoguri, amintiri*, Ed. Astra, Brasov.

Eliade, M. (1991), *Memorii (1907-1960)*, **I**, **II**, Ed. Humanitas, Bucuresti.

Eliasberg, Nora (1968), *Operele lui Brancusi la expozitia din Moscova*, in *Colocviul Brancusi—Bucuresti, 13-15 octombrie 1967,* Ed. Meridiane, Bucuresti.

Elimann, R. (1959), *James Joyce*, Oxford University Press, New York.

Elsen, A.E. (1974), *Origins of Modern Sculpture: Pioneers and Premises*, G. Braziller, New York.

Enescu, T. (1991), *Momentul 1910 in istoria artei moderne*, Studii si Cercetari de Istoria Artei, seria Arta Plastica, Bucuresti, tom **38**.

Epstein, J. (1940), *Let There Be Sculpture*, M. Joseph Publishers, London.

Epstein, J. (1955), *An Autobiography*, Hulton Press, London.

Estienne, C. (1956), *Perennité de l'art moderne*, Combat-Art, Paris, *1,* 9 janvier.

Farrell, J.T. (1965), *Brancusi*, Tribuna, Cluj, **9**, *40*, 7 octombrie.

Faure, E. (1970), *Istoria artei*, **V** *Arta moderna*, Ed. Meridiane, Bucuresti.

Fierens, P. (1933), *Sculpteurs d'aujourd'hui*, Éd. des Chroniques du Jour, Paris.

Filler, M. (1979), *The Gov. Nelson A. Rockefeller Empire State Plaza, Albany, NY / Halicarnassus on the Hudson,* Progressive Architecture, New York, 5, May.

Firoiu, V. (1969), *Din nou acasa ... Convorbiri cu Henri Coanda*, Ed. Tineretului, Bucuresti.

Fisher, Barbara (2004), *Mistress of Modernism: The Life of Peggy Guggenheim*, The Boston Globe, Boston, 17 October.

Floda, L. (1986), *An Interview with Isamu Noguchi on Brancusi*, Journal of the American Romanian Academy of Arts and Sciences, Davis (CA), *8-9*.

Florea, V. (1980), *Arta romaneasca moderna si contemporana*, Ed. Meridiane, Bucuresti.

Florea, V. (1985), *L'art roumain*, **II**. *Moderne et contemporaine*, Ed. Meridiane, Bucuresti.

Fondane, B. (1929), *Brancusi*, Cahiers de l'Étoile, Paris, **II**, *11,* septembre-octobre.

Ford, H., éd. (1989), *This Must Be the Place: Memoirs of Montparnasse by Jimmie 'the Barman' Charters, as Told to Morrill Cody,* Collier Books, New York.

Fortunato (1928), *Artisti olteni*, Arhivele Olteniei, Craiova, **VII**, *37-38*, mai-august.

Fortunescu, C.D. (1943), *Arta in Oltenia*, Ed. Ramuri, Craiova.

Francastel, P. (1954), *Brancusi*, in *Les Sculpteurs célèbres*, Éd. d'Art, Lucien Mazenoc, Paris.

Frank, W., ed. (1934), *America and Alfred Stieglitz: A Collective Portrait,* The Literary Guild, New York.

Frumuselu, Doina (2007), *Brancusi: O bibliografie nesfarsita / Brancusi: An Endless Bibliography*, Ed. AGIR, Bucuresti.

Frumuselu, Doina (2012), *Brancusi in His Time and in Ours*, Ed. Eurostampa, Timisoara.

Frumuselu, Doina (2012), *Brancusi. Fiul campului si Mars Borghese*, Aisberg, Brasov, serie noua, revista murala, **IV**, *10*, octombrie.

Frumuselu, Doina (2012), *Brancusi. Portretul lui Gheorghe Chitu?*, Aisberg, Brasov, serie noua, revista murala, **IV**, *3*, mai.

Frumuselu, Doina (2013), *Brancusi: the Beginner*, RCR Editorial, Bucharest.

Frumuselu, Doina, ed. (2014), *Brancusi in the Exhibitions from Romania*, RCR Editorial, Bucharest.

Frumuselu, Doina (2014), *Brancusi: Testimonies*, RCR Editorial, Bucharest.

Fry, R. (1913), *The Allied Artists Exhibition*, The Nation, London, 2 august.

Fulton Margolis, Marianne, ed. (1978), *Camera Work: A Pictorial Guide*, Dover Publications, New York.

Fundoianu, B. (1925), *Brancusi*, Contimporanul, Bucuresti, **IV**, *52,* ianuarie.

Fundoianu, B. (1930), *Privelisti / poeme / cu un portret inedit de C. Brancusi*, Ed. Cultura Nationala, Bucuresti.

G.L.S. (1938), *Sculptors Guild Show Continues in Brooklyn; Open Until Nov. 27 Exhibit Well Arranged Not Confined to Nudes,* The Washington Post, Washington, D.C., 20 November.

G.M. (1954), *Verpasste Gelegenheiten,* Die Weltwoche, Zürich, **XXI**, 10 Dezember.

Geist, S. (1964), *Looking for Brancusi in Romania,* Arts Magazine, New York, *10*, October.

Geist, S. (1966), *"Numai ochi" / "Domnisoara Pogany" de Brancusi in lumina unor documente inedite,* Contemporanul, Bucuresti, *36(1039),* 9 septembrie.

Geist, S. (1966), *O coloana la sfarsit,* Tribuna, Cluj, **10**, *8,* 24 februarie (republicat in *Colocviul Brancusi—Bucuresti, 13-15 octombrie 1967,* Ed. Meridiane, Bucuresti).

Geist, S. (1968), *Brancusi. A Study of the Sculpture,* Grossman Publishers, New York (Studio Vista ltd., London, 1968; Hacker Art Books, New York, 1983).

Geist, S. (1968), *Indicatii biografice in sculptura lui Brancusi,* in *Colocviul Brancusi—Bucuresti, 13-15 octombrie 1967,* Ed. Meridiane, Bucuresti.

Geist, S. (1975), *Brancusi. The Sculpture and Drawings,* Harry N. Abrams, Inc., New York.

Geist, S. (1978), *Brancusi. The Kiss,* Icon Editions Harper & Row Publishers, New York.

Geist, S., Pascu, A. (1985), *Délicatesse de Brancusi,* Éd. du Regard, Paris.

George, W. (1936), *Les tendances actuelles de la sculpture. Brancusi,* in *Encyclopédie française,* **XVII**, Paris.

George, W. (1951), *Grandeur et solitude de Constantin Brancusi,* Art et industrie, Paris, *22.*

Georgescu-Gorjan, St. (1964), *Biografia si perspectivele Coloanei Infinite,* Ramuri, Craiova, *12,* 30 decembrie.

Georgescu-Gorjan, St. (1964), *The Genesis of the Column Without End,* Revue Roumaine d'Histoire de l'Art, série BeauxArts, Bucarest, Tome **I**.

Georgescu-Gorjan, St. (1965), *Marturii despre Brancusi,* Studii si Cercetari de Istoria Artei, seria Arta Plastica, Bucuresti, tom **12**, *1.*

Georgescu-Gorjan, St. (1965), *Memoria locurilor,* Ramuri, Craiova, *3, 23* martie.

Georgescu-Gorjan, St. (1965), *Realizarea Coloanei infinite*, Arta plastica, Bucuresti, *2*.

Georgescu-Gorjan, St. (1978), *Schita Coloanei Infinite facuta de Constantin Brancusi si montarea ei la Targu-Jiu*, Fotografia, Bucuresti, *121*, ianuarie-februarie.

Georgescu-Gorjan, St. (1979), *Brancusi et ses colonnes infinies—Nouvelles contributions*, Revue Roumaine d'Histoire de l'Art, série Beaux-Arts, Bucarest, Tome **XVI**.

Georgescu-Gorjan, St. (1988), *Amintiri despre Brancusi*, Ed. Scrisul Romanesc, Craiova.

Georgescu-Gorjan, St. (1996), *Templul din Indor*, Ed. Eminescu, Bucuresti.

Georgescu-Gorjan, St. (2005), *Am lucrat cu Brancusi*, Ed. Universalia, Bucuresti.

Ghenie, A. (1927), *Brancusi*, Gorjanul, Targu-Jiu, 25 decembrie.

Ghiata, P., Sachelarie, C. (1965), *Maria Tanase si cantecul romanesc*, Ed. Muzicala, Bucuresti.

Giedion, S. (1948), *Mechanization Takes Command: A Contribution to Anonymous History*, Oxford University Press, New York.

Giedion, S. (1956), *Architektur und Gemeinschaft,* in seria Rowohlts Deutsche Enzyklopädie: das Wissen des 20. Jahrhunderts im Taschenbuch mit enzyklopädischem Stichwort, 18, Rowohlt Verlag, Hamburg (first publication in 1936; issue in english language—*Architecture. You and Me*, Harvard University Press, Cambridge, 1958).

Giedion-Welcker, Carola (1937), *Moderne Plastik: Elemente der Wirklichkeit, Masse und Auflockerung*, Dr. H. Girsberger Verlag, Zürich.

Giedion-Welcker, Carola (1948), *Constantin Brancusi Weg,* Werk, Winterthur, *10*, October.

Giedion-Welcker, Carola (1949), *Constantin Brancusi*, Horizon, London, **XIX**, March.

Giedion-Welcker, Carola (1954), *Sept pionniers de la sculpture moderne*, Werk, Winterthur, *9*, September.

Giedion-Welcker, Carola (1957), *Zum Tode von Constantin Brancusi*, National Zeitung, Sonntags-Beilage, Basel, *137*, 24 März.

Giedion-Welcker, Carola (1958), *Constantin Brancusi (1876-1957)*, Benno Schwabe & Co., Basel-Stuttgart (Éd. du Griffon, Neuchâtel, 1959; George Braziller Publishers, New York, 1959).

Giglioli, E. (1957), *Hommage à Brancusi*, Les Lettres françaises, Paris, *664*, 28 mars.

Gindertael, R.V. (1956), *Brancusi l'inaccessible*, Cimaise, Paris, *3*, janvier-février.

Giroiu, Ioana (1938), *De vorba cu sculptorul Constantin Brancusi*, Timpul, Bucuresti, **II**, 1 august.

Giry, Stéphanie (2002), *An Odd Bird*, Legal Affairs, The Magazine at the Intersection of Law and Life, http://www.legalaffairs.org/issues/September-October-2002/.

Goldberger, P., Lambert, Phyllis, Lavnin, Sylvia (2010), *Modern Views*, Assouline Publishers, New York.

Golding, J. (1994), *Visions of the Modern*, Thames & Hudson Publishers, London.

Goldwater, R. (1954), *The Arensberg Collection for Philadelphia*, The Burlington Magazine, London, *620*, November.

Goldwater, R. (1974), *Primitivismul in arta moderna*, Ed. Meridiane, Bucuresti.

Gombrich, E.H. (1973), *Arta si iluzie*, Ed. Meridiane, Bucuresti.

Gombrich, E.H. (1975), *O istorie a artei*, Ed. Meridiane, Bucuresti.

Green Harris, Ruth (1929), *Paintings and Sculpture Shown in Paris*, The New York Times, New York, 31 March.

Greenough, Sarah, ed. (2000), *Modern Art and America: Alfred Stieglitz and His New York Galleries*, National Gallery of Art, Washington, D.C.

Gregg, F.J. (1918), *New Works of Art, Native and Foreign*, New York Herald, New York, 29 September.

Gremer, J. (1914), *Arta si problemele ei*, Ed. Meridiane, Bucuresti.

Grigorescu, D. (1977), *Brancusi*, Ed. Stiintifica si Enciclopedica, Bucuresti.

Grigorescu, D. (1980), *Constantin Brancusi*, Ed. Meridiane, Bucuresti.

Grigorescu, D. (1984), *Brancusi and the Romanian Roots of His Art*, Ed. Meridiane, Bucuresti.

Grigorescu, D. (1999) *Brancusi si arta secolului XX*, Ed. Gramar, Bucuresti.

Grigorescu, D. (2001), *Brancusi si arta moderna*, Ed. Universal DALSI, Bucuresti.

Gross, J.R., Bohan, R.L. (2006), *The Société Anonyme: Modernism for America*, Yale University Press, New Haven.

Grozea, I. (1917), *Convorbiri artistice—"Tinerimea artistica"*, Romania ilustrata, Bucuresti, aprilie-iunie.

Gruia, I. (1907), *A sasea expozitie a "Tinerimii artistice"*, Secolul, Bucuresti, 27 aprilie.

Gruia, I. (1909), *Expozitia "Tinerimii artistice"*, Secolul, Bucuresti, 3 aprilie.

Gruia, I. (1910), *A IX-a expozitie a "Tinerimii artistice"*, Secolul, Bucuresti, 29 aprilie.

Gruia, I. (1910), *Un mare eveniment artistic*, Secolul, Bucuresti, 15 aprilie.

Guggenheim, Peggy (1980), *Out of This Century: Confessions of an Art Addict*, André Deutsch Publishers, London.

Guggenheim, Peggy, ed. (1942), *Art of This Century: 1910-1942*, Art of This Century, New York.

Guilbert, C. G. (1957), *Propos de Brancusi (1876-1957)*, Prisme des Arts, Paris, *12*, mai.

H.T.F. (1955), *C. Brancusi*, Frankfurter Allgemeine Zeitung, Frankfurt, 12 März.

Habasque, G. (1959), *L'Armory Show*, L'Œil, Paris, 59, février.

Hajdu, É. (1957), *Hommage à Brancusi*, Les Lettres françaises, Paris, *664*, 28 mars.

Hajdu, É. (1968), *Discutii*, in *Colocviul Brancusi—Bucuresti, 13-15 octombrie 1967*, Ed. Meridiane, Bucuresti.

Han, O. (1965), *Rencontre avec Brancusi*, Revue Roumaine d'Histoire de l'Art, série Beaux-Arts, Bucarest, Tome II.

Han, O. (1970), *Dalti si pensule*, Ed. Minerva, Bucuresti.

Hansen, Arlen J. (1990), *Expatriate Paris: A Cultural and Literary Guide to Paris of the 1920s*, Arcade Publishing, New York (reprint in Skyhorse Publishing Inc., New York, 2014).

Hansen, H. (1928), *The First Reader. Reverberations*, New York World, New York, 18 February.

Hasnas, N. (1938), *O munca chibzuita*, Cuvantul Gorjului, Targu-Jiu, I, 18, 9 octombrie.

Haulica, D. (1967), *Brancusi ou l'anonimat du génie*, Ed. Meridiane, Bucuresti.

Haulica, D. (2004), *Variatiuni la Brancusi*, Observator Cultural, Bucuresti, *201-202*, 1 ianuarie.

Hébert (1926), *Notes d'un curieux / Le Salon du franc*, Le Gaulois, Paris, 30 octobre.

Heitkamt, E. (1927), *Brancusi's Modern Art Easy for Critic Understand...*, Chicago Herald and Examiner, Chicago, January.

Herbé, P. (1946), *Visite à Brancusi*, L'Architecture d'aujourd'hui, Paris, numéro hors-série.

Hetzler, Florence M. (1974), *Easter and Western Language, Thought and Reality Meet in the Philosophy and Art of Constantin Brancusi*, in *Death and Creativity*, Health Science Publ. Corp., New York.

Hetzler, Florence M. (1976), *Brancusi: Meditation Monument at Indore India*, Scarsdale, New York.

Hetzler, Florence M. (1976), *Cu Noguchi, despre Brancusi si Indore*, Secolul 20, Bucuresti, *10-12(189-191),* octombrie-decembrie.

Hetzler, Florence M., ed. (1992), *Art and Philosophy: Brancusi: The Courage to Love*, Peter Lang Publishers, New York.

Hickok, G. (1927), *Brancusi, Modernist Sculptor Bows Meekly to Kracke's Stand Barring His Work from U.S.*, Brooklyn Eagle & Brooklyn Times, New York, 12 March.

Hinoveanu, I. (2001), *Memorialul Brancusi. Pasi pe nisipul eternitatii sau cazna legamantului cu demiurgul: Antologie, documente, scrisori*, Ed. ALMA, Craiova.

Hoctin, Luce (1957), *Grandeur et solitude de Brancusi*, Arts et spectacles, Paris, 27 mars.

Hoctin, Luce (1957), *Le testament de Brancusi, le plus grand sculpteur, depuis Rodin a légué son atelier à la France*, Art, Paris, 16 avril.

Hoffman, Malvina (1939), *Sculpture Inside and Out*, W. W. Norton & Co., New York.

Hofmann, W. (1954), *Malerei im 20. Jahrhunderts*, Prestel Verlag, München.

Hofmann, W. (1968), *Discutii*, in *Colocviul Brancusi—Bucuresti, 13-15 octombrie 1967,* Ed. Meridiane, Bucuresti.

Housez, Judith (2006), *Marcel Duchamp*, Éd. Grasset, Paris.

Howe, R.W. (1949), *Constantin Brancusi. The Man Who Doesn't Like Michelangelo. Interview*, Apollo, London, **XLIX**, May.

Hulten, P., Dumitrescu, Natalia, Istrati, A. (1986), *Brancusi*, Éd. Flammarion, Paris.

Humbert, Agnes (1954), *La sculpture contemporaine au Musée National d'Art Moderne de Paris*, Éd. Albert Morancé, Paris.

Huszár, V. (1918), *Aesthetische beschouwing V (bij bijlage XVI)*, De Stijl, Leyda, **1**, *12*, oktober.

Huxley, A. (1929), *Das Land*, Der Querschnitt, Berlin (Propyläen Verlag), **IX**, Heft *12*, Dezember.

Huyghe, R. (1961), *L'art et l'homme*, **III**, Librairie Larousse, Paris.

Huyghe, R. (1971), *Puterea imaginii*, Ed. Meridiane, Bucuresti.

Huyghe, R. (1981), *Dialog cu vizibilul*, Ed. Meridiane, Bucuresti. I.N.T. (1913), *Sculptura noastra*, Seara, Bucuresti, 23 mai.

Iacob, X. (1975), *"Visam sa cioplesc direct in stanca...". Brancusi in insemnarile dr. Nicolae Hasnas*, Coloana, Targu-Jiu, decembrie.

Iancu, M. (1925), *Brancusi*, Contimporanul, Bucuresti, **IV**, *52*, ianuarie.

Iancu, M. (1926), *La Brancusi*, Contimporanul, Bucuresti, **V**, *64*, ianuarie.

Iancu, M. (1929), *Brancusi, sculptorul tainelor*, Contimporanul, Bucuresti, **VIII**, *83*, 27 octombrie.

Ioan, O.G. (1909), *La VIIIe Exposition de la "Tinerimea artistica"*, L'Indépendance Roumaine, Bucarest, 26 avril.

Ioan, O.G. (1910), *La IXe Exposition de la "Tinerimea artistica"*, L'Indépendance Roumaine, Bucarest, 29 avril.

Ionescu, E. (1959), *Témoignages sur Brancusi*, Les Cahiers du Musée de Poche, Paris, décembre.

Ionescu, E. (1962), *Notes et contre-notes*, Éd. Gallimard, Paris.

Ionescu, A.S. (1999), *Invatamantul artistic romanesc 1830-1892*, Ed. Meridiane, Bucuresti.

Ionescu, R. (1966), *Muzeul de Arta al Academiei. Colectia G. Oprescu*, Revista Muzeelor, Bucuresti, tom **3**, *2*.

Ionescu, R. (1967), *Cu Milita Petrascu despre Brancusi*, Familia, Oradea, *11*, noiembrie.

Ionescu, Ruxandra (1975), *Toma Gh. Tomescu* (album), Muzeul de Arta din Ploiesti.

Iorga, N. (1926), *Romania in chipuri si vederi*, Ed. Cultura Nationala, Bucuresti.

Iorga, N. (1968), *Scrieri despre arta*, Ed. Meridiane, Bucuresti.

Ivascu, G. (1956), *Expozitia Brancusi*, Contemporanul, Bucuresti, **40**, decembrie.

Jacovski, A. (1935), *Brancusi*, Axis—a quarterly review of contemporary abstract painting and sculpture, London, *3,* July.

Jaffé, H.L.C. (1956), *De Stijl, 1917-1931, The Dutch Contribution to Modern Art*, J. M. Meulenhoff, Amsterdam.

Jalea, I. (1956), *Brancusi*, Contemporanul, Bucuresti, *40(522)*, 5 octombrie.

Jeanjaquet, M.A. (1908), *"Tinerimea artistica"*, La Roumanie, Bucuresti, 3 aprilie.

Jeanjaquet, M.A. (1908), *La jeunesse artistique—Ouverture de la 7-ème exposition*, La Roumanie, Bucuresti, 11 mars.

Jeanjaquet, M.A. (1912), *Cronica artistica / Expozitia artistilor in viata /— Salonul Oficial*, Noua Revista Romana, Bucuresti, **XII**, *9*, 10 iunie.

Jeanjaquet, M.A. (1912), *Le Salon officiel*, La Roumanie, Bucuresti, 9 mai.

Jianu, I. (1938), *Brancusi. O lectie de arta, o lectie de viata*, Jurnalul Doamnei, Bucuresti, **3**, 15 noiembrie.

Jianu, I. (1946), *Constantin Brancusi. Marturii,* Lumina si coloare, Bucuresti, *1*, mai (reprint in Revista Fundatiilor Regale, Bucuresti, 1946, **XIII**, *9*, septembrie).

Jianu, I. (1957), *Brancusi à Bucarest*, Les Lettres françaises, Paris, *657*, 7-13 février.

Jianu, I. (1963), *Brancusi*, Arted, Éd. d'Art, Paris.

Jianu, I. (1983), *Constantin Brancusi—viata si opera*, Ed. Stiintifica si Enciclopedica, Bucuresti.

Jianu, I., Noica, C. (1976), *Introduction à la sculpture de Brancusi*, Arted, Éd. d'Art, Paris.

Jianu, I., Xuriguera, G., Lardera, A. (1982), *La sculpture moderne en France depuis 1950*, Arted, Éd. d'Art, Paris.

Jones, C. (1999), *Nancy Cunard: An Inventory of Her Collection at the Harry Ransom Humanities Research Center*, University of Texas at Austin.

Joseph, E. (1930/1933), *Dictionnaire biographique des artistes contemporains, 1910-1930*, **I**, Éd. d'Art, Paris.

K.C. (1957), *Frère de Socrate*, L'Express, Paris, 24 mai.

Kamadeva (1912), *Preumblari artistice. La Ateneu, Salonul oficial. Critica si realitatea*, Conservatorul, Bucuresti, 30 mai.

Keller, H. (1957), *Brancusi, ein Klassiker unserer Zeit*, Neue Zürcher Zeitung. Literatur und Kunst. Sonntagsausgabe Nr. 1001, 1003, Zürich, 7, *4*.

Kesser, A. (1957), *Erfahrungen in Brancusi*, Neue Zürcher Zeitung. Literatur und Kunst. Sonntagsausgabe Nr. 1001, 1003, Zürich, 7, *4*.

Készman, J. (2004), *Egy világraszóló magyar / Az art déco egyetemes nagykövete: Miklós Gusztáv (1888, Budapest—1967, Oyonnax)*, Artmagazin, mai, www.artmagazin.hu.

KONG (1914), *Expozitia "Tinerimii artistice"*, Epoca, Bucuresti, 10 aprilie.

Kozmutza, Ottilie de (1906), *Un artiste roumain à Paris*, L'Indépendance Roumaine, Bucarest, 5 décembre.

Kramer, H. (1979), *Beyond the Avant-garde*, The New York Times, New York, 4 November.

Kramer, H. (1979), *Brancusi, the Sculptor as Photographer*, David Grob Ltd. Publisher, London.

Krauss, Rosalind (1990), *Forms of Ready-made: Duchamp and Brancusi*, in *Passages in Modern Sculpture*, The MIT Press, Cambridge (MA).

Kulterman, U. (1956), *Brancusi—der Vater der Modernen Skulptur*, Baukunst und Werkform, Nürnberg, *164-166*, März.

Kulterman, U. (1957), *Constantin Brancusi—ein bildernisches Genie aus des 20. Jahrhunderts*, Kunstwerk, Baden-Baden, **XI**, *1*, Juli.

Lafranchis, J. (1965), *Marcoussis,* Éd. du Temps, Paris.

Lambert, J.C. (1994), *Marta Pan: de la sculpture au paysage ou la pensée sculpturale*, Éd. du Cercle d'Art, Paris.

Lambert, Phyllis (2013), *Building Seagram*, Yale University Press, New Haven & London.

Lamster, M. (2013), *A Personal Stamp on the Skyline*, The New York Times, New York, 3 April.

Langui, E. (1960), *50 ans d'art moderne*, DuMont Buchverlag, Köln.

Lardera, B. (1948), *Visita a Brancusi*, Il Nuovo Corriere, Florence, 26 aprile.

Lassaigne, J., Cogniat, R., Zahar, M., eds. (1948), *Panorama des arts: 1947*, Éd. Aimery Somogy, Paris.

Le Corbusier (1984), *L'Espace indicible,* in *Savina, dessins et sculptures,* Fondation Le Corbusier et Philippe Sers, Paris.

Le Corbusier (1984), *Savina, dessins et sculptures,* Fondation Le Corbusier et Philippe Sers, Paris.

Lemny, Doina (2005), *Constantin Brancusi (biographie),* Éd. Oxus, Paris.

Lemny, Doina (2012), *Brancusi au-delà de toutes les frontières*, Éd. Fage, Lyon.

Lemny, Doina (2020), *L-au intalnit pe / Ils ont rencontré Brancusi*, Ed. Vremea, Bucuresti.

Lemny, Doina, Velescu, C.R., eds. (2004), *Brancusi inedit: insemnari si corespondenta romaneasca,* Ed. Humanitas, Bucuresti.

Lévy, Sophie, ed. (2003), *American Artists in Paris 1918-1939: A Transatlantic Avant-garde*, Musée d'Art Américain, France & University California Press, Berkeley.

Lewis, D. (1957), *Constantin Brancusi*, Alec Tiranti, London.

Lieberman, A. (1969), *The Artist in His Studio*, Viking Press, New York.

Lipsi, M. (1957), *Hommage à Brancusi*, Les Lettres françaises, Paris, *664*, 28 mars.

LK (1926), *In New York Galleries*, The New York Times, New York, 21 November.

Londraville, R., Londraville, Janis (2001), *Dear Yeats, Dear Pound, Dear Ford: Jeanne Robert Foster and Her Circle of Friends*, Syracuse University Press, New York.

Loy, Mina (1922), *Brancusi's Golden Bird*, The Dial, New York, **LXXIII**, *5*, November.

Luclu, E. (1910), *A noua expozitie a "Tinerimii artistice"*, Revista democratiei romane, Bucuresti, 2 mai.

Lunacearski, A. V. (1928), *Arta pariziana pe Prechistenka*, Proektor, Moscova, 43(161), in *Dialog despre arta (antologie, traducere si prefata de Vasile Florea)*, Ed. Meridiane, Bucuresti, 1975.

M.D. (1907), *Miscarea artistica,* Convorbiri critice, Bucuresti, *8-10*, 15 aprilie.

M.M. (1923), *Constantin Brancusi. A Summary of Many Conversations*, The Arts, New York, **IV**, *1*, 4 July.

M.V. (1930), *Roemeensche Kunst in Het Stedelijk Museum Beeldhouwerk en Tapyten*, Algemen Handeblad, Amsterdam, 11 mei.

MA (1920), *Arta romana. A III-a expozitie*, Adeverul, Bucuresti, 3 aprilie.

Magura, I. (1906), *Lettres de Paris. Les Roumains aux Salons,* L'Indépendance Roumaine, Bucarest, 20 mai.

Maillard, L. (1899), *Études sur quelques artistes originaux / Auguste Rodin / Statuaire*, H. Floury, Libraire-Éditeur, Paris.

Mallet-Stevens, R. (2008), *Architecture. Villa Noailles*, Quintet magazine, Genève, 30 janvier.

Man Ray (1963), *Self-Portrait*, André Deutsch Publishers, London.

Mandrescu, A. (1966), *Le Musée d'Art de Craiova*, Ed. Meridiane, Bucuresti.
Maniu, A. (1913), *Cronica artistica. A XII-a expozitiune a Societatii "Tinerimea Artistica"*, Noua Revista Romana, Bucuresti, **XIII**, *23-24*, 7-14 aprilie.
Maniu, A. (1929), *Salonul Desenului*, Rampa, Bucuresti, **XIV**, *3541*, 8 noiembrie.
Maniu, A. (1930), *Brancusi*, Dimineata, Bucuresti, 12 octombrie.
Maniu, A. (1933), *Fel de fel / Brancusi*, Universul, Bucuresti, **50**, *26*, 29 ianuarie.
Maniu, A. (1935), *Cioplitorul,* in *Focurile primaverii si flacari de toamna*, Fundatia pentru Literatura si Arta, Bucuresti.
Manu, E. (1976), *5 scrisori ilustrate de la Constantin Brancusi*, Romania literara, Bucuresti, *8*, 19-25 februarie.
Marchiori, G. (1965), *The Peggy Guggenheim Collection*, Studio International, London, January.
Marchiori, G. (1968), *Brancusi la Targu-Jiu*, Arta plastica, Bucuresti, *1*.
Marchis-Bölöni, Otilia (2011), *Cartea suferintelor*, Ed. Dacia, Cluj-Napoca.
Margineanu, N. (1957), *Fecunditate. Opera sculptorului C. Brancusi*, Tribuna, Cluj-Napoca, **1**, *8*, 31 martie.
Marter, Joan, ed. (2011), *The Grove Encyclopedia of American Art*, **I**, The Oxford University Press, New York.
Martinescu, P. (1943), *Un gran escultor rumano C. Brancusi*, Solidaridad Nacional, Barcelona, 31 agosto.
Maxy, M.H. (1925), *Tendinte noi in arte. Cubismul si constructivismul*, Foaia Tinerimii, Bucuresti, **IX**, *6*, 15 martie.
Maxy, M.H. (1931), *Brancusi, ilustrator de carti avangardiste la noi*, Integral, Bucuresti, *33*, februarie.
Maxy, M.H. (1931), *Contributiuni sumare la cunoasterea miscarii moderne dela noi*, Unu, Bucuresti, **IV**, *33*, februarie.
Maxy, M.H. (1966), *Chez lui, Brancusi réalise et se réalise*, La Roumanie d'aujourd'hui, Bucuresti, février.
McAlmon, R., Boyle, Kay (1984), *Being Geniuses Together 1920-1930*, North Point Press, New York.
McBride, H. (1914), *Brancusi*, The Sun, New York, 22 March.

McBride, H. (1926), *Brancusi's Sculptures at the Brummer Galleries: Simplifications of Sculptor's Work. Test for the Imagination*, The New York Sun, New York, **XCIV**, 20 November.

McBride, H. (1927), *Modern Art*, The Dial, New York, **LXXXII**, February.

McLintock, A.H., ed. (1966), *Expatriates—Biographies*, in *An Encyclopaedia of New-Zealand*, http://www.teara.govt.nz.

Medianu, Apriliana (1930), *Maestrul Brancusi*, Curentul literar si artistic, Bucuresti, **III**, *972*, 6 octombrie.

Mereuta, I. (1966), *Omagiu uriasului*, Viata studenteasca, Bucuresti, 1 martie.

Merrill, Flora (1926), *Brancusi, the Sculptor of Spirit, Would Build 'Infinite Column' in Park,* New York World, New York, 3 October.

Michailescu, C. (1928), *Arta romana*, Politica, Bucuresti, **III**, 19 martie.

Michailescu, C. (1928), *C. Brancusi*, Universul literar, Bucuresti, **XLIV**, *17*, 22 aprilie.

Micheli, M. de (1966), *I maestri della scultura / Brancusi*, Fabbri, Milano.

Micheli, M. de (1968), *Avangarda artistica a secolului XX*, Ed. Meridiane, Bucuresti.

Mignot-Ogliastri, C. (1986), *Anna de Noailles: une amie de la Princesse Edmond de Polignac*, Éd. Méridiens Klincksieck—Fondation Singer-Polignac, Paris.

Mihaescu, G. (1930), *Expozitia de arta romaneasca...*, Curentul literar si artistic, Bucuresti, **III**, *910*, 11 august.

Mihalovici, M. (1987), *Amintiri despre Enescu, Brancusi si alti prieteni*, Ed. Eminescu, Bucuresti.

Milian Minulescu, Claudia (1937), *Sinteza si spirit romanesc*, Adeverul, Bucuresti, 4 November (reprint in Gorjanul, TarguJiu, **XIV**, *42*, 8 November).

Miller, Sanda (1995), *Constantin Brancusi*, Oxford University Press, New York.

Miller, Sanda (2001), *Brancusi,* Phaidon Press, London.

Miller, Sanda (2007), *Brancusi's Women: Constantin Brancusi Died 50 years Ago This Month*, Apollo, London, 1 March.

Miller, Sanda (2010), *Constantin Brancusi*, Reaktion Books, London.

Minulescu, I. (1925), *Constantin Brancusi,* Integral, Bucuresti, **I**, *2*, 1 aprilie.

Minulescu, I. (1930), *Strofe pentru toata lumea*, Ed. Cultura Nationala, Bucuresti.

Mocioi, I. (1970), *Se destainuie unul din prietenii lui Brancusi—Dr. Micu Marcu, din Targu-Jiu*, Gazeta Gorjului, Targu-Jiu, 26 septembrie.

Mocioi, I. (1980), *Imprejurarile edificarii la Targu-Jiu a Ansamblului sculptural al lui Constantin Brancusi*, Gorjul turistic, O.J.T. Gorj, Targu-Jiu, iulie.

Mocioi, I. (2003), *Brancusi,* **I** Viata, **II** *Opera*, Ed. Spicon & Drim Edit, Targu-Jiu.

Mocioi, I. (2004), *Insemnari despre Brancusi*, Ed. Spicon & Drim Edit, Targu-Jiu.

Mocioi, I., ed. (1971), *Brancusi: Ansamblul sculptural de la Targu-Jiu—documentar*, C.J.C.E.S. Gorj, Targu-Jiu.

Mocioi, I., ed. (1975), *Marturii despre Brancusi*, C.J.C.E.S. Gorj, Targu-Jiu.

Moeschler, V. (1995), *Brancusi est l'inventeur de la sculpture moderne*, Tribune de Genève, Genève, 163.

Moholy-Nagy, L. (1929), *Von Material zu Architektur*, Bauhausbücher, Band 14, Albert Langen, München.

Moholy-Nagy, L. (1947), *Vision in Motion*, Paul Theobald Publishers, Chicago.

Mohor, I. (1938), *Adevarul inainte de toate*, Gorjanul, Targu-Jiu, 9 octombrie.

Mola, Paola (2000), *Studi su Brancusi*, Solchi, Milano.

Moldovanu, C. (1982), *In corespondenta*, Ed. Minerva, Bucuresti.

Montale, E. (1953), *Visita al bisbetico Brancusi detto "Fidia senza l'aneddoto"*, Corriere della Sera, Roma, 1 maggio.

Moore, H. (1934), *The Sculptor's Aims*, in *Unit One*, ed. Herbert Read, Gassell Publishers, London.

Moore, H. (1937), *The Sculptor Speaks*, The Listener, London, 18 August.

Moore, H. (1938), *Sculpture*, in *Art in England*, R. S. Lambert, Penguin Books Ltd., London.

Morand, P. (1927), *Brancusi*, Contimporanul, Bucuresti, **VI**, *76*, mai-iunie.

Morand, P. (1928), *C. Brancusi si strainatatea*, Universul literar, Bucuresti, **XLIV**, *17*, 22 aprilie.

Morand, P. (1931), *Brancusi, Papiers d'identité*, Éd. Grasset, Paris.

Morand, P. (1957), *Adieu à Brancusi*, Arts et spectacles, Paris, 20-26 mars.

Morarescu, D. (2002), *Lizica Codreanu si avangarda pariziana*, Ed. Aritmos, Bucuresti.

Morice, C. (1909), *Scrisori din Paris. Salonul de toamna*, Luceafarul, Sibiu, **VIII**, *5*, 1 martie.

Morris, G.L.K. (1938), *Art Chronicle: The Architectural Evolution of Brancusi*, Partisan Review, New York, **V**, 3, August-September.

Mosescu, O. (1973), *Alte vitralii*, **3**, Ed. Litera, Bucuresti.

Muller, J.É. (1969), *Arta moderna*, Ed. Stiintifica, Bucuresti.

Munteanu, B. (1957), *Discours à l'enterrement de Brancusi. Une sculpture toute pétrie de poésie,* La Nation Roumaine, Paris, **X**, *168,* avril.

Murnu, G. (1908), *Expozitia anuala a "Tinerimei artistice"*, Luceafarul, Sibiu, **VII**, *9-10*, 1-15 mai.

Murnu, G. (1908), *Expozitia VII a "Tinerimei artistice"*, Viata Romaneasca, Bucuresti, **9**, *4*, aprilie.

Murnu, G. (1909), *A VIII-a expozitie a "Tinerimii artistice"*, Luceafarul, Sibiu, **VIII**, *10*, 16 mai.

Murnu, G. (1913), *Expozitia a 12-a a Tinerimii artistice*, Luceafarul, Sibiu, **XII**, *11*, 1 iunie.

Neagoe, P. (1977), *Sfantul din Montparnasse: roman despre viata sculptorului roman Constantin Brancusi*, Ed. Dacia, ClujNapoca.

Negru, M. (1913), *A XII-a Expozitie a soc. "Tinerimea Artistica"*, Universul Literar, Bucuresti, **XXX**, *14*, 7 aprilie.

Negru, M. (1913), *De la Societatea "Tinerimea artistica"*, Universul, Bucuresti, 1 aprilie.

Nenitescu, S.I. (1927), *Pe marginea unui catalog*, Adeverul, Bucuresti, 27 februarie.

Newton, E. (1952), *A Critic Wiretaps Alexander Calder*, The New York Times, New York, 10 August.

Newton, E. (1954), *British Portraits*, The New York Times, New York, 25 April.

Nicoara, I. (1910), *Expozitia "Tinerimea artistica"*, Facla, Bucuresti, 10 mai.

Nicoara, M. (1963), *Marturii despre Brancusi*, Tribuna, Cluj, **7**, *47*, 21 noiembrie.

Nicoara, M. (1966), *Insemnari,* Familia, Oradea, februarie.

Nicolaescu-Plopsor, C.S. (1967), *"Brancusii" de la Craiova*, Astra, Brasov, *10*, octombrie.

Nicolaescu-Plopsor, C.S. (1989), *Cateva amintiri despre "Brancusii" de la Craiova*, Manuscriptum, Bucuresti, **XX**, *4(77)*.

Nicolescu, B. (2011), *Brancusi si Gurdjieff* (I), Convorbiri literare, Iasi, *3*, martie.

Nicolescu, B., Beekman Taylor, P. (2005), *Brancusi et Gurdjieff*, Ligeia, Paris, *57-60*, janvier-juin.

Niggl, R. (1996), *Eckart Muthesius 1930: Der Palast des Maharadschas in Indore—Architektur und Interieur / The Maharaja's Palace in Indore—Architecture and Interior*, Arnoldsche Verlagsanstalt GmbH, Stuttgart.

Noël (1930), *L'exposition d'art roumain moderne. Le vernissage à la Galérie Giroux à Bruxelles,* Neptune, Bruxelles, 20 juillet.

Noguchi, I. (1970), *Brancusi*, Chronique de l'Art vivant, Paris, février.

Oeri, Georgine (1956), *Constantin Brancusi in Amerika*, Werk, Winterthur, *6*.

Oprea, P. (1960), *Constantin Brancusi. Données biographiques*, Cahiers d'art, Paris, *33-35*.

Oprea, P. (1964), *Constantin Brancusi, bursier*, Tribuna, Cluj-Napoca, **VIII**, 22 octombrie.

Oprea, P. (1965), *Colectia de arta plastica "Alexandru Bogdan-Pitesti"*, Revista Muzeelor, Bucuresti, tom **2**, *1*.

Oprea, P. (1969), *Societati artistice bucurestene*, Ed. Meridiane, Bucuresti.

Oprea, P. (1972), *Intimități brancușiene*, Revista Muzeelor, Bucuresti, tom **9**, *4*.

Oprea, P. (1972), *Portretul lui Carol Davila de Constantin Brancusi*, Studii muzeale, Bucuresti, **IV**, *6*, iunie.

Oprea, P. (1976), *Colectionari de arta bucuresteni*, Ed. Meridiane, Bucuresti.

Oprea, P. (2001), *Doua perioade din istoriografia artei romanesti moderne si contemporane*, Ed. Maiko, Bucuresti.

Oprescu, G. (1935), *Roumanian Art from 1800 to Our Days*, Editor John Kroon, A.B. Malmö Ljustrycksanstalt.

Oprescu, G. (1954), *Sculptura statuara romaneasca*, Ed. de Stat pentru Literatura si Arta, Bucuresti.

Oprescu, G. (1965), *Sculptura romaneasca*, Ed. Meridiane, Bucuresti.

Oprescu, G. (1966), *Consideratii asupra artei moderne*, Ed. Meridiane, Bucuresti.

Oprescu, G. (1966), *Scrieri despre arta*, Ed. Meridiane, Bucuresti.

Oprescu, G. (1967), *Un chapitre peu connu de la vie sociale et artistique du Paris de la "belle époque"*, Gazette des BeauxArts, Paris, VIe période, **LXX**, *1182-1183*, juillet-août.

Oprescu, G. (1968), *Amintiri, evocari*, Ed. pentru Literatura, Bucuresti.

Oprescu, G. (1968), *Contributii la biografia lui Brancusi*, in *Colocviul Brancusi—Bucuresti, 13-15 octombrie 1967*, Ed. Meridiane, Bucuresti.

Oprescu, G., coord. (1959), *Artele plastice in Romania dupa 23 august 1944*, Ed. Academiei R.P.R., Bucuresti.

Owens, Mitchell (1997), *Art Deco Enough for a Maharajah*, The New York Times, New York, 22 May.

Ozenfant, A. (1928), *Art, bilan des arts modernes en France*, Éd. Jean Budry, Paris.

Ozenfant, A. (1931), *Foundations of Modern Art*, John Rodker Publishers, London. P.N. (1912), *Deschiderea salonului oficial*, Minerva, Bucuresti, 8 mai.

P.N. (1913), *Cronica artistica. Sculptura in expozitia "Tinerimii artistice"*, Minerva, Bucuresti, 21 aprilie.

Pach, W. (1925), *The Masters of Modern Art*, Viking Press & B. W. Huebsch, New York.

Pach, W. (1926), *Art: Brancusi*, The Nation, New York, **123**, *3204*.

Paleolog, T. (1976), *De vorba cu Brancusi despre "Calea Sufletelor Eroilor"*, Ed. Sport-Turism, Bucuresti.

Paleolog, V.G. (1937), *Sculptorul Brancusi*, Arhivele Olteniei, Craiova, **XVI**, *92-94*, iulie-decembrie.

Paleolog, V.G. (1938), *C. Brancusi,* Tipografia *Ramuri*, Craiova.

Paleolog, V.G. (1943), *Un sculptor al lumii*, Meridian, Craiova, aprilie.

Paleolog, V.G. (1944), *Cartea a doua despre C. Brancusi*, Ed. Ramuri, Craiova.

Paleolog, V.G. (1947), *Brancusi, valeur internationale*, Arcades, Bucarest, *1,* janvier-mars.

Paleolog, V.G. (1947), *C. Brancusi*, Ed. Forum, Bucuresti.

Paleolog, V.G. (1964), *Bilantul unui sfert de veac. Plecarea din tara la drum spre cucerirea lumii*, Inainte, Craiova, 27 septembrie.

Paleolog, V.G. (1964), *Brancusi. 1905-1907. Ani de tensiune si tranzitie*, Inainte, Craiova, 20 decembrie.

Paleolog, V.G. (1964), *Ecoul amintirilor. Un tovaras de drum spre cucerirea lumii*, Inainte, Craiova, 4 octombrie.

Paleolog, V.G. (1964), *Intaia opera muzeala "Vitellius" —C. Brancusi fecit, Craiova, 1896*, Inainte, Craiova, 16 august.

Paleolog, V.G. (1964), *Intaia si a doua fuga a lui Brancusi din Hobita*, Inainte, Craiova, 5 iulie.

Paleolog, V.G. (1965), *Cele trei "gresuri" ale lui Brancusi*, Inainte, Craiova, 21 februarie.

Paleolog, V.G. (1965), *Despre cele cinci opere ale lui Brancusi din Muzeul de Arta din Craiova*, Inainte, Craiova, 21 noiembrie.

Paleolog, V.G. (1965), *Piatra de hotar—despre un inedit iconografic din opera lui C. Brancusi,* Inainte, Craiova, 12 decembrie.

Paleolog, V.G. (1965), *Totul despre ciclul feminin in opera lui C. Brancusi*, Inainte, Craiova, 18 aprilie.

Paleolog, V.G. (1966), *Descoperirea unei opere de Brancusi,* Inainte, Craiova, 20 noiembrie.

Paleolog, V.G. (1966), *Unde incepe marele Brancusi*, Contemporanul, Bucuresti, 18 februarie.

Paleolog, V.G. (1967), *Activitatea urbanistica a lui C. Brancusi in 1937 la Targu-Jiu*, Inainte, Craiova, 12 octombrie.

Paleolog, V.G. (1967), *Brancusi si Scoala de Meserii,* Inainte, Craiova, 2 noiembrie.

Paleolog, V.G. (1967), *Doua lucrari inedite de Brancusi,* Inainte, Craiova, 13 iunie.

Paleolog, V.G. (1967), *Génèse de la Via Sacra de Tirgu-Jiu*, Académie R.S.R., Centre d'Histoire de Philologie et d'Éthnographie, Craiova.

Paleolog, V.G. (1967), *Tineretea lui Brancusi*, Ed. Tineretului, Bucuresti.

Paleolog, V.G. (1968), *Noi marturii inedite despre Brancusi*, Inainte, Craiova, 11 februarie.

Paleolog, V.G. (1968), *O exceptionala descoperire: Macheta arhitravei "Portii Sarutului"*, Inainte, Craiova, 28 iulie.

Paleolog, V.G. (1969), *Despre procesul lui Brancusi din 1926-1928 cu vama americana*, Tribuna, Cluj, **13,** *36,* 4 septembrie.

Paleolog, V. G. (1970), *Din genetica inspiratiei lui Brancusi*, Inainte, Craiova, 14 iunie.

Paleolog, V.G. (1971), *Brancusi in America*, Ramuri, Craiova, 2, februarie.

Paleolog, V.G. (1971), *Procesul dus de Brancusi impotriva administratiei SUA (1926-1928)*, Ramuri, Craiova, 6, 15 iunie.

Paleolog, V.G. (1971), *Un document biografic si portretistic in "Informatica bibliografica C. Brancusi"*, Inainte, Craiova, 6 august.

Paleolog, V.G. (1974), *Date noi despre viata si opera lui Brancusi*, Inainte, Craiova, 17 iulie.

Paleolog, V.G. (1976), *Din cateva convorbiri cu Brancusi*, in *Omagiu—100—Brancusi*, C.J.C.E.S. Gorj, Targu-Jiu.

Paleolog, V.G. (1976), *L-am cunoscut pe Brancusi*, Tribuna Romaniei, Bucuresti, **V**, *79*, 15 februarie.

Paleolog, V.G. (1976/2002), *Brancusi-Brancusi,* **I**/1976, **II**/2002, Ed. Scrisul Romanesc, Craiova.

Paleolog, V.G. (1996), *Procesul sculpturii moderne—eseuri*, Ed. Fundatiei Constantin Brancusi, Targu-Jiu.

Pamfil, F. (1928), *Manifest*, Unu, Bucuresti, **I**, 1, aprilie.

Pana, S. (1976), *Prezenta lui Constantin Brancusi in publicatiile romanesti de avangarda*, Arta, Bucuresti, *4*.

Pandrea, P. (1943), *Brancusi. Prezentare*, Meridian, Craiova, aprilie.

Pandrea, P. (1945), *Portrete si controverse*, **I**, Colectia Meridiane, Ed. Bucur Ciobanu, Bucuresti.

Pandrea, P. (1968), *Joyce—Brancusi a Parallel*, Romanian Review, Bucuresti, 2 februarie.

Pandrea, P. (2010), *Brancusi. Amicii si inamicii. Sociologia lui Brancusi*, Ed. Vremea, Bucuresti.

Pandrea, P. (2010), *Brancusi. Pravila de la Craiova. Etica lui Brancusi,* Ed. Vremea, Bucuresti.

Parker, T.H. (1927), *Studio Windows*, Times, Hartford, Conneticut, 2 February.

Passuth, Kristina (1976), *Gehört Brancusi zur Avangarde,* in *C. Brancusi. Plastiken—Zeichnungen, Duisburg, 11 Juli – 5 September*, W. Lehmbruck Museum, Duisburg.

Passuth, Krisztina (2001), *Brancusi, Joseph Brummer et le primitivisme*, Lucrarile Colocviului international *Brancusi la apogeu. Noi perspective,* Éd. Univers Enciclopedic, Bucuresti.

Patterson, Augusta O. (1926), *Arts and Decoration*, Town and Country, New York, 15 March.

Paulvé, D. (2003), *La Ruche. Un siècle d'art à Paris*, Éd. Gründ, Paris.

Paun, Silvia (2001), *Constantin Brancusi et la mémoire des héros de la grande union de la Roumanie*, Lucrarile Colocviului international *Brancusi la apogeu. Noi perspective,* Ed. Univers Enciclopedic, Bucuresti.

Pavel, Amelia (1968), *Cateva marturii despre Brancusi in critica romaneasca a epocii*, in *Colocviul Brancusi—Bucuresti, 13-15 octombrie 1967*, Ed. Meridiane, Bucuresti.

Pavel, Amelia (1976), *Brancusi si curentele artei europene la inceputul secolului XX*, in *Omagiu—100—Brancusi*, C.J.C.E.S. Gorj, Targu-Jiu.

Pavel, Amelia (2001), *Brancusi et l'art allemand au début du XX-e siècle*, Lucrarile Colocviului international *Brancusi la apogeu. Noi perspective,* Ed. Univers Enciclopedic, Bucuresti.

Payne, R. (1942), *Constantin Brancusi*, World Review, London, October.

Payne, R. (1949), *A Meeting with Brancusi*, World Review, London, October.

Pearson, J. (2000), *Constantin Brancusi: Sculpting Within the Essence of Things*, Crescent Moon Publishing, London.

Pedrazo, M. (1957), *Brancusi morto*, Journal da Brazel, Rio de Janeiro, abril.

Penders, Anne-Françoise (1995), *Brancusi, la photographie ou l'atelier comme "groupe mobile"*, Éd. La Lettre volée, Bruxelles.

Pestisanu, G. (1976), *Brancusi in amintirea unora dintre cei ce l-au cunoscut*, in *Omagiu—100—Brancusi*, C.J.C.E.S. Gorj, Targu-Jiu.

Petrascu, G. (1929), *"Pavilionul Artei"*, Revista literara a liceului Sf. Sava, Bucuresti, **4**, *1*, decembrie.

Petrascu, Milita (1925), *Brancusi*, Contimporanul, Bucuresti, **IV**, *52*, ianuarie.

Petrascu, Milita (1925), *Nota despre sculptura*, Contimporanul, Bucuresti, **IV**, *60,* septembrie.

Petrascu, Milita (1925), *Procedee noi*, Contimporanul, Bucuresti, **IV**, *62,* octombrie.

Petrascu, Milita (1926), *Initiere in misterele unei expozitii,* Contimporanul, Bucuresti, **V**, *65*, martie.

Petrascu, Milita (1957), *Amintiri despre Brancusi,* Arta plastica, Bucuresti, *3*.

Petrascu, Milita (1976), *L-am cunoscut pe Brancusi*, Tribuna Romaniei, Bucuresti, **V**, *79*, 15 februarie.

Petrescu, C. (1928), *Sculptorul*, Universul literar, Bucuresti, **XLIV**, *17*, 22 aprilie.

Petrescu, P. (1983), *Arcade in timp*, Ed. Eminescu, Bucuresti.

Petringenaru, A. (1964), *Pasi spre Brancusi*, Contemporanul, Bucuresti, 19 iunie.

Petringenaru, A. (1966), *Brancusi, locuinta, obiectele*, Cronica, Iasi, **I**, *2*, 19 februarie.

Petringenaru, A. (1968), *Ansamblul monumental de la Targu-Jiu,* in *Colocviul Brancusi—Bucuresti, 13-15 octombrie 1967,* Ed. Meridiane, Bucuresti.

Petringenaru, A. (1983), *Imagine si simbol la Brancusi*, Ed. Meridiane, Bucuresti.

Phair, G. (1926), *Critic Finds Modern Art Is What it Isn't*, New York American, New York, 25 November.

Phoenix (1898), *Expozitia de la Craiova*, Albina, Bucuresti, **II**, 6, 8 noiembrie.

Pierron, S. (1930), *L'art à Bruxelles. Exposition d'Art roumain moderne. II. Les sculpteurs*, Neptune, Bruxelles, 2 août.

PL (1930), *Les expositions d'art roumain moderne*, Le peuple, Bruxelles, 21 juillet.

Plat, Hélène (1994), *Lucie Delarue-Mardrus: Une femme de lettres des années folles*, Éd. B. Grasset, Paris.

Pogorilovschi, I. (1976), *Comentarea capodoperei. Ansamblul sculptural Brancusi de la Targu-Jiu*, Ed. Junimea, Iasi.

Pogorilovschi, I. (1976), *Fantana lui Haret*, Luceafarul, Bucuresti, **XVII,** 6-7.

Pogorilovschi, I. (1995), *Brancusi arhitect—proiecte nerealizate, templul iubirii-templul maharanei-templul eliberarii*, Brancusi, Targu-Jiu, **I**, 4, decembrie.

Pogorilovschi, I. (2000), *Brancusi, apogeul imaginarului. Comentarea capodoperei de la Targu-Jiu*, Ed. Fundatiei *Constantin Brancusi*, Targu-Jiu.

Pogorilovschi, I. (2005), *Brancusi: Sophrosyne or Wisdom of the Earth / Brancusi Sophrosyne sau Cumintenia Pamantului*, Universalia Publishers, New York.

Pogorilovschi, I. (2007), *Brancusi: Geneza*, Universalia Publishers, New York.

Pollack, R. (1960), *Brancusi's Sculpture vs. His Homemade Legend*, Artnews, New York, February.

Pollack, R. (1988), *Shaman and Showman. An Intimate Portrait of the Legendary Romanian Sculptor Constantin Brancusi*, Art & Antiques, New York, May.

Pop, T. (1976), *Despre Constantin Brancusi*, Flacara, Bucuresti, 2, 17 ianuarie.

Popa, V. I. (1924), *Saptamana plastica*, Adeverul, Bucuresti, 1 martie.

Pora, N. (1909), *Expozitia "Tinerimii artistice"*, Minerva, Bucuresti, 29 martie.

Pora, N. (1910), *A IX-a expozitie "Tinerimea artistica"*, Minerva, Bucuresti, 16 aprilie.

Pora, N. (1910), *Miscarea artistica. Expozitiile artei, arta moderna*, Seara, Bucuresti, 24 ianuarie.

Pora, N. (1911), *Muzeul Simu*, Calendarul Minervei pe 1911, Ed. Minerva, Bucuresti.

Pora, N. (1912), *Deschiderea salonului oficial*, Minerva, Bucuresti, 8 mai.

Pora, N. (1913), *Cronica artistica. Sculptura in expozitia "Tinerimii Artistice"*, Minerva, Bucuresti, 21 aprilie.

Pora, N. (1913), *Deschiderea expozitiei "Tinerimea Artistica"*, Minerva, Bucuresti, 1 aprilie.

Pora, N. (1914), *Miscarea artistica pe 1913. Expozitia "Tinerimii artistice"*, Calendarul Minervei, Bucuresti.

Potopin, I. (1970), *Convorbiri cu oameni despre oameni—C. S. Nicolaescu-Plopsor despre Constantin Brancusi*, Magazin, Bucuresti, 1 august.

Pound, E. (1921), *Constantin Brancusi*, The Little Review, New York, **VIII**, *1*, autumn.

Pound, E. (1957), *Brancusi,* All'Insegna del Pesce d'Oro, Milan.

Pound, E. (1959), *Témoignages sur Brancusi*, Les Cahiers du Musée de Poche, Paris, *3*.

Pound, E. (1985), *Brancusi and Human Sculpture*, in Catalogue *Pound's Artists, Ezra Pound and the Visual Arts in London, Paris and Italy*, Kettle's Yard Gallery, Cambridge, June 14-August 4; Tate Gallery, London, 11 October – 10 November.

Pralea, N. (1908), *Expozitie "Tinerimea artistica",* Secolul, Bucuresti, 4 aprilie.

Preston, S. (1951), *Yesterday and Today*, The New York Times, New York, 23 September.

Preston, S. (1957), *Ancients to Moderns*, The New York Times, New York, 20 January.

Preston, S. (1957), *Modern Masters*, The New York Times, New York, 31 May.

Preston, S. (1957), *Rodin and Friends*, The New York Times, New York, 26 April.

Prodan, C. (1937), *Sculptura, pictura si gravura romaneasca / Prelegeri tinute de d-l Const. Prodan in zilele de 7, 14 si 28 Martie 1936 / Sulptura romaneasca*, Almanahul Ateneului Roman pentru 1936, Tipografia Independenta, Bucuresti.

Prut, C. (1976), *Geniul lui Brancusi*, Contemporanul, Bucuresti, **38**, 17 septembrie.

Przybós, J. (1966), *La Targu-Jiu*, Gazeta literara, Bucuresti, 3 martie.

Przybós, J. (1969), *Brancusi*, Cronica, Iasi, **IV**, *20*, mai.

Puicouyoul, P. (1997), *Constantin Brancusi, l'Exposition*—film, VHS, Center Pompidou, Paris.

Purcaru, I. (1980), *Brancusi la el acasa*, Flacara, Bucuresti, *7,* 14 februarie.

Puscariu, S. (1968), *Calare pe doua veacuri. Amintiri din tinerete (1895-1906)*, Ed. pentru Literatura, Bucuresti.

Putnam, S. (1947), *Paris Was Our Mistress,* in *Memoirs of a Lost and Found Generation*, Viking Press, New York.

Quirot, Odile (1997), *La beauté en question / Les minutes du procès de "Brancusi contre les États-Unis" portées à la scène par Eric Vigner,* Nouvel Observateur Hebdo, Paris, *1679*, 9 jan.

Radian, M. (1967), *Asa l-am cunoscut pe Brancusi—de vorba cu pictorul Bohdan Urbanowicz,* Magazin, Bucuresti, 21 octombrie.

Radulescu, N.N. (1981), *Brancusi, fotograful sculpturilor sale*, Flacara, Bucuresti, *1(1334)*, 1 ianuarie.

Ragon, M. (1956), *L'aventure de l'art abstrait*, Éd. Robert Laffont, Paris.

Ramsden, E.H. (1949), *20th Century Sculpture*, Pleiades Books, London.

Ramsden, E.H. (1953), *Sculpture: Theme and Variations "Toward a Contemporary Aesthetic"*, Lund Humphries, London.

Rascoe, B. (1927), *Daybook of a New Yorker*, Baltimore Evening Sun, Baltimore, 7 March.

Ravici, V. (1909), *Expozitia societatii "Tinerimea artistica" (La Ateneul din Bucuresti), aprilie 1909*, Arta romana, Iasi, aprilie.

Ravici, V. (1910), *A IX-a expozitie de pictura si sculptura a societatii "Tinerimea artistica" (in local propriu langa Primaria Capitalei)*, Arta romana, Iasi, mai-iunie.

Ray, Man (1963), *Self-Portrait*, André Deutsch Publishers, London.

Raynal, D. (2008), *Maurice Raynal: La bande à Picasso*, Éd. Ouest-France, Rennes.

Raynal, M. (1933), *Dieu—table—cuvette. Les ateliers de Brancusi, Despiau, Giacometti, Laurens, Lipchitz, Maillol, photographiés par Brassaï*, Minotaure, Paris, *3-4*, décembre.

Read, H., ed. (1952), *Barbara Hepworth: Carvings and Drawings*, Lund Humphries, London.

Read, H. (1956), *The Art of Sculpture*, Faber & Faber, London.

Read, H. (1957), *Brancusi, 1876-1957*, The Listener, London, April.

Réau, L. (1946), *L'art roumain*, Librairie Larousse, Paris.

Reiss, Carole (2008), *Villa Noailles de Mallet-Steven*, 3 janvier, http://www.quintet.ch/.

REMBRANDT (1912), *Salonul oficial*, Flacara, Bucuresti, 16 iunie.

REMBRANDT (1913), *A XII-a expozitie de pictura si sculptura a Societatii "Tinerimea Artistica"*, Flacara, Bucuresti, 6 aprilie.

Renaud, R.E. (1935), *African Art Exposition a Study in Primitive Influence; World's Most Complete Collection of Native Work,* The Washington Post, Washington, D.C., 5 May.

Ressu, C. (1913), *Note de arta. Expozitia "Tinerimii artistice",* Facla, Bucuresti, 6 aprilie.

Ressu, C. (1967), *Insemnari*, Ed. Meridiane, Bucuresti.

Rezeanu, P. (1982), *Brancusi si Craiova. Cartograme*, Amfiteatru, Bucuresti, **XVII**, 8 August.

Rezeanu, P. (2001), *"La Craiova m-am nascut a doua oara",* Ramuri, Craiova, *2-3*, februarie-martie.

Rezeanu, P. (2001), *Brancusi la Craiova*, Ed. ARC 2000, Bucuresti.

Rezeanu, P. (2012), *Brancusi. Tatal nostru,* Ed. Autograf MJM, Craiova.

Riegler-Dinu, E. (1938), *Povesteste Brancusi*, Seara, Bucuresti, 27 octombrie.

Ritchie, A.C. (1952), *Sculpture of the Twentieth Century*, The Museum of Modern Art, New York.

Ritchie, A.C. (1955), *Sculpture of the 20th Century, Who's New and Why*, The Museum of Modern Art, New York, September.

Robert Foster, Jeanne (1922), *New Sculptures by Constantin Brancusi: A Note on the Man and the Formal Perfection of His Carvings,* Vanity Fair, New York, **XVIII**, *3*, May.

Robert Foster, Jeanne (1926), *It's Clever, But Is it Art? Is Asked by the Critics of Brancusi*, New York Herald Tribune, New York, 21 February.

Roché, H.P. (1954), *Hommage à John Quinn, collectionneur*, La Parisienne, Paris, août-sept.

Roché, H.P. (1957), *L'enterrement de Brancusi,* in *Hommage à Brancusi,* Éd. de Beaune, Paris.

Roché, H.P. (1957), *Souvenirs sur Brancusi*, L'Œil, Paris, *29*, 15 mai.

Romanescu, I. (1939), *Brancusi si arta romaneasca*, Cuvantul Gorjului, Targu-Jiu, **II**, *20-21*, 15-27 August.

Ronnebeck, A. (1928), *Spirit of Old Masters Dominates the Moderns / Surprising Decision of New York Customs Officials Provokes a Caustic Comment from Some Leading U.S. Painters*, News, Denver.

Rosu, Dona (1976), *Mi-a spus ca gloria il oboseste*, Romania pitoreasca, Bucuresti, **V**, 2(50), februarie.

Roszak, T. (1955), *Problems of Modern Sculpture*, in *7 Arts*, The Falcon's Wing Press, Indian Hills, *3*.

Rouve, P. (1976), *Brancusi: Renasterea Trans-Renasterii*, Secolul 20, Bucuresti, *10-12(189-191)*, octombrie-decembrie.

Rowell, Margit (2003), *Brancusi contre les États-Unis*, Éd. Adam Biro, Paris.

Rowell, Margit, Paléologue, A. (1999), *Brancusi vs. United States. The Historic Trial, 1928*, Diane Pub. Co.—Vilo International.

Rupea, R. (1972), *O lucrare necunoscuta a lui Brancusi / relief in ghips "Al. Davila"*, Contemporanul, Bucuresti, *17*, 21 aprilie.

Rusan, R. (2006), *O discutie la Masa Tacerii*, Ed. LiterNet, Bucuresti.

Russell, J. (1966), *Great Sculptor. Fine Gallery*, The Sunday Times, London, 6 November.

Russu Sirianu, V. (1969), *Vinurile lor... Ore traite cu George Enescu, Constantin Brancusi, Mihail Sadoveanu, Octavian Goga, George Cosbuc, Panait Istrati...*, Ed. pentru Literatura, Bucuresti. S. (1929), *Deschiderea Salonului oficial*, Universul, Bucuresti, 4 noiembrie.

S.C. (1924), *Expozitia "Contimporanul" (insemnari)*, Punct, Bucuresti, 2 decembrie.

S.P. (1949), *The New and Old*, The New York Times, New York, 29 May.

Saarinen, Aline B. (1955), *A Critic's Collection*, The New York Times, New York, 23 January.

Saarinen, Aline B. (1955), *Revival of Rodin—and of Sentiment*, The New York Times, New York, 20 March.

Saarinen, Aline B. (1955), *The Strange Story of Brancusi*, The New York Times Magazine, New York, 23 October.

Saarinen, Aline B. (1958), *The Proud Possessors: The lives, times and tastes of some adventurous American art collectors*, Random House, New York.

Salles, G.A., Cassou, J. (1957), *Paroles prononcées devant le cercueil de Brancusi dans L'Église roumaine de la Rue Jean de Beauvais, le 19 mars 1957*, in *Hommage à Brancusi*, Éd. de Beaune, Paris.

Salmon, A. (1919), *La jeune sculpture française,* Société des Trente, Albert Messein éditeur, Paris.

Salmon, A. (1922), *Propos d'atelier*, Éd. G. Crès & C-ie, Paris.

Salvy, G.J. *Un carnet vénitien*, Éd. du Regard, Paris, 2001.

Salzmann, S. (1976), *Brancusi si Lehmbruck*, in *Catalogul sculpturii germane, 1900-1933 Sculptura si grafica*, Muzeul de Arta al R.S.R., Bucuresti.

Salzmann, S. (1976), *Das Skulpturale Ensemble von Targu-Jiu*, in *C. Brancusi Plastiken—Zeichnungen, Duisburg, 11 Juli-5 September*, W. Lehmbruck Museum, Duisburg.

San Lazzaro, G. di (1957), *Brancusi*, Revue le XX-e Siècle, Paris, *9*.

Sandburg, C. (1922), *Brancusi*, in *Slabs of the Sunburnt West*, Harcourt, Brace and Company, New York.

Sanzio (1907), *Expozitia "Tinerimea artistica"*, Literatura si arta romana, Bucuresti, **XI**, *1*, 25 aprilie.

Sava, I. (1928), *Expozitia jubiliara a "Tinerimii artistice"*, Universul literar, Bucuresti, **XLIV**, *46*, 11 noiembrie.

Sawelson-Gorse, Naomi (1993), *The Art Institute of Chicago and the Arensberg Collection*, Art Institute of Chicago Museum Studies, One Hundred Years at the Art Institute: A Centennial Celebration, **19**, *1*.

Schafer Simmers, H. (1955), *Sculpture in Europe Today*, California University Press, Berkeley.

Schiff, G. (1957), *Das Atelier Brancusi*, Die Weltwoche, Zürich, **XXIV**, 13 Januar.

Schildt, G. (1958), *Colloqui con Brancusi*, La Biennale di Venezia, Venetia, **VIII**, *32*, Iuglio-Settembre.

Schileru, E. (1957), *Constantin Brancusi* (I, II), Gazeta literara, Bucuresti, I/*11*, 13 martie; II/*13*, 28 martie.

Schileru, E. (1971), *Scrisoare de dragoste*, Ed. Meridiane, Bucuresti.

Schintee, I. (1964), *Alfabetul Brancusian*, Inainte, Craiova, 9 August.

Schintee, I. (1964), *Brancusi*, Ramuri, Craiova, *1*, ianuarie.

Schintee, I. (1964), *Date noi despre Brancusi*, Ramuri, Craiova, 8 August.

Schintee, I. (1967), *Exegeza brancusiana*, Ramuri, Craiova, 2 February.

Schmitz, M. (1930), *Une exposition d'art roumain à Bruxelles*, Revue le XX-e Siècle, Paris, 27 juillet.

Schneider, P. (1962), *Brancusi*, L'Express, Paris, 5 avril.

Schneider, P. (1966), *Unde incepe marele Brancusi*, Contemporanul, Bucuresti, 18 februarie.

Schneider, P. (1988), *Le coq et les vautours*, L'Express, Paris, 15 avril.

Schobel, Doina (1981), *Expozitie retrospectiva Camil Ressu, pictura si grafica*, catalog, Musée d'Art de la R.S.R., Bucuresti.

Schulman, R. (2006), *Romany Marie: The Queen of Greenwich Village*, Butler Books, Louisville.

Schwarz, J. (2002), *Literature and the Visual Arts: The Brazilian Roaring Twenties*, Institute of Latin American Studies, University of Texas Libraries, Austin, http://lanic.utexas.edu/.

Seckler, D. (1950), *Brancusi's Fish Bought by New York's Museum of Modern Art*, The Art News, New York, *49*, March.

Sedlmayr, H. (1955), *Die Revolution den Modernen Kunst*, in *Rowohlts Deutsche Enzyklopëdie*, **I**, Verlag Rowohlt, Hamburg.

Seiwert, F.W. (1929), *Constantin Brancusi, der Bildhauer*, A bis Z, Köln, *2*.

Seiwert, F.W. (1931), *Kunstform—Zweckform*, A bis Z, Köln, *18*.

Senila-Vasiliu, Mariana (1985), *Bursier la Paris*, Ateneu, Bacau, *6*, iunie.

Senila-Vasiliu, Mariana (1998), *Ionel Jianu—ultimul interviu*, Brancusi, Targu-Jiu, **IV**, *1(13)*.

Senila-Vasiliu, Mariana (2006), *Cutia cu prejudecati / "Tarania" lui Brancusi, o falsa interpretare*, Cafeneaua literara, Pitesti, **IV**, *3(33)*, martie.

Seuphor, M. (1950), *L'art abstrait, ses origines, ses premiers maîtres*, Éd. Maeght, Paris.

Seuphor, M. (1956), *Un musée militant*, l'Œil, Paris, juin.

Severus, I.P. (1910), *Un vernisaj mult asteptat. "Tinerimea artistica"*, Falanga literara si artistica, Bucuresti, 13 aprilie.

Shanes, E. (1989), *Constantin Brancusi*, Abbeville Press, New York.

Sicherman, B., Green, C.H., eds. (1980), *Notable American Women: The Modern Period*, Harvard University Press, Cambridge (MA).

Siegfried, W. (1957), *Ultima intalnire cu Brancusi*, Informatia Bucurestiului, Bucuresti, 2 aprilie.

Silver, K.E. (1989), *Esprit de Corps: The Art of the Parisian Avant-garde and the First World War, 1914-1925*, Princeton University Press, Princeton.

Simi, G.J. (1957), *Decadence in Art?,* The Washington Post and Times Herald, Washington, D.C., 7 April.

Simionescu-Ramniceanu, M. (1924), *Istoria artelor*, Ed. Cultura Nationala, Bucuresti.

Sinculici, I.L. (2014), *Dosarul Brancusi de la Scoala de Meserii din Craiova*, Portal-Maiastra, Targu-Jiu, **X**, *1(38)*.

Smantanescu, D. (1967), *Documente si amintiri despre Brancusi*, Arges, Pitesti, martie.

Smantanescu, D. (1971), *Noi contributii privind viata si activitatea sculptorului din Hobita*, Coloana (supliment socialcultural editat de Gazeta Gorjului), Targu-Jiu, mai.

Smantanescu, D. (1999), *L-am cunoscut pe Constantin Brancusi*, Literatorul, Bucuresti, **IX**, *4-5(337-338)*.

Smith, Katharine (1934), *In Washington. Art Gallery,* The Washington Post, Washington, D.C., 21 January.

Soby, J.T. (1954), *The Arensberg Collection*, The Saturday Review, New York, 6 November.

Soby, J.T. (1955), *Brancusi Exhibition at Guggenheim*, The Saturday Review, New York, 3 December.

Soby, J.T. (1957), *Constantin Brancusi,* in *Modern Art and the New Past,* Oklahoma University Press, Norman.

Sollier, R. de (1967), *Sculptura moderna incepe cu Brancusi,* Contemporanul, Bucuresti, 17 martie.

Sollier, R. de (1968), *Stiinta si natura: Aparitia unei forme noi*, in *Colocviul Brancusi—Bucuresti, 13-15 octombrie 1967*, Ed. Meridiane, Bucuresti.

Sorban, R., Nanu, Adina, Schileru, E., Constantin, P. (1964), *100 de ani de la infiintarea Institutului de Arte Plastice "Nicolae Grigorescu" din Bucuresti 1864-1964*, Ed. Meridiane, Bucuresti.

Soroceanu, T. (1928), *Arta romana*, Universul literar, Bucuresti, **XLIV**, *17*, 22 aprilie.

Soroceanu, T. (1930), *Pinacoteca Statului*, Boabe de Grau, Bucuresti, **I**, *4*, iunie.

Spear, Athena Tacha (1966), *A Contribution to Brancusi Chronology*, The Art Bulletin, New York, *3*, March.

Spear, Athena Tacha (1969), *Brancusi's Birds*, New York University Press, New York.

Spear, Athena Tacha (1971), *Exhibition Review*, The Art Quarterly, New York, 2.

Spiteris, T. (1968), *Discutii*, in *Colocviul Brancusi—Bucuresti, 13-15 octombrie 1967,* Ed. Meridiane, Bucuresti.

Stanculescu, Nina (1988), *Doi artisti care au lucrat in atelierul lui Brancusi (Amedeo Modigliani, Isamu Noguchi)*, Synthesis, Ed. Academiei R.S.R., Bucuresti, **XV**.

Stanculescu, Nina (2001), *Brancusi—Duchamp*, Luceafarul, Bucuresti, *38(484)*, 1 noiembrie.

Stanculescu, Nina, ed. (1984), *Izvoare si cristalizari in opera lui Brancusi*, Ed. Stiintifica si Enciclopedica, Bucuresti.

Stavarus, I. (1967), *Brancusi, documente inedite*, Luceafarul, Bucuresti, **VIII**, *8*, 25 februarie.

Stefan, C. (1985), *La noapte, cotidianul*, Ed. Eminescu, Bucuresti.

Stefanica, G., Nicoara, M. (1963), *O romanca, secretara lui Anatole France,* Tribuna, Cluj-Napoca, 22 noiembrie.

Steichen, E. (1962), *Brancusi vs. United States*, Art in America, New York, *1*.

Steichen, E. (1963), *A Life in Photography*, Doubleday & Company, New York.

Sterescu, S. [F. Storck] (1907), *Cronica artistica. Expozitiunea "Tinerimea artistica"*, Viata literara si artistica, Bucuresti, 13 mai.

Sterescu, S. [F. Storck] (1966*), Scurt popas langa pretutindenarul Brancusi*, Inainte, Craiova, 4 decembrie.

Sterian, P. (1929), *Cronica plastica*, Gandirea, Bucuresti, **IX**, *9*.

Sterian, P. (1929), *Gravura si desen. Salonul oficial*, Cuvantul, Bucuresti, 5 noiembrie.

Sterian, P. (1930), *Cronica plastica / Artistii romani din Paris / La duhul apelor adanci (Brancusi)*, Gandirea, Bucuresti, **X**, *6-7*.

Stieglitz, A. (1963), *A Life in Photography—Edward Steichen, MoMA, New York*, W. H. Allen Publishers, London.

Stirbu, T. (2004), *"Jupuitul" lui Brancusi*, Clujeanul, Cluj-Napoca, 26 August.

Stircea-Craciun, Matei (2009), *Brancusi: limbajele materiei*, Ed. Anima, Bucuresti.

Sulzberger, M. (1930), *Les Expositions à la Galerie Giroux. L'art roumain*, L'Étoile Belge, Bruxelles, 23 juillet.

Švrček, J.B. (1947), *Sochařstvi Francia*, Rovnost, Prague, 7 December.

Sweeney, J.J. (1955), *The Brancusi Touch*, The Art News, New York, **54**, *XI*, November.

Sweeney, J.J. (1962), *Added Perception That Only Sculpture Gives*, The New York Times, New York, 27 May.

Sweeney, J.J. (1972), *La Brancusi acasa*, Inainte, Craiova, 8 octombrie.

Sweeney, J.J. (1976), *Arta si copilarie*, Secolul 20, Bucuresti, *10-12(189-191)*, octombrie-decembrie.

T.Gr. (1913), *Expozitiunea "Tinerimii artistice"—o manifestare cu care ne putem mandri*, Viitorul, Bucuresti, 3 aprilie.

T.Gr. (1929), *Salonul Oficial de desen si gravura*, Viitorul, Bucuresti, 9 noiembrie.

Tabart, Marielle, ed. (1995), *Brancusi l'inventeur de la sculpture moderne,* Coll. Découvertes, Éd. Center Pompidou & Gallimard, Paris.

Tabart, Marielle, ed. (1997), *L'atelier Brancusi, Album*, Les Carnets de l'atelier Brancusi, Éd. Center Pompidou, Paris.

Tabart, Marielle, ed. (1998), *Leda*, Les Carnets de l'Atelier Brancusi, Éd. Center Pompidou, Paris.

Tabart, Marielle, ed. (1999), *Brancusi: Le Baiser*, Les Carnets de l'atelier Brancusi, Éd. Center Pompidou, Paris.

Tabart, Marielle, ed. (2002), *Brancusi: Le Portrait?*, Les Carnets de l'atelier Brancusi, Éd. Center Pompidou, Paris.

Tabart, Marielle, Lemny, Doina, eds. (1998), *Brancusi: La Colonne sans Fin*, Les Carnets de l'atelier Brancusi, Éd. Center Pompidou, Paris.

Tabart, Marielle, Lemny, Doina, eds. (1999), *Brancusi: Princesse X*, Les Carnets de l'atelier Brancusi, Éd. Center Pompidou, Paris.

Tabart, Marielle, Lemny, Doina, eds. (2000), *Brancusi & Duchamp: Regards historiques*, Les Carnets de l'atelier Brancusi, Éd. Center Pompidou, Paris.

Tabart, Marielle, Lemny, Doina, eds. (2001), *Brancusi: L'Oiseau dans l'espace*, Les Carnets de l'atelier Brancusi, Éd. Center Pompidou, Paris.

Tabart, Marielle, Lemny, Doina, eds. (2003), *La dation Brancusi, Dessins et Archives*, Éd. Center Pompidou, Paris.

Tanasescu, T. (1928), *Evenimentele plastice. "Arta romana"*, Viata literara, Bucuresti, **III**, *80*, 30 martie.

Taslauanu, O.C. (1907), *Sculptorul Brancusi*, Luceafarul, Sibiu, 1907, **VI**, *4-5*, 1 martie.

Teodorovici, D. (2010), *Dialogik zwischen Tradition und Moderne*, dizertatie Städtebau-Institut der Universität Stuttgart.

Timon [M. Simionescu-Ramniceanu] (1914), *Cronica artistica. Expozitia "Tinerimea Artistica" (A XIV-a)*, Noua Revista Romana, Bucuresti, **XIV**, 20 aprilie.

Tiucra, T. (1934), *Brancusi*, Hotarul, Arad, **I**, *4*, aprilie.

Tiucra, T. (1936), *Opera lui Constantin Brancusi*, Hotarul, Arad, **III**, *1*, ianuarie.

Tiucra, T. (1938), *Sufletul si viata romaneasca in arta*, Innoirea, Arad, **I**, *21*, 15 iulie.

Tomkins, C. (1966), *The World of Marcel Duchamp: 1887-*, Time-Life Books, New York.

Tonitza, N. (1964), *Scrieri despre arta*, Ed. Minerva, Bucuresti.

Torynopol, V. (1950), *Vrajitorul din Montparnasse*, Gazeta literara, Bucuresti, *1*, 1 ianuarie.

Trier, E. (1955), *Moderne Plastik: von Auguste Rodin bis Marino Marini*, Büchergilde Gutenberg, Frankfurt.

Trier, E. (1955), *Zeichnungen und Radierung. Einführung von Eduard Wilhelm Lehmbruck*, P. Piper & Co., München.

Trier, E. (1968), *Brancusi si Lehmbruck*, in *Colocviul Brancusi—Bucuresti, 13-15 octombrie 1967*, Éd. Meridiane, Bucuresti.

Tucker, W. (1970), *Four Sculptors. Part I. Brancusi*, Studio International, London, April.

Tucker, W. (1970), *The Man Who Created Modern Sculpture*, The Guardian, London, 25 November.

Tucker, W. (1973), *The Hand Changed the Forms*, The Daily Telegraph Magazine, London, 20 July.

Tucker, W. (1974), *Early Modern Sculpture. Rodin, Degas, Matisse, Brancusi, Picasso, González*, Oxford University Press, New York.

Tucker, W. (1974), *The Language of Sculpture*, Thames & Hudson Publishers, London.

Tucker, W. (1975), *Brancusi in Romania*, Studio International, London, March-April.

Tugui, P. (2001), *Dosarul Brancusi*, Ed. Dacia, Cluj-Napoca.

Turner, E.H. (1988), *American Artists in Paris, 1919-1929*, Umi Research Press, Ann Arbor.

Tzara, T. (1975), *Œuvres complètes*, **I**, 1912-1924, Éd. Flammarion, Paris.

Tzigal, V. (1968), *Konstantin Brankusi—Zarubezhnye mastera XX veka*, Tvorcestvo, Moscow, *8*.

Tzigara-Samurcas, A. (1910), *Cronica artistica. Expozitia "Tinerimii artistice"*, Convorbiri literare, Iasi, **2**, *2*, aprilie.

Tzigara-Samurcas, A. (1991). *Memorii,* **I**, 1872-1910, Ed. Grai si suflet—Cultura nationala, Bucuresti.

Tzigara-Samurcas, A. (2003), *Memorii*, **3**, 1919-1930, Ed. Meridiane, Bucuresti.

Urbanowicz, B. (1968), *Vizita mea la Brancusi—decembrie 1956*, in *Colocviul Brancusi—Bucuresti, 13-15 octombrie 1967*, Ed. Meridiane, Bucuresti.

Uscatescu, J. (1958), *Constantin Brancusi*, Ateneo, Madrid.

Uscatescu, J. (1976), *Brancusi y el arte del siglo*, Ed. Reus, Madrid.

V. (1930), *Exposition*, L'Évantail, Bruxelles, 3 août.

Vainer, N. (1968), *Brancusi e outros maestres da escultura Romena*, Grafica Record Editóra, Rio de Janeiro.

Valentiner, W.R. (1946), *Origins of Modern Sculpture*, G. Wittenborn Publishers, New York.

Vallier, Dora (1954), *La vie fait l'œuvre de Fernand Léger*, Cahiers d'art, Paris, *2*.

Vallier, Dora (1982), *L'intérieur de l'art. Entretiens avec Braque, Léger, Villon, Miró, Brancusi*, Éd. du Seuil, Paris.

Vallier, Dora (1995), *Chez Brancusi, vendredi 4 mai 1956*, Éd. de l'Échoppe, Paris.

Van Hook, Katrina (1946), *April Brings New Exhibits for Washington's Art Lovers*, The Washington Post, Washington, D.C., April 7.

Velescu, C.R. (1992), *Iconologie si existenta la Constantin Brancusi*, Revista Muzeelor, Bucuresti, tom **29**, *3*.

Velescu, C.R. (1993), *Brancusi initiatul*, Ed. Editis, Bucuresti.

Velescu, C.R. (1994), *Le temple de la délivrance de Constantin Brancusi, substitut de l'atelier de l'artiste entendu comme œuvre globale—le rôle du commanditaire dans la réalisation du projet de l'ensemble d'Indore*, Künstlerbilder /

Images de l'artiste, Colloque du Comité International d'Histoire de l'Art, Université de Lausanne, 9-12 juin (Peter Lang, Berne, 1998).

Velescu, C.R. (1996). *Brancusi alchimist*, Ed. Editis, Bucuresti.

Velescu, C.R. (2013), *Marcel Duchamp, Constantin Brancusi, Victor Brauner: leurs rencontres et les retombées sur leurs œuvres*, Revue Roumaine d'Histoire de l'Art, série Beaux-Arts, Bucarest, Tome **L**.

VERAX (1910), *Viata Sociala, Mai,* Noua Revista Romana, Bucuresti, **VIII**, *8*, 30 mai.

Vessereau, Marguerite (1930), *Roumanie. Terre du dor*, Les Presses Universitaires de France, Paris.

Vianu, T. (1924), *Prima expozitie internationala a "Contimporanului"*, Miscarea literara, Bucuresti, 6 decembrie.

Vianu, T. (1938), *Sculptura romaneasca*, Arta si tehnica grafica, Bucuresti, *4-5* (reprint in *Opere,* **12**, Ed. Minerva, Bucuresti, 1985).

Vida, G. (1995), *Brancusi: monographies allemandes*, Revue Roumaine d'Histoire de l'Art, série Beaux-Arts, Bucarest, Tome **XXXII**.

Vinea, I. (1925), *Pasarea Maiastra* (poem, 1920), Contimporanul, Bucuresti, **IV**, *52,* ianuarie.

Vintila, P. (1972), *Milita*, Ed. Eminescu, Bucuresti.

Vitner, I. (1981), *Popas langa Notre-Dame*, Ed. Cartea Romaneasca, Bucuresti.

Vitrac, R. (1929), *Constantin Brancusi*, Cahiers d'art, Paris, *8-9*.

Vlasiu, I. (1947), *Da si nu, fragment dintr-un jurnal intim (1937-1938)*, Revista literara, Bucuresti, *13*.

Vlasiu, I. (1968), *Aspecte generale in opera lui Brancusi*, in *Colocviul Brancusi—Bucuresti,13-15 octombrie 1967,* Ed. Meridiane, Bucuresti.

Vlasiu, I. (1970), *In spatiu si timp. Pagini de jurnal*, Ed. Dacia, Cluj-Napoca.

Vlasiu, I. (1976), *L-am cunoscut pe Brancusi*, Tribuna Romaniei, Bucuresti, **V**, *79*, 15 februarie.

Vlasiu, Ioana (2001), *Brancusi and His Disciples. An Insight into Brancusian Pedagogy*, Lucrarile Colocviului international *Brancusi la apogeu. Noi perspective,* Ed. Univers Enciclopedic, Bucuresti (reprint in Revue Roumaine d'Histoire de l'Art, série Beaux-Arts, Bucarest, Tome **XXXVIII**).

Vogt, A.G. (1957), *Brancusis Polituren*, Neue Zürcher Zeitung. Literatur und Kunst. Sonntagsausgabe Nr. 1001, 1003, Zürich, **7**, *4*.

Vollmer, H. (1953), *Allgemeines Lexikon der Bildenden Künstler des XX. Jahrhunderts*, **I** (A-D), Seemann, Leipzig.

Voronca, I. (1929), *Plante si animale. Terase*, Collection Integral, Imprimerie Union, Paris.

VR (1930), *Sympathies roumaines*, Le Courrier belge, Bruxelles, 9 août.

VT (1924), *Prima expozitie internationala "Contimporanul"*, Miscarea literara, Bucuresti, 6 decembrie.

Wachtova, Lida (1968), *Brancusi in Cehoslovacia*, in *Colocviul Brancusi—Bucuresti, 13-15 octombrie 1967,* Ed. Meridiane, Bucuresti.

Watson Crane, Jane (1949), *A "Monumental" Sculpture Show,* The Washington Post, Washington, D.C., 22 May.

Watson, F. (1926), *The Gallic Spirit*, World New York City, New York, 21 November.

Watson, F. (1926), *What Is the Sculpture?* The Art News, New York, **25**, *10*, 11 December.

Watson, F. (1928), *The Curious Case of Brancusi*, The Arts, New York, **XIII**, *5*, May.

Watson, S. (1991), *Armory Show Scoreboard*, in *Strange Bedfellows: The First American Avant-Garde*, Abbeville Press, New York.

Wehrli, R. (1957), *Erinnerungen an einen Besuch*, Neue Zürcher Zeitung. Literatur und Kunst. Sonntagsausgabe Nr. 1001, 1003, Zürich, **7**, *4*.

Weld, J.B. (1986), *Peggy: The Wayward Guggenheim*, Dutton Adult, New York.

Wescott, G. (1925), *Picasso, Matisse, Brancusi and Arthur Lee: An American Novelist Passes an Afternoon in a Sculptor's Studio in New York*, Vanity Fair, New York, **XXI**, June.

Westheim, P. (1922), *Bildhauer in Frankreich*, Das Kunstblatt, Potsdam, **VI**, *2*.

Wilenski, R.H. (1945), *The Modern Movement in Art*, Faber & Faber Publishers, London.

Williams, Marguerite B. (1926), *Here and There in the Art World*, Chicago News, Chicago, 29 December.

Williams, W.C. (1955), *C. Brancusi: First Major Retrospective Exhibition at Solomon R. Guggenheim Museum*, The Arts, New York, 30 November.

Wilson, A. (1923), *A Visit to Brancusi's*, The New York Times Book Review and Magazine, New York, 19 August.

Wood, Beatrice (1992), *Visit to Brancusi,* The Smithsonian Institution, Archives of American Art Journal, *4*.

Zadkine, O. (1957), *Hommage à Brancusi*, Les Lettres françaises, Paris, *664*, 28 mars.

Zahar, M. (1940), *In Brancusi's Studio*, Studio International, London, February.

Zahn, L. (1956), *Kleine Geschichte der Modernen Kunst,* Verlag Ullstein Taschenbücher, Ullstein Buch, **92**, Frankfurt.

Zambaccian, K.H. (1943), *Note despre sculptorii Brancusi si Medrea*, in *Pagini de arta*, Casa Scoalelor, Bucuresti.

Zambaccian, K.H. (1946), *Alexandru Bogdan-Pitesti*, Revista Fundatiilor Regale, Bucuresti, **XIII**, 8 August.

Zambaccian, K.H. (1956), *Insemnarile unui amator de arta*, Ed. pentru Literatura, Bucuresti.

Zayas, M. de (1998), *How, When, and Why Modern Art Came to New York*, ed. F.M. Naumann, The MIT Press, Cambridge (MA).

Zarnescu, C. (1980), *Aforismele si textele lui Brancusi*, Ed. Scrisul Romanesc, Craiova.

Zarnescu, C. (2001), *Brancusi si civilizatia imaginii, anii revolutionari 1907-1918*, Ed. Dacia, Cluj-Napoca.

Zarnescu, C., ed. (2001), *Brancusi si Transilvania—antologie*, Ed. Grinta, Cluj-Napoca.

Zervos, C. (1934), *Réflexions sur Brancusi. À propos de son exposition à la Galerie Brummer de New York (17 novembre 1933-13 janvier 1934)*, Cahiers d'art, Paris, *1-4*.

Zervos, C. (1938), *Histoire de l'art contemporaine*, Éd. Cahiers d'art, Paris.

Zervos, C., ed. (1957), *Constantin Brancusi: sculptures, peintures, fresques, dessins*, Éd. Cahiers d'art, Paris.

Zimbru, O. (1910), *A noua expozitie a "Tinerimii artistice"*, Luceafarul, Sibiu, **IX**, *11-12*, 1-16 iunie.

Zorach, W. (1926), *The Sculptures of Constantin Brancusi*, The Arts, New York, **IX**, March.

***(1898), *Expozitia regionala din Craiova*—Prin posta de la corespondentul nostru special, Adeverul, Bucuresti, 16 octombrie.

***(1898), *Expozitiunea agricola si industriala*, Vointa Craiovei, Craiova, 21 octombrie.

***(1903), *Informatiuni,* Gazeta artelor, Bucuresti, 11 mai.

***(1903), *Informatiuni*, Vointa nationala, Bucuresti, 17 mai.

***(1903), *Un bust lui Davilla*, Adeverul, Bucuresti, 28 octombrie.

***(1907), *Calendarul "Minervei" pe anul 1907*, Anul al IX-lea, Institut de Arte Grafice si Editura, Bucuresti.

***(1907), *Deschiderea expozitiei "Tinerimea artistica"*, Secolul, Bucuresti, 18 martie.

***(1907), *Ecouri (Vernisajul expozitiei "Tinerimea artistica")*, Vointa nationala, Bucuresti, 16 martie.

***(1910), *"Tinerimea artistica": Luchian, Artachino, Spaethe si altii*, Seara, Bucuresti, 8 decembrie.

***(1910), *Artistice*, Falanga literara si artistica, Bucuresti, 11 aprilie.

***(1910), *Impresii de la "Tinerimea artistica"*, Universul, Bucuresti, 9 mai.

***(1910), *Informatiuni literare si culturale 1903-1910*, ed. W. Krafft, Sibiu.

***(1912), *Cronica artistica. De la Salonul Oficial*, Ordinea, Bucuresti, 23 mai.

***(1912), *Informatiuni*, Vointa nationala, Bucuresti, 28 septembrie.

***(1913), *Buy Cubist Pictures While Critics Cavil*, Chicago Record-Herald, 29 March.

***(1913), *Cubist Art Exhibit Ends "At the Stake"*, Chicago Record-Herald, 17 April.

***(1914), Stieglitz Collection, National Gallery of Art, Washington, D.C., *Two Installation Photographs by Alfred Stieglitz of the Brancusi Exhibition at the Little Galleries of the Photo-Secession*, 12 March-1 April 1914.

***(1915), *Colectiunea artistica a Statului din Palatul Ateneului. Pictura si sculptura*, Ministerul Cultelor si Instructiei Publice, Bucuresti.

***(1917), *Allies of Sculpture Exhibition*, The American Art News, New York, 8 December.

***(1920), *Pour l'indépendance de l'art*, Le journal de peuple, Paris, 25 février.

***(1923), *Cronici / Idei, oameni & fapte: Un critic de arta german despre Brancusi*, Gandirea, Bucuresti, **III**, 5, 1 noiembrie.

***(1924), *Prima expozitie plastica moderna organizata de revista "Contimporanul"*, Contimporanul, Bucuresti, **III**, *48*.

***(1925), *Calendarul Minerva pe anul 1925*, Ed. Cartea Romaneasca, Bucuresti.

***(1925), Catalogue Général Officiel *Exposition Internationale des Arts Décoratifs et Industriels Modernes*, avril-octobre, Paris.

***(1926), *Arta moderna. Constantin Brancusi*, Rampa, Bucuresti, 8 noiembrie.

***(1926), *Brancusi in New York*, The New York Telegram Editorial, New York, 16 February.

***(1926), *Brancusi Returns Here for Display...*, The New York World, New York, 30 September.

***(1926), *Brancusi to Show His Provoking Art...*, New York World, New York, 9 November. ***(1926), *Brancusi, Grimm and Bartlett Exhibits*, New York World, New York, 21 February.

***(1926), *Brancusi*, The New York Times, New York, 28 February.

***(1926), *Brancusi*, The New York World, New York, 14 November.

***(1926), *Constantin Brancusi*, The Art News, New York, 28 November.

***(1926), *Exhibition of Modern Art at Brooklyn Museum*, Citizen Brooklyn, New York, 28 November.

***(1926), *La vente aux enchères des œuvres exposées au Salon du Franc rapporta 850.000 francs au Trésor*, Le Matin, Paris, 30 octobre.

***(1926), *Many Brancusi's Sold at Brummer's*, The Art News, New York, 11 December.

***(1926), *Many Types of Art Are Now on Exhibition*, The New York Times, New York, 28 February.

***(1926), *Modern Art Poisoning Minds and Morals; Science Condemns Strange Pictures and Statues of the Cubists and Futurists as the Work of Unbalanced Minds and an Evil Influence on Everybody Who Admires Them*, The Washington Post, Washington, D.C., 26 December.

***(1926), *New York's Statues Called "Ridiculous". Brancusi, Regarded as Rodin's Most Brilliant Pupil, Here to Exhibit His Work. Our Architecture "Poetic" Likes Our Skyscrapers, Considers Grand Central Terminal "Most Beautiful"*, The New York Times, New York, 3 October.

***(1926), *Queer, But Art!*, New York Mirror, New York, 24 November.

***(1926), *Sculpture by Brancusi*, New York American, New York, 18 November.

***(1926), *The Abstract Sculpture of Brancusi*, New York Brooklyn Eagle, New York, 23 February.

***(1926), *Tri-National Sculpture Exhibition*, The New York Times, New York, 7 February.

***(1927), *"Art" Not Art, so US's Taxes "Bird"*, New York American, New York, 24 February.

***(1927), *Arts / Controversial Art*, Time, New York, 7 March.

***(1927), *Assail Duty Levy on "Bird of space"*, The New York Times, New York, 22 October.

***(1927), *Bird*, The New York Review of Books, New York, 31 October.

***(1927), *Brahma, Brancusi for Buffalo*, The Art News, New York, 23 April.

***(1927), *Brancusi Bronzes Defended by Cubist*, The New York Times, New York, 27 February.

***(1927), *Brancusi Must Pay Duty on Sculpture*, New York Brooklyn Eagle, New York, 24 February.

***(1927), *Brancusi No Artist, Customs Men Hold*, The New York Times, New York, 24 February.

***(1927), *Brancusi's Art Is Not Art, Federal Customs Men Rule…*, The New York Evening Post, 23 February.

***(1927), *Constantin Brancusi, un studiu asupra sculptorului*, Propasirea, Ploiesti, mai.

***(1927), *Customs Officers Say Pieces of Art Are Only Bronze*, Morning Telegraph, New York, 25 February.

***(1927), *His Sculpture Not "Art"*, New York Mirror, New York, 24 February.

***(1927), *Modern Art Displayed by International Exhibit at Toronto Art Gallery*, Globe, Toronto, 6 April.

***(1927), *Of Brancusi and the Triumph of the Egg*, The Chicago Evening Post Magazine of the Art World, Chicago, 4 January.

***(1927), *Society Gulps Hard at Brancusi Eggs*, Chicago Herald and Examiner, 23 January.

***(1928), *Brancusi Work Duty Free*, The New York Times, New York, 28 November.

***(1928), *Custom House Aesthete*, Time, New York, 17 December.

***(1928), *Fresh Paint. A Just Decision*, The Arts, New York, **XIII**, 14 December.

***(1928), *Metropolitan Duped, Flayed*, Time, New York, 17 December.

***(1928), *Modernist Sculptor Hails United States as New Cradle of Art*, The Washington Post, Washington, D.C., 8 January.

***(1928), *Procesul artei lui Brancusi, in fata tribunalului din New York*, Rampa, Bucuresti, 21 ianuarie.

***(1929), *"Art" Ruling Wins Sculptors Praise. Gertrude Whitney Aided in Decision on Brancusi's Protoplasmic "Bird"*, New York Evening Post, New York, 7 January.

***(1929), *Complete Prices of Davies Dale*, The Art News, New York, 29 April.

***(1929), *Le sculpteur Brancusi n'est pas un contrebandier*, L'Intransigéant, Paris, 8 janvier.

***(1929), *Vernisajul Salonului Oficial de gravura si desen*, Rampa, Bucuresti, *4*.

***(1929), *Vestiar*, Unu, Bucuresti, ianuarie.

***(1930), *Constantin Brancusi. Aforisme despre arta* (traducere de Dan Botta), Vremea. Politica, sociala, culturala (suplimentul Vremea plastica), Bucuresti, **III**, *144*, 9 noiembrie.

***(1930), *Constantin Brancusi. Poveste cu haiduci* (traducere de Dan Botta), Vremea. Politica, sociala, culturala (suplimentul Vremea plastica), Bucuresti, **III**, *141*, 30 octombrie.

***(1930), *Expozitia de arta romana din Bruxelles*, Epoca, Bucuresti, 7 August.

***(1930), *L'Exposition d'art roumain*, Le Peuple, Bruxelles, *1*, 24 juillet.

***(1930), *Minerva. Enciclopedie*, Ed. Minerva, Cluj.

***(1930), *My Thirty Years' War: An Autobiography by Margaret Anderson*, Covici, Friede Publishers, New York.

***(1930), *Pinacoteca statului* (catalog), Ateneul Roman, Bucuresti.

***(1930), *Roemeensche Kunst Gemeentemuseum*, Nieuwe Rotterdamsche Courant, Rotterdam, 11 mei.

***(1930), *Romania la Expozitia de la Bruxelles*, Dreptatea, Bucuresti, 7 August.

***(1933), *Brancusi Sculpture Exhibited; Brancusi's Sculpture Is Shown in New York*, The Washington Post, Washington, D.C., 10 December.

***(1934), *Art, Once Barred, Given to Museum*, The New York Times, New York, 12 August. ***(1935), *Un monument eroismului gorjenesc*, Gorjanul, Targu-Jiu, *42*.

***(1937), *Carvers & Casters*, Time, New York, 13 December.

***(1938), *Black-outs*, Time, New York, 25 April.

***(1940), *Exhibit Shows House Shaped Like a Snail; New York Display Portrays Numerous Uses Made of Shell*, The Washington Post, Washington, D.C., 24 November.

***(1942), *Artist Descending to America*, Time, New York, 7 September.

***(1946), *Temptation of Peggy*, Time, New York, 12 March.

***(1949), *20th Century Art from the Louise and Walter Arensberg Collection, Exhibition, First Showing of the Pioneer Collection of Modern Art, Including Four Versions of Marcel Duchamp's Nude Descending a Staircase and Sculpture of Constantin Brancusi*, Museum News Releases Index for 1939-1998, The Art Institute of Chicago, Chicago, *59, 62-64,* 13 September.

***(1949), *20th Century Art from the Louise and Walter Arensberg Collection, Exhibition Preview Featuring Mr. Marcel Duchamp; Notes on the Collection and Works Represented; Brancusi's Sculpture, Shown in Special Installation; Catalogue, Designed by Paul Rand and Published by AIC with Essays by AIC Curator Katharine Kuh and AIC Director Daniel Catton Rich*, Museum News Releases Index for 1939-1998, The Art Institute of Chicago, Chicago, *59, 62-64,* 10 October.

***(1950), *Passionate Pioneer*, Time, New York, 18 December.

***(1950), *The Great Armory of 1913*, Life, New York, 16 January.

***(1951), *The Fast Way*, Time, New York, 23 April.

***(1953), *Light on Dark*, Time, New York, 5 October.

***(1954), *Litterary Essays of Ezra Pound*, Faber & Faber, London.

***(1955), *Great Recluse. Brancusi and Art Come from Hiding* (photographs by Bernhard Moosbrugger), Life, New York, **39**, *23*.

***(1955), *Master of Form*, Time, New York, 14 November.

***(1957), *Constantin Brancusi, Sculptor Famed for Free Forms, Is Dead*, The New York Times, New York, 16 March.

***(1957), *Constantin Brancusi*, The Washington Post and Times Herald, Washington, D.C., 19 March.

***(1957), *Constantin Brancusi (necrolog)*, Scanteia si Romania libera, Bucuresti, 20 martie.

***(1957), *Funeraliile sculptorului Constantin Brancusi*, Romania libera, Bucuresti, 22 martie.

***(1968), *Isamu Noguchi, A Sculptor's World*, Harper & Row Publishers, New York.

***(1971), *Brancusi impotriva Statelor Unite* (traducere de P. Comarnescu), Ed. Dacia, Cluj-Napoca.

***(1971), *Liceul industrial de mecanica agricola Craiova—100 ani, 1871-1971,* Craiova.

***(1976), *Noguchi on Brancusi*, Craft Horizons, New York, 1976, *4*.

***(1976), *Omagiu—100—Brancusi* (antologie ingrijita de C. Baleanu si I. Mocioi), Comitetul pentru cultura si arta al judetului Gorj, Targu-Jiu.

***(1976), *Omagiu lui Brancusi*, volum editat de revista Tribuna, Cluj-Napoca.

***(1997), *Brancusi, acum,* comunicari stiintifice prezentate in cadrul simpozionului *Brancusiana 96*, organizat la Targu-Jiu, Ed. Fundatiei *Constantin Brancusi*, Targu-Jiu.

***(2010), Catalogul *Charles et Marie-Laure de Noailles / Une vie de mécènes*, Avant-première, Paris, Vitrines du Palais Royal, Ministère de la Culture et de la Communication, du 1er au 11 mars 2010 / puis à Hyères, à partir du 2 juillet 2010 à Saint-Bernard, www.villanoailles-hyeres.com/

***(2015), *Juana Müller 1911-1952 destin d'une femme sculpteur*, sous la direction de Sabrina Dubbeld, Somogy Éditions d'Art, Paris.

***International Resin Modelers Association, www.internationalresinmodellers.com/

***Interpretive Resource, The Art Institue of Chicago—Ryerson and Burnham Libraries, http://www.artic.edu/

***Katherine S. Dreier Papers / Société Anonyme Archive at the Beinecke Rare Booke and Manuscript Library at Yale University

***The Eleanor Roosevelt Papers, The George Washington University, Washington, D.C., https://www.gwu.edu/

***The New York Public Library, archives@manuscripts, John Quinn papers 1901-1926

***Warm Ashes: The Life and Career of Mary Reynolds, The Art Institue of Chicago—Ryerson and Burnham Libraries, http://www.artic.edu/

List/Source of Illustrations

Fig. 1. Tismana Monastery, 1860 / engraving by D. Lancelot, *Le tour du monde, Premier semestre,* Librairie Hachette et C-ie, Paris, 1868, p. 340

Fig. 2. Village surrounding Targu-Jiu, 1860 / engraving by D. Lancelot, *Le tour du monde, Premier semestre,* Librairie Hachette et C-ie, Paris, 1868, p. 342

Fig. 3. *Constantin Brancusi* house museum of Hobita, reconstituted in 1971 / postcard, I. P. Arta Grafica, Bucharest

Fig. 4. Coppice of Bistrita River / postcard, unknown author

Fig. 5. Targu-Jiu at the end of the 19th century / http://romania-online.blogspot.ro

Fig. 6. Central area of Slatina town / postcard, unknown author

Fig. 7. Train station of Craiova / http://memorielocala.aman.ro

Fig. 8. Pitesti train station area / http://www.info-pitesti.ro/

Figs. 9a-c. Churches of Craiova, 1908: a—Madonna Dudu; b—St. Elijah; c—Saint Trinity / 1908 Ramuri magazine calendar, Craiova

Fig. 10. Workshops of the School of Crafts, Craiova / V. Constantinescu, 1937

Fig. 11. Minutes of the Commission attributing stipends in the School of Crafts in Craiova, 31 August 1895 / B. Brezianu, 1974

Fig. 12. Letter of Brancusi to the mayor of Pestisani, 20 August 1895 / private collection

Fig. 13. *Beetle* / ROMSIT Co. SA Fund

Fig. 14. Guarantee deed signed by Brancusi's mother, Pestisani, 1 January 1896 / B. Brezianu, 1974

Fig. 15. Brancusi wearing the uniform of the School of Crafts in Craiova / B. Brezianu, 1964

Figs. 16a, b. Wood pieces executed outside the curriculum, Craiova, 1896: a—*loom* / I. Schintee, 1964; b—*lotto pieces* / B. Brezianu, 1976

Fig. 17. Aspects of the sculpted walls of a marble box to keep holy oil, Craiova, 1896 / ROMSIT Co. SA Fund

Fig. 18. Donation deed to priest G. Haiduc from St. Elijah Church in Craiova, 12 July 1896 / private collection

Fig. 19. Brancusi in the School of Crafts, Craiova, 1897 / B. Brezianu, 1974

Fig. 20. Vienna, 1897 / http://kunstmuseum-hamburg.de/wien-alte-stadtansichten/

Figs. 21a, b. Wood pieces executed in the School of Crafts shop, Craiova: a—*frame* / V.G. Paleolog, 1967; b—*corner chair* / B. Brezianu, 1974

Fig. 22. *Prayer* / ROMSIT Co. SA Fund

Fig. 23. Priest C. Smantanescu's house with pillars carved by Brancusi, Curtisoara Museum / D. Smantanescu, 1967

Fig. 24. Brancusi near his colleagues upon graduation of the School of Crafts, Craiova, June 1898 / M. Deac, 1966

Fig. 25. Lucilla Chitu, Craiova / 1908 Ramuri magazine calendar, Craiova

Figs. 26a, b. Bucharest: a—University Palace during construction / photo by Satmary, Literary and artistic calendar 1909, Bucharest; b—letterhead of the School of Beaux Arts / National University of Arts Bucharest, Elena Dumitrescu, 2013

Fig. 27. Professor sculptor I. Georgescu during a perspective class, School of Beaux Arts in Bucharest, 1896-97 / National University of Arts Bucharest, Elena Dumitrescu, 2013

Fig. 28. Buzesti Street, Bucharest / www.bucurestiivechisinoi.ro

Fig. 29. Adeverul, Bucharest, 16 October 1898

Fig. 30. Albina, Bucharest, 8 November 1898

Fig. 31. Ion Campineanu Street where Osvald's beer and spirits pub was found, Bucharest / www.bucurestiivechisinoi.ro

Fig. 32. Monument of Tudor Vladimirescu by C. Balacescu, Targu-Jiu / 1908 Ramuri magazine calendar, Craiova

Figs. 33a, b. Drawings by Brancusi after the monument of Tudor Vladimirescu / I. Croitoru collection, B. Brezianu, 1976

Fig. 34. Brancusi in the studio of the School of Beaux Arts, Bucharest, 1899-1901 / National University of Arts Bucharest, unknown author

Fig. 35. *Madonna* / ROMSIT Co. SA Fund

Figs. 36a, b. Brancusi next to his colleagues in the studio of the School of Beaux Arts, Bucharest, 1901 / National University of Arts Bucharest, unknown author

Fig. 37. *Brancusi* by Th. Pallady, Bucharest, 1900 / B. Brezianu, 1998

Fig. 38. Brancoveanu Hospital of Bucharest where the School of Beaux Arts students attended artistic anatomy classes / www.bucurestiivechisinoi.ro

Fig. 39. Studio of the School of Beaux Arts, Bucharest, 1901 / National University of Arts Bucharest, unknown author

Fig. 40. Sale-purchase deed of a marble woman's head, Craiova, 27 September 1901 / private collection

Figs. 41a, b. Brancusi self-portraits, Bucharest, 1901-1902 / I. Croitoru collection, B. Brezianu, 1976

Fig. 42. 1902 Typographic Almanac, Bucharest

Fig. 43. Elisabeta Blvd, Bucharest / www.bucurestiivechisinoi.ro

Fig. 44. Ana Stefanescu, Bucharest, 1903 / P. Comarnescu, 1972

Figs. 45a, b. Rovine Regiment no. 26, Craiova, 1902: a—Brancusi's conscription order / private collection; b—barracks of the regiment / http://memorielocala.aman.ro

Fig. 46. Graduation Diploma of the School of Beaux Arts, Bucharest, 24 September 1902 / M. Deac, 1966

Fig. 47. House of G. Ionescu, Craiova, 1902 / Ramuri, 1981, *1*

Figs. 48a, b. Trusteeship of Madonna Dudu Church, Craiova: a—Brancusi's letter, 30 January 1902 / private collection; b
Brancusi and N. Titulescu as scholars, 1902-1903 / European Foundation Titulescu www.titulescu.eu

Fig. 49. Ion Georgescu-Gorjan (a) and his bust (b), Craiova, 1902 / a—St. Georgescu-Gorjan archive; b—M. Deac, 1966

Fig. 50. Letter of Brancusi to the Trusteeship of Madonna Dudu Church, Craiova, 1902 / B. Brezianu, 1976

Figs. 51a-c. Bucharest, 1903: a—Athenaeum Palace / postcard, unknown author; b—Adeverul, 7 May; c—Gazeta Artelor, 11 May

Fig. 52. Letter of the School of Beaux Arts students, Bucharest, 14 May 1903 / Elena Dumitrescu, 2013

Figs. 53a-d. General Doctor Carol Davila, Bucharest: a—Adeverul, 28 October 1903; b—Davila's photograph / Albina, 8 February 1898; c— bust; d—bas-relief / Brancusi Fund of MNAM, Paris

Fig. 54. Vienna, 1904 / http://tramway.at/

Fig. 55. Brancusi on the way to Paris, 1904 / Luceafarul, 1 March 1907

Fig. 56. Munich, 1904 / https://www.stadtbild-deutschland.org/

Fig. 57. Provisional bridge, Basel, 1904 / collection.hht.net.au

Fig. 58. Rack bar railroad, Langres, 1904 / www.delcampe.net

Figs. 59a, b. Paris, 1904: a—East Station; b—Cité Condorcet Street / paris1900.lartnouveau.fr

Figs. 60a, b. Paris, 1904: a—Brancusi working as dishwasher / Brancusi Fund of MNAM, Paris, unknown author; b—Chartier Beer House / photo by André Kertész

Figs. 61a, b. Paris, 1904: a—Romanian Orthodox Church / P.P.C. Paris; b—Brancusi parish clerk / V.G. Paleolog, 1967

Fig. 62. Place de la Bourse, Paris, 1905 / paris1900.lartnouveau.fr

Fig. 63. View from the home-studio of Brancusi, Paris, 1905 / B. Brezianu, 1964

Fig. 64. Place Dauphine, Paris / paris1900.lartnouveau.fr

Figs. 65a, b. Paris, 1905-1906: a—National School of Beaux Arts / paris1900.lartnouveau.fr; b—Brancusi next to his colleagues / Brancusi Fund of MNAM, Paris, unknown author

Fig. 66. School grade given to Brancusi by Professor A. Mercié, Paris, 1 July 1905 / B. Brezianu, 1964

Fig. 67. *Leaf of the Life* / Museum of Banat, Timisoara

Fig. 68. Closerie des Lilas, Paris / paris1900.lartnouveau.fr

Fig. 69. L'Aérophile, Paris, 1906, *9*

Figs. 70a, b. Traian Vuia (a) and his portrait (b), Paris / a—http://www.imperialtransilvania.com/; b—private collection, photo by Olivier Brunet

Figs. 71a, b. *General Romanian Exhibition*—1906, Bucharest: a—general view / postcard, Ad. Maier & D. Stern Publishers, 1906; b—pavilion of doctor D. Gerota / Calendar Minerva, 1907

Fig. 72. Card sent to I. Gheorghian-Popescu, Paris, 28 September 1906 / E. Manu, 1976

Fig. 73. Sofia, wife of painter S. Popescu, and Otilia Cosmuta in Brancusi's studio of 16 Place Dauphine, Paris / M. Deac, 1966

Fig. 74. 1906 Bucharest Yearbook

Fig. 75. Commitment to make the funerary ensemble of Buzau, Paris, 18 April 1907 / Bulletin of Bucharest, edited by the Chamber of Notaries Public, May-June 2010

Fig. 76. Montparnasse Street, Paris / paris1900.lartnouveau.fr

Fig. 77. Daniel Poiana and his daughter Alicia in Brancusi's studio of 54 Montparnasse Street, Paris, 1907 / Brancusi Fund of MNAM, Paris, unknown author

Fig. 78. Luceafarul, Sibiu, 1 March 1907

Fig. 79. 1908 Ramuri magazine calendar, Craiova

Fig. 80. Victoria and Nicolae Vaschide and many other friends in Brancusi's studio, Paris, 1907 / Brancusi Fund of MNAM, Paris, unknown author

Figs. 81a, b. Paris, 1907: a—*Prayer* / *Romania in chipuri si vederi,* 1926; b—*Kiss* / P. Hulten, Natalia Dumitrescu, A. Istrati, 1986

Fig. 82. Luceafarul, Sibiu, 1 February 1908

Fig. 83. Brancusi ill with typhoid fever—drawing by L. Biju, Paris, 18 February 1908 / V.G. Paleolog, 1967

Fig. 84. Luceafarul, Sibiu, 1 May 1908

Fig. 85. Luceafarul, Sibiu, 1 October 1908

Fig. 86. Bateau Lavoir, Paris / www.theartsadventurer.com

Figs. 87a, b. Paris: a—Léonie Ricou / F.T. Bach, Margit Rowell, Ann Temkin, 1995; b—*Madame L.R.* / photo by Brancusi, Brancusi Fund of MNAM, Paris

Fig. 88. Raspail Blvd, Paris / paris1900.lartnouveau.fr

Figs. 89a, b. Paris: a—Baroness Renée Irana Frachon / F.T. Bach, Margit Rowell, Ann Temkin, 1995; b—*Sleeping Muse* / photo by Brancusi, Brancusi Fund of MNAM, Paris

Fig. 90. Luceafarul, Sibiu, 1 March 1909

Fig. 91. Façade of the building from 7 Delta Street, Paris / www.secretmodigliani.com

Figs. 92a-d. *Brancusi* by Modigliani—drawings and paintings: a—*Portrait of Brancusi Seated in an Armchair*, 1908-1909; b—*Portrait of Brancusi*, 1909 / Sotheby's, London; c—*Portrait of Constantin Brancusi*, 1909 / Doris Krystof, 2000; d—*The Cellist*, 1909 / *Modigliani paintings, drawings, sculpture, with an introd. by James Thrall Soby. The Museum of Modern Art, New York, in collaboration with the Cleveland Museum of Art,* New York, 1951; e—*Portrait of Brancusi*, 1909-1910 / Smithsonian Libraries (photographed by P.A.) Juley & Son, O. Patani, *Amedeo Modigliani, Catalogo Generale: Sculture e Disegni 1909-1914*, Leonardo Editore, Milan, 1992, cat. 48); f—*Bearded Man Seated*, 1909-1910 / The Fitzwilliam Museum, Cambridge

Fig. 93. *De Modi Oiseau de nuit* / private collection, photo by Olivier Brunet

Fig. 94. Queen Elisabeth of Romania and Princess Maria at the exhibition entrance, Bucharest, 1910 / Noua Revista Romana, 1910, *2-3*

Fig. 95. Luceafarul, Sibiu, 1-16 June 1910

Figs. 96a, b. Margit Pogany, 1910—a / S. Geist, 1968; *Miss Pogany*—b / http://armoryshow.si.edu/

Fig. 97. *Bust of Painter Nicolae Darascu* and *Sleep* in the Simu Museum, Bucharest / Minerva Romanian Encyclopedia, 1929

Fig. 98. Colony of artists *La Ruche*, Paris / paris1900.lartnouveau.fr

Figs. 99a, b. Aurel Vlaicu pilot of *Vlaicu No. I* airplane, Bucharest, June 1910—a / S. Miloran, 1962; *Maiastra* in the garden of Katherine S. Dreier's West Redding home (CT)—b / Brancusi Fund of MNAM, Paris, unknown author

Fig. 100. Brancusi, H. Coanda and his wife near the *Coanda-10* airplane, Paris Air Show, 1910 / International Resin Modelers Association, http://www.internationalresinmodellers.com/

Fig. 101a, b. Montparnasse Cemetery, Paris: a—The *Kiss* on the tomb of Tatiana Rashevskaia / photo by Brancusi, Brancusi Fund of MNAM, Paris; b—the epitaph engraved by Brancusi on the pedestal / V.G. Paleolog, 1967

Figs. 102a, b. Corneliu Cosmuta—a / B. Brezianu, 1976; *Prometheus*—b / S. Geist, 1968

Figs. 103a, b. Jean-Baptiste Charcot surrounded by penguins at the South Pole, 1908—a / http://ilyaunsiecle.blog.lemonde.fr/; *Three Penguins*—b / photo by Brancusi, Brancusi Fund of MNAM, Paris

Fig. 104. La Rotonde, Paris / paris1900.lartnouveau.fr

Fig. 105. Brancusi working at the forge in the studio courtyard, Paris, 1912 / photo by Brancusi, Brancusi Fund of MNAM, Paris

Fig. 106. Châtillon Avenue, Paris / paris1900.lartnouveau.fr

Figs. 107a, b. Agnes E. Meyer, 1910—a / photo by Ed. Steichen; *Study for the Portrait of Mrs. Eugene Meyer Jr.*—b / photo by Brancusi, Brancusi Fund of MNAM, Paris

Fig. 108. Denise Poiret with *Maiastra*, Paris, 1921 / photo by Man Ray, http://www.manray-photo.com

Fig. 109. Oscar Wilde's tomb, Père Lachaise Cemetery, Paris—funerary monument covered with a cloth by the police / http://blog.dorant.gayattitude.com

Figs. 110a-d. Echoes in the media, New York, February 1913: a—New York American; b—The International Press; c—The Brooklyn Daily Eagle; d—New York Tribune

Figs. 111a, b. Chicago Daily Tribune, 1913: a—17 February; b—17 April

Fig. 112. *Maiastra* in Ed. Steichen's garden, Voulangis / photo by Ed. Steichen, 1920-1923

Fig. 113. *Brancusi* by C. Ressu, Bucharest, 1913 / Seara, 28 April 1914

Fig. 114. Zlatá Praha, Prague, 13 March 1914

Figs. 115a, b. Guillaume Apollinaire's epitaph written at the death of H. Rousseau (a) engraved in 1913 by Brancusi and O. de Zarate on the tombal stone (b) / a, Les Soirées de Paris, 1914, *20-27*; b, photo by G. Goutierre, http://www.lessoireesdeparis.com/

Fig. 116. Brancusi working to the *Gate,* Paris, 1915 / photo by Brancusi, Brancusi Fund of MNAM, Paris

Fig. 117. 291 Gallery, New York, before 1913 / Sarah Greenough et al., 2001

Figs. 118a, b. New York, March 1914: a—The Brooklyn Daily Eagle; b—The Sun

Fig. 119. The funerary ensemble in Dumbrava Cemetery, Buzau / V.G. Paleolog, 1967

Fig. 120. *Fountain of Narcissus* in Brancusi's studio, Paris / photo by Brancusi, Brancusi Fund of MNAM, Paris

Fig. 121. *Cubists and Post-Impressionism* by A.J. Eddy, Chicago, 1914

Fig. 122. View from the Modern Gallery window toward The New York Public Library / M. de Zayas, Fr. M. Naumann, 1998

Figs. 123a, b. Paris at the beginning of the 20th century: a—Impasse Ronsin; b—Odessa Street / paris1900.lartnouveau.fr

Figs. 124a, b. Marie Bonaparte—a / Les Modes, Paris, 1907, *81*; *Princesse X*—b / photo by Brancusi, Brancusi Fund of MNAM, Paris

Fig. 125. Camera Work, New York, October 1916

Fig. 126. The Sun, New York, 5 November 1916

Figs. 127a, b. Wood sculptures in Brancusi's studio, Paris, 1914-1916: a—*Gate;* b—*Bench* / photos by Brancusi, Brancusi Fund of MNAM, Paris

Fig. 128. *Child in the World*, mobile group in Brancusi's studio, Paris / photo by Brancusi, Brancusi Fund of MNAM, Paris

Fig. 129. La Renaissance politique, économique, littéraire et artistique, Paris, 15 September 1917

Fig. 130. Miss Vanderbilt, Miss Payne Thompson and Miss Canfield, members of the organizing committee in the exhibition hall of Ritz Carlton Hotel, New York, 1917 / http://www.gettyimages.com/

Fig. 131. De Stijl, Leiden, 1918, *12*

Fig. 132. *La Roumanie en images*, I, Paris, 1919

Fig. 133. *Brancusi* by G. de Zayas, 1919 / http://artgallery.yale.edu/

Fig. 134. Maria Brancusi, Hobita / unknown author

Fig. 135. *Little French Girl* in Katherine S. Dreier's West Redding home (CT), 1941 / photo by J. Schiff, http://artgallery.yale.edu/

Fig. 136. *Drie Voordrachten over de Nieuwe Beeldende Kunst* by Th. van Doesburg, Amsterdam, 1919

Fig. 137. Le Journal du peuple, Paris, 25 February 1920

Fig. 138. Poster of the *Manifeste cannibale dada* by Fr. Picabia, Paris, 27 March 1920 / DADAphone, Paris, 1920, *7*

Figs. 139a, b. *Festival dada*, Paris, 26 May 1920: a—poster / www.ieef.org; b—Gaveau Hall / https://oss.adm.ntu.edu.sg/sria0002/art-cinema-dada-filmmaking/

Fig. 140. *A Hand* / photo by Brancusi, Brancusi Fund of MNAM, Paris

Fig. 141. Mina Loy and Peggy Guggenheim, Paris, 1920 / vogue.it

Fig. 142. Brancusi in front of the studio, Paris, 1920s / Yale University Library, Beinecke Digital Collections, http://brbldl.library.yale.edu/, photo by Katherine S. Dreier

Figs. 143a, b. *Yellow Bird* (a, photo of 1941) and *Leda* (b, photo of 1948) in the Katherine S. Dreier's West Redding home (CT) / photos by J. Schiff, http://artgallery.yale.edu/

Fig. 144. *The Golden Bird "After Brancusi"* by G. Antheil, New York, 1921

Fig. 145. Poster of the *Excursions et visites dada*, Paris, 14 April 1921 / dadasurr.blogspot.com

Figs. 146a, b. Brancusi together with Jeanne Robert Foster (a) and J. Quinn (b), Paris, 1921 / a, R. Londraville, Janis Londraville, 2001; b, New York Public Library

Fig. 147. Brancusi in his studio, Paris, 1921 / photo by Brancusi, Brancusi Fund of MNAM, Paris

Fig. 148. *Modern Tendencies in Sculpture* by L. Taft, Chicago, 1921

Fig. 149. *A History of European and American Sculpture: From the Early Christian Period to the Present Day* by C.A. Post, **II**, Cambridge (MA), 1921

Fig. 150. The Little Review, New York, September 1921

Fig. 151. Brancusi, Maja Chrusecz, Mina Loy, Jane Heap and Margaret Anderson in the sculptor's studio, Paris, 1921 / photo by Brancusi, Brancusi Fund of MNAM, Paris

Figs. 152a, b. Paris: a—*Réveillon cacodylate* participants, 31 December 1921 / Vente des archives de la cantatrice Marthe Chenal (1881-1947), le 8 juin 2009, Alde, maison de ventes, Salle Rossini, Paris; b—*L'Œil cacodylate* collage / William A. Camfield, 1970

Figs. 153a, b. New York, 1922: a—The New York Herald, 26 March; b—Vanity Fair, May

Fig. 154. Gaîté Street, Paris / paris1900.lartnouveau.fr

Fig. 155. Erik Satie in Brancusi's studio, Paris, 1922 / photo by Brancusi, Brancusi Fund of MNAM, Paris

Figs. 156a, b. Brancusi's studio, Paris: a—Lizica Codreanu dancing, 1922; b—*Sorceress* / photos by Brancusi, Brancusi Fund of MNAM, Paris

Figs. 157a, b. Drawings by Brancusi: a—ideogram of the *Kiss* with dedication for Edith Taylor / B. Nicolescu, 2011; b—*Dimitrie Cuclin* / I. Barsan, 2005

Fig. 158. Universul literar, Bucharest, 1942, *29*

Figs. 159a, b. Caraiman Hotel, Sinaia—a / Romania ilustrata, 1926, July; Cathedral and Episcopal Palace, Ramnicu Valcea—b / postcards, unknown authors

Figs. 160a, b. Eileen Lane: a—in the popular costume of Gorj, Hobita, 1922; b—*Eileen* / photos by Brancusi, Brancusi Fund of MNAM, Paris

Fig. 161. Satie, Quinn, Brancusi, and Roché on the golf course of Fontainebleau, Paris, 1922 / photo by Jeanne Robert Foster, L'Œil de la photographie, Paris, 15 February 2015

Fig. 162. *Fish* / photo by Brancusi, Brancusi Fund of MNAM, Paris

Fig. 163. *Brancusi's Golden Bird* by Mina Loy, The Dial, New York, November 1922

Fig. 164. *Brancusi*, in *Slabs of the Sunburnt West* by C. Sandburg, New York, 1922

Fig. 165. Der Querschnitt, Berlin, 1923, *3-4*

Fig. 166. The Arts, New York, July 1923

Figs. 167a, b. Brancusi's studio, Paris, 1923: a—*Bird in Space*; b—*White Negress* / photos by Brancusi, Brancusi Fund of MNAM, Paris

Fig. 168. Outdoor party around Paris attended among others by Léger, Lizica Codreanu and Brancusi / B. Brezianu, 1998, unknown author

Fig. 169. Brancusi on the golf course of Chantilly with Roché, Jeanne Robert Foster and Satie, Paris, 1923 / photo by J. Quinn, Mary E. Davis, 2006

Fig. 170. Swedish Ballet at Champs-Élysées Theater, Paris, 1923 / https://gallica.bnf.fr/blog/12072018/amities-de-fernandleger

Figs. 171a, b. Nancy Cunard, 1924—a / photo by Man Ray; *Sophisticated Young Lady*—b / photo by Brancusi, Brancusi Fund of MNAM, Paris

Figs. 172a, b. Bal Banal, Paris, 14 March 1924: a—poster by A. Brodovitch with drawings by Picasso and Brancusi / artnet.com; b—Bullier Hall / http://dadaparis.blogspot.com/

Figs. 173a, b. Bal Olympique, Paris, 11 July 1924: a—program / catalog.quittenbaum.de; b—façade of the Olympia Tavern program / gallica.bnf.fr

Fig. 174. Georgette Leblanc, Léger and Polaire in Brancusi's studio, Paris, 1924 / Der Querschnitt, 1924, Bild 4

Fig. 175. Contimporanul, Bucharest, 1924, *45*

Figs. 176a, b. *Brancusi* by M.H. Maxy (a) and J. Mattis-Teutsch (b) / wikiart.org

Fig. 177a, b. Paris, 1924: a—The Transatlantic Review, *6*; b—*Dictionnaire Critique et Documentaire des Peintres, Sculpteurs, Dessinateurs et Graveurs de tous les temps et de tous les pays* coordinated by E. Bénézit

Figs. 178a, b. Paris: a—ballet dancer S. Lifar / https://pleasurephoto.wordpress.com; b—*The Beginning of the World* / photo by Brancusi, Brancusi Fund of MNAM, Paris

Figs. 179a, b. Brancusi's studio, Paris, 1924: a—*Cock*; b—the sculptor carving a *Column* / photos by Brancusi, Brancusi Fund of MNAM, Paris

Figs. 180a, b. *Temple of the Crocodile*, 1924: a—on the Saint-Raphaël beach; b—in the studio, Paris / photos by Brancusi, Brancusi Fund of MNAM, Paris

Fig. 181. *Brancusi* by E. Walsh, Poetry—A Magazine of Verse, Chicago, octobre 1924

Fig. 182. Contimporanul, Bucharest, 1925, *1*

Fig. 183. Integral, Bucharest, 1925, *2*

Fig. 184. Brancusi at the celebration of his birthday in the Rotonde, Paris, 19 February 1925. From left to right: M. Mihalovici, L. Delarue-Mardrus, Dr. Mardrus, O. Cosmuta, G. Bölöni, Th. Aladar / Brancusi Fund of MNAM, Paris, unknown author

Fig. 185. This Quarter, Paris, May 1925

Fig. 186. Augustus John, Brancusi and F.O. Dobson at the National Portrait Gallery, London, 1925 / npg.org.uk

Fig. 187. Sturm, Berlin, October 1925

Figs. 188a, b. Cruise ships: a—France; b—De Grasse / www.frenchlines.com

Fig. 189. Brevoort Hotel, New York / http://collections.mcny.org

Fig. 190. Invitation to the Firemen's Gala, New York, 27 February 1926

Fig. 191. *Firemen's Dinner for Brancusi* by A. Calder, New York, 1926 / The catalogue Alexander Calder, Whitney Museum of America Art, New York, 17 February-3 May 1981

Fig. 192. Contimporanul, Bucharest, 1926, *1*

Fig. 193. *Brancusi* by M. Iancu / M. Tita, bursa.ro, 2013

Figs. 194a, b. *Romania in chipuri si vederi*, Bucharest, 1926 with photographic reproductions of Brancusi's woks—a; *La Roumanie en images*, **I**, Paris, 1922—b

Figs. 195a, b. Brancusi erected the *Column* in Ed. Steichen's garden, Voulangis, 1926b / photos by Ed. Steichen

Fig. 196. Brancusi, Marthe Lebherz and sisters Codreanu, Paris, 1926 / photo by Brancusi, Brancusi Fund of MNAM, Paris

Fig. 197. Pásmo, Prague, 1926, *9-10*

Figs. 198a, b. Paris cruise ship—a / www.frenchlines.com; Brancusi and Ed. Steichen's dog on the deck of the cruise ship—b / photo by Brancusi, Brancusi Fund of MNAM, Paris

Fig. 199. *Bird in Space* for which court trial was opened with the American customs / photo by Ed. Steichen, ca. 1920

Figs. 200a, b. Marie Romany (a) and her famous tavern of Greenwich Village (b), New York / J. Whitaker, 2010

Fig. 201. Brochure by Katherine S. Dreier, New York, 1926 / beinecke.library.yale.edu/

Fig. 202. Brancusi, New York, 1926 / photo by A. Stieglitz, Yale University Library, Beinecke Digital Collections, http://brbl-dl.library.yale.edu/

Fig. 203. Rochambeau cruise ship / www.frenchlines.com

Fig. 204. *Transformations: Critical and Speculative Essays on Art* by R. Fry, London, 1926

Fig. 205. *The Analysis of Art* by D.H. Parker, New Haven, 1926

Fig. 206. Oswaldo de Andrade, Tarsila do Amaral, Yvette Farkou, F. Léger, Brancusi, M. Gauthier, Paris, 1926 / A. A. Amaral, 2003, unknown author

Figs. 207a, b. Brancusi's gifts at Tarsila's wedding, Paris, 1926: a—ideogram of the *Kiss* / www.revistapiaui.estadao.com.br/; b—view of Tarsila's living room with *Prometheus* on the table, São Paulo, 1929 / A.A. Amaral, 2003

Figs. 208a, b. Hyères: a—Villa Noailles, 1929 / postcard, Villa Noailles collection, unknown author; b—*Sleeping Muse* in the garden of the villa—b / https://www.villanoailles-designparade.com/

Fig. 209. Integral, Bucharest, 1926, *9*

Fig. 210. Cahiers d'art, Paris, 1927, *2*

Fig. 211. *Bust of Painter Nicolae Darascu* exhibited in the State Art Gallery, Bucharest / Boabe de grau, 1930, *4*

Fig. 212. ReD, Prague, October 1927-July 1928

Figs. 213a, b. Edward Steichen's garden, Voulangis, 1927: a—Man Ray and Brancusi; b—Brancusi disassembling the *Column* / photogrammes of 35 mm film by Man Ray, Brancusi Fund of MNAM, Paris

Fig. 214. American Weekly (Chicago Herald-Examiner), 13 March 1927

Fig. 215. *Newborn* / photo by Brancusi, Brancusi Fund of MNAM, Paris

Fig. 216. De Stijl, Leiden, 1927, Jubileum Serie XIV, *79-84*

Figs 217a, b. Brancusi and Marthe Lebherz on the beach of Nice, 1928 / photos by Brancusi, Brancusi Fund of MNAM, Paris

Fig. 218. Unu, Bucharest, April 1928

Fig. 219. Universul literar, Bucharest, 1928, *17*

Fig. 220. Poster of the international exhibition at the Little Review Gallery, New York, 1928 / Brancusi Fund of MNAM, Paris

Figs. 221a, b. *White Negress* II exhibited in Helena Rubinstein's house, Paris: a—apartment on Raspail Blvd, 1930s / photo by Dora Maar, http://brunoclaessens.com/; b—beauty parlor, 1950s / photo by P. Kowaliski, Helena Rubinstein Foundation Photographs, https://fitdil.fitnyc.edu/

Fig. 222. Brancusi, Paris, 1928 / *Portraits André Kertész*, edited by Nicolas Ducrot, 1979

Fig. 223. U.S. Supreme Court Justices that judged the trial of the *Bird in Space*, New York, 1928. Seated (l to r)—J.C. McReynolds, O.W. Holmes, Jr., W.H. Taft (27th President of U.S. 1909-13), W. Van Devanter, L. Brandeis; Standing (1 to r)—Ed. Sanford, G. Sutherland, P. Butler, H.F. Stone / unknown author, 1925, www.oyez.org

Fig. 224. Duchamp, Mary Reynolds and Brancusi, Villefranche-sur-Mer, 1929 / Reynolds, Mary, Collection, 1892-1972 (bulk 1941-1964), digital-libraries.saic.edu/

Fig. 225. *Portrait of James Joyce* by Brancusi, in *Tales Told of Shem and Shaun* by J. Joyce, Paris, 1929 / The Black Sun Press, Paris, 1929

Fig. 226. Transition, Paris, 1929, *16-17*

Fig. 227. Cahiers d'art, Paris, 1929, *8-9*

Fig. 228. Cahiers de l'Étoile, Paris, 1929, *11*

Fig. 229. Death mask of S. Diaghilev polished by Brancusi, Paris, 1929 / photo by Man Ray

Fig. 230. Brancusi drawings, in *Plante si animale: terase* by I. Voronca, Paris, 1929 / Collection Intégral, Imprimerie Union, Paris, 1929

Fig. 231. *Danaide* exhibited in J. Doucet's house, Neuilly-sur-Seine, 1929 / photo by P. Legrain, 1929

Fig. 232. *Von Material zu Architektur* by L. Moholy-Nagy, Munich, 1929

Fig. 233. Der Querschnitt, Berlin, 1929, *12*

Fig. 234. Brancusi together with Margit and V. Brauner, Impasse Ronsin, Paris, 1930 / photo by Brancusi, Brancusi Fund of MNAM, Paris

Fig. 235. Grand Hotel du Boulevard, Bucharest / www.bucurestiivechisinoi.ro

Fig. 236. *Partenza*, in *Strofe pentru toata lumea* by I. Minulescu, Bucarest, 1930

Figs. 237a, b. Vera Moore—a / J. Moore archive; *Brancusi* by O. Kokoschka, Paris, 1930—b / Brancusi Fund of MNAM, Paris

Fig. 238. *Portrait of B. Fundoianu* by Brancusi, in *Privelisti / poeme* by B. Fundoianu, Bucharest, 1930 / Cultura Nationala Publishers, Bucharest, 1930

Figs. 239a, b. Adeverul, Bucharest, 1930: a—4 July; b—9 October

Fig. 240. Praesens, Warsaw, 1930, *2*

Fig. 241. *My Thirty Years' War: An Autobiography by Margaret Anderson*, New York, 1930

Fig. 242. Letter to T.G. Tomescu, Paris, 16 February 1931 / Ruxandra Ionescu, 1975

Fig. 243. Maharajah of Indore and his wife, Cannes, 1930 / photo by Man Ray, https://www.asianart.com/

Figs. 244a-c. *Birds in Space* of the maharajah of Indore: a—bronze; b, c—marble / photos by Brancusi, Brancusi Fund of MNAM, Paris

Fig. 245. Brancusi on the terrace of the Villa Marguerite, Villefranche-sur-Mer, 1931 / photo by Brancusi, Brancusi Fund of MNAM, Paris

Figs. 246a, b. Brancusi's studio, Paris, 1932: a—Florence Meyer; b—*Miracle* / photos by Brancusi, Brancusi Fund of MNAM, Paris

Fig. 247. Brancusi's letter to Florence Meyer, Paris, 28 July 1933 / http://www.binocheetgiquello.com

Fig. 248. *Portrait of Brancusi* by Lilly Steiner, 1929 / Formes, 1932, *24*

Fig. 249. *Bird in Space* in the music salon of Helena Rubinstein's apartment, Paris, 1933 / photo by B. Elkouken, Vogue, 1933, January

Fig. 250. *Sculptor at Rest, Reclining Model, and Sculpture* by Picasso, Paris, March 1933 / https://brucemuseum.org/

Fig. 251. Beach of Saint-Jean-de-Luz / www.saintjeandeluz.fr

Fig. 252. *Sculpteurs d'aujourd'hui* by P. Fierens, Paris, 1933

Fig. 253. Minotaure, Paris, 1933, *3-4*

Fig. 254. *King of Kings* in Brancusi's studio, Paris / photo by Brancusi, Brancusi Fund of MNAM, Paris

Fig. 255. *Modern Sculpture* by H. Maryon, London, 1933

Figs. 256a, b. *Brancusi* by Anne Harvey, Paris, 1934 / (a) Exhibition catalogue *Family Line, drawings and paintings by Anne Harvey, Jason Harvey and Steven Harvey*, 10 January-23 February 2002, New York Studio School of Drawing, Painting and Sculpture; (b) Exhibition catalogue *Anne Harvey: Private Life*, Steven Harvey Fine Art Projects, 10 May-11 June 2017, New York

Figs. 257a, b. *Anne Harvey* by Brancusi, 1934 / (a) photo by Brancusi, Brancusi Fund of MNAM, Paris; (b) drawing in pencil and pastel on cardboard by Brancusi, Brancusi Fund of MNAM, Paris

Fig. 258. Cahiers d'art, Paris, 1934, *1-4*

Fig. 259. Abstraction création art non figuratif, Paris, 1934, *3*

Fig. 260. Stone fireplace made by Brancusi in M. Raynal's house, Quincy Voisins / http://www.artnet.com

Fig. 261. Axis, London, 1935, *3*

Fig. 262. *Bird in Space/Brancusi*, in *Time Has No Shadow* by Katherine Garrison Chapin, New York, 1922

Fig. 263. Minotaure, Paris, 1936, *8*

Fig. 264. Transition, Paris, 1936, *25*

Fig. 265. Tatarescus' manor house from Poiana / Sanda Negropontes-Tatarescu archive

Fig. 266. Brancusi and architect O. Doicescu, Bucharest, 1936 / http://octavdoicescu.blogspot.ro/

Fig. 267. *Brancusi* by Milita Petrascu, Bucharest / http://andreidoicescu.blogspot.ro/

Fig. 268. Catalogue *Museum of Living Art, New York University, A.E. Gallatin Collection*, New York, 1937

Figs. 269a, b. Universal Exhibition, Paris, 1937: a—Romania's Pavilion / www.delcampe.net; b—Romania's representatives among whom Brancusi, Th. Pallady, D. Gusti, Elena Vacarescu / O. Badina, O. Neamtu, 1967

Fig. 270. Juana Müller working in Brancusi's studio, Paris, 1937 / Sabrina Dubbeld, 2015

Fig. 271. *Moderne Plastik* by Carola Giedion-Welcker, Zürich, 1937

Fig. 272. Brancusi with Irina Codreanu and Milita Petrascu (first row), Arethia Tatarescu (second row, middle) and two other members of the Women's League of Gorj County, Poiana, 1937 / unknown author

Fig. 273. Circle, London, 1937

Fig. 274. Arhivele Olteniei, Craiova, July-December 1937

Figs. 275a, b. Targu-Jiu, 1937: a—outside market; b—sketch of the *Column* and of the architectural-decorative elements, drawing by Brancusi—b / St. Georgescu-Gorjan archive

Figs. 276a, b. Brancusi's accommodation places in Targu-Jiu, 1937-38: a—Royal Hotel; b—Ganescu house / postcards, unknown authors

Figs. 277a, b. Stones arranged by Brancusi in the Ganescu courtyard, Targu-Jiu: a—mill stones; b—river stone / P. Comarnescu, 1963

Fig. 278. Stones arranged by Brancusi in the manor house garden of the Tatarescus, Poiana, 1937 / photo by Brancusi, Brancusi Fund of MNAM, Paris

Figs. 279a, b. Petrosani, 1937: a—Central Workshops; b—2 Closca Street / St. Georgescu-Gorjan archive

Figs. 280a, b. Central Workshops of Petrosani, 1937: a—carving the wood module for the mold; b—assembling the *Column* for integration tests / St. Georgescu-Gorjan archive

Fig. 281. Plan of Targu-Jiu town indicating the monuments (drawing by T. Paleolog) / T. Paleolog, 1976

Figs. 282a, b. Heroes' Road Street after urban planning, Targu-Jiu / postcards, unknown author

Fig. 283. Donation deed to the Targu-Jiu Town Hall by the Women's League, 20 October 1937 / State Archives, Gorj County, Fund of the Targu-Jiu Municipality

Figs. 284a, b. Targu-Jiu: a—access stairs to the *Endless Column* (reconstitution by I. Alexandrescu) / I. Mocioi, 2004; b—the square project with the zodiac around the *Endless Column* (reconstitution by T. Paleolog) / T. Paleolog, 1976

Fig. 285. Adeverul, Bucharest, 4 November 1937

Figs. 286a, b. Brancusi supervising the *Column* work, Targu-Jiu, November 1937: a—supervising the *Column* work / photo by St. Georgescu-Gorjan

Fig. 287a-c. Patriarch Miron Cristea, Prime Minister G. Tatarescu and his wife Arethia (a, b), and Brancusi (c) participating to the inauguration of St. Apostles' Church, Targu-Jiu, 8 November 1937 / a—Realitatea ilustrata, Bucharest, 17 November 1937; b, c—unknown author

Fig. 288. Ambassador Hotel, Bucharest / www.bucurestiivechisinoi.ro

Fig. 289. Column with double capital (1930-33)—model of the *Temple of Deliverance* from Indore, Paris / photo by Brancusi, Brancusi Fund of MNAM, Paris

Figs. 290a, b. Indore: a—The Manik Bagh Palace / R. Niggl, 1996; b—*Birds in Space* of marble in the palace, 1968 / Catalogue *Modern Masters*, Phillips, Auction 27 April 2016, London

Figs. 291a, b. Brancusi in India, January 1938—a / Catalogue *Modern Masters*, Phillips, Auction 27 April 2016, London, unknown author; book edited by Florence M. Hetzler, New York, 1992—b

Figs. 292a, b. Brancusi in Egypt, 1938 / Carola Giedion-Welcker, 1981

Figs. 293a, b. Conte Biancamano cruise ship—a / www.ssmaritime.com; Brancusi on board, February 1938—b / Brancusi Fund of MNAM Paris

Fig. 294. Residence of the Tatarescus, Bucharest / February 1940, photo by Margaret Bourke-White, The LIFE Picture Collection / Getty Images

Figs. 295a, b. Targu-Jiu, 1938: a—building site organized in the public garden / unknown author; b—Brancusi cutting the stone by saw mill / photo by doctor Micu G. Marcu

Figs. 296a-c. *Gate of Kiss*, Targu-Jiu, 1938: a—before sculpting; b—during work; c—after the work / unknown author

Figs. 297a, b. Gorj County in the 1930s: a—women washing their laundry in the Jiu River, Targu-Jiu / http://romaniaonline.blogspot.ro; wood carpenters—b / Sociologie Romaneasca, May 1936

Fig. 298. Document of the Targu-Jiu Town Hall, 9 July 1938 / State Archives, Gorj County, Fund of the Targu-Jiu Municipality, 1938

Fig. 299. A bank carved from tree trunk, provisionally located in the Public garden, Targu-Jiu / T. Paleolog, 1976

Figs. 300a, b. Targu-Jiu, 1938: a—Brancusi near stonecutter I. Alexandrescu carving a stone bank / photo by doctor Micu G. Marcu; b—stone bank and chairs / unknown author

Fig. 301. Brancusi taking the photograph of the *Column*, Targu-Jiu, 1938 / photo by doctor Micu G. Marcu

Figs. 302a, b. Targu-Jiu, 1938: a—*Table of Silence* / photo by Brancusi, Brancusi Fund of MNAM, Paris; b—*Lonely Table* / I. Mocioi, 2004

Fig. 303. Partisan Review, New York, 1938, *3*

Fig. 304. Letter of the Women's League, Targu-Jiu, 27 October 1938 / State Archives, Gorj County, Fund of the Targu-Jiu Municipality

Figs. 305a, b. Aspects from the inauguration of the sculptural ensemble of Targu-Jiu, 1938 / unknown author

Figs. 306a, b. Ciucea: a—Octavian Goga's Castle / Realitatea ilustrata, 11 May 1938; b—funerary monument in Brancusi's vision (reconstituted by P. Comarnescu) / C. Cublesan, 2006

Fig. 307. Athenaeum Palace Hotel, Bucharest / www.bucurestiivechisinoi.ro

Figs. 308a, b. Saftica, near Bucharest, 1938: a—Brancusi and the Gerotas at their manor house / photo by D.D. Gerota, B. Brezianu Fund, George Oprescu Institute of Art History Bucarest; b—Brancusi in Gerota's garden / B. Brezianu, 1976

Fig. 309. *C. Brancusi* by V.G. Paleolog, Craiova, 1938

Fig. 310. Manor house of V.G. Paleolog from Corlate / I. Hinoveanu, 2005

Figs. 311a, b. Le Havre, 1939: a—Champlain cruise ship / www.frenchlines.com; b—Le Petit Havre, 21 April

Figs. 312a, b. World's Fair New York, 1939: Suzana Doicescu, Brancusi and Maria Tanase (a) at the opening of the
Romanian Pavilion (b) / a—Stamp Collection of the Romanian Academy Library; b—Museum of the City of New York, collections.mcny.org

Fig. 313. Elsa Schiaparelli's model between Brancusi sculptures, MoMA, New York, 1939 / photo by Louise Dahl-Wolfe, http://artgallery.yale.edu/

Figs. 314a, b. Brancusi in Long Island, 1939 together with: a—Marion Willard and architect A. Aalto in architect W.K. Harrison's garden; b—S. Giedion and Marion Willard / Carola Giedion-Welcker, 1981

Figs. 315a, b. Isamu Noguchi in Gorj County, 1981: a—near the *Endless Column* of Targu-Jiu; b—in front of the gate from the memorial house of Hobita / B. Brezianu Fund, George Oprescu Institute of Art History Bucharest

Fig. 316. St. Moritz Hotel of New York / www.allposters.com

Fig. 317. *Sculpture: Inside and Out* by Malvina Hoffman, New York, 1939

Fig. 318. Peggy Guggenheim and *Maiastra*, on the terrace of her Parisian house, 1940 / photo by A. Rogi, https://www.artforum.com/

Fig. 319. Dacia rediviva, Bucharest, 1942, *6*

Fig. 320. *Danaide* / photo by Brancusi, Brancusi Fund of MNAM, Paris

Figs. 321a, b. Catalogue MoMA by A. H. Barr Jr., New York: a—1942 edition; b—1948 edition

Figs. 322a, b. Craiova, 1943: a—Meridian, *17-18-19*; b—*Cartea a doua despre C. Brancusi* by V.G. Paleolog

Fig. 323. Jean Mihail Palace, Craiova / postcard, unknown author

Figs. 324a, b. Terrestrial and air means of transport manufactured by US companies, 1943-45 / unknown author, Brancusi Fund of MNAM, Paris

Fig. 325. "Kinetic" corner in Brancusi's studio, Paris, 1943 / photo by Brancusi, Brancusi Fund of MNAM, Paris

Fig. 326. Revista Fundatiilor Regale, Bucharest, 1944, *12*

Fig. 327. Brancusi, H. Moore, F. McEwen (British Council), H. Read, and P. Eluard at the British Council Gallery, Paris, 1945 / *Henry Moore: Writings and Conversations*, edited by Alan Wilkinson, University of California Press, Berkeley and Los Angeles, 2002

Fig. 328. *Milestone* in Brancusi's studio, Paris / photo by Brancusi, Brancusi Fund of MNAM, Paris

Figs. 329a, b. Brancusi in his studio gate frame, Paris, 1946 —a / photo by Wayne Miller; young Gorj peasants at the house gate, at the beginning of the 20th century—b / postcard, unknown author

Fig. 330. *Portrete si controverse* by P. Pandrea, **I**, Bucharest, 1945

Fig. 331. Brancusi, T. Tzara and an unknown person, Paris, 1946 / photo by Ralph Morse / The LIFE Picture Collection / Getty Images

Fig. 332. Brancusi and Enescu at Romania's Legation (screen capture), Paris, 1947 / cotidianul.tv

Figs. 333a, b. Paris: a—sculptor C. Antonovici and painter A. Istrati in the Brancusi's studio, 1947 / photo by Brancusi, Brancusi Fund of MNAM, Paris; b—recommending certification given to C. Antonovici by Brancusi, 9 May 1951 / C. Eleancu, 1997

Fig. 334. *Brancusi* by C. Antonovici / Doina Uricariu, V. Bulat, 2011

Fig. 335. *C. Brancusi* by V.G. Paleolog, Bucharest, 1947

Fig. 336. Arcades, Bucharest, 1947, *1*

Fig. 337. Brancusi and F.X. Lalanne in front of the studio, Paris, 1948 / photo by J. Ph. Lalanne, Brancusi Fund of MNAM, Paris

Fig. 338. The *Cock* IV in Brancusi's studio, Paris / photo by Brancusi, Brancusi Fund of MNAM, Paris

Figs. 339a, b. *Maiastra* (a) and *Bird in Space* (b) in the garden of Palazzo Venier dei Leoni, Venice / Catalogue *The Peggy Guggenheim Collection Venice*, Palazzo Venier dei Leoni, 1979, Venice

Fig. 340. *Collection of the Société Anonyme: Museum of Modern Art 1920*, New Haven, 1950

Fig. 341. *Musée national d'art moderne: catalogue—guide*, Paris, 1950

Fig. 342. Minutes of the 7 March 1951 session of the Language Science, Literature, and Art Section from the Academy of the People's Republic of Romania, Bucharest / Zig-Zag, Bucharest, 1993, *45*

Figs. 343a, b. Request for approval to demolish the *Endless Column*, Bucharest, 30 June 1951—a / www.isciv.ro; *Column* in the 1950s—b / unknown author

Fig. 344. *The Arts and Their Interrelations* by Th. Munro, New York, 1951

Fig. 345. *Sculpture of the Twentieth Century* by A.C. Ritchie, New York, 1952

Fig. 346. *Art in Modern Architecture* by Eleonor Bittermann, New York, 1952

Fig. 347. Katherine S. Dreier with Coco, and *Leda*, West Redding (CT) / Aline B. Saarinen, 1958

Fig. 348. *The Passionate Years* by Caresse Crosby, New York, 1953

Fig. 349. Cahiers d'art, Paris, 1955, *30*

Fig. 350. Life, New York, 5 December 1955

Fig. 351. *King of Kings* in "dialogue" with a fan, PMA, 1956 / unknown author, http://philamuseum.tumblr.com/

Figs. 352a, b. *Brancusi* by Florica Cordescu Jebeleanu, Paris, 1956—a / *Omagiu lui Brancusi*, 1976; cover of the Tanarul Scriitor magazine, Bucharest, November 1956—b

Figs. 353a, b. Sigfried Giedion: a—*Architektur und Gemeinschaft,* Hamburg, 1956; b—*Architecture. You and Me*, Cambridge (MA), 1958

Fig. 354. Silvana Mangano at the MoMA, New York, 1956 / photo by Eve Arnold, Magnum Photos Agency, New York

Fig. 355. *The Art of Sculpture* by H. Read, London, 1956

Fig. 356. *Brancusi* by Milita Petrascu, Bucharest, 1956 / http://andreidoicescu.blogspot.ro/

Fig. 357. Steaua, Cluj, 1957, *2*

Fig. 358. Lifeless body of Brancusi in his studio, Paris / photo by R. Descharnes

Fig. 359. Life, New York, 1 April 1957

Fig. 360. L'Œil, Paris, 1957, *29*

Fig. 361. *Brancusi* by Ezra Pound, Milan, 1957

Fig. 362. *Constantin Brancusi, sculptures, peintures, fresques, dessins*, Paris, 1957

Fig. 363. *Brancusi* by D. Lewis, London, 1957

Endnotes

[1] P. Comarnescu, (1972) *Brancusi. Mit si metamorfoza in sculptura contemporana* [Brancusi. Myth and Metamorphosis in Contemporary Sculpture], Meridiane Publishers, Bucharest, p. 279.

[2] P. Pandrea, *Brancusi. Amintiri si exegeze* [Brancusi. Memories and Exegesis], Vremea Publishers, Bucharest, 2009, p. 31.

[3] Apriliana Medianu, (1930) *Maestrul Brancusi* [Master Brancusi], Curentul literar si artistic, Bucharest, **III**, *972*, 6 October, pp. 3–4. Brancusi on his father: "He has been to Craiova, having reached as far as Bucharest. In those days houses had only a little bull's eye opening, covered with paper. As soon as he returned from his travel to town he introduced an innovation: he had the windows enlarged, and made them open. All the others followed his example."

[4] P. Comarnescu, *op. cit.*, p. 36. Petre Ceaureanu, professor at Constantin Brancusi High School from Pestisani: "Brancusi told father that, had he kept his sheep, he would make his portrait in clay. Indeed he modelled various clay faces, taking it from the river bank."

[5] I. Jianu, (1963) *Brancusi*, Arted, Éd. d'Art, Paris, p. 23. "Il suivit ainsi une école plus âpre et plus utile que l'école officielle: celle de la nature et de la vie. Durant les hivers rudes, il aimait modeler, dans la neige abondante, aux cristaux étincelants, des formes inventées par sa riche fantaisie d'enfant. [...] Brancusi avoua plus tard que l'image de son enfance des sculptures faites dans la neige, l'a poursuivi tout le long de sa vie."

[6] P. Comarnescu, *op. cit.*, p. 29. Vasile Blendea-Trifu about Brancusi: "When he was a little boy he kept playing pranks and did not like grazing the pigs. [...] When he ran away from the pigs he went to the Bistrita River and filled his bag of river stones, so it was always torn. Some other times he started carving sticks with his pocket knife, as he always kept it with him."

[7] V.G. Paleolog, (1967) *Tineretea lui Brancusi* [Brancusi's Youth], Tineretului Publishers, Bucharest, pp. 32–33.

[8] P. Comarnescu, *op. cit.*, p. 30.

[9] V.G. Paleolog, *op. cit.*, p. 41.

[10] V.G. Paleolog, *op. cit.*, p. 43. Brancusi: "We used to close at one o'clock at night, once with the last train to Bucharest at ten minutes to one, and we had to be up at half past four for the mixed Severin train, both merchandise and people. We could have slept well from 1 to 4 if only carriage men had left us alone in the winter, but they knocked their whip knobs in our windows and asked us to open up and let them in to get warm with some alcohol and hot wine, to chase away the morning cold. And they knocked! And knocked! Even dead people could get awake, truly dead, let alone poor us apprentices who were only dead beat."

[11] V.G. Paleolog, *op. cit.*, p. 43.

[12] P. Pandrea, *op. cit.*, p. 30.

[13] P. Hulten, Natalia Dumitrescu, Al. Istrati, (1986) *Brancusi*, Éd. Flammarion, Paris, p. 57.

[14] ibidem

[15] St. Georgescu-Gorjan, *Biografia si perspectivele Coloanei Infinite* [Biography and Endless Column's Perspectives], Ramuri, Craiova, 1964, *12*, 30 December, pp. 8–9.

[16] V.G. Paleolog, *op. cit.*, p. 43

[17] P. Comarnescu, *op. cit.*, p. 36

[18] Eugenia Cioroianu, (2001) *Pasi spre infinit. Istoricul Colegiului Tehnic de Arte si Meserii "Constantin Brancusi" (1871–1948)* [Steps to Infinity, History of Constantin Brancusi Technical College of Art and Crafts (1871–1948)], **I**, Aius Publishers, Craiova, pp. 17–18.

[19] P. Comarnescu, *op. cit.*, p. 68

[20] B. Brezianu, *Opera lui Brancusi in Romania* [Brancusi's Work in Romania], Romanian Academy Publishers, Bucharest, 1974, p. 13.

[21] I.L. Sinculici, (2014) *Dosarul Brancusi de la Scoala de Meserii din Craiova* [Brancusi File from the School of Crafts from Craiova], Portal-Maiastra, Targu-Jiu, **X**, *1(38)*, pp. 2–4.

[22] V.G. Paleolog, *op. cit.*, pp. 35–36. Brancusi: "From wood I got to sculpture and stone after wood, which is also confirmed by the development stages of sculpture [...], Xoanan receiving stone patterns, serving it. Stone was nothing else but the passing of a thought, already told, in a more durable material: stone or burnt clay, but also defeated by human technique because it resisted, but a different opposition than that of docile perishable wood, or later the ingot from the Bronze Age."

[23] Al. Balintescu, *Contributii documentare referitoare la Constantin Brancusi* [Documentary Contributions About Constantin Brancusi], in *Catalogue of the Museum of Art Craiova*, 1967.

[24] B. Brezianu, *op. cit.*, p. 270.

[25] P. Comarnescu, *op. cit.*

[26] Doina Frumuselu, ed., *Brancusi: The Beginner*, RCR Editorial Publishers, Bucharest, 2013, pp. 104–108, 119–120. Letter to the Headman of Pestisani, Gorj County (private collection):

Town Hall of Pestisani Village / Mr. Headman, / I the undersigned Constantin Brancusi son of this village and currently student with the trade school of Craiova I join in good will Your proposal to make a bust in front of the Town Hall for which I kindly ask you to bring forth a block of white marble of which I shall make the bust. The pedestal will be 2.5 m made of stone and also I await the bust representation. In consequence thereof I have also attached the sketch of the monument besides which please accept as present this marble beetle that I have made and signed. / Yours devoted / Constantin Brancusi / 1895, August 20

To Mr. Brancusi / I assume the honor and responsibility / to bring you shortly all that is necessary / to the monument and I take pleasure in / the result you have obtained so far in school. / Thank you for your present / Headman

[27] V.G. Paleolog, *op. cit.*, p. 51.

[28] State Archives, Dolj County, Fund of the Prefect's Office of Dolj County, 1896 (B. Brezianu, *Brancusi in Romania*, Romanian Academy Publishers, Bucharest, 1976, p. 271):

Guarantee deed / Whereby I the undersigned Maria wife and tutor of the estate of late Nicolae C.

Brancusi domiciled in village Pestisani, region Tismana, Gorj County I declare that for my son Brancusi Constantin who got stipend in the School of Crafts of Dolj County in the speciality of sculpture, I will answer for any expenses made with this student in case he will not attend fully such courses to their end, or he will be expelled from school for bad conduct. The set sum will be covered by applying the supervision law without having the right of law court or any claim; and in exchange the county is obliged to keep him in school until courses end.

In witness thereof I have issued this, signed by me by finger-stamping and authenticated accordingly.

1896, January 1

Maria wife of late Nicolae C. Brancusi and guardian of the estate of under age children of the deceased from village Pestisani

[29] B. Brezianu, *op. cit.*, p. 13.

[30] I. Schintee, *Date noi despre C. Brancusi* [New Data on C. Brancusi], Inainte, Craiova, 8 August 1965, p. 2.

[31] B. Brezianu, *op. cit.*, p. 200.

[32] Doina Frumuselu, ed., *op. cit.*, pp. 109–118, 121. Donation deed to priest G. Haiduc from St. Elijah's Church in Craiova (private collection):

Donation deed / I the undersigned Constantin Brancusi son of Maria and of late Nicolae, domiciled in Pestisani village Tismana region Gorj County, currently student with the trade school of Craiova Town in the sculpture section, have the great honor to give this box for the holy oil to Father G. Haiduc priest of St. Elijah Church of Craiova, in remembrance of me and my family and for his assistance. / Yours devoted / C. Brancusi / July 12, 1896

Written before me today July 12, 1896 / to be kept on the saint table of the saint altar / Parish Pr.

[33] State Archives, Dolj County, Fund of the Prefect's Office of Dolj County, 1896 (P. Comarnescu, *op. cit.*, p. 214):

Romania / Year 1896 month December 23 / General Council Dolj / Steering Council of the School of Crafts / No. 373 / Mr. Prefect, / The 7 stipend holder students of our school whose names are provided overleaf have remained in the school premises during the 8 days' vacation for the winter holy days of Christmas because they come from distant towns and their parents have poor means, this being the reason why we are kindly asking you to provide the order authorising their food during such vacation in order to maintain their canteen quotas. / Looking forward to receiving your answer please receive, Prefect, the expression of our highest esteem and consideration./ Director / Accountant / C. Stanciulescu / To the kind attention of Mr. Prefect of Dolj County

[34] P. Comarnescu, *op. cit.*, p. 215.

[35] Oltenia's Metropolitan Seat Review digital archives, Craiova, crestinortodox.ro, accessed 20 June 2014.

[36] W. Hofmann, (1968) *Discutii* [Debates], in *Colocviul Brancusi—Bucuresti, 13–15 octombrie 1967* [*Colloquium Brancusi—Bucharest, 13–15 October 1967*], Meridiane Publishers, Bucharest, pp. 152–155. W. Hofmann, director of the Modern Art Museum of Vienna, assumed that the factory where Brancusi worked "could be the famous Thonet house, which around the mid 19th century established in Vienna quite an important enterprise of wood bending, in order to provide it with extreme sinuosity.".

[37] V.G. Paleolog, *op. cit.*, pp. 68–69.

[38] V.G. Paleolog, (1967) *Doua lucrari inedite de Brancusi* [Two Unknown Works by Brancusi], Inainte, Craiova, 13 June, p2.

[39] B. Brezianu, *op. cit.*, pp. 215–217.

[40] Doina Frumuselu, ed., *op. cit.*, pp. 161–185.

[41] P. Comarnescu, *op. cit.*, pp. 69–70. Talk with Professor Dan Smantanescu recorded by the art critic on 14 September 1969.

[42] Doina Frumuselu, ed., *Brancusi: Testimonies*, RCR Editorial Publishers, Bucharest, 2014, pp. 25–29. Professor Dan Smantanescu in the TV broadcast *Hourglass with images*, May 1999, producer George Radu Serafim.

[43] V.G. Paleolog, *op. cit.*, p. 61.

[44] Doina Frumuselu, (2012) *Brancusi in His Time and in Ours*, Eurostampa Publishers, Timisoara, p. 14.

[45] B. Brezianu, (1969) *Debutul lui Brancusi—Craiova, 1898* [Brancusi's Debut—Craiova, 1898], Contemporanul, Bucharest, **53**, *40*, 3 October.

[46] P. Comarnescu, *op. cit.*, p. 272. "We hereby certify that Brancusi Constantin graduated successfully all the theoretical and practical five years' courses of our school in the sculpture section, always showing application both in practice and in theory, being of exemplary conduct. In witness thereof we release him this certificate to serve him in case of need."

[47] V.G. Paleolog, *op. cit.*, pp. 51–52. Brancusi: "I have learned whole-heartedly and managed to acquire solid knowledge, thus getting rid of hearsay learning and using the available books, tools and moreover people competent to teach me, as I needed a long time to discard the wrong saw pulling that I used and match it instead with my breath, as well as the hatchet and chisel keeping my head high and swelling up my chest."

[48] P. Comarnescu, *op. cit.*, p. 74. "In Craiova, waiter and shop assistant, he worked 18 hours a day. He did that several years in the pub, in the grocery store, etc. But that only hardened him; and he speaks about that time but not in hatred. *Frotter le diamant*. Such experiences polished and strengthened him, he says. He also attended art and trade courses."

[49] B. Brezianu, *op. cit.*, p. 163.

[50] R. Sorban, Adina Nanu, E. Schileru, P. Constantin, (1964) *100 de ani de la infiintarea Institutului de Arte Plastice "Nicolae Grigorescu" din Bucuresti 1864–1964* [100 Years from the Establishment of the Plastic Arts Institute Nicolae Grigorescu], Meridiane Publishers, Bucharest, p. 68.

[51] V.G. Paleolog, *op. cit.*, p. 90.

[52] P.I. David, deacon, (1972) *Constantin Brancusi in cultura romaneasca si arta universala* [C. Brancusi in Romanian Culture and Universal Art], Review of the Metropolitan Seat of Oltenia, Craiova, **XXIV**, *11–12*, November-December, pp. 978–997.

[53] P. Comarnescu, *op. cit.*, p. 33. Brancusi: "I am not afraid of the future because I know I will always be capable of earning my daily bread. I have done it since childhood. If I can no longer sculpt I would go into the wide world and sing. And I can manage!" (Information from a letter sent by Ionel Jianu to P. Comarnescu).

[54] *Expozitia regionala din Craiova—Prin posta de la corespondentul nostru special* [The Regional Exhibition of Craiova—By Post from Our Special Correspondent], Adeverul, Bucharest, 16 October 1898, p. 4. "In a corner by the entrance a very good bust of the former minister, late Chitu, can be seen, which was artistically worked by Mr. C. Brancusi."

[55] *Expozitiunea agricola si industriala* [Agricultural and Industrial Exhibition], Vointa Craiovei, Craiova, 21 October 1898. "On the left side of the entrance door sits a very well done bust, of the former minister G. Chitu: this bust deserves all the more attention as it has been done by a beginner, Mr. C. Brancusi."

[56] Phoenix, (1898) *Expositia de la Craiova* [The Exhibition of Craiova], Albina, Bucharest, **II**, *6*, 8 November, pp. 181–182. "The bust of Gheorghe Chitu, made by Mr. Brancusi, has been exhibited by the door."

[57] T. Arghezi, (1946) *Din viata lui Stefan Luchian* [From the Life of Stefan Luchian], Lumina si Coloare, Bucharest, *1*, May (reprint in *Pensula si dalta* [Brush and Chisel], Meridiane Publishers, Bucharest, pp. 282–284).

[58] P. Comarnescu, *op. cit.*, p. 90.

[59] Adeverul, Bucharest, 24 December 1898, p. 3.

[60] Adeverul, Bucharest, 24 December 1899, p. 2.

[61] *Marea carte a Craiovei* [Great Book of Craiova], Sitech Publishers, Craiova, 2007, p. 276.

[62] P. Comarnescu, *op. cit.*, p. 280.

[63] B. Brezianu, *op. cit.*, pp. 164, 165.

[64] R. Sorban, Adina Nanu, E. Schileru, P. Constantin, *op. cit.*, p. 68.

[65] P. Comarnescu, *op. cit.*, pp. 272–273.

[66] Doina Frumuselu, *op. cit.*, pp. 131–158.

[67] Doina Frumuselu, *op. cit.*, pp. 121–129. Testimony of Professor priest Petre I. David, dated March 2000.

[68] P. Comarnescu, *op. cit.*, p. 84. Ion Croitoru, musicologist: "He needed music. He played the violin every time he felt like it. More than that: he went to concerts and participated in the rehearsals of the choral society *Carmen*."

[69] B. Brezianu, *op. cit.*, pp. 14–15.

[70] B. Brezianu, *op. cit.*, p. 275.

[71] B. Brezianu, *Brancusi in Romania*, All Publishers, Bucharest, 1998, p. 69.

[72] V.G. Paleolog, *op. cit.*, pp. 90–94.

[73] B. Brezianu, *op. cit.*, p. 275.

[74] B. Brezianu, *op. cit.*, pp. 209, 217.

[75] Doina Frumuselu, ed., *op. cit.*, p. 123. Sale–purchase deed (private collection): *Paid / 27 September 1901 / Sale–purchase deed / Has been concluded today 27 September 1901 between Constantin Brancusi student with the School of Beaux Arts of Bucharest into the sculpture section, who sculpted a woman's head in marble sized 24 x 10 x 15 and signed in the left side: C. Brancusi 1901, upon order of Mrs. Popescu Stanca from Craiova, 13B Marea Unire Street. / This deed required for authentication has been executed before me Silviu Simonovici notary of Craiova Town, Mrs. Popescu handing 600 (six hundred lei) to Mr. Brancusi, in witness thereof*

I authenticate and sign together with the other two. Stamps of 10+25 ban were charged. / Silviu Simonovici, notary / Constantin Brancusi, seller / Stanca Popescu, purchaser

[76] Typographic Almanac, Bucharest, 1902.

[77] P. Comarnescu, *op. cit.*, p. 83.

[78] M. Deac, (1996) *Romanul Brancusi* [Romanian Brancusi], Thausib Publishers, Sibiu, p. 178.

[79] Dumitru Brancusi family archive.

[80] P.I. David, *op. cit.*

[81] B. Brezianu, *op. cit.,* p. 277.

[82] B. Brezianu, *op. cit.,* p. 278.

[83] Doina Frumuselu, ed., *op. cit.*, p. 124. Letter to the Trusteeship of Madonna Dudu Church requesting monetary aid (private collection):
To be forwarded to the assembly for budget establishment in 1902–1903 to provide Mr. Brancusi with study aid./ January 30, 1902 / Messrs Trustees, / I the undersigned Constantin Brancusi graduate of the Fine Arts School of Bucharest, sculpture section, hereby attach the certification of the School Principal ascertaining I still attend the classes available for practical training. / With utmost respect I kindly ask you to provide some study aid for 1902–1903 in the quantum You deem appropriate, and since I am in Bucharest during the year attending courses I shall authorise Mr. Ion Georgescu Gorjan merchant of Craiova to receive on my behalf the money I hope you will provide me with. / With highest regards, yours devoted / Constantin Brancusi / January 30, 1902

[84] St. Georgescu-Gorjan's testimony in Ramuri magazine, Craiova, 1981, *1*, January.

[85] St. Georgescu-Gorjan, (1965) *Marturii despre Brancusi* [Testimonies on Brancusi], Studii si Cercetari de Istoria Artei, seria Arta Plastica, Bucharest, **12**, *1*, p. 68.

[86] B. Brezianu, *op. cit.*, p. 279.

[87] P. Comarnescu, *op. cit.*, p. 92. "Of the 12 photos mentioned by Brancusi, we do not know whether all have been kept. We have only a few of them, which were reproduced by the commentators of Brancusi's creation, as best they could."

[88] *Editia de dimineata / Informatiuni* [Morning edition / News], Adeverul, Bucharest, 7 May 1903, p. 2.

[89] *Informatiuni* [News], Gazeta Artelor, Bucharest, 11 May 1903, p. 7. "can serve very much in secondary and superior schools where *myology* is taught. It is the first sculpture of this kind in our country and deserves everyone's attention."

[90] Elena Dumitrescu, (2013) *Ecorseul Brancusi—Gerota—istoria unei lucrari realizate la Scoala de Belle Arte din Bucuresti* [Brancusi's Écorché—Gerota, the History of a Sculpture Made in the School of Beaux Arts of Bucharest], UNARTE Publishers, Bucharest, p. 51.

[91] O. Han, (1970) *Dalti si pensule* [Chisels and Brushes], Minerva Publishers, Bucharest, pp. 572–577.

[92] C. Ressu, *Insemnari* [Writings], Meridiane Publishers, Bucharest, 1967. "I have known Brancusi less then as he was about to leave the country, having left us with a nice ecorse as memory, which he has worked together with his anatomy professor, doctor Gerota."

[93] G. Oprescu, (1968) *Amintiri, evocari* [Recollections, Evocations], Literature Publishers, Bucharest, pp. 85–86. "Initially the original was executed in three copies, of which one was given to the Art School of Iasi, another to Dr. Gerota's sanatorium, which was destroyed in WWI and the third stayed with the School of Bucharest, for students' instruction. It also underwent accidents and nowadays can be found in three pieces. Several copies were cast in gypsum after it, though, of which one is still with the school."

[94] Mihaela Antoce, *Dimitrie Gerota si "Jupuitul" lui Brancusi* [D. Gerota and Brancusi's Écorché], http://www.medicalstudent.ro/, 27 November 2008, accessed 14 July 2009. "Benefitting of professor Gerota's support Brancusi executed four copies that went to: doctor D. Gerota, college *Carol I* of Craiova, Anatomy Museum of Iasi and the Medical Faculty of Cluj. It seems there has been one more copy that belonged to the School of Beaux Arts then went to the stocks of the Medical Faculty of Bucharest."

[95] The testimony of Professor Ion Albu, in *"Jupuitul" lui Brancusi* [Brancusi's Écorché] by T. Stirbu, Clujeanul, ClujNapoca, 26 August 2004, http://old.clujeanul.ro/, accessed 5 August 2014.

[96] *Un bust lui Davila* [A Bust of Davila], Adeverul, Bucharest, 28 October 1903, p. 3.

[97] B. Brezianu, *op. cit.*, pp. 18, 102–103.

[98] P. Oprea, *Portretul lui Carol Davila de Constantin Brancusi* [Portrait of Carol Davila by Constantin Brancusi], Studii muzeale [Museum Studies], Bucharest, 1972, **IV**, *6*, June, pp. 36–38.

[99] V.G. Paleolog, *op. cit.*, p. 106. Brancusi: "It would have been easy but prostitute work, which could have got me the few coins I needed for a train fare ticket to Paris. But something that was growing within for several years now has just burst forth and I couldn't take it any longer. I turned about face with no military salute, to doctor Gerota's utmost panic and fear…and away I went, mumbling about their origins."

[100] Ion Croitoru's testimony of 11 March 1964, Bucharest (B. Brezianu, *op. cit.*, p. 74).

[101] I.C. Bercus, (1981) *Legaturile lui Brancusi cu medicii si medicina* [Brancusi's Connections with Doctors and Medicine], in *Trecut si viitor in medicina—studii si note* [Past and Future in Medicine, Studies and Notes], under the care of G. Bratescu, Medical Publishers, Bucharest, Archives of the History Medical College from the

Faculty of Medicine in Craiova (The letter was not handwritten by Brancusi, habitual practice of that time—A/N):

Chairman, / The undersigned sculptor, graduate of the fine arts school, having got abroad for studies and since my monetary situation is highly aggravated I have put up for sale the latest reproduction of the «écorché» (after the Antinous' statue), sculpted under coordination of dr. Gerota; however, after some painful experience I am convinced artistic pieces cannot find buyers in our country, because these last several years I only managed to place 2 reproductions to the Minister of Public Instruction and 1 to the Institute for Military Medicine, but my circumstances require my quick departure so being in this torment I took up your idea to have the forementioned latest copy of the écorché displayed in the headquarters of the «Medical Students' Society» and this is quite so seasonal, given the reasons for such action— the affairs of the Medical Students' Society, the results it obtained in the harsh conditions of our country, so it is natural to accept my offer as the écorché fits wonderfully with the grand library, with the Society's collections and it only seems awaiting the inquisitive stares of its members! / Shall I add that my monetary claim is one of the most modest? There is no need, this is understood. / Having cleared up my mind thinking this offer is accepted, please receive, Chairman, the expression of my highest regards. / C. Brancusi, Bucharest, May 17, 1904

[102] V.G. Paleolog, *op. cit.*, pp. 113, 114.

[103] P. Pandrea, (1976) *Brancusi. Amintiri si exegeze* [Brancusi, Memories and Exegeses], Meridiane Publishers, Bucharest, p. 24.

[104] I. Jianu, (1946) *Constantin Brancusi: Marturii* [Constantin Brancusi: Testimonies], Revista Fundatiilor Regale [The Review of Royal Foundations], Bucharest, **XIII**, new series, *9*, September, pp. 41–44.

[105] Ioana Giroiu, *De vorba cu sculptorul Constantin Brancusi* [Talking with Sculptor Constantin Brancusi], Timpul, Bucharest, 1938, **II**, 1 August, p. 2.

[106] V.G. Paleolog, *op. cit.*, p. 126.

[107] P. Hulten, Natalia Dumitrescu, Al. Istrati, *op. cit.*, p. 65.

[108] B. Brezianu, *op. cit.*, p. 18.

[109] Th. Cornel, *Figuri contimporane din Romania: Dictionar biografic ilustrat / Figures contemporaines de Roumanie: Dictionnaire biographique illustré*, Socec Printing House, Bucharest, 1911, p. 446.

[110] State Archives, Bucharest, Fund of the Ministry of Cults and Public Instruction, 1905 (B. Brezianu, *op. cit.*, p. 280).

[111] Otilia Marchis-Bölöni, *Cartea suferintelor* [The Book of Suffering], Dacia Publishers, Cluj-Napoca, 2011, pp. 8–9.

[112] Mariana Vida, *Arte vizuale / O eleva a lui Bourdelle: Margareta Cosaceanu-Lavrillier* [Visual Arts / Bourdelle's Apprentice: Margareta Cosaceanu-Lavrillier], Observator Cultural, Bucharest, 2006, *317–318*, 20 April.

[113] B. Brezianu, *op. cit.*, p. 19.

[114] State Archives, Bucharest, Fund of the Ministry of Cults and Public Instruction, 1905 (B. Brezianu, *op. cit.*, p. 283).

[115] B. Brezianu, *op. cit.*, p. 17.

[116] P. Pandrea, *op. cit.*, p. 37. Brancusi: "I entered Mercié's studio as a student, and reached there to high technical dexterity. I was making a sculpture a day, Rodin like. I could no longer stay near master Mercié, although he loved me. I did what he did. I was uncounsciously imitating Rodin, like Mercié, but I could see the pastiche. I was miserable. Those were the most difficult years, when I searched for my path; I found again my own path. I left Mercié and he was upset, but I had to look for my own road. I have reached simplicity, peace, and joy through inner difficulties…"

[117] State Archives, Bucharest, Fund of the Ministry of Cults and Public Instruction, 1906 (B. Brezianu, *op. cit.*, p. 284).

[118] B. Brezianu, *op. cit.*, p. 286.

[119] P. Comarnescu, *op. cit.*, p. 113. In the letter of 12 November 1964 he sent to P. Comarnescu, Professor C. Nedelcu remembers this time period: "In 1904–1906 as a student in Paris I befriended Brancusi, and even paid him a visit in his attic of Quartier Latin. He came to our student gatherings of the League, whose secretary I was, in a salon of the Voltaire coffee shop in front of the Odéon Theatre. I also met him on Sundays in the Romanian Church of Jean-de-Beauvais and every other holiday when he assisted Father Stefanu, the parochial priest, for the liturgy. I asked him whether he was also theologian. He answered: *No, but even back home I used to sing at the lectern during services and am no sexton as malicious people call me here.* I answered: *You know, I also helped the priest…back in my Banat village…* He trusted me as a friend seeing my serious quiet behavior, matching his kindness and sobriety, the essence of his nature was sincere and careful, and he was orderly in his acts and attitudes, all showing an original profound independent personality, devoid of any ostentation and oddity."

[120] Liliana Brad, (2013) *"Frunza" lui Brancusi se ascunde de urmasii lui Traian Vuia* [Brancusi's "Leaf" Is Hiding from the Successors of Traian Vuia], Romania libera, Bucharest, 14 May 2013.

[121] Marielle Tabart, (1997) *L'atelier Brancusi*, Les Carnets de l'atelier Brancusi, Centre Pompidou, Paris, p. 249.

[122] B. Brezianu, (1964) *Inceputurile lui Brancusi* [The Beginning of Brancusi], Secolul 20, Bucharest, **3**, March, pp. 145–169.

[123] *L'Aéroplane à moteur de M. Vuia*, L'Aérophile, Paris, 1906, **14**, *9*, septembre, p. 195.

[124] D. Antoniu, G. Cicos, I. Buiu, D. Hadarca, P. Sandachi, (2006) *Pionieri ai aviatiei mondiale—Traian Vuia si epoca sa* [Pioneers of World Aviation—Traian Vuia and His Epoch], Vivaldi Publishers, Bucharest.

[125] Doina Frumuselu, (2014) *A Life Between Two Centuries*, RCR Editorial, Bucharest.

[126] I. Magura [Nicolae Vaschide], *Lettres de Paris. Les Roumains aux Salons*, L'Indépendance Roumaine, Bucarest, 20 mai 1906.

[127] Marie Bengescu, *Les artistes roumains au Salon de la Société Nationale des Beaux-Arts et à celui des artistes français,* L'Indépendance Roumaine, Bucarest, 17 mai 1908.

[128] E. Manu, (1976) *5 scrisori ilustrate de la Constantin Brancusi* [Five Illustrated Letters from Constantin Brancusi], Romania literara, Bucharest, *8*, 19–25 February, p. 17.

[129] Ottilie de Kozmutza, *Un artiste roumain à Paris*, L'Indépendance Roumaine, Bucarest, 5 décembre 1906. Rodin "fait grand cas du talent de Brancusi."

[130] B. Brezianu, *op. cit.*, pp. 17–18.

[131] Ioana Giroiu, *op. cit.*, p. 2.

[132] V.G. Paleolog, *op. cit.*, pp. 140–141.

[133] Ottilie de Kozmutza, *op. cit.* J'espère présenter bientôt Brancusi à maître Rodin.

[134] V. Firoiu, (1969) *Din nou acasa … Convorbiri cu Henri Coanda* [Home Again… Talking with Henri Coanda], Tineretului Publishers, Bucharest, pp. 226–229.

[135] In Bulletin of Bucharest, edited by the Chamber of Notaries Public, 2010, May–June, Doina Rotaru, Chairperson of the Notaries' Chamber of Bucharest, writes about the contract that Brancusi concluded with Elisa Stanescu where the artist proved very attentive in drawing up the contractual clauses.

Commitment / Between the undersigned Elisa Petre Stanescu, proprietor, domiciled in Buzau town, 20 Dobrogei Street (Romania) and Constantin Brancusi sculptor, domiciled in Paris, 16 Place Dauphine (France) has been executed the following agreement: / I. I Constantin Brancusi commit to personally carry out to the account of Mrs. Elisa P. Stanescu a funerary monument for the above set price, namely seven thousand five hundred Lei (N° 7500), which includes the execution of such monument comprising as below specified, as well as the transport from Paris to Buzau station (Romania). / The monument comprises the following pieces: / a. A stone pedestal reaching 2 m high up to 2 m 50, / b. An allegorical figure representing a woman weeping near a pedestal, / c. A bust with the arms, resembling the photos that Mrs. Stanescu will provide. Both the figure and the bust will be cast in bronze and they should exceed the natural size as much as need be. The deadline to make the sculptures will be the end of February nineteen hundred and eight (1908) at the latest. / II. I Elisa P. Stanescu commit to provide Mr. C. Brancusi for the work I have entrusted him to execute with the above set price, namely seven thousand five hundred Lei (N° 7.500), payable upon set dates as follows: / Five hundred Lei (500) in May [new calendar] 1907 in Paris, and afterwards one hundred fifty Lei each month until September the same year—1907. / Beginning with October the same year

I commit sending two hundred fifty Lei each month until the sculpture is ready to be dispatched to be cast in gypsum, time when I will send Mr. C. Brancusi the amount of one thousand Lei necessary to make the gypsum variant. The remaining amount up to seven thousand five hundred Lei, sum which was set as fixed price, will be sent in a lump sum at the end of January 1908 nineteen hundred and eight, when the bronze casting is planned. / Mr. C. Brancusi cannot execute gypsum casting until he has received my written agreement. / Executed today 18 April [new calendar] 1907 in Paris, in two copies signed by both parties, each party receiving one. / Constantin Brancusi / Elisa Petre Stanescu

[136] O.C. Taslauanu, (1907) *Sculptorul Brancus* [Sculptor Brancus], Luceafarul, Sibiu, **VI**, *4–5*, 1 March, p. 87.

[137] Carola Giedion-Welcker, *op. cit.*, p. 26.

[138] Th. Cornel, *Artisti romani la Paris. Despre cativa artisti care expun la "Saloanele" din 1907* [Romanian Artists in Paris; About a Few That Exhibited in the 1907 "Salons"], Adeverul, Bucharest, 16 April 1907, p. 1.

[139] Otilia de Cozmutza, *Scrisori din Paris* [Letters of Paris], Luceafarul, Sibiu, 1908, **VII**, *3*, 1 February, pp. 49–50.

[140] Ramuri, Craiova, (1908) **I**, 1 January, p. 20. "Finally Craiova will have the bust of poet Traian Demetrescu. Mr. Victor Popp had an agreement thereto with sculptor C. Brancusi from Oltenia who is now in Paris."

[141] V.G. Paleolog, *op. cit.*

[142] G. Murnu, (1908) *Expozitia anuala a "Tinerimii Artistice"* [Annual Artistic Youth Exhibition], Luceafarul, Sibiu, **VII**, *9–10*, 1–15 May, pp. 209–213.

[143] Otilia de Cozmuta, (1908) *Scrisori din Paris. Saloanele* [Letters of Paris: the Salons], Luceafarul, Sibiu, **VII**, *19*, 1 October, pp. 458–460.

[144] G. Oprescu, (1967) *Un chapitre peu connu de la vie sociale et artistique du Paris de la "belle époque,"* Gazette des Beaux-Arts, Paris, **LXX**, *1182–1183*, juillet–août, pp. 121–124. "[Léonie Ricou] riche, belle, cultivée, bien informée sur l'art et la littérature, s'affollant pour toute chose nouvelle, mais de constitution délicate."

[145] Marielle Tabart, Doina Lemny, eds., (2003) *La Dation Brancusi. Dessins et archives*, Éd. Centre Pompidou, Paris, p. 210.

[146] Marielle Tabart, Doina Lemny, eds., *op. cit.*, p. 208.

[147] T. Arghezi, *op. cit.*

[148] I. Cuciurea, *Brancusi fotograf* [Brancusi Photographer], Steaua, Cluj-Napoca, 1974, **XXV**, *1*, January, pp. 53–54.

[149] P. Hulten, Natalia Dumitrescu, Al. Istrati, *op. cit.*, p. 281.

[150] C. Morice, (1909) *Scrisori din Paris. Salonul de toamna* [Letters of Paris: the Autumn Salon], Luceafarul, Sibiu, **VIII**, *5*, 1 March, p. 5.

[151] B. Brezianu, *op. cit.*, p. 19.

[152] Cecilia Cutescu-Storck, (1966) *O viata daruita artei* [A Life Dedicated to Art], Meridiane Publishers, Bucharest, pp. 74–75.

[153] B. Brezianu, *op. cit.*, p. 19.

[154] Doina Frumuselu, ed., *op. cit.*, pp. 226–232.

[155] B. Brezianu, *op. cit.*, p. 128.

[156] P. Comarnescu, *op. cit.*, p. 21.

[157] F.T. Bach, Margit Rowell, Ann Temkin, (1995) *Constantin Brancusi: 1876–1957*, Éd. Gallimard & Centre Pompidou, Paris, p. 120.

[158] N. Pora, (1911) *Muzeul Simu* [Museum Simu], Calendar Minerva—1911, 13th Year, Minerva Publishers, Bucharest, pp. 112–126.

[159] A. Buican, (2006) *Brancusi: O biografie* [Brancusi: A Biography], Artemis Publishers, Bucharest, p. 134.

[160] R. Rusan, (2006) *O discutie la masa tacerii* [Conversation at the Table of Silence], LiterNet Publishers, Bucharest, p. 72, accessed 15 February 2011. Vasile G. Paleolog: "My name was Vasile Gheorghiescu, but when my next door neighbor, a young Italian looking just like an ephebus and energetically carving stone in front of his studio asked me my name and nationality I introduced myself as *Constantinopolitan* and gave him my mother's name: Paleolog. Modigliani however discovered my true identity when I handed over the documents to the landlord. *Are you Romanian? My master is also Romanian: Brancusi.* A few days later I was about to enter my room when I heard Modigliani's voice as he leaned over his stone, hammer in hand: *Ecco-lo!* [There he is!] A man was standing next to him in the doorframe, looking at me carefully as if trying to get a quick impression. He bade me approach and talk to him. He asked me who I was and I just repeated the same story: Constantinopolitan of imperial origin. *I was born in the village*, replied harshly Brancusi and started speaking Romanian. I could not help accepting his play; but only a few moments later—during which time I slipped some very specific phrases of the Jiu River area—Brancusi burst out: *I've got you, you were born in Oltenia!* I was stupefied: *Yes, in Craiova! Are you of Craiova? What family?* After a few days I came to his studio holding some pineapple like a trophy and Modigliani was bringing Italian wine. But unfortunately I irritated him again, because I imprudently told him about the lesson on Michelangelo that professor Seailles taught us the day before. Having stood the challenge (I completely ignored his idiosyncrasy for the *muscular terribleness*), Brancusi caught me by the chest (he thought I provoked him on purpose) and told me some terrible words I can still recall. *Just you listen here—* continued Brancusi *—you should learn from me that art is not supposed to frighten but to approach people!* Modigliani who had been dosing in the meantime woke up in due time to separate us…"

[161] E. Carafoli, (1960) *Aurel Vlaicu, pionier al aviatiei romanesti* [A. Vlaicu, Pioneer of Romanian Aviation], Society Spreading Science and Culture, Bucharest.

[162] *Omagiu lui Brancusi* [Homage to Brancusi], volume edited by Tribuna, Cluj-Napoca, 1976, p. 245. Brancusi: "I intended to remind (by the *Kiss*) not only this single pair of lovers but also all other (anonymous) pairs that have loved each other in this world—before leaving it…Each one of my sculptures was motivated (at first) by very deep sentiment."

[163] C. Craciunoiu, G.P. Sandachi, *Henri Coanda… si avioanele sale 1910–2010* [Henri Coanda… and His Planes 1910–2010], Modelism Publishers, Bucharest, 2010.

[164] International Resin Modellers Association, www.internationalresinmodellers.com, accessed 25 July 2015.

[165] V. Firoiu, *op. cit.*, pp. 226–229.

[166] V.G. Paleolog, *Brancuși–Brancusi,* **I**, Scrisul Romanesc Publishers, Craiova, 1976, p. 25. Epitaph engraved with Cyrillic letters by Brancusi on the plinth of the funerary stele "Taniushka Rachevskaia / born on April 6, 1887 / deceased November 22, 1910 / most beloved and adored / I cannot stop looking at her."

[167] Th. Cornel, *op. cit.*

[168] C. Cosmuta, *Cu Brancusi* [With Brancusi], Ramuri, Craiova, 1965, *6,* 15 June, p. 22. Corneliu Cosmuta remembers how he posed to Brancusi for the *Prometheus*: "standing, one arm stretched forward, the other towards the back and my head high. The sculpture was made in clay and Brancusi would tell me various legends or sing."

[169] A. Buican, *op. cit.*, pp. 144–145.

[170] G. Apollinaire, *Le Salon des Indépendants / Fin de la promenade à travers les Salles du quai d'Orsay*, L'Intransigeant et le Journal de Paris, 3 avril 1912, p. 2. "Brancusy [sic], sculpteur délicat et très personnel, dont ses œuvres sont les plus raffinées."

[171] B. Brezianu, *op. cit.*, p. 20.

[172] T. Arghezi, *Expozitia Societatii "Tinerimea Artistica"* ["Artistic Youth" Exhibition], in *op. cit.*, p. 35. "However we cannot fail recording something which regards especially our most personal sculptor, Brancusi. From Paris where he lives this emulator of Rodin sent to the *Artistic Youth* some of his sculptures, having also sent others to the *Official Salon*, which will open soon in the Athenaeum. Painter Harlescu is in the same situation as, being invited like Brancusi to participate, he divided his artworks in two for both exhibitions. At the last moment, and therefore when the invitation had been answered the *Youth* Society just sat, pondered and decided. So it decided for painter Harlescu and sculptor Brancusi not to exhibit any more, on infidelity grounds. Being Society members, their colleagues cannot see them mentioned in the official State catalogue. The mentality of the *Youth* Society is thus self defined and our comments are superfluous."

[173] N. Pora, *Deschiderea salonului oficial* [Opening the Official Salon], Minerva, Bucharest, 8 May 1912.

[174] Marielle Tabart, Doina Lemny, eds., *op. cit.*, p. 224.

[175] I. Jianu, *op. cit.*, p. 65.

[176] P. Hulten, Natalia Dumitrescu, Al. Istrati, *op. cit*, p. 92. Brancusi: "En voilà une sculpture! La sculpture dorénavant ne doit pas être inférieure à cela!"

[177] Dora Vallier, (1954) *La vie fait l'œuvre de Fernand Léger*, Cahiers d'art, Paris, **29**, 2, p. 140.

[178] *Poiret*, The Metropolitan Museum of Art, New York, 2007.

[179] P. Hulten, Natalia Dumitrescu, Al. Istrati, *op. cit.*, p. 286.

[180] R. Wenrich, ed., (2015) *Die Medialität der Mode: Kleidung als kulturelle Praxis. Perspektiven für eine Modewissenschaft*, ebook, wwwtranscript-verlag.de, p. 157.

[181] S. Geist, (1968) *Brancusi. A Study of the Sculpture*, Studio Vista ltd., London, p. 3.

[182] Catalogue *International Exhibition of Modern Art—The Armory Show*, 17 February–15 March 1913, The Association of American Painters and Sculptors, edited by Vreeland Advertising Press.

[183] T.E. Powers, (1913) *Art at the Armory by Powers*, New York American, 22 February.

[184] J. Nilsen Laurvik, (1913) *Is It Art? Post-Impresionism, Futurism, Cubism*, The International Press, New York.

[185] *Examples of New Art Now on Exhibition*, The Brooklyn Daily Eagle, New York, 27 February 1913, p. 19.

[186] R.C., (1913) *Matters of Art*, New York Tribune, 23 February, p. 6.

[187] S. Watson, (1991) *Armory Show Scoreboard*, in *Strange Bedfellows: The First American Avant-garde*, Abbeville Press, New York.

[188] F.T. Bach, Margit Rowell, Ann Temkin, *op. cit.*, p. 53.

[189] *Buy Cubist Pictures While Critics Cavil*, Chicago Record-Herald, 29 March 1913, p. 14.

[190] *Students Burning Futurist Art and Celebrating Cubist' Departure*, Chicago Daily Tribune, 17 April 1913, p. 3.

[191] Harriet Monroe, (1913) *Bedlam in Art*, The Chicago Sunday Tribune, Chicago, 1 February 1913.

[192] E. Steichen, (1963) *A Life in Photography*, Doubleday & Company, New York.

[193] Doina Frumuselu, ed., (2014) *Brancusi in Exhibitions from Romania*, RCR Editorial, Bucharest.

[194] I. Jianu, (1938) *Brancusi. O lectie de arta, o lectie de viata* [Brancusi, Lesson of Art, Lesson of Life], Jurnalul Doamnei, Bucharest, **3**, 15 November (resumed in *Constantin Brancusi—viata si opera* [Constantin Brancusi—Life and Work], Scientific & Encyclopaedic Publishers, Bucharest, 1983, p. 73).

[195] W. Hausenstein, *Die bildende Kunst der Gegenwart. Malerei, Plastik, Zeichnung*, Deutsche Verlags-Anstalt, Stuttgart und Berlin, 2. Aufl., 1920, p. 33. "Brancusi einer der interessantesten Geister der neuen Skulptur."

[196] R. Fry, (1913) *The Allied Artists Exhibition*, The Nation, London, 2 Augustpp. 676–677. "Constantin Brancusi's sculptures have not, I think, been seen before in England. His three heads are the most remarkable works of sculpture at the Albert Hall. Two are in brass and one in stone. They show a technical skill which is almost disquieting, a skill which might lead him, in default of any overpowering imaginative purpose, to become a brilliant *pasticheur*. But it seemed to me that there was evidence of passionate conviction; that the simplification of forms was no mere exercise in plastic design, but a real interpretation of the rhythm of life. These abstract ovoid forms into which he compresses his heads give a vivid presentment of character; they are not empty abstractions, but filled with a content which has been clearly and passionately apprehended."

[197] G. Apollinaire, *Inscription pour le tombeau du peintre Henri Rousseau le Douanier*, Les Soirées de Paris, 1914, **2**, *20–27*, janvier, p. 29. "En 1913, enfin, le sculpteur Brancusy [sic] et le peintre Ortiz de Zarate gravèrent sur la pierre tombale cette épitaphe que j'avais inscripte au crayon: Gentil Rousseau tu nous entends/ Nous te saluons/ Delaunay sa femme Monsieur Queval et moi/Laisse passer nos bagages en frachise à la porte du ciel/ Nous t'apporterons des pinceaux des couleurs des toiles/ Afin que tes loisirs sacrés dans la lumière réelle/ Tu les consacres à peindre comme tu tiras mon portrait/ La face des étoiles."

[198] Sarah Greenough, ed., (2000) *Modern Art and America: Alfred Stieglitz and His New York Galleries*, National Gallery of Art, Washington D.C., p. 563.

[199] *Brancusi Sculpture at the Photo Secession*, The Brooklyn Daily Eagle, New York, 19 March 1914, p. 12.

[200] *What is Happening in the World of Art*, The Sun, New York, 22 March 1914, p. 2.

[201] A/rghezi/ T/udor/, *Cronica picturala. "Tinerimea artistica." Expozitie* [Painting Chronicle: Artistic Youth: Exhibition], Seara, Bucharest, 1914, **IV**, *1540*, 28 April (*op. cit.*, pp. 115–124). "Brancusi is a beginner, if not absolutely the first beginner. He is in every way a new man that thought of and searched for a long time, while others lived happily, the place where art's justice might cross the new intuition. And he is brand new because, having awaken inside the mysterious silence a creature brings into the world, unaware it might have found out something of the past, assumedly his own, and anyhow of the universe's whence it comes by all means searching the woman's womb, the wind, seeds, and the land; since agitating itself in honor of the Greeks and of the French the world's huge wave found a new expression, a Brancusi expression."

[202] T/udor/.A/rghezi/., *Tabula rasa. Arta si arta* [Tabula rasa: Art and art], Seara, Bucharest, 1914, **IV**, *1590*, 23 June (*op. cit.*, pp. 125–127). "Such organ players and

greengrocers of art have the difficulties alleviated for them which talents cannot overcome without sacrifice and exhaustion. They are received as friends, treated like prophets and, standing up from the chair occupied thanks to high-up ignorance, many of them leave with a purse of gold obtained by curved backs and methodical bootlicking."

[203] P. Pandrea, *op. cit.*, pp. 25–26. Brancusi: "Mortun refused my archaic fountain. I was left holding it in my arms, with great inner anguish. I saw Haret wearing a tailcoat in front of the University, soldierly aligned in a statue parade—quite an architectonic and plastic horror."

[204] Marielle Tabart, Doina Lemny, eds., *op. cit.*, pp. 114–115.

[205] A. Buican, *op. cit.*, p. 187.

[206] P. Hulten, Natalia Dumitrescu, Al. Istrati, *op. cit.*, p. 100.

[207] A. Duravel, (1916) *Expositions*, L'Élan, Paris, 8, janvier, p. 16.

[208] *Katalog Grafiki Konstantego Brandla*, Muzeum Uniwersyteckie Toruń, 2005, p. 15.

[209] *The World of Art*, The Brooklyn Daily Eagle, New York, 13 March 1916, p. 11.

[210] M. de Zayas, (1996) *How, When, and Why Modern Art Came to New York*, ed. F.M. Naumann, The MIT Press, Cambridge (MA), pp. 99, 102.

[211] S. Geist, *op. cit.*, p. 56.

[212] K.E. Silver, (1989) *Esprit de Corps: The Art of the Parisian Avant-garde and the First World War, 1914–1925*, Princeton University Press, Princeton.

[213] H. McBride, (1916) *News and Comment in the World of Art*, The Sun, New York, 5 November, p. 12.

[214] Marielle Tabart, Doina Lemny, eds., *op. cit.*, p. 112.

[215] *Of Varied Interest / Exhibition of Society of Independent Artists*, The Brooklyn Daily Eagle, New York, 31 March 1917, p. 7.

[216] K.E. Silver, *op. cit.*, pp. 167–185.

[217] Marielle Tabart, Doina Lemny, eds., *op. cit.*, pp. 136–137.

[218] *"Allies of Sculpture" Exhibition*, American Art News, New York, **16**, *9*, 8 December 1917, p. 2.

[219] Royal Cortissoz, (1917) *Art as a Scourge and Art as Confectionery*, New York Tribune, 9 December 1917, p. 3.

[220] H. McBride, (1917) *News and Comment in the World of Art / Allies of Sculpture at the Ritz-Carlton*, The Sun, New York, 9 December 1917, p. 12.

[221] P. Hulten, Natalia Dumitrescu, Al. Istrati, *op. cit.*, p. 116.

[222] V. Huszár, (1918) *Aesthetische beschouwingen V (bij bijlage XVI)*, De Stijl, Leiden, **1**, *12*, Oktober, pp. 147–150.

[223] Marie Bengescu, (1919) *L'Art en Roumanie*, in *La Roumanie en images*, **I**, coord. Petre Antonescu, Imprimeries A.G. L'Hoir, Paris, pp. 194–197.

[224] P. Vintila, (1972) *Milita*, Eminescu Publishers, Bucharest, pp. 33–36. "Brancusi would show up, wearing sabots and expensive camel hair jerseys—both summer and winter—and canvas trousers. Before realising how he looked like he dominated by the manner in which he stretched out his arm. Whatever is stereotype gesture with most persons was almost commitment to friendship with him, which acknowledged people can and should be more than animated puppets to each other—but living communicative radiant beings. Then you managed seeing a man with sharp smiling eyes, fleshy well delineated mouth almost fully covered by his moustache, regular straight nose and a beard turned white too soon that mixed with his thick slightly undulating hair. Two deep traits from nose to mouth make him look sometimes like a disappointed child, in contrast with the shining energy of his eyes."

[225] A. Salmon, (1919) *La jeune sculpture française,* Société des Trente, Albert Messein éditeur, Paris.

[226] Marielle Tabart, Doina Lemny, eds., *op. cit.*, p. 142.

[227] Marielle Tabart, Doina Lemny, eds., *op. cit.*, pp. 114–115.

[228] Th. van Doesburg, *Drie Voordrachten over de Nieuwe Beeldende Kunst*, Maatschappij voor goede en goedkoope lectuur, 1919, Amsterdam, p. 98. Tot een aesthetische oplossing, waarbij de volumen werkelijk als zoodanig en (niet als lichaams[spier]-volumen) tot een kunstconceptie leiden, kwam het eerst in de 20ste eeuw met Archipenko, Boccioni, Brancusi, e.a.

[229] R. Rusan, *op. cit.*, p. 78.

[230] R. Devigne, *op. cit.* Brancusi: "Ma statue, Monsieur, vous le comprenez, n'est-ce pas, c'est la femme, c'est l'Éternel féminin de Goethe réduit à son essence […]. Ensuite, montrant une photographie, il continua: Ce fut ma première ébauche, monsieur. Cinq ans, j'ai travaillé, j'ai simplifié et j'ai fait dire à la matière l'inexprimable. […]. Pour dégager cette entité, pour ramener dans le domaine sensible ce type éternel des formes éphémères, cinq ans j'ai simplifié et raboté mon œuvre. Et je crois, enfin vainqueur, avoir dépassé la matière. D'ailleurs, c'est tellement dommage de gâter une belle matière en y creusant des petits trous pour les yeux, les cheveux, les oreilles. Et ma matière est si belle en ces lignes sinueuses qui brillent comme de l'or pur et qui résument en un seul archétype toutes les effigies féminines de la terre."

[231] *Pour l'indépendance de l'art*, Le journal de peuple, Paris, 25 février 1920.

[232] *DADAphone*, Paris, 1920, 7, mars.

[233] M. Dachy, (1994) *Dada et les dadaïsmes*, Éd. Gallimard, Paris.

[234] www.dadart.com, accessed 2 February 2015.

[235] Regina Teixeira de Barros, (1969) *Tarsila do Amaral: Cronología*, in The Catalogue *Tarsila: 50 anos de pintura*, São Paulo.

[236] New York Tribune, 9 May 1920, p. 7.

²³⁷ S. Geist, *op. cit.*, p. 76. "*A hand* is a reminiscence of A Muse or Mlle. Pogany. Carved in a sliver of marble, a variation at the wrist inflicts its long taper. It is the hand become object. It seems to embody not so much the anatomical member as the sense of a caress. Inevitably it opposes itself to the individualized, gesticulating Hands of Rodin."

²³⁸ Doina Frumuselu, (2016) *Brancusi Perceived by His Contemporaries, and Commented on by Posterity*, Doctoral Dissertation in Visual Arts, George Enescu National University of Arts, Iasi, (published in 2017).

²³⁹ Peggy Guggenheim, (1987) *Out of This Century: Confessions of an Art Addict*, Universe Publishing, New York.

²⁴⁰ Marielle Tabart, Doina, Lemny, eds., *op. cit.*, pp. 148–149.

²⁴¹ S. Geist, *op. cit.*, p. 204.

²⁴² A. Buican, *op. cit.*, pp. 253, 256–257.

²⁴³ The New York Public Library, archives@manuscripts, John Quinn papers 1901–1926, accessed 16 July 2014.

²⁴⁴ www.adirondackreview.homestead.com, accessed 2 March 2014.

²⁴⁵ Arlen J. Hansen, *Expatriate Paris: A Cultural and Literary Guide to Paris of the 1920s*, Arcade Publishing, New York, 1990.

²⁴⁶ S. Benstock, *Women of the Left Bank: Paris, 1900–1940*, University of Texas Press, Austin, 1986.

²⁴⁷ H. O'Neal, *Berenice Abbott: American Photographer*, McGraw-Hill, New York, 1982.

²⁴⁸ L. Taft, *Modern Tendencies in Sculpture*, 1921, p. 27.

²⁴⁹ C.R. Post, *A History of European and American Sculpture: From the Early Christian Period to the Present Day*, **II**, Harvard University Press, Cambridge (MA), 1921, pp. 268–269.

²⁵⁰ E. Pound, *Brancusi*, The Little Review, New York, 1921, **VIII,** *1*, autumn, pp. 3–7. "In the case of the ovoid, I take it Brancusi is meditating upon pure form free from all terrestrial gravitation; form as free in its own life as the form of the analytic geometers; and the measure of this success in this experiment (unfinished and probably unfinishable) is that from some angles at least ovoid does come to life and appear ready to levitate. (Or this is perhaps merely a fortuitous anecdote, like any other expression)."

²⁵¹ Germaine Everling, (1970) *L'Anneau de Saturne*, Fayard, Paris, p. 167.

²⁵² Marie-Claude Chaudonneret, (2007) *Les artistes étrangers à Paris, de la fin du Moyen Âge aux années 1920*, Peter Lang Publishers, Bern.

²⁵³ P. Westheim, (1922) *Bildhauer in Frankreich*, Das Kunstblatt, Potsdam, **VI**, *2*, pp. 53–56.

[254] *Cronici / Idei, oameni & fapte: Un critic de arta german despre Brancusi* [Chronicles / Ideas, People & Facts: A German Art Critic about Brancusi], Gandirea, Bucharest, 1923, **III**, *5*, 1 November, p. 103.

[255] H. McBride, (1922) *News and Reviews of Art—Modern French Works in Striking Show / Part of the Notable John Quinn Collection on View in the Sculptor's Gallery the Most Interesting Exhibition of the Kind of the Season*, The New York Herald, 26 March 1922, p. 10.

[256] Jeanne Robert Foster, (1922) *New Sculptures by Constantin Brancusi: A Note on the Man and the Formal Perfection of His Carvings*, Vanity Fair, New York, **XVIII**, *3*, May, pp. 68, 124. "He is modest in speaking of his work, but one feels that he has attained serene confidence in the beauty and significance of his own creation.;" "He will astonish of wit and knowledge."

[257] Irina Codreanu, *Ucenicie la Brancusi* [Apprenticeship with Brancusi], in *op. cit.*, p. 57. "I have met him in a small district theatre on Gaîté Street […] that sheltered several performance halls. At that time such theatre would perform social plays, in extremely direct popular style, usually written by one of the actors such as famous Monthéus, l'ami du peuple as he liked to call himself. Brancusi was very fond of such kind of theatre. He went there until the last world war."

[258] *Le Gala des artistes roumains au Théâtre Mogador*, Comœdia, Paris, 23 janvier 1923, p. 2.

[259] D. Morarescu, (2002) *Lizica Codreanu si avangarda pariziana* [Lizica Codreanu and Parisian Vanguard], Aritmos Publishers, Bucharest, pp. 51–56.

[260] Cella Delavrancea, *O vizita in Atelierul lui Brancusi* [A Visit to Brancusi's Studio], in *Mozaic in timp* [Mosaic Over Time], Eminescu Publishers, Bucharest, 1973, pp. 135–139. "We were in a dusty courtyard with wood studios and open doors, showing stone and marble blocks, cement heaps and a few men working scantily dressed, wearing paper caps. In the bottom to the left was Brancusi's studio. He was waiting for us. He opened the door to us and two small blue eyes pierced me from the shadowy deep sockets. Slyness, suspicion and a touch of hostility could be read in those eyes […] We got inside. Brancusi examined me ruthlessly. Everything was lively with him, his grey beard, loose hair, working clothes, or swift hands. Brass objects of various shapes stood up like reed on different whitewashed brick shelves and some ovoid melons of the same material stood on a chest and shone so bright that I could not help hearing their cello vibrations. I could no longer refrain and said: *They are so alive!* Brancusi smiled. All of a sudden we were closer. *Yes indeed, I polish them for months on end with my own hands, until they turn alive. Look here the portrait of a young lady.* At that, he placed my finger on a melon where one could see the simplified drawing of an exophthalmic eye. A bulky saw-like brass piece stood before me that vertically towered all the other objects. Brancusi asked: *What do you say about it, do you like it? If you can guess what it is I will invite you to lunch*

and we'll have mushrooms cooked by me. I looked well and could hear a far away croaky voice. *Cock-a-doodle-doo the rooster cries*, I answered. Brancusi's eyes shone and he offered a malicious smile: *Bravo! Nobody else has sensed before this brass is singing. So I was not wrong. You proved to me that I succeeded. Thank you…I will cook a great lunch for you.* […] We parted after deciding the lunch date. I was very happy when I left. Everybody knew Brancusi did not accept someone so easily in his private circle."

[261] P. Beekman Taylor, (2004) *Gurdjieff's America: Mediating the Miraculous*, Lighthouse Editions Ltd.

[262] B. Nicolescu, P. Beekman Taylor, *Brancusi et Gurdjieff*, Ligeia, Paris, 2005, *57–60*, janvier–juin, pp. 84–92.

[263] B. Nicolescu, *Brancusi si Gurdjieff* [Brancusi and Gurdjiefff] (I), Convorbiri literare, Iasi, 2011, *3*, March.

[264] I. Barsan, *Convorbiri cu Dimitrie Cuclin—filosof, muzician, scriitor* [Talks with D. Cuclin—Philosopher, Musician, Writer], 2nd edition reviewed and added, Grai si Suflet—Cultura Nationala Publishers, Bucharest, 2005. The first edition of 1995 received the prize of the Romanian Academy.

[265] Lucia Dem. Balacescu, (1942) *Cronica plastica. Colectia Al. Bogdan-Pitesti (introducere)* [Plastic Chronicle: Al. Bogdan—Pitesti Collection (Introduction)], Universul literar, Bucharest, **LI**, *29*, 18 July, p. 3.

[266] S. Geist, (1975) *Brancusi. The Sculpture and Drawings*, Harry N. Abrams, Inc. Publishers, New York, p. 176.

[267] B. Brezianu, *op. cit.*, p. 256.

[268] P. Vintila, *op. cit.* pp. 35–36. Milita Petrascu about Eileen Lane: "A fairy sat on the bench; […] a snow-white Irish woman with antique regular traits, dark blue big mysterious eyes with thick eyelashes; her black hair was combed with a parting and a bun in the back above a long neck as white as the face. Brancusi was looking at her enraptured.;" "Brancusi was extremely sensitive to feminine beauty. More than a woman's appearance the combination of plastic elements providing harmony acquired sacred meaning to him."

[269] P. Hulten, Natalia Dumitrescu, Al. Istrati, *op. cit.*, p. 147.

[270] R. Rusan, *op. cit.,* p. 51.

[271] ibidem.

[272] P. Hulten, Natalia Dumitrescu, Al. Istrati, *op. cit.*, p. 148.

[273] P. Vintila, *op. cit.*, p. 36.

[274] Aline & Eero Saarinen papers, 1906–1977. Archives of American Art, Smithsonian Institution. https://www.aaa.si.edu/collections/items/detail/erik-satie-john-quinn-constantin-brancusi-and-henripierre-roche-14380

[275] J. Cocteau, *Le solitaire d'Arcueil / Pour la tombe d'Erik Satie*, Comœdia, Paris, 17 mai 1926, p. 1. "L'atelier de Brancusi ressemble à un paysage de préhistoire: des

troncs d'arbre, des blocs de pierre, un four où le maître de maison, homme primitif, grille les viandes au bout d'une pointe de fer. Aux quatre coins, le Brontosaure a déposé des œufs, et des statues miroitantes attirent les belles Américaines comme des oiseaux. Satie se plaisait dans ce décor."

[276] P. Comarnescu, *op. cit.*, pp. 24, 279.

[277] Mina Loy, (1922) *Brancusi's Golden Bird*, The Dial, New York, **LXXIII**, pp. 507–508.

[278] *Brancusi's Golden Bird* by Mina Loy translated in Romanian by V. G. Paleolog, C. Brancusi, Forum Publishers, Bucharest, 1947, republished with the Foundation Scrisul Romanesc, Craiova, 2002.

[279] C. Sandburg, *Brancusi*, in *Slabs of the Sunburnt West*, Harcourt, Brace and Company, New York, 1922.

[280] A. Dreyfus, (1923) *Constantin Brancusi*, Der Querschnitt, Berlin, **III**, *3–4*, pp. 119–121. "Brancusi ist ein Eigenbrödler; er hat keine Schüler, aber seine Einwirkung auf die neuere Kunst ist schon jetzt erheblich. Lehmbruck's gotisierende Frauenkörper sind ohne Brancusi nicht denkbar. Lipschitz läßt die von Brancusi mit den Sinnen gefundenen, mit Instinkt angewandten plastischen Gesetze in geometrischen Formeln erstarren.
Lipschitz ist ein Intellekt, kein Schöpfer. Arckipenko, Zadkine, andere unter den Jüngeren, haben das Gold, das Brancusi prägte, in Scheidemünze umgewechselt in Umlauf gebracht. Es ist nur Gerechtigkeit, das festzustellen."

[281] M.M., (1923) *Constantin Brancusi: A Summary of Many Conversations,* The Arts, New York, **IV**, *1*, July, pp. 14–29.

[282] A. Wilson, (1923) *A Visit to Brancusi's*, The New York Times Book Review and Magazine, New York, 19 August 1923, p. 23.

[283] J.P. Colleyn, L. Homberger, *Ciwara, chimères africaines*, www.quaibranly.fr, accessed 11 May 2015.

[284] H. Van den Berg, Irmeli Hautamäki, B. Hjartarson, T. Jelsbak, R. Schönström, P. Stounbjerg, Tania Ørum, Dorthe Aagesen, eds., (2013) *A Cultural History of the Avant-garde in the Nordic Countries 1900–1925*, Rodopi Publishers, Amsterdam, p. 132.

[285] Marielle Tabart, Doina Lemny, eds., (1924) *op. cit.*, p. 154. The last letter from Brancusi archives to collector John Quinn who died on July 28.

[286] G.J. Salvy, (2001) *Un carnet vénitien*, Éd. du Regard, Paris.

[287] Anne Chisholm, *Nancy Cunard: A Biography*, Alfred A. Knopf, New York, 1979, p. 31.

[288] Searcher Ceasinger, *The Greatest Coup of the Age*, Der Querschnitt, Berlin, 1924, Bild 4, pp. 47–48.

[289] R. Radiguet, *Œuvres complètes*, Éd. Omnibus, Paris, 2012.

[290] B. Brezianu, *op. cit.*, p. 26.

[291] The Little Review, New York, autumn–winter, 1924–1925, pp. 17–18.

[292] V.G. Paleolog, *Brancusi, Brancusi*, **II**, Scrisul Romanesc Publishers, Craiova, 2002, p. 110. Brummer Joseph was "Born in Botosani (town in the north-eastern part of Romania—A/N), established in the USA at the beginning of the century. He founded the Brummer Art Galleries in New York."

[293] Contimporanul, Bucharest, 1924, **III**, *50–51*, December.

[294] E. Walsh, *Brancusi*, cap. *Brancusi and others*, Poetry—A Magazine of Verse, Chicago, 1924, **XXV**, *1*, octombrie, pp. 25–26. "He is the man who, needing marble, / was offered shadows, / and taking them / made marble. / He is the man who, needing stone, / was offered water, / and taking it / made stone. / He is the man who, needing bronze, / was offered fire, / and taking it / made bronze. / He is the Niagara of the ages—no man can explain: / This is where he begins; this is where he ends."

[295] I. Minulescu, (1925) *Constantin Brancusi,* Integral, Bucharest, **I**, *2*, 1 April, p. 8.

[296] Integral, Bucharest, 1925, **I**, *3*, p. 3.

[297] Integral, Bucharest 1925, **I**, 4, pp. 5, 7, 12.

[298] Integral, Bucharest, 1925, **I**, *5*, pp. 8, 9.

[299] This Quarter, Paris, 1925, **I**, *1*, Spring.

[300] M. Mihalovici, *Amintiri despre Enescu, Brancusi si alti prieteni* [Memories about Enescu, Brancusi and Other Friends], Eminescu Publishers, Bucharest, 1987, p. 97.

[301] M. Mihalovici, *op. cit.*, p. 99. "At a certain moment he wanted me very much to write a book on him because Fondane, Benjamin Fondane (Fundoianu) had this intention and Brancusi refused him. […] And for several weeks—I can still recall him in the studio of 10, Impasse Ronsin, perhaps in 1925–1926, in his small bedroom, lying on the sofa and myself with a pile of white sheets of paper was sitting at the table, while he was dictating things from his life, which I tried to arrange."

[302] Mariana Vida, *op. cit.*

[303] Calendar Minerva 1925, Cartea Romaneasca Publishers, Bucharest, pp. 130–131.

[304] libertyellisfoundation.org, accessed 15 February 2014.

[305] *Brancusi in New York*, The New York Telegram Editorial, New York, 16 February 1926.

[306] Flora Merrill, *Brancusi, the Sculptor of the Spirit, Would Build "Infinite Column" in Park*, New York World, New York, 3 October 1926, p. 4. Brancusi: "I couldn't built the city any better. When I approached New York on the boat I had the impression of seeing my studio on a large scale. All the buildings look like these blocks. It is very beautiful."

[307] F.T. Bach, Margit Rowell, Ann Temkin, *op. cit.*, p. 381.

[308] F.T. Bach, Margit Rowell, Ann Temkin, *op. cit.*, p. 60.

[309] Catalogue Alexander Calder, Whitney Museum of America Art, New York, 17 February–3 May 1981.

[310] Le Petit Havre, Le Havre, 31 March 1926.

[311] Contimporanul, Bucharest, 1926, **V**, *64*, January, p. 3.

[312] N. Iorga, (1926) *Romania in chipuri si vederi* [Romania in Faces and Images], Cultura Nationala Publishers, Bucharest.

[313] S. Geist, *op. cit.*, p. 71.

[314] *The Letters of T.S. Eliot*, **3**, 1926–1927, Faber & Faber Ltd., London, 2012, p. 199.

[315] Marielle Tabart, Doina Lemny, eds., *op. cit.*, pp. 214–215.

[316] Hébert, *Notes d'un curieux / Le Salon du franc*, Le Gaulois, Paris, 30 octobre 1926, p. 3.

[317] *La vente aux enchères des œuvres exposées au Salon du Franc rapporta 850.000 francs au Trésor*, Le Matin, Paris, 30 octobre 1926, p. 2.

[318] F.T. Bach, Margit Rowell, Ann Temkin, *op. cit.*, p. 62.

[319] Margit Rowell, A. Paléologue, (1999) *Brancusi vs. United States. The Historic Trial, 1928,* Diane Pub. Co.–Vilo International.

[320] *New York's Statues Called 'Ridiculous'. Brancusi, Regarded as Rodin's Most Brilliant Pupil, Here to Exhibit His Work. Our Architecture 'Poetic' Likes Our Skyscrapers, Considers Grand Central Terminal 'Most Beautiful'*, The New York Times, New York, 3 October 1926, p. 1. "Constantin Brancusi, modernist sculptor, whose work has caused a storm of controversy on both sides of the Atlantic, and who is to hold an exhibition here in November and December, declared yesterday that he did not care for the statues in the public squares and parks of New York, although he had found many specimens of architecture here very pleasing."

[321] Flora Merrill, *Brancusi, the Sculptor of the Spirit, Would Build "Infinite Column" in Park*, New York World, New York, 3 October 1926, p. 4. Brancusi: "I would like to make my column in Central Park. It would be greater than any building, three times higher than your obelisk in Washington, with a base correspondingly wide sixty meters or more. It would be made of metal. In each pyramid there would be apartments and people would live there, and on the very top I would have my bird—a great bird poised on the top of my infinite column."

[322] I.H. Brown, (1924) *Gypsy Fires in America; A Narrative of Life Among the Romanies of the United States and Canada.../ With Many Illustrations from Photos*, Harper New York & London.

[323] R. Schulman, (2006) *Romany Marie: The Queen of Greenwich Village,* Butler Books, Louisville.

[324] V.G. Paleolog, *op. cit.*, p. 9. "In 1970 while in the National Museum of Modern Art of Paris I found among the unstudied documents of Brancusi the model of a coffee fortune telling manual that Mary Romany dictated to Harry Kemp, being illustrated with photos taken by Brancusi when the three of them had had countless talks about the dreg marks of their cups."

[325] La Petit Havre, Le Havre, 3 décembre 1926.

[326] Marielle Tabart, Doina Lemny, eds., *op. cit.*, pp.118–119.

[327] R. Fry, (1926) *Transformations: Critical and Speculative Essays on Art*, Chatto & Windus, London, p. 76. "In this connection, it is interesting that among the many instances of Chinese influence on modern Western art we may note a tendency among contemporary sculptors to accept this ovoid schema. Brancusi is, of course, the most striking example."

[328] D.H. Parker, *The Analysis of Art,* Yale University Press, New Haven, p. 6. "Or when, for example, we look at MacMonnies' Bacchante, it is as if the divinely frenzied girl and her child were alive in our presence and we were witnesses of their ecstasy in the festival of the god. To induce us to make believe this is the triumph of the artist. But equally, when we look at Brancusi's Miss Pogany, for all the geometrization of the head, we get a feeling of reality. So, likewise, we demand of every novel and play, every dramatic and narrative poem, that it create the semblance of reality."

[329] S. Geist, (1982) *Brancusi / Sarutul* [Brancusi / The Kiss], Meridiane Publishers, Bucharest, pp. 66–67.

[330] Carole Reiss, (2008) *Villa Noailles de Mallet-Steven*, 3 janvier 2008, http://www.quintet.ch/, accessed 4 June 2014.

[331] Catalogue *Charles et Marie-Laure de Noailles / Une vie de mécènes*, Avant-première, Paris, Vitrines du Palais Royal, Ministère de la Culture et de la Communication, du 1er au 11 mars 2010 / puis à Hyères, à partir du 2 juillet 2010 à Saint-Bernard, www.villanoailles-hyeres.com, accessed 24 April 2015.

[332] Integral, Bucharest, 1926, **II**, 9, 1 December.

[333] P.B. Franklin, ed., (2016) *The Artist and His Critic Stripped Bare: The Correspondence of Marcel Duchamp and Robert Lebel*, Getty Research Institute, Los Angeles, 2016, p. 296.

[334] Dorothy Dudley Harvey, (1927) *Brancusi,* The Dial, New York, **LXXXII,** February, pp. 123–130.

[335] Dorothy Adlow, *C. Brancusi*, Drawings and Design, London, 1927, **II**, February, pp. 37–41. "Remind [Brancusi] of the beauty of classical drapery, the power of Michelangelo's muscle…he will answer briefly. He pinches the flesh of his wrist, makes a funny face, and mutters *biftek*…he identifies his subject [in his own sculptures] with what is real and elemental in its nature.He tries to differentiate it from everything else, and give it a unique character. As for the representation of every external fact, clothes, limbs, facial features, all of this is *biftek*…People are afraid, they are content with the external, with clothing and flesh, with what is physical and not mental. Of course, it is not easy to give what is purely mental a tangible form, and so artists resort to the simplest way of conveying their thoughts. They proceed to exult in the grandeur of draperies, in exaggerated movement, in sentimentality, *biftek*."

[336] *Isamu Noguchi, A Sculptor's World,* Harper & Row Publishers, New York, 1968. "He spoke no English, and I no French. Communication was through the eyes, through gesture and through the materials and tools to be used. Brancusi would show me for instance precisely how a chisel should be held and how to true a plane of limestone. He would show me by doing it himself, indicating that I should do the same."

"Wherever he was, everything had to be all white. He wore white, his beard was then already white. He had two white dogs that he fed with lettuce floating in milk. My memory of Brancusi is always of whiteness and of his bright and smiling eyes."

[337] R. Schulman, (2006) *Romany Marie: The Queen of Greenwich Village*, Butler Books, Louisville, pp. 109–110.

[338] L. Vauxcelles, *Beaux-Arts/Le Salon des Tuileries au Palais de Bois*, Excelsior, Paris, 28 avril 1927, p. 5. (cet hermétique Brancusi (si grave, si sérieux pourtant, mais dont *l'Oiseau*, luisant de reflets, posé sur un carton à chapeaux en plâtre, demeure à mes yeux une troublant énigme))

[339] A. Dreyfus, (1927) *Constantin Brancusi*, Cahiers d'art, Paris, **2**, 2, pp. 69–75.

[340] S.I. Nenitescu, foreword to the catalogue of the *Exposition d'art roumain—Congrès de la Presse Latine,* Bucharest, 30 September–10 October 1927. "Brancusi is the greatest sculptor and we will be able to call him ours in all his abstract sides and with his entire will-power for free art. Being passionate for material, he joins the handicraftsman's joy and the constructive impetus of the visionary."

[341] T. Soroceanu, *Pinacoteca Statului* [State Art Gallery], Boabe de grau, Bucharest, 1930, **I**, *4*, June, p. 214. "an exhibition was hurriedly set up whose organizers went in a hurry to the collectors to gather representative works of Romanian art."

"His small volume creations have got domineering power and easily acquire monumental dimensions by understanding them."

"Homage albums are dedicated to Brancusi in England, in America—poems, in Germany—the inspirations of modern sculptural art and although he has no rival in Romania the Art Gallery has got only two of his older sculptures."

[342] J. Honzl, *Taneční masky primitivů* [Dance Masks of Primitive People], ReD, Prague, October 1927–July 1928, pp. 146–152.

[343] San Antonio Light, 25 December 1927. "How They Know It's *A Bird* and Are Sure It is *Art* / Illuminating Testimony of Sculptors, Painters and Admirers of the *Modernist School* in the U.S. Customs Court Explaining Why They Think Mr. Brancusi's Famous *Bird in Flight* Is Not Meaningless Junk."

[344] Marielle Tabart, Doina Lemny, eds., *op. cit.*, p. 224.

[345] Marielle Tabart, Doina Lemny, eds., *op. cit.*, pp. 186–187.

[346] T. van Doesburg, *Brancusi*, De Stijl, Leiden, 1927, Jubileum, series XIV, *79–84*, pp. 85–86.

³⁴⁷ C. Petrescu, *op. cit.*, p. 270.

³⁴⁸ C. Michailescu, *C. Brancusi*, Universul literar, Bucharest, 1928, **XLIV**, *17*, 22 April, pp. 270–271. To C. Michailescu Brancusi remained "the child of our realms, a peasant's son from the heart of a province full of sensuality and life."

³⁴⁹ Apriliana Medianu, *op. cit.*, pp. 3–4.

³⁵⁰ E. Riegler-Dinu, *op. cit.*, p. 2.

³⁵¹ *The Inaugural Exhibition of the New Museum of Art Fairmount European and American Sections,* Bulletin of the Pennsylvania Museum, Philadelphia, 1928, **23**, *119*, March, pp. 1–31.

³⁵² M. Raynal, *La sculpture au Salon des Tuileries*, L'Intransigeant, Paris, 21 mai 1928, p. 5.

³⁵³ A. Buican, *op. cit.*, p. 379.

³⁵⁴ M. Mihalovici, *op. cit.*, p. 97.

³⁵⁵ The catalogue of French Exhibition of Contemporary Art, State Modern Art Museum of Moscow, September–October 1928. A.V. Lunacearski about Brancusi: "One of the most faithful followers of the plastic purity principle. His trend towards plenitude and roundness of form brings him to certain elementary volume."

³⁵⁶ A.V. Lunacearski, *Arta pariziana pe Prechistenka* [Parisian Art on Prechistenka], Proektor, Moscow, 1928, *43(161)*, in *Dialog despre arta* [Dialogue on art] (antology, translation, foreword by Vasile Florea), Meridiane Publishers, Bucharest, 1975, pp. 174–175.

³⁵⁷ Michèle Fitoussi, *Helena Rubinstein: The Woman Who Invented Beauty*, Gallic Books, London, 2014.

³⁵⁸ V.G. Paleolog, *Procesul sculpturii moderne—eseuri* [Court Trial of Modern Sculpture—Essays], Foundation Constantin Brancusi Publishers, Targu-Jiu, 1996.

³⁵⁹ U.S. Treasury Department, Customs court, 3rd Division, Protest 209109-G, C. Brancusi v. U.S., New York, October 21, 1927–March 23, 1928 (stenographic minutes in the library of the Museum of Modern Art, New York), accessed 11 April 2015.

³⁶⁰ *Warm Ashes: The Life and Career of Mary Reynolds*, The Art Institue of Chicago—Ryerson and Burnham Libraries, http://www.artic.edu/reynolds/essays/godlewski3.php, accessed 18 August 2014.

³⁶¹ *Interpretive Resource*, The Art Institue of Chicago—Ryerson and Burnham Libraries, http://www.artic.edu/, accessed 18 August 2014.

³⁶² *Marcel Duchamp* edited by Anne d'Harnoncourt and Kynaston McShine, The Museum of Modern Art and Philadelphia Museum of Art, New York, 1973, p. 20.

³⁶³ R. Vitrac, (1929) *Constantin Brancusi*, Cahiers d'art, Paris, **4**, *8–9*, pp. 383–397. "Le temps travaille par les mains dw Brancusi. Il n'y a pas, il ne peut pas y avoir d'œuvre de Brancusi. De temps en temps, il nous propose l'état d'une sculpture, c'est un poisson, c'est un cheval, mais aussitôt il reprend la pierre ou le bronze, les polit

pendant deux ans, trois ans, dix ans et le poisson—1910 devient le poisson—1929, ce dernier plus mince, plus brillant, prêt à rejoindre les eaux vives, bref, échappant de plus en plus aux mains qui l'aimèrent."

[364] B. Fondane, (1929) *Brancusi*, Cahiers de l'Étoile, Paris, **II**, *11*, septembre–octobre, pp. 708–725.

[365] E. Shanes, *Constantin Brancusi*, Abbeville Press, New York, 1989, p. 105. Vera Moukhina: "I think that the significance of Brancusi's œuvre first lies in his regard for the materials used. Secondly, the Romanian artist had a pure conception about sculptural forms. He returned to the primeval and almost magic sense of the symbols rendering by his work to sculpture its whole aesthetic oneness."

[366] http://catalogue.bnf.fr/ark:/12148/cb39747287s, accessed 14 March 2016.

[367] I. Voronca, (1929) *Plante si animale: terase* [Plants and Animals: Terraces], Coll. Intégral, Imprimerie Union, Paris.

[368] J. Készman, (2004) *Egy világraszóló magyar / Az art déco egyetemes nagykövete: Miklós Gusztáv (1888, Budapest—1967, Oyonnax)*, Artmagazin, May 2004, pp. 48–51, www.artmagazin.hu, accessed 7 May 2005.

[369] F.W. Seiwert, (1929) *Constantin Brancusi, der Bildhauer*, A bis Z, Köln, *2*, pp. 5–7.

[370] L. Moholy-Nagy, (1929) *Von Material zu Architektur*, Bauhausbücher, Band 14, Albert Langen Verlag, München.

[371] A. Huxley, (1929) *Das Land*, Der Querschnitt, Berlin (Propyläen Verlag), **IX**, Heft *12*, Dezember, pp. 864–868.

[372] W. George, (1930) *Chroniques / L'Art à Paris*, Formes, Paris, *2*, février 1930, p. 13: L'ove et la sphère, symbole de l'infini, telles sont les limites exactes de Brankusi, ce statuaire esclave de l'idée d'absolu.

[373] M. Raynal, (1929) *Une exposition de sculpture internationale*, L'Intransigeant, Paris, 2 decembrie 1929, p. 5.

[374] M. Zahar, (1930) *Chroniques / L'Art à Paris*, Formes, Paris, *2*, février, p. 14: "Brancusi dans sa souffrance de ne point trouver de forme encore assez pure semble déjà limer, limer éperdûment jusqu'aux sensations géométriques."

[375] I. Vitner, (1981) *Popas langa Notre-Dame* [A Halt Near Notre-Dame], Cartea Romaneasca Publishers, Bucharest, pp. 56–57.

[376] http://en.museuberardo.pt/, accessed 25 March 2014.

[377] Marguerite Vessereau, (1930) *Le rythme essentiel*, in *Roumanie terre du dor*, Presses Universitaires de France, Paris, pp. 115–124.

[378] I. Minulescu, (1930) *Strofe pentru toata lumea* [Stanzas for Everyone], Cultura Nationala Publishers, Bucharest, pp. 91–92.

[379] Apriliana Medianu, *op. cit.*, pp. 3–4. Brancusi: "None (nobody helped me—A/N). Everything came out from me as hey all sprang out of me. Art is mystery, it is belief not formula. When art is done according to some theory it is false. We should

completely destroy ourselves, detach fully from all human impertinence. Beauty can be discovered only like this. Art is neither modern nor old, it is art. But time is improving the human spirit—while the spirit itself asks for it. Nowadays I hear people talking of all sorts of currents in art. It is like a sort of universal bedlam. Art has never developed but in great religious eras. When the religious sentiment decreases, decadence follows. Whatever is created by philosophy and religion is happiness, light, liberty."

[380] C. Baillat, *Vera Moore, pianiste, de Dunedin à Jouy-en-Josas*, Collection Univers musical, Éd. L'Harmattan, Paris, 2012.

[381] http://lesamisdeveramoore.jimdo.com/, accessed 14 May 2014.

[382] M. Mihalovici, *Amintiri despre Enescu, Brancusi si alti prieteni* [Memories of Enescu, Brancusi and Other Friends] (edition and introduction by V. Rapeanu, notes & comments by Alice Mavrodin and V. Rapeanu), Eminescu Publishers, Bucharest, 1987, p. 100. "[Oskar Kokoschka] came to Brancusi: he brought a canvas with him, leaned it against the wall and painted it with his finger. […] It stayed as he began that day because Brancusi did not like it. […] He enjoyed precise things."

[383] *L'Age d'Or*, a film by Luis Buñuel, pressbook compiled by Elliott Stein, pressbook, Kino International, New York.

[384] Sanda Miller, (2007) *Brancusi's Women: Constantin Brancusi Died 50 Years Ago This Month*, Apollo, London, 1 March 2007.

[385] *Constantin Brancusi. Poveste cu haiduci* [Constantin Brancusi, Brigand Story], translated by Dan Botta, Vremea. Politica, sociala, culturala (Supplement Vremea plastica)], Bucharest, 1930, **III**, *141*, 30 October, p. 4.

[386] *Constantin Brancusi. Aforisme despre arta* [Constantin Brancusi, Aphorisms on Art], translated by Dan Botta, Vremea. Politica, sociala, culturala (Supplement Vremea plastica), Bucharest, 1930, **III**, *144*, 9 November, p. 5.

[387] L. Boz, (1930) *Brancusi*, Adeverul, Bucharest, 4 July 1930, p. 2.

[388] H. Blazian, (1930) *Sculptorul Constantin Brancusi* [Sculptor Constantin Brancusi], Adeverul, Bucharest, 9 October 1930, pp.1, 2.

[389] *My Thirty Years' War: An Autobiography by Margaret Anderson*, Covici, Friede Publishers, New York, 1930, pp. 253–255. "After dinner he brings out his coffee machine, grinds and makes a thick black Turkish coffee. Then someone always asks if he will sing and play his violin. / Oh, we will see—later. *Si tout marche bien*. / By which he means if everyone always is, he brings out the violin and plays folk songs with Romanian abandon and the smile of a child. He sings to you in a soft timid laughing voice. He dances in his heavy sabots. He produces a small drum and makes Duchamp beat it. He dances wildly on the stone floor. Leger sits with his head on one hand and with the other beats the rhythms on the stone table. He always looks lonely. A young Dadaist (this being 1923) declaims his opinions. Léger looks at him patiently. I agree with you, he says, bringing down his fist on the table. I agreed with

you fifteen years ago. / Tzara talks about the abstract heart and sings to please Brancusi. Duchamp smiles obligingly at everything that is said, whether it is funny or not. / At midnight Brancusi decides to take flashlights. He becomes instantly as serious as if he were beginning a piece of sculpture. He spends an hour adjusting his apparatus to suit him and in examining his audience with a view to good lighting. He seats himself with the group and by an arrangement of long cords takes the picture so as to include himself. / By one in the morning, he decides that the night will be lost unless the party will spend it with him in the streets of Paris. Tzara suggests going to the Opera to tear down the statues and put up Brancusis in their places. / Paris will be surprised in the morning, and happier, he says. / Brancusi leads the way through the streets. He stops at cafes where there is music, talks with everyone, drinks with everyone, dances in the middle of the floor. He is not in the least drunk. He is happy. / By seven o'clock in the morning he has led you to the Bois. He lies down flat on the wet grass by the lake with the intention of catching a duck and taking it home to roast. He suggests taking a boat down the Seine to Rouen. Everyone refuses this. So he takes you instead to the Halles for onion soup."

[390] Brancusi's letter sent to T. Tomescu, 16 February 1931, notified by G. Nicodinescu and published by Ruxandra Ionescu in *Toma Gh. Tomescu* album, Art Museum of Ploiesti. "Dear Tomescu, / I received your registered letter and the one sent through Marbé, with respect to Caragiale's monument. / If I have full freedom and enough time it would be like a duty to me to thank the spirit of Caragiale. / Do you remember how impatiently we were waiting for his artists? / As far as the fee is concerned, I cannot know without doing a draft project. Therefore send me please a brief sketch indicating the width of the place where they want the monument and what is built around it. / Your friend, / C. Brancusi, / 11 Impasse Ronsin Paris XV-ème."

[391] B. Brezianu, (2001) *Brancusi, sapte prilejuri pierdute* [Brancusi, Seven Failed Opportunities], in *Brancusi si Transilvania* [Brancusi and Transylvania], antology by C. Zarnescu, Grinta Publishers, Cluj-Napoca, pp. 104–108.

[392] P. Comarnescu, (1966) *Atelierele pariziene ale lui Brancusi* [Brancusi's Parisian Studios], Tribuna, Cluj-Napoca, **10**, 29 December, p. 8. "We were amazed by the desolating air of the dwellings, looking like post floods or earthquakes. The studios arranged at random showed only ground floors, or one floor or at least a high garret with pointed roof. Some had immense glass partitions; others looked like simple sheds with wide wooden doors. Roofs were quite fantastic. Everything had an air of poverty, improvisation, sometimes ingeniously added by an artist in a momentary successful moment. Only the tall lean trees reminded nature of its nobility. However there were small alleys with trees and vegetation, especially around Brancusi's rooms, sovereign of this citadel, surrounded—alas!—by rudimentary wattle. A fragment of wall and an iron gate could be seen only on one side…"

[393] H.P. Roché, (1957) *Souvenirs sur Brancusi*, l'Œil, Paris, *29*, 15 mai, pp. 12–17.

[394] *Barbara Hepworth: Carvings and Drawings* with an introduction by Herbert Read, Lund Humphries, London, 1952. Barbara Hepworth: "I felt the force of Brancusi's personality and his so decided manner of carving stone and wood" and the studio impressed her by "the balance between the form to be and the finished sculptures, the humanity animating them, the full unity between form and matter."

[395] Letter of 28 July 1933, sent by Brancusi to Mlle Florence Meyer Plainstrasse 18 A bei Klose Salzburg Autriche, http://www.binocheetgiquello.com/, accessed 19 May 2016. "Envoie-moi un mot chère Florence et dismoi ce que tu fais. Je t'embrasse avec tout l'amour et je t'envoie un tas de baisers. Brancusi"

[396] Letters from a private collection cited by R. Varia, (2003) *Brancusi in universul sau. Morice III, seducator, fotograf, sculptor* [Brancusi in His Universe. Morice III, Seducer, Photographer, Sculptor], Observator cultural, *165–166*, April.

[397] Formes, Paris, 1932, *24*, avril, p. 265.

[398] *The Sculptor Speaks: Jacob Epstein to Arnold L. Haskell, a Series of Conversations on Art*, Doubleday, Doran and Company, Inc., New York, 1932, pp. 117–134. A volume with the same title was published in 1931, William Heinemann, London.

[399] R.H. Wilenski, *The Meaning of Modern Sculpture: An easy on some original sculpture of the present day together with some account of the methods of professional disseminators of the notion that certain sculptors in ancient Greece were rhe first and the last to achieve perfection in sculpture*, Frederick A. Stokes Company Publisers, New York, p. 91. "The pioneer experiments and researches were made quite early in the present century by the Romanian sculptor Brancusi who is still living. / Brancusi started to explore geometry, the science which deals with relations of magnitude; he set out to fashion objects with the permanent universal meaning of the geometric symbols as distinguished from meanings that are local and topical. He made sculptures which had meaning only in their shapes—spirals which held the spectator fascinated, ovoids in stone or brass which created an uncanny sensation of permanence and finality by the sheer interplay of their constituent forms. He turned his back completely upon naturalism. His only utterance with which I am acquainted is: 'Je ne veux pas faire de bifteck'—an attitude towards beauty of form which was precisely that of Socrates in the Philebus."

[400] *L'architecture et le décor*, Vogue, Paris, 1933, janvier, pp. 55–57.

[401] brucemuseum.org, accessed 7 March 2015.

[402] V.G. Paleolog, *op. cit.*, p. 35.

[403] *La vie artistique à l'étranger*, La Revue de l'Art, Paris, 1933, **LXIV**, *346*, juin, p. 384.

[404] *Informations*, La Revue de l'Art, Paris, 1933, **LXIII**, *341*, janvier, p. 214.

[405] *Les échos d'art*, Art et décoration, Paris, 1933, **LXII**, janvier, p. IX.

[406] E. Bucuta, *Cronica / Carti, conferinte, congrese, expozitii: Expozitii de arta* [Chronicle / Books, Conferences, Congresses, Exhibitions: Art Exhibitions], Boabe de Grau, Bucharest, 1933, **IV**, *10*, October, p. 627. "Two halls gather the plastic art of Bucharest. One lives on its old fame and has to go back step-by-step in front of happy competition. This is the Romanian Athenaeum and the true exhibition place it embodied. The other one is the Dalles Foundation. The Romanian Academy, which ponders whether it should provide an artistic section besides the existing historical, literary and scientific ones. Today, it shelters and opens the way to new art. Painting and sculpture are displayed in one wing, and Bach, Haydn, and the entire modern musical life are displayed in the other. Enescu has entered, at great pains. Brancusi, Petrascu, and Pallady are waiting. It is impossible for the Romanian Academy not to find out, at least through the Dalles Foundation, if there exists a Romanian artistic creation that is equivalent, if not stronger, to the literary one. If discovered, if should acquire the same high recognition."

[407] Marielle Tabart, Doina Lemny, eds., *op. cit.*, pp. 201–204.

[408] P. Fierens, *Sculpteurs d'aujourd'hui*, Éd. Chroniques du jour, Paris, 1933. Fierens on Brancusi: "spiritualise la matière ou, ce qui revient au même, donne à l'esprit le plus ailé, le plus détaché de la terre, sa consistance et sa configuration."

[409] M. Raynal, (1933) *Dieu—table—cuvette. Les ateliers de Brancusi, Despiau, Giacometti, Laurens, Lipchitz, Maillol, photographiés par Brassaï*, Minotaure, Paris, **IV**, *3–4*, décembre, pp. 39–53.

[410] H. Maryon, (1933) *Modern Sculpture: Its Methods and Ideals, with 354 illustrations*, Sir Isaac Pitman & Sons, LTD, London, p. 163.

[411] Le Rapin, (1934) *De Braque à Dali à Bruxelles*, Comœdia, Paris, 22 marsp. 3.

[412] Catalogue of the exhibition *Anne Harvey: Private Life* at Steven Harvey Fine Art Projects, 10 May–11 June 2017.

[413] S. Geist, *op. cit.*, p. 66.

[414] C. Zervos, (1934) *Réflexions sur Brancusi / À propos de son exposition à New York (17 Novembre 1933–13 Janvier 1934)*, Cahiers d'art, Paris, **9**, *1–4*, pp. 80–83.

[415] Abstraction création art non figuratif, Paris, 1934, *3*, p. 6.

[416] D. Raynal, (2008) *Maurice Raynal: La bande à Picasso*, Éd. Ouest-France, Rennes, p. 106.

[417] St. Georgescu-Gorjan, (1965) *Realizarea Coloanei infinite* [The construction of the Endless Column], Studii si Cercetari despre Istoria Artei, serie Arta Plastica, Bucharest, *2*, p. 105.

[418] The letter is in the manuscripts section of the Romanian Academy Library, inventory number 146912/1966.

[419] A. Jakovski, (1935) *Brancusi*, Axis, London, *3*, July, pp. 3–4.

[420] A.H. Barr Jr., *Brancusi*, in *Cubism and Abstract Art*, The Museum of Modern Art, New York, 1936, pp. 116–120.

[421] Mariana Vida, (2005) *Constantin Brancusi dessinateur*, Ligeia. Dossiers sur l'art, Paris, **XVIII**, *57–58–59–60*, janvier–juin, p. 128.

[422] É. Tériade, (1936) *La peinture surréaliste*, Minotaure, Paris, **8**, juin, pp. 4–17.

[423] P. Anghel, (1972) *Convorbiri culturale* [Cultural discussions], Eminescu Publishers, Bucharest, p. 34. Sanda Negropontes-Tatarescu, daughter of Arethia and of Gheorghe Tatarescu, is speaking about Brancusi: "In Poiana, as I told you, he looked much at the Parang Mts., he meditated, and he played with stones. He was very warm and voluble whenever he saw you understood what he was thinking or wanting. Above all he was droll Oltenia born; he liked jokes of every kind. But all of a sudden he could turn quiet and smoke. His beard impressed me—it was a yellow whirl…At such times he looked like a force of nature and everybody in the house observed his recollection, unforeseen and threatening as the whims of some Jupiter Tonans."

[424] http://andreidoicescu.blogspot.ro/, accessed 12 March 2011.

[425] C. Brancusi, (1952) *Hommage à Rodin*, Quatrième Salon de la Jeune Sculpture, Musée Rodin, Paris, p. 22. "Depuis Michel-Ange, les sculpteurs voulaient faire du grandiose. Ils ne réussissaient à faire que du grandiloquent. Inutile de citer des noms. Au XIXe siècle, la situation de la sculpture était désespérée. Rodin arrive et transforme tout. Grâce à lui, l'homme redevient la mesure, le module d'après lequel s'organize la statue. Grâce à lui, la sculpture redevient humaine dans ses dimensions et dans la signification de son contenu. L'influence de Rodin fut et reste immense. Tandis qu'il était encore vivant, et que j'exposais à la Nationale des Beaux-Arts dont il était président, des amis et des protecteurs, dont la reine, essayèrent, sans me consulter, de me faire admettre dans son atelier. Rodin accepta de me prendre comme élève. Mais moi je refusais, car il ne pousse rien sous les grands arbres. Mes amis étaient fort gênés, ignorants qu'ils étaient de la réaction de Rodin. Quand ce dernier apprit ma décision, il dit tout simplement: «Dans le fond il a raison, il est aussi entête que moi». Rodin avait une attitude modeste devant son art. Lorsqu'il termina son Balzac, qui reste le point de départ incontestable de la sculpture moderne, il déclara: C'est maintenant que je voudrais commencer à travailler." [Beginning with Michelangelo sculptors wanted creating the grandiose, but they only managed grandiloquence. It is useless to provide any name. In the 19th century sculpture was in a desperate situation. Rodin has arrived and changed everything. Thanks to him man became again the measure, the module organizing the statue. Due to him, sculpture became human again in its dimensions and significant contents. Rodin's influence has been and still is immense. In his lifetime, when I exhibited in the National Society of Beaux-Arts that he chaired some friends and protectors, among whom my queen, have attempted without telling me to have me admitted in his studio. Rodin accepted to take me as apprentice; but I was declining, because nothing can grow in the shadow. My friends were quite embarrassed and ignored Rodin's

reaction. When he heard my decision he simply said: *After all he is right, he is as stubborn as I*. Rodin had modest attitude in his art. When he finished his *Balzac*, which remains the incontestable beginning of modern sculpture, he declared: *It is now I would like to begin working*].

[426] Caresse Crosby, (1953) *The Passionate Years*, The Dial Press, New York, p. 185. "I became a frequent visitor to Brancusi's whitewashed atelier. It was in the rue de Vaugirard and was reached by a long thin passage as so many of these hidden work places are. It was on the ground, of course, with a small open area before it. The sliding doors admitted one to a fresh high-raftered room. Brancusi's work stood all about, much of it unfinished, and tools and chips and hammers were in evidence. Also in the center a big white oven opened its door, and since it was autumn, it was red with coals. My first luncheon with him, *à deux*, was unforgettable. On his work table he spread a white sheet of crispest tissue paper to serve as tablecloth, in the center to hold it in place one of his chiseled marble gems. A plump pullet was roasting on the coals, and huge potatoes baking there too. We drank Rosé from the Midi, and ended the feast with strawberry jam and *hearts of cream*. He was a darling, and he cut up the pullet with a sculpting knife. He was in white linen, and I was in black velvet. Together we pulled the wishbone—I don't remember who got the wish."

[427] E. Schileru, (1957) *Constantin Brancusi*, Gazeta literara, Bucharest, **IV**, *13*, 28 March, p. 5.

[428] Cahiers d'art, Paris, 1955, **vol. 30**. Papers on Brancusi: Christian Zervos—*Constantin Brancusi*, p. 153; Dora Vallier—*Vendredi 4 mai 1956 chez Brancusi*, p. 168; Jean Arp—*La colonne sans fin*, p. 174; *Hommages à Brancusi*, p. 178; *Propos de Brancusi—Bibliographie de Brancusi*, p. 243.

[429] M. Lamster, (2013) *A Personal Stamp on the Skyline*, The New York Times, 3 April 2013.

[430] Phyllis Lambert, (2013) *Building Seagram*, Yale University Press, New Haven & London, pp. 240–247.

[431] S. Starling, *Tableaux pour une exposition, 2013–2014*, Musée d'art contemporain de Montréal, p. 25.

[432] Dorothy Adlow, *Brancusi and Modern Sculpture*, Christian Science Monitor, Boston, 29 October 1955, p. 10. "The name of Constantin Brancusi is associated with the first striking departures of modern sculpture. The Romanian sculptor had already approached the absolute of geometric form before some of our rebellious talents in plastic art were born. The starting contribution of Brancusi first came when the styles of cubism and abstraction were formulating."

[433] Press Release, Solomon R. Guggenheim Museum, New York, 1955. J.J. Sweeney: "the importance of such a comprehensive exhibition of the sculptor's work to a just appreciation of Brancusi's genius. Only such a cross-section of his art can bring out the full justice the variety of work, his dedicated love of materials wood, stone, metal

and his simple, direct yet subtly imaginative interpretation of them.," accessed 11 July 2015.

[434] Aline Saarinen, (1955) *Strange Story of Brancusi*, New York Times Magazine, 23 October 1955. Brancusi: "Without the Americans, I would not have been able to produce all this or even to have existed."

[435] *Great Recluse. Brancusi and Art Come from Hiding* (photographs by Bernhard Moosbrugger), Life, New York, **39**, *23*, pp. 131–132, 135–136, 139.

[436] Doina Lemny, (2020) *Irène et Pascu Atanasiu, décembre 1994*, in *L-au intalnit pe / Ils ont rencontré Brancusi*, Vremea Publishers, Bucharest, pp. 31–42.

[437] I. Mereuta, (1966) *Omagiu uriasului* [Hommage au géant], Viata studenteasca, Bucarest, 1er mars 1966.

[438] B. Brezianu, *op. cit.*, p. 41.

[439] Doina Lemny, *op. cit.*, p. 41.

[440] P. Tugui, *op. cit.*, p. 132.

[441] F.T. Bach, Margit Rowell, Ann Temkin, *op. cit.*, p. 386. Brancusi: "Si cela peut être fait en acier inoxydable poli, ce sera une des merveilles du monde."

[442] P. Hulten, Natalia Dumitrescu, Al. Istrati, *op. cit.*, p. 263.

[443] S. Geist, *O coloana la sfarsit* [A Column at Its End], in *op. cit.*, pp. 185–187.

[444] P. Tugui, *op. cit.*, p. 130.

[445] Cover of the Tanarul scriitor review, Bucharest, 1956, **V**, 11 November.

[446] S. Giedion, *Architektur und Gemeinschaft,* series Rowohlts Deutsche Enzyklopädie: das Wissen des 20. Jahrhunderts im Taschenbuch mit enzyklopädischem Stichwort, 18, Rowohlt Verlag, Hamburg, 1956; English version *Architecture. You and Me*, Harvard University Press, Cambridge (MA), 1958, p. 77. "In magnificent simplicity this clastic vertical seems to lunge directly upward and claim possession of all space: *Bird created to penetrate the heavenly vault* in the words of Brancusi. It required thirty years of labor before this sculpture came to its final form. *Simplicity is not an end in art, but one arrives at simplicity in spite of oneself, in approaching the real sense of things* (Brancusi). [...] The achievement of men like Le Corbusier, Mondrian, or Brancusi compels us to believe, surely, that we are indeed approaching a brighter era; one in which grace is expressed in life as it is in art."

[447] H. Read, (1956) *The Art of Sculpture*, The A. W. Mellon Lectures in the Fine Art, National Gallery of Art, Washington, Faber and Faber, London, pp. 110–111.

[448] Doina Schobel, *Expozitie 276 etrospective Camil Ressu, pictura si grafica* [Retrospective Exhibition Camil Ressu, Painting and Graphics], Museum of Art of Romania, Bucharest, 1981—catalogue. On 20 January 1957 painter Camil Ressu wrote the following letter: *"Dear Brancusi, / Perhaps you have heard an exhibition opened in Bucharest for you. The exhibited pieces are older, which could be found around here: Child Head, Darascu's portrait, etc. Unfortunately these sculptures*

cannot by far represent you as they should. / Our artists love you and especially the young ones cherish your work from hear-say rather than by sight, and they look eagerly at the reproductions of your works shown in foreign publications, they know your success in the United States and follow lovingly your every step. / They know you have been carrying the fame of the Romanian carver's creative genius in the whole world for half a century now and regret your work so spread in other parts of the world is almost absent in our country. / Such regret we do not have your works near us to admire while also admiring you is the unanimous sentiment of all our artists and art lovers. / I am content to share with you this impression, which is a distant echoing chorus bringing you homage from your people. / I am thinking whether, you are willing, we might not have something from your life's work in this country you so much loved and so brilliantly represented. / I wish you many happy returns of the day and fruitful activity now that you turned 80 on 22 February 1956 / Yours, C. Ressu / 20 January 1957, Bucharest / Dear Brancusi, please convey my best sentiments to our Istrati colleagues."

[449] G. Ivascu, (1956) *Expozitia Brancusi* [Brancusi Exhibition], Contemporanul, Bucharest, **40**, December, p. 4. "The artist's Bust executed by Milita Petrascu is seen at the entrance of the hall, with glass windows arranged so as to pay homage to Brancusi's exhibit's in French, English, Italian and German publications of specific studies, accompanied by many reproductions."

[450] P. Tugui, *op. cit.*, p. 142.

[451] I. Frunzetti, (1957) *Expoziţia Brancusi* [Brancusi Exhibition], Steaua, Cluj, **VIII**, *2(84)*, February, pp. 111–114.

[452] P. Hulten, Natalia Dumitrescu, Al. Istrati, *op. cit.*, p. 114.

[453] Testimony of Archbishop T. Ionescu of 17 August 1974, reproduced by deacon P. I. David in *Arta si cultura, coordonatele eternitatii unui popor. Centenarul nasterii lui Constantin Brancusi (1876–1976)* [Art and Culture, Coordinates of Eternity for a People: Centenary of Constantin Brancusi's Birth (1876–1976)], Romanian Orthodox Church, Bucharest, 1976, *3–4*, pp. 323–331. Brancusi: "I die with no peace in my heart to be so far from my country, and I am very sorry to rot in a foreign land, far from my most beloved mother."

Archbishop T. Ionescu about the artist's funeral: "We then took him to Montparnasse Cemetery where he told me he wanted to rest."

[454] W. Siegfried, (1957) *Ultima intalnire cu Brancusi* [Last meeting with Brancusi], Informatia Bucurestiului, Bucharest, **IV**, *1139*, 2 April, p. 2.

[455] R. Bogdan, (2002) *Despre un fals istoriografic—Constantin Brancusi n-a propus niciodata vreo donatie statului roman* [About a historical-biographical forgery—C. Brancusi never proposed a donation to the Romanian state], Observator Cultural, Bucharest, *102*, 5 February.

[456] Doina Lemny, *op. cit.*, p. 36.

⁴⁵⁷ *Funeraliile sculptorului Constantin Brancusi* [Burial of Sculptor Constantin Brancusi], Romania libera, Bucharest, 22 March 1957, p. 4. News release from the Romanian Press Agency Agerpres: "On 19 March took place in Paris the funeral of the great Romanian sculptor Constantin Brancusi. Such a funeral ceremony was performed in the Romanian Orthodox Church of Paris, before a great number of admirers, among whom many representatives of the artistic medium in France; also participant was a delegation of the Legation from the People's Republic of Romania in Paris, headed by Gheorghe Pascu, ad-interim chargé d'affaires that deposited a crown of flowers on behalf of the Legation. Another crown of flowers was provided by the Romanian Union of Plastic Artists."

⁴⁵⁸ Carola Giedion-Welcker, (1981) *Constantin Brancusi (1876–1957)*, Meridiane Publishers, Bucharest, p. 114.

⁴⁵⁹ H.P. Roché, *L'enterrement de Brancusi*, in *Hommage à Brancusi*, Éd. de Beaune, Paris, 1957, pp. 26–29.

⁴⁶⁰ P. Tugui, *op. cit*, pp. 148–149.

⁴⁶¹ R. Bogdan, *op. cit.*

⁴⁶² D. Lewis, *Constantin Brancusi*, Alec Tiranti Publishers, London, 1957, p. 34.

⁴⁶³ P. Schneider, *Brancusi*, L'Express, Paris, 5 avril 1962.

⁴⁶⁴ Victoria Dragu Dimitriu, Povesti ale Doamnelor din Bucuresti [Stories of Ladies in Bucharest], Vremea Publishers, Bucharest, 2008, p. 316.

⁴⁶⁵ Funerary monument devised by Brancusi, reconstituted by Petru Comarnescu, in *Brancusi si Goga la Ciucea* [Brancusi and Goga in Ciucea] by C. Cublesan, Orasul, Cluj-Napoca, 2006, *3*, August

⁴⁶⁶ G.I. Bodea, INVESNICIREA lui Octavian Goga la Ciucea [Immortalising O. Goga in Ciucea], Vremi Publishers, Cluj-Napoca, 2010. Veturia Goga: "In the summer of 1938 I went to Ciucea with Brancusi, who was in the country for the Tg. Jiu project which was towards the end. He was impressed by the pictureasque location of the complex and told me: I want to make Goga's tomb. Now I have to go to Paris, but I come back in a few months and will work here. I thanked him but asked for a sketch to work by with the local experts. He answered: I use no sketch, I just take the hammer in my hand and similarly finish. / And so he worked, as we all know… Unfortunately Brancusi had no opportunity to provide another monument to the country. I waited for two months, then the artist informed me he could not come immediately, but he would certainly come next spring. I couldn't wait any longer so I started the work with architect G. M. Cantacuzino."

⁴⁶⁷N. Prelipceanu, *Un minut sau o viata* [A Minute or A Lifetime], Transilvania, Sibiu, 1981, *3*.

⁴⁶⁸ C. Cublesan, *Brancusi si Goga, la Ciucea* [Brancusi and Goga in Ciucea], in *Brancusi si Transilvania* [Brancusi and Transylvania], Grinta Publishers, Cluj-Napoca, 2001

⁴⁶⁹ P. Tugui, *Dosarul Brancusi* [Brancusi File], Dacia Publishers, Cluj-Napoca, 2001, p. 137.

⁴⁷⁰ Ioana Giroiu, *op. cit.*, p. 2.

⁴⁷¹ R. Boureanu, *Constantin Brancusi. O clipa afara din timp* [Constantin Brancusi, One Moment Out of Time], Romania, 1938, 9 November (reprint in *Funia de nisip* [Sand Cord], Cartea Romaneasca Publishers, Bucharest, 1972, pp. 281–284).

⁴⁷² Le Petit Havre, Le Havre, 21 April 1939.

⁴⁷³ P. Pandrea, *op. cit.*, p. 339.

⁴⁷⁴ *Art in Our Time / an Exhibition to Celebrate the Tenth Anniversary of the Museum of Modern Art and the Opening of its New Building Held at the Time of the New York World's Fair 1939* / Museum of Modern Art, MoMAExh_0085_89_MasterChecklist.pdf, accessed 20 April 2015. "The great sculptor of abstract forms which are beautiful in themselves rather than as representations of nature."

⁴⁷⁵ S. Giedion, Space, Time and Architecture: The Growth of a New Tradition, Harvard University Press, Cambridge (MA), 1967, pp. 665–667.

⁴⁷⁶ Monika Schäfer, *Carola Giedion-Welcker: Grande Dame de klassischen Moderne*, Artensuite, Zürich, 2007, *10*, October, pp. 10–11, http://www.ensuite.ch/, accessed 15 April 2012.

⁴⁷⁷ S. Giedion, *Raum, Zeit, Architektur: Die Entstehung einer neuen Tradition*, Birkhäuser Verlag GmbH, Basel, 2015,
p. 352. "Während der New Yorker Weltausstellung 1939 waren wir mit Aalto und Brancusi eines Sonntags bei ihm in seinem Landhaus auf Long Island; auch war er ein persönlicher Freund von Fernand Léger."

⁴⁷⁸ S. Giedion, op. cit., p. 621. "When Aalto was in the United States in 1939, building the Finnish Pavilion for the New York World's Fair, he and I were once sitting together with Brancusi, the sculptor. Brancusi had been telling of some work that he had done for an Indian Maharajah when Aalto suddenly exclaimed, I see now, Brancusi! You stand at the crossroads of Asia and Europe! Finland is also at the crossroads of East and West, but for the moment we would only stress the fact that many remnants of primeval and medieval times still remain alive there and intermingle with modern civilization. This double nature is instilled in Aalto too, and gives creative tension to his work."

⁴⁷⁹ Carola Giedion-Welcker, op. cit., pp. 38–39. "[A. Aalto] undoubtedly understood correctly the position and double essence of Brancusi's work, which he situated at the crossroads of the Orient and the Occident."

⁴⁸⁰ F.T. Bach, Margit Rowell, Ann Temkin, op. cit., p. 66.

[481] Noguchi on Brancusi, Craft Horizons, New York, 1976, 4. "I believe it was when I saw him in 1935 that he told me that Ingersoll had arranged with the Budd Company near Philadelphia, which makes the railroad cars, to execute a large Endless Column in welded stainless steel. Brancusi would have none of this; it went against everything he believed in."

[482] B. Brezianu, op. cit., pp. 18–22

[483] Malvina Hoffman, Sculpture: Inside and Out, W. W. Norton Publishers, New York, 1939, p. 53.

[484] M. Deac, Brancusi. Interviu la Venetia cu Peggy Guggenheim in palatul de pe Canale Grande [Brancusi, Interview with Peggy Guggenheim in Venice, in the Canal Grande Palace], Flacara, Bucharest, 1965, 3, 16 January. "For years I had wanted to buy a bronze by Brancusi, but had not been able to afford one. A piece by Brancusi would have boosted up my collection. I spent months negotiating with the artist to set up this acquisition. It was all for nothing since perhaps he could not part with his Bird in Space and asked for such a price as to force me give it up. I gave it up but not before a terrible row with my friend. After such conflict, I disappeared from Brancusi's life for a few months and in the meantime managed to buy a Bird which the sculptor had made long before. I bought it from Paul Poiret's sister. However, I was pining for a Bird in Space, which was so particular and beautiful. / I went to his studio and talked again. This time Brancusi softened. Then for weeks he kept polishing the Bird in Space: nobody surpassed his finishing technique. By the time he had finished the Germans were near Paris. Before leaving to New York I went to the studio to take my sculpture. Tears were streaming down Brancusi's face, and I was genuinely touched. I never knew why Brancusi was so upset: but I assumed it was because I was parting with his favourite bird."

[485] Peggy Guggenheim, op. cit., pp. 211–212. "For years I had wanted to buy a Brancusi bronze, but had not been able to afford one. Now the moment seemed to have arrived for this great acquisition. I spent months becoming more and more involved with Brancusi before this sale was actually consummated. I had known him for sixteen years, but I never dreamed I was to get into such complications with him. It was very difficult to talk prices to Brancusi, and if you ever had the courage to do so, you had to expect him to ask you some monstrous sum. I was aware of this and hoped my excessive friendship with him would make things easier. But in spite of all this we ended up in a terrible row, when he asked four thousand dollars for the Bird in Space."

"Brancusi was a marvellous little man with a beard and piercing dark eyes. He was half astute peasant and half real god. He made you very happy to be with him. It was a privilege to know him; unfortunately he got too possessive and wanted all of my name. He called me Pegitza… Formerly he had taken beautiful young girls travelling with him. He now wanted to take me but I would not go. […] He had been back to

Romania, his own country, where the government had asked him to build public monuments. He was very proud of this. Most of his life he had been very austere and devoted entirely to his work. He had sacrificed everything to this, and had given up women for the most part to the point of anguish. In his old age he felt it very much and was very lonely. He had a persecution complex and always thought people were spying on him. Brancusi used to dress up and take me out to dinner when he did not cook for me. He loved me very much..."

"Brancusi polished all his sculptures by hand. I think that it is the main reason they are so beautiful. This Bird in Space was to give him several weeks' work. By the time he had finished, the Germans were near Paris, and I went to fetch it in my little car to have it packed and shipped away. Tears were streaming down Brancusi's face, and I was genuinely touched. I never knew why he was so upset, but assumed it was because I was parting with his favourite bird."

[486] J. Epstein, Let There Be Sculpture, G.P. Putnam's Sons, New York, pp. 40–41, 123–127, 207–208

[487] D. Haulica, Variatiuni la Brancusi [Variations to Brancusi], Observator Cultural, Bucharest, 2004, 201–202, 1 January. Brancusi: "If Henri Rousseau had stayed in his native town most likely he would have achieved nothing. As an artist he was born in Paris, it was there he found his friends who, understanding and loving him, also helped him achieve his work. The homage to Henri Rousseau, as Guillaume Apollinaire expressed it and as carved on his gravestone is, by its moving simplicity, an expression of the ambient created around the painter. Taking his bones elsewhere means unrooting him. Henri Rousseau's soul, his memory, his ashes belong to Paris."

[488] N. Agarbiceanu, In atelierul mesterului [In Brancusi's Studio], Secolul 20, Bucharest, 1976, 10–12(189–191), p. 267.

[489] P. Westheim, op. cit

[490] O.W. Cisek, Limpeziri / Arta romaneasca [Clarifications / Romanian Art], Dacia Rediviva, Bucharest, 1942, II, 6, June, pp. 13–14. "he starts from simple forms of wood carving, characteristic to popular art, and from some ancient Tracian elements thus discovering such road before Archipenko and Lehmbruck, as also underlined by Paul Westheim. His European significance cannot be contested."

[491] Lorraine Welling Lanmon, William Lescaze, Architect, The Art Alliance Press, Philadelphia, 1987

[492] Marielle Tabart, Doina Lemny, eds., op. cit., p. 223. Inventaire des archives personnelles de Constantin Brancusi / Correspondance avec des particuliers / Correspondance avec de proches: "Lescaze, William et Mary, 14 f., 1926–1955"

[493] P. Comarnescu, Valoarea romaneasca si universala a sculpturii lui C. Brancusi [Romanian and Universal Value of C. Brancusi's Sculpture], Revista Fundatiilor Regale, Bucharest, 1944, XI, 6, June, pp. 624–656. "[Brancusi] is the genial expression of the absolute Romanian naturism. He reached achievement with the

culture of his people, finding its essence and major virtualness. His genius was however anticipated, through the young age of Romanian culture and with the return of aged cultures to the same sources."

"If in general human heads interested Brancusi more than the carnal body, we should not forget a sculpture with sober pathos such as Prayer […]. It is a more concrete piece, where the circumscribed matter is not prevailing […], with surfaces of pure sensuality that even Egyptians could have coveted as well as the classical Hellenes, with volume that provides monumentality and geology to the flesh. The Prayer, a youth sculpture, shows a kneeling feminine Nude with the superior part of the body and the head bowed in prayer."

[494] P. Comarnescu, Ilustratii din opera lui C. Brancusi [Illustrations from C. Brancusi's Work], Revista Fundatiilor Regale, Bucharest, 1944, XI, 12, December, pp. 695–696.

[495] P. Comarnescu, Alte ilustratii dupa opera lui C. Brancusi [Other Illustrations of C. Brancusi's Work], Revista Fundatiilor Regale, Bucharest, 1945, XII, 2, February, pp. 468–469. "As Brancusi has few sculptures in the country these photographs are helpful, at least as a suggestion, and incentive to long to know better his creation".

[496] P. Pandrea, Portrete si controverse [Portraits and Controversies], I, Meridiane Collection, Bucur Ciobanu Publishers, Bucharest, 1945, pp. 95–173. "[Oltenia] reservoir of energy, where Romania provides herself constantly of."
"[Oltenians] are oscillating in their heart between the speculative kind and the purely speculator one. This means between the pedlar and the man with Brancusi's Maiastra Bird…"

[497] cotidianul.tv, Bucharest, video clip posted on 2 April 2015, accessed 14 May 2016.

[498] Certificate given by Brancusi to sculptor Constantin Antonovici:
C. Brancusi Sculptor / 11 Impasse Ronsin / Paris 15ème
I the undersigned certify that Mr Antonovici Constantin has great talent for sculpture and he works strenuously.
C. Brancusi / Paris, May 9, 1951

[499] Mary-Elizabeth Andrews, 'Memory of the Nation': Making and Re-making German History in the Berlin Zeughaus, PhD Thesis, The University of Sidney, 2014, p. 251, Andrews_ME_Thesis.pdf, accessed 20 December 2015.

[500] V.G. Paleolog, Constantin Brancusi, Forum Publishers, Bucharest, 1947. The original content of the book: Atteindre un nouveau plan de la réalité / Digression / Confluences I / Ensemble I, Ensemble II / Confluences II / Suite / Parallèlement / Saint bird by Lucian Blaga (in Romanian) / Brancusi's Golden Bird by Mina Loy (in English) / Note I / Note II / La sculpture, cette nouvelle métaphysique

[501] V.G. Paleolog, Brancusi, valeur internationale, Arcades, Bucarest, 1947, 1, janvier–mars.

⁵⁰² I. Jianu, G. Xuriguera, A. Lardera, La sculpture moderne en France depuis 1950, Arted, Éd. d'Art, Paris, 1982.

⁵⁰³ J.-C. Lambert, Marta Pan: de la sculpture au paysage ou la pensée sculpturale, Éd. du Cercle d'Art, Paris, 1994

⁵⁰⁴ I. Jianu, G. Xuriguera, A. Lardera, op. cit.

⁵⁰⁵ W. Grimes, François-Xavier Lalanne, Sculptor of Surrealistic Animals, Is Dead at 81, The New York Times, New York, 13 December 2008.

⁵⁰⁶ P. Annigoni, Arriva a Palazzo Strozzi il baraccone della Guggenheim, Il Mattino dell'Italia Centrale, Firenze, 20 febbraio 1949

⁵⁰⁷ P. Bargellini, Le Commissioni della Signora Peggy, Il Mattino dell'Italia Centrale, Firenze, 11 marzo 1949.

⁵⁰⁸ M. Seuphor, ed., L'Art abstrait, ses origines, ses premiers maîtres, Éd. Maeght, Paris, 1950.

⁵⁰⁹ Karl-Jean Longuet et Simone Boisecq, De la sculpture à la cité rêvée – catalogue d'exposition, Musée d'Art de Reims, 10 mars–6 juin 2011

⁵¹⁰ Katherine Kuh, Twentieth Century Art from the Louise and Walter Arensberg Collection, Bulletin of the Art Institute of Chicago (1907–1951), 43, 3 (Sep. 15, 1949), pp. 52–57.

⁵¹¹ http://au.wow.com/wiki/Walter_Conrad_Arensberg, accessed 12 May 2016.

⁵¹² Document published in Zig-Zag magazine, Bucharest, 1993, 45, November:
The Academy of the People's Republic of Romania / Section of Language Science, Literature and Arts
Bucharest, 125 Calea Victoriei / Minutes 10 / of the March 7, 1951 meeting / Acad. M. Sadoveanu chaired the meeting / Participants: Acad. Gh. Calinescu, I. Iordan, Camil Petrescu, Al. Rosetti, Al. Toma,
G. Oprescu, Jean Al. Steriadi, V. Eftimiu and comrade Geo Bogza, Prof. Al. Graur, Prof. I. Jalea, I. Panaitescu-Perpessicius and K.H. Zambaccian / Academician Gala Galaction and comrade Lucian Grigorescu motivated their absence. / 1/ The minutes of the 28 February meeting was read and approved.
/ 2/ Acad. I. Iordan about the activity report of February 1951 of the Linguistic Institute and Acad. G. Oprescu about the minutes of the 1 March meeting of the Art History Institute. / 3/ Professor Jalea read the completion of his account on sculptor C. Brancusi, providing also many boards and publications with reproductions from Brancusi. / Summarising his ideas from his previous report on Sobolev's book Leninist theory of artistic formalism comrade Jalea reminded us he has been quoting Paciurea and Brancusi as examples of formalism in sculpture in our country. / This being the case of a talented artist fluctuating between realism and extreme formalism, Brancusi's situation should be discussed as it raises important issues. / Academician Calinescu took into account the communication of Prof. Jalea and found that Brancusi cannot be considered creator in sculpture because he does not express

himself using the essential characteristic means of such art. He explained realism in the sense of Soviet artistic creators as superior transposing of reality not photographical reproduction of it, as they understand it in leftist manner. / He concluded showing it was futile to go on talking about Brancusi.

Acad. Oprescu said the communication of comrade Calinescu cleared up some important issues. He shows the data and facts quoted by him on Brancusi, a less known character, show his absent sincerity and illustrate him as talented person providing great expectations in the first part of his activity but who, under the influence of fashionable sculptors from Paris cultivating the indefinite and cubism he became formalist, even when he uses elements from popular art, speculating by bizarre means the morbid tastes of the bourgeois society. / Acad. V. Eftimiu specified that comrade Jalea wanted to rehabilitate Brancusi's valid works in his communication. / Prof. Graur was against admitting the sculptures of Brancusi in the Art Museum of the People's Republic of Romania since artistic anti-democrats gang up around him. He asked the section to discuss in the future solved problems published by the author and proposed to the section for discussion. / Comrade K. Zambaccian and Acad. Victor Eftimiu, coming back to sculptor Paciurea, showed his 'chimeras' were protest against the reality of that moment and Paciurea finished as realist with his busts, among whom that of Tolstoy. / Acad. Camil Petrescu pointed out the merit of comrade Jalea's communication to have occasioned interesting discussions and provided problems of particular significance. / He announced the future meeting would specify some nuances of art formalism. / The meeting was closed at 19:00 h. / Secretary of the Section, / Acad. Mihail Sadoveanu.

[513] History and Civilisation Magazine, County Department of Culture and National Heritage Calarasi, www.isciv.ro.
Art Committee / from the / Council of Ministers / Plastic Arts Section / 123528 / 951 / June 30, 1951 / To the / Scientific Commission of Museums / Historical and Artistic Monuments / from the Academy of the People's Republic of Romania / 125 Calea Victoriei / Please find hereby attached: / a/ Letter of the Ministry of Internal Affairs, Department of Communal and Local Industry Husbandry no. 3963/40659 of 1951, with respect to the demand to pull down the metallic column of sculptor Brancus from Targu-Jiu town / b/ Letter no. 2/345 of the Ministry of Transports, General Division of Procurement and Distributions A.M.T./1951, with respect to the demand to assemble back the commemorating monument made by sculptor Baraschi from railroad station Predeal. c/ Letter No. 20792/1951 of the Ministry of Public Instruction with respect to the old Arms of Arges County on the façade of the high school in Pitesti. / Kindly please endorse. / Director / Head of department

[514] Th. Munro, The Arts and Their Interrelations / A Survey of the Arts and an Outline of Comparative Aesthetics, The Liberal Arts Press, New York, 1951, p. 8 (first edition,1949; reprint, 1950).

515 C. Brancusi, Hommage à Rodin, Quatrième Salon de la Jeune Sculpture, Musée Rodin, Paris, 1952, p. 22. "Depuis Michel-Ange, les sculpteurs voulaient faire du grandiose. Ils ne réussissaient à faire que du grandiloquent. Inutile de citer des noms. Au XIXe siècle, la situation de la sculpture était désespérée. Rodin arrive et transforme tout. Grâce à lui, l'homme redevient la mesure, le module d'après lequel s'organise la statue. Grâce à lui, la sculpture redevient humaine dans ses dimensions et dans la signification de son contenu. L'influence de Rodin fut et reste immense. Tandis qu'il était encore vivant, et que j'exposais à la Nationale des Beaux-Arts dont il était président, des amis et des protecteurs, dont la reine, essayèrent, sans me consulter, de me faire admettre dans son atelier. Rodin accepta de me prendre comme élève. Mais moi je refusais, car il ne pousse rien sous les grands arbres. Mes amis étaient fort gênés, ignorants qu'ils étaient de la réaction de Rodin. Quand ce dernier apprit ma décision, il dit tout simplement: «Dans le fond il a raison, il est aussi entête que moi». Rodin avait une attitude modeste devant son art. Lorsqu'il termina son Balzac, qui reste le point de départ incontestable de la sculpture moderne, il déclara: «C'est maintenant que je voudrais commencer à travailler»." [Beginning with Michelangelo sculptors wanted creating the grandiose, but they only managed grandiloquence. It is useless to provide any name. In the 19th century sculpture was in a desperate situation. Rodin has arrived and changed everything. Thanks to him man became again the measure, the module organising the statue. Due to him sculpture became human again in its dimensions and significant contents. Rodin's influence has been and still is immense. In his lifetime, when I exhibited in the National Society of Beaux-Arts that he chaired some friends and protectors, among whom my queen, have attempted without telling me to have me admitted in his studio. Rodin accepted to take me as apprentice; but I was declining, because nothing can grow in the shadow. My friends were quite embarrassed and ignored Rodin's reaction. When he heard my decision he simply said: After all he is right, he is as stubborn as I. Rodin had modest attitude in his art. When he finished his Balzac, which remains the incontestable beginning of modern sculpture, he declared: It is now I would like to begin working].

516 Caresse Crosby, The Passionate Years, The Dial Press, New York, 1953, p. 185. "I became a frequent visitor to Brancusi's whitewashed atelier. It was in the rue de Vaugirard and was reached by a long thin passage as so many of these hidden work places are. It was on the ground, of course, with a small open area before it. The sliding doors admitted one to a fresh high-raftered room. Brancusi's work stood all about, much of it unfinished, and tools and chips and hammers were in evidence. Also in the center a big white oven opened its door, and since it was autumn, it was red with coals. My first luncheon with him, à deux, was unforgettable. On his work table he spread a white sheet of crispest tissue paper to serve as tablecloth, in the center to hold it in place one of his chiseled marble gems. A plump pullet was roasting

on the coals, and huge potatoes baking there too. We drank Rosé from the Midi, and ended the feast with strawberry jam and hearts of cream. He was a darling, and he cut up the pullet with a sculpting knife. He was in white linen, and I was in black velvet. Together we pulled the wishbone – I don't remember who got the wish."

[517] E. Schileru, Constantin Brancusi, Gazeta literara, Bucharest, 1957, IV, 13, 28 March, p. 5.

[518] Cahiers d'art, Paris, 1955, vol. 30. Papers on Brancusi: Christian Zervos – Constantin Brancusi, p. 153; Dora Vallier – Vendredi 4 mai 1956 chez Brancusi, p. 168; Jean Arp – La colonne sans fin, p. 174; Hommages à Brancusi, p. 178; Propos de Brancusi – Bibliographie de Brancusi, p. 243

[519] M. Lamster, A Personal Stamp on the Skyline, The New York Times, 3 April 2013.

[520] Phyllis Lambert, Building Seagram, Yale University Press, New Haven & London, 2013, pp. 240–247.

[521] S. Starling, Tableaux pour une exposition, 2013–2014, Musée d'art contemporain de Montréal, p. 25

[522] Dorothy Adlow, Brancusi and Modern Sculpture, Christian Science Monitor, Boston, 29 October 1955, p. 10. "The name of Constantin Brancusi is associated with the first striking departures of modern sculpture. The Romanian sculptor had already approached the absolute of geometric form before some of our rebellious talents in plastic art were born. The starting contribution of Brancusi first came when the styles of cubism and abstraction were formulating."

[523] Press Release, Solomon R. Guggenheim Museum, New York, 1955. J.J. Sweeney: "the importance of such a comprehensive exhibition of the sculptor's work to a just appreciation of Brancusi's genius. Only such a cross-section of his art can bring out the full justice the variety of work, his dedicated love of materials wood, stone, metal and his simple, direct yet subtly imaginative interpretation of them.", accessed 11 July 2015.

[524] Aline Saarinen, Strange Story of Brancusi, New York Times Magazine, 23 October 1955. Brancusi: "Without the Americans, I would not have been able to produce all this or even to have existed."

[525] Great Recluse. Brancusi and Art Come from Hiding (photographs by Bernhard Moosbrugger), Life, New York, 1955,
39, 23, pp. 131–132, 135–136, 139.

[526] Doina Lemny, Irène et Pascu Atanasiu, décembre 1994, in L-au intalnit pe / Ils ont rencontré Brancusi, Vremea Publishers, Bucharest, 2020, pp. 31–42.

[527] I. Mereuta, Omagiu uriasului [Hommage au géant], Viata studenteasca, Bucarest, 1er mars 1966.

[528] B. Brezianu, op. cit., p. 41

[529] Doina Lemny, op. cit., p. 41.

[530] P. Tugui, op. cit., p. 132.

531 F.T. Bach, Margit Rowell, Ann Temkin, op. cit., p. 386. Brancusi: "Si cela peut être fait en acier inoxydable poli, ce sera une des merveilles du monde."
532 P. Hulten, Natalia Dumitrescu, Al. Istrati, op. cit., p. 263
533 S. Geist, O coloana la sfarsit [A Column at Its End], in op. cit., pp. 185–187.
534 P. Tugui, op. cit., p. 130.
535 Cover of the Tanarul scriitor review, Bucharest, 1956, V, 11 November.
536 S. Giedion, Architektur und Gemeinschaft, series Rowohlts Deutsche Enzyklopädie: das Wissen des 20. Jahrhunderts im Taschenbuch mit enzyklopädischem Stichwort, 18, Rowohlt Verlag, Hamburg, 1956; English version Architecture. You and Me, Harvard University Press, Cambridge (MA), 1958, p. 77. "In magnificent simplicity this clastic vertical seems to lunge directly upward and claim possession of all space: Bird created to penetrate the heavenly vault in the words of Brancusi. It required thirty years of labor before this sculpture came to its final form. Simplicity is not an end in art, but one arrives at simplicity in spite of oneself, in approaching the real sense of things (Brancusi). […] The achievement of men like Le Corbusier, Mondrian, or Brancusi compels us to believe, surely, that we are indeed approaching a brighter era; one in which grace is expressed in life as it is in art."
537 H. Read, The Art of Sculpture, The A. W. Mellon Lectures in the Fine Art, National Gallery of Art, Washington, Faber and Faber, London, 1956, pp. 110–111
538 Doina Schobel, Expozitie retrospectiva Camil Ressu, pictura si grafica [Retrospective Exhibition Camil Ressu, Painting and Graphics], Museum of Art of Romania, Bucharest, 1981 – catalogue. On 20 January 1957 painter Camil Ressu wrote the following letter: "Dear Brancusi, / Perhaps you have heard an exhibition opened in Bucharest for you. The exhibited pieces are older, which could be found around here: Child Head, Darascu's portrait, etc. Unfortunately these sculptures cannot by far represent you as they should.
/ Our artists love you and especially the young ones cherish your work from hear-say rather than by sight, and they look eagerly at the reproductions of your works shown in foreign publications, they know your success in the United States and follow lovingly your every step. / They know you have been carrying the fame of the Romanian carver's creative genius in the whole world for half a century now and regret your work so spread in other parts of the world is almost absent in our country. / Such regret we do not have your works near us to admire while also admiring you is the unanimous sentiment of all our artists and art lovers. / I am content to share with you this impression, which is a distant echoing chorus bringing you homage from your people. / I am thinking whether, you are willing, we might not have something from your life's work in this country you so much loved and so brilliantly represented. / I wish you many happy returns of the day and fruitful activity now that

you turned 80 on 22 February 1956 / Yours, C. Ressu / 20 January 1957, Bucharest / Dear Brancusi, please convey my best sentiments to our Istrati colleagues."

[539] G. Ivascu, Expozitia Brancusi [Brancusi Exhibition], Contemporanul, Bucharest, 1956, 40, December, p. 4. "The artist's Bust executed by Milita Petrascu is seen at the entrance of the hall, with glass windows arranged so as to pay homage to Brancusi's exhibit's in French, English, Italian and German publications of specific studies, accompanied by many reproductions."

[540] P. Tugui, op. cit., p. 142.

[541] I. Frunzetti, Expoziţia Brancusi [Brancusi Exhibition], Steaua, Cluj, 1957, VIII, 2(84), February, pp. 111–114.

[542] P. Hulten, Natalia Dumitrescu, Al. Istrati, op. cit., p. 114.

[543] Testimony of Archbishop T. Ionescu of 17 August 1974, reproduced by deacon P. I. David in Arta si cultura, coordonatele eternitatii unui popor. Centenarul nasterii lui Constantin Brancusi (1876–1976) [Art and Culture, Coordinates of Eternity for a People: Centenary of Constantin Brancusi's Birth (1876–1976)], Romanian Orthodox Church, Bucharest, 1976, 3–4, pp. 323–331. Brancusi: "I die with no peace in my heart to be so far from my country, and I am very sorry to rot in a foreign land, far from my most beloved mother."
Archbishop T. Ionescu about the artist's funeral: "We then took him to Montparnasse Cemetery where he told me he wanted to rest."

[544] W. Siegfried, Ultima intalnire cu Brancusi [Last meeting with Brancusi], Informatia Bucurestiului, Bucharest, 1957,
IV, 1139, 2 April, p. 2.

[545] R. Bogdan, Despre un fals istoriografic – Constantin Brancusi n-a propus niciodata vreo donatie statului roman [About a historical-biographical forgery – C. Brancusi never proposed a donation to the Romanian state], Observator Cultural, Bucharest, 2002, 102, 5 February.

[546] Doina Lemny, op. cit., p. 36.

[547] Funeraliile sculptorului Constantin Brancusi [Burial of Sculptor Constantin Brancusi], Romania libera, Bucharest, 22 March 1957, p. 4. News release from the Romanian Press Agency Agerpres: "On 19 March took place in Paris the funeral of the great Romanian sculptor Constantin Brancusi. Such a funeral ceremony was performed in the Romanian Orthodox Church of Paris, before a great number of admirers, among whom many representatives of the artistic medium in France; also participant was a delegation of the Legation from the People's Republic of Romania in Paris, headed by Gheorghe Pascu, ad-interim chargé d'affaires that deposited a crown of flowers on behalf of the Legation. Another crown of flowers was provided by the Romanian Union of Plastic Artists."

[548] Carola Giedion-Welcker, Constantin Brancusi (1876–1957), Meridiane Publishers, Bucharest, 1981, p. 114.

[549] H.P. Roché, L'enterrement de Brancusi, in Hommage à Brancusi, Éd. de Beaune, Paris, 1957, pp. 26–29.
[550] P. Tugui, op. cit, pp. 148–149
[551] R. Bogdan, op. cit.
[552] D. Lewis, Constantin Brancusi, Alec Tiranti Publishers, London, 1957, p. 34.
[553] P. Schneider, Brancusi, L'Express, Paris, 5 avril 1962.